NORAGAMI
STRAY GOD

ADACHITOKA

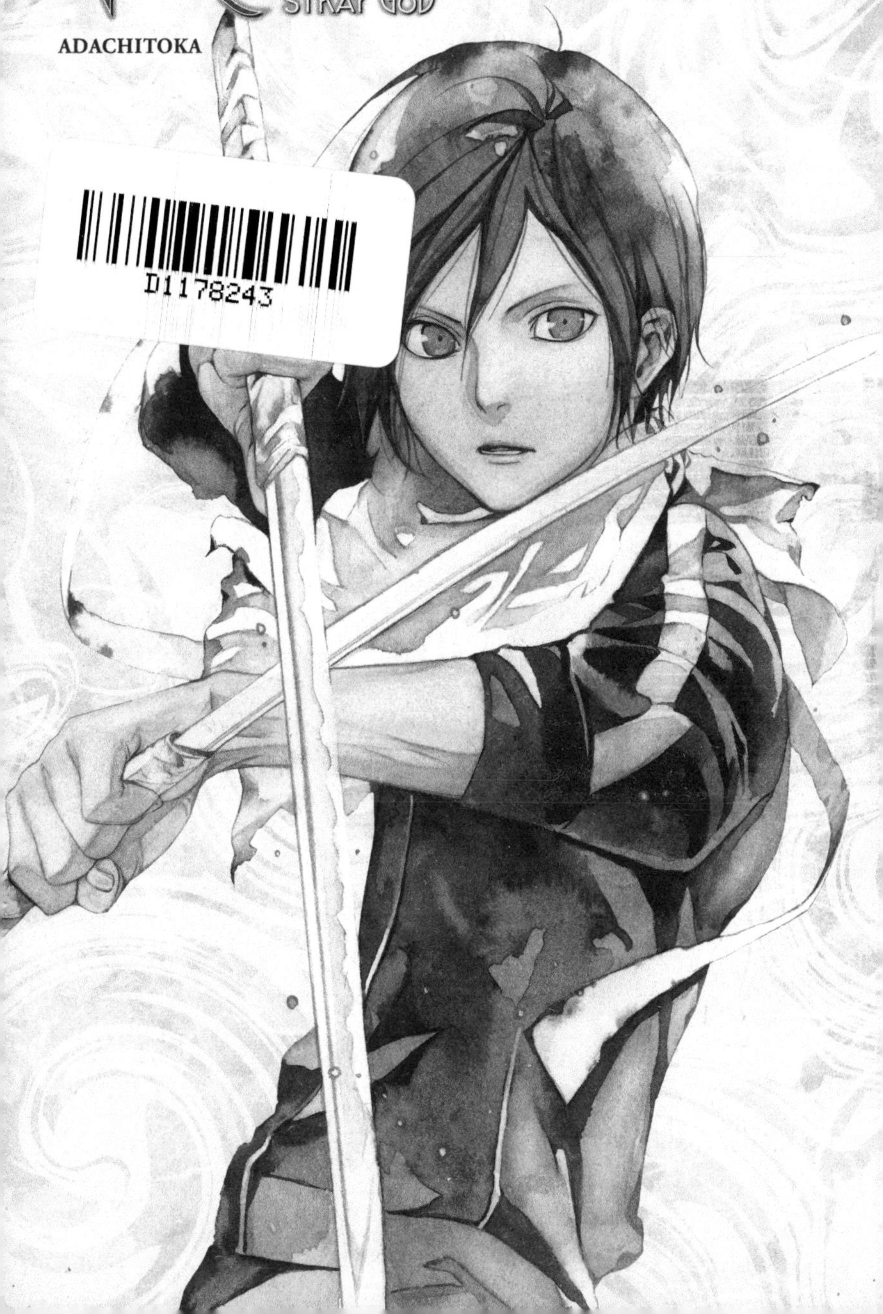

characters

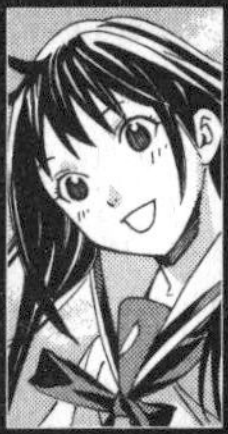

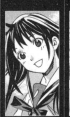

HIYORI IKI

A high school student who has become half ayakashi.

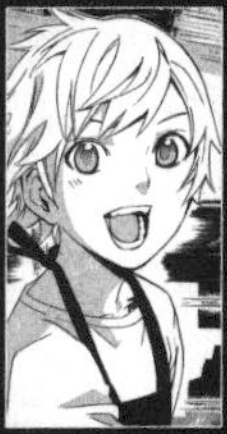

YUKINÉ

Yato's shinki who turns into a sword.

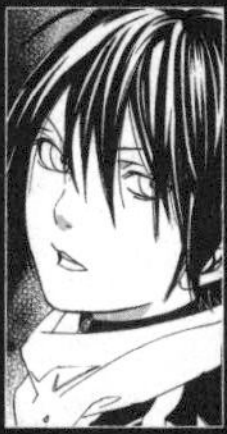

YATO

A minor deity who always wears a sweatsuit.

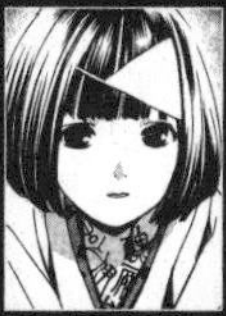

STRAY

A shinki who serves an unspecified number of deities.

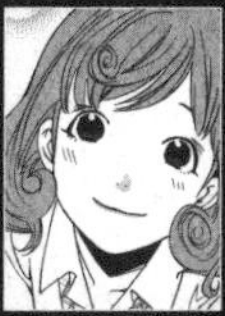

KOFUKU

A goddess of poverty who calls herself Ebisu after the god of fortune.

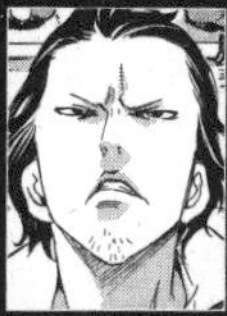

DAIKOKU

Kofuku's shinki who summons storms.

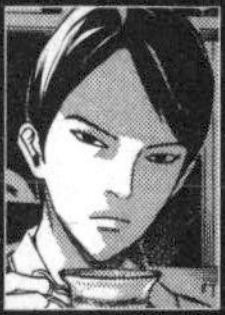

EBISU

A no-nonsense businessgod, one of the Seven Gods of Fortune.

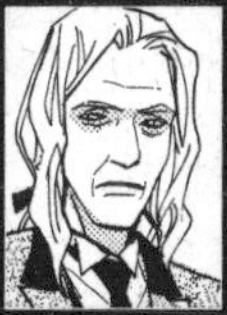

IWAMI

Ebisu's shinki and guide.

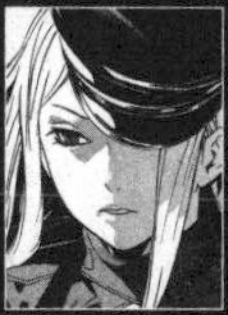

BISHA-MONTEN

A powerful warrior god, one of the Seven Gods of Fortune.

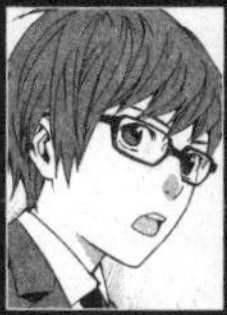

KAZUMA

A navigational shinki who serves as guide to Bishamon.

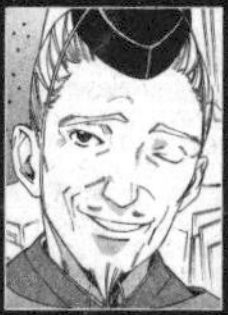

TENJIN

The god of learning, Sugawara no Michizane.

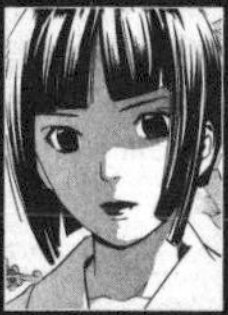

MAYU

Formerly Yato's shinki, now Tenjin's shinki.

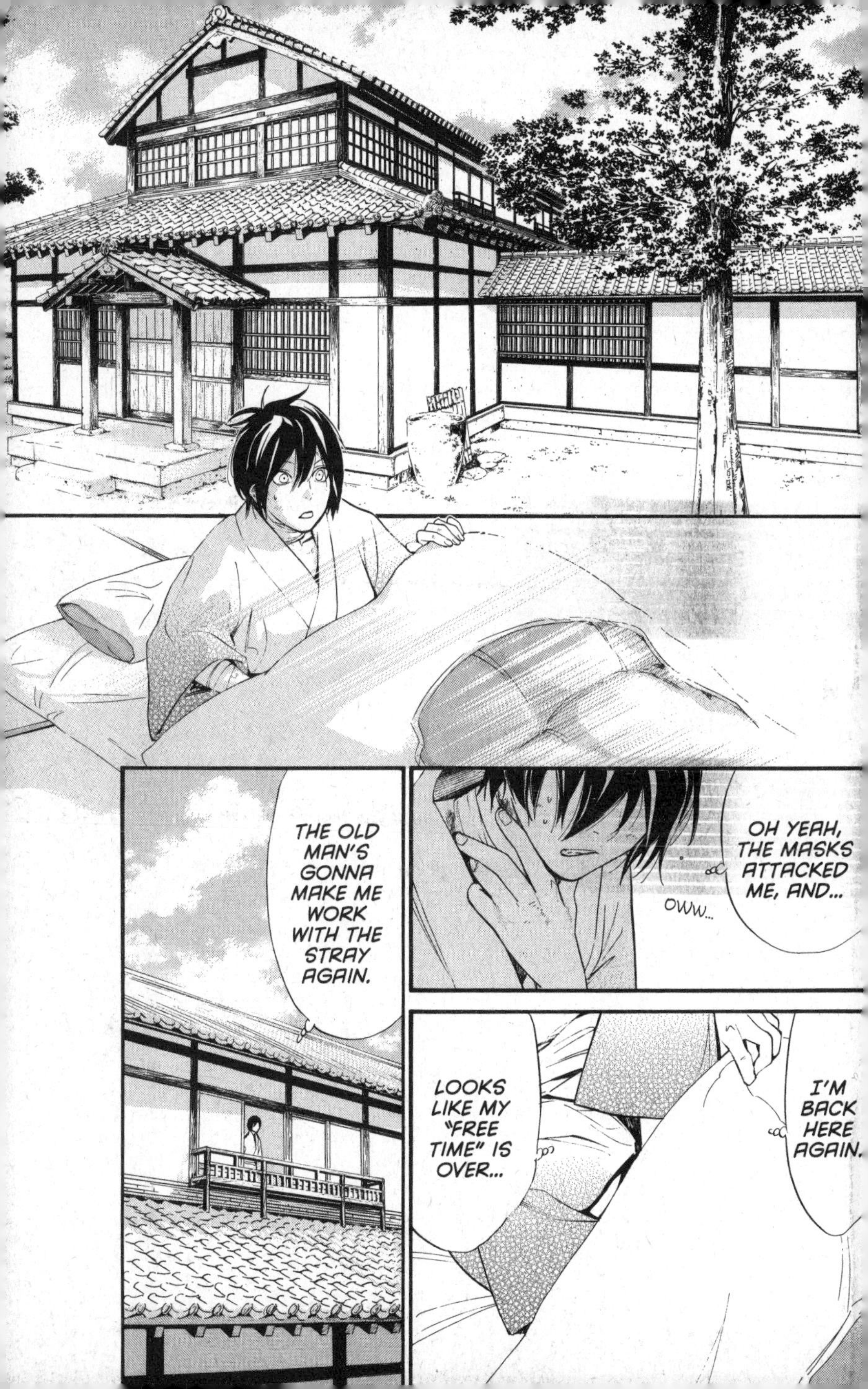
OH YEAH, THE MASKS ATTACKED ME, AND...
OWW...
I'M BACK HERE AGAIN.
LOOKS LIKE MY "FREE TIME" IS OVER...
THE OLD MAN'S GONNA MAKE ME WORK WITH THE STRAY AGAIN.

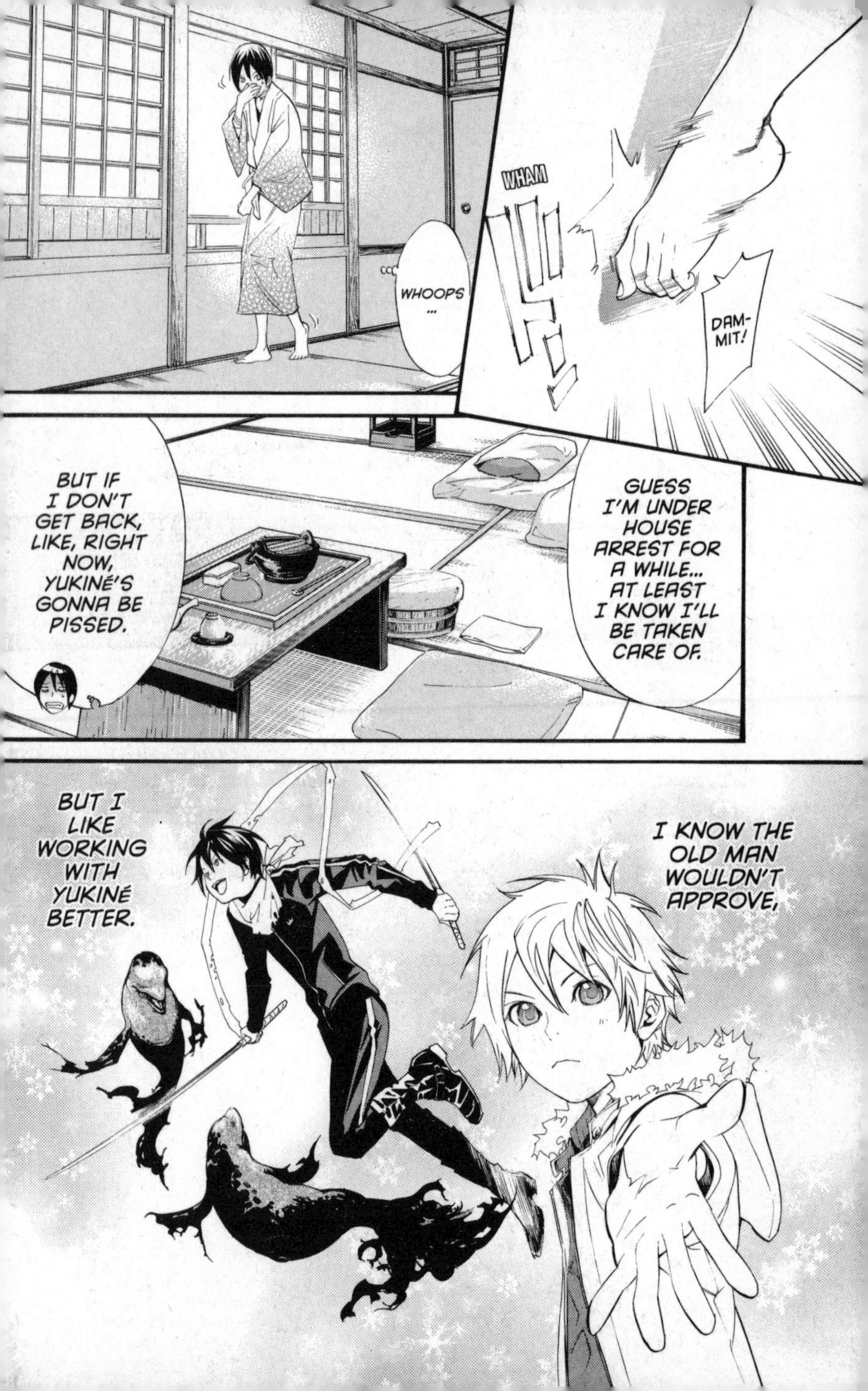
WHAM
DAM-MIT!
WHOOPS ...
GUESS I'M UNDER HOUSE ARREST FOR A WHILE... AT LEAST I KNOW I'LL BE TAKEN CARE OF.
BUT IF I DON'T GET BACK, LIKE, RIGHT NOW, YUKINÉ'S GONNA BE PISSED.
I KNOW THE OLD MAN WOULDN'T APPROVE,
BUT I LIKE WORKING WITH YUKINÉ BETTER.

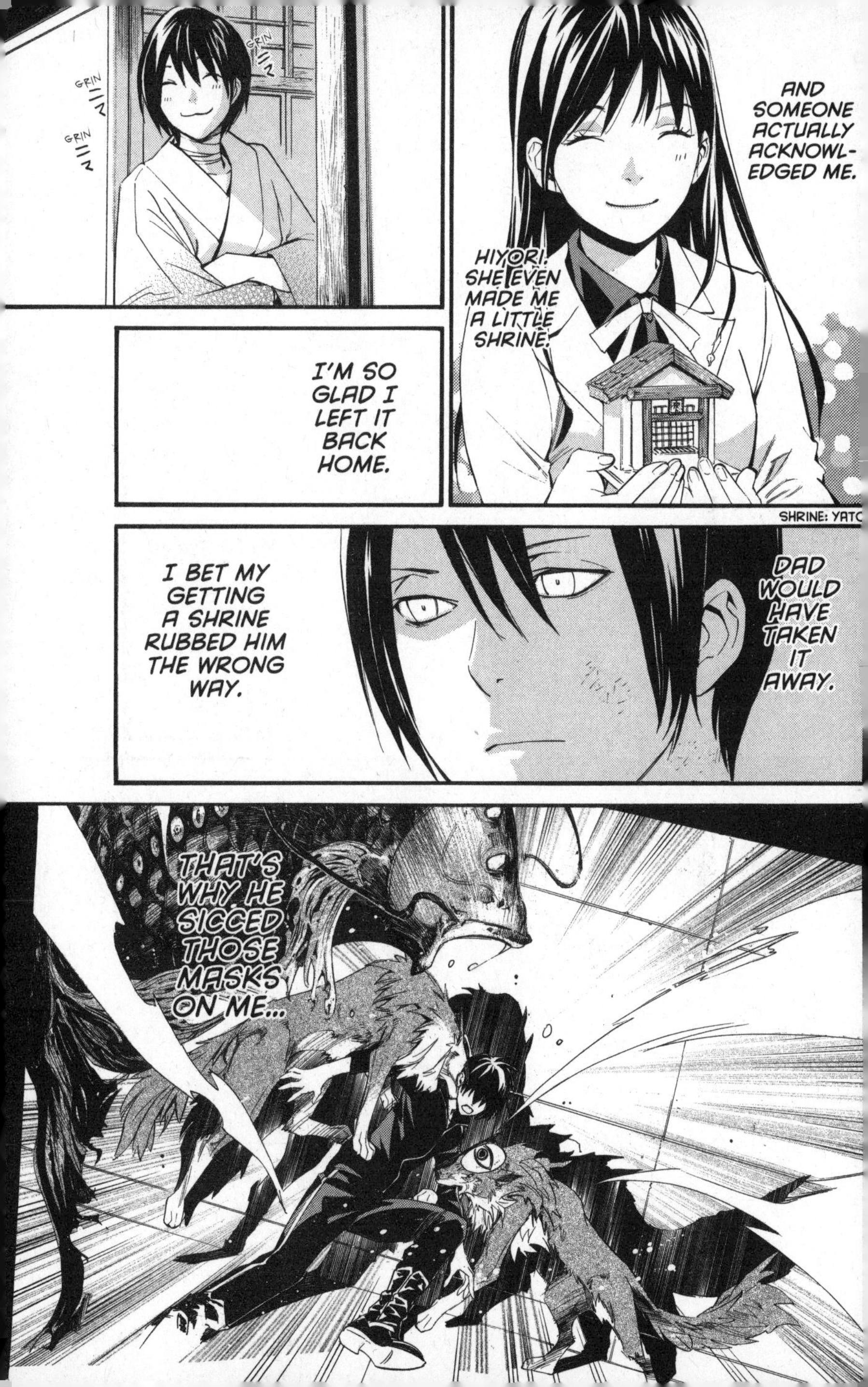
AND SOMEONE ACTUALLY ACKNOWL-EDGED ME.
HIYORI. SHE EVEN MADE ME A LITTLE SHRINE.
SHRINE: YAT
GRIN
GRIN
GRIN
I'M SO GLAD I LEFT IT BACK HOME.
DAD WOULD HAVE TAKEN IT AWAY.
I BET MY GETTING A SHRINE RUBBED HIM THE WRONG WAY.
THAT'S WHY HE SICCED THOSE MASKS ON ME...

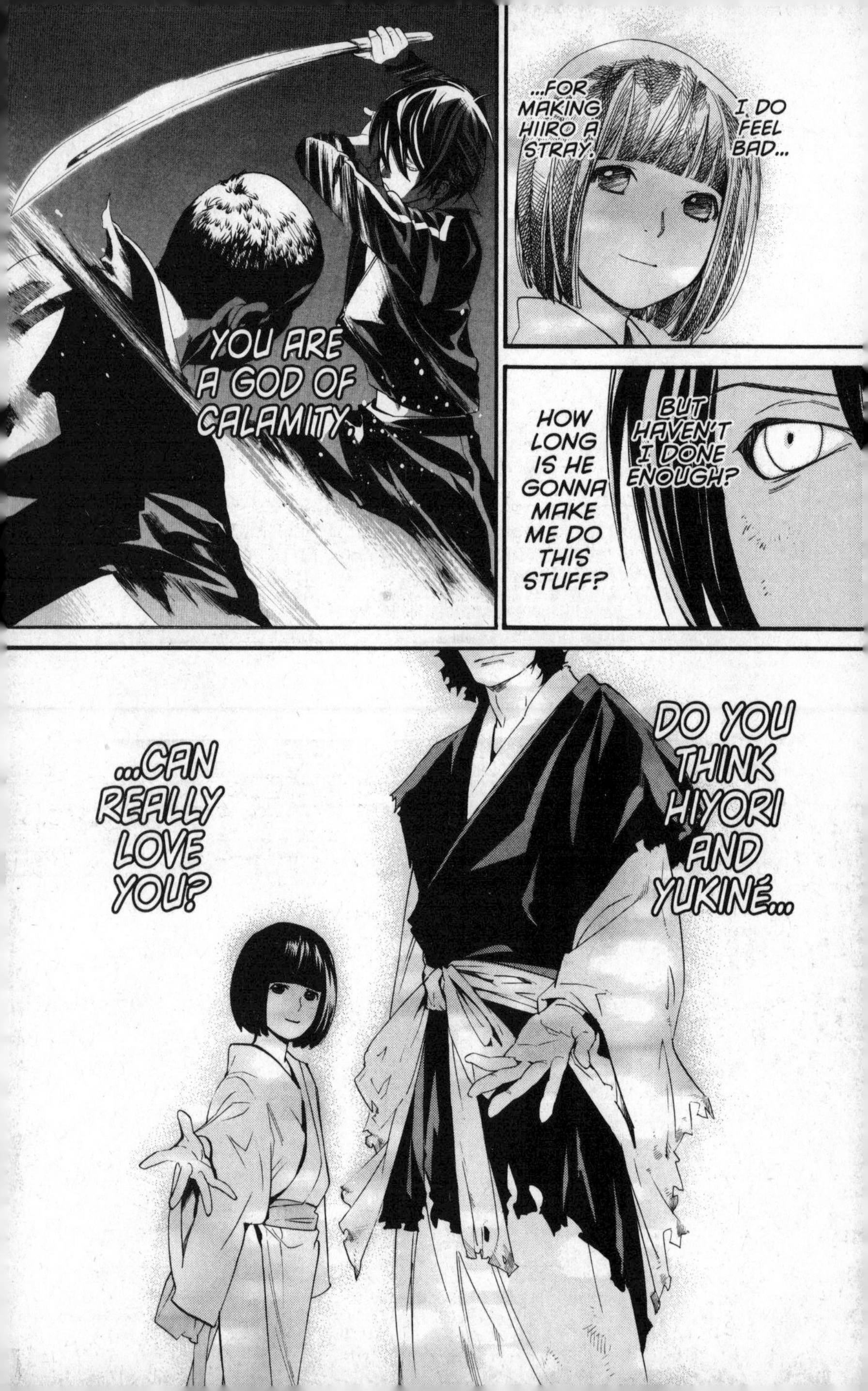
I DO FEEL BAD...
...FOR MAKING HIIRO A STRAY.
BUT HAVEN'T I DONE ENOUGH?
HOW LONG IS HE GONNA MAKE ME DO THIS STUFF?
YOU ARE A GOD OF CALAMITY.
DO YOU THINK HIYORI AND YUKINÉ...
...CAN REALLY LOVE YOU?

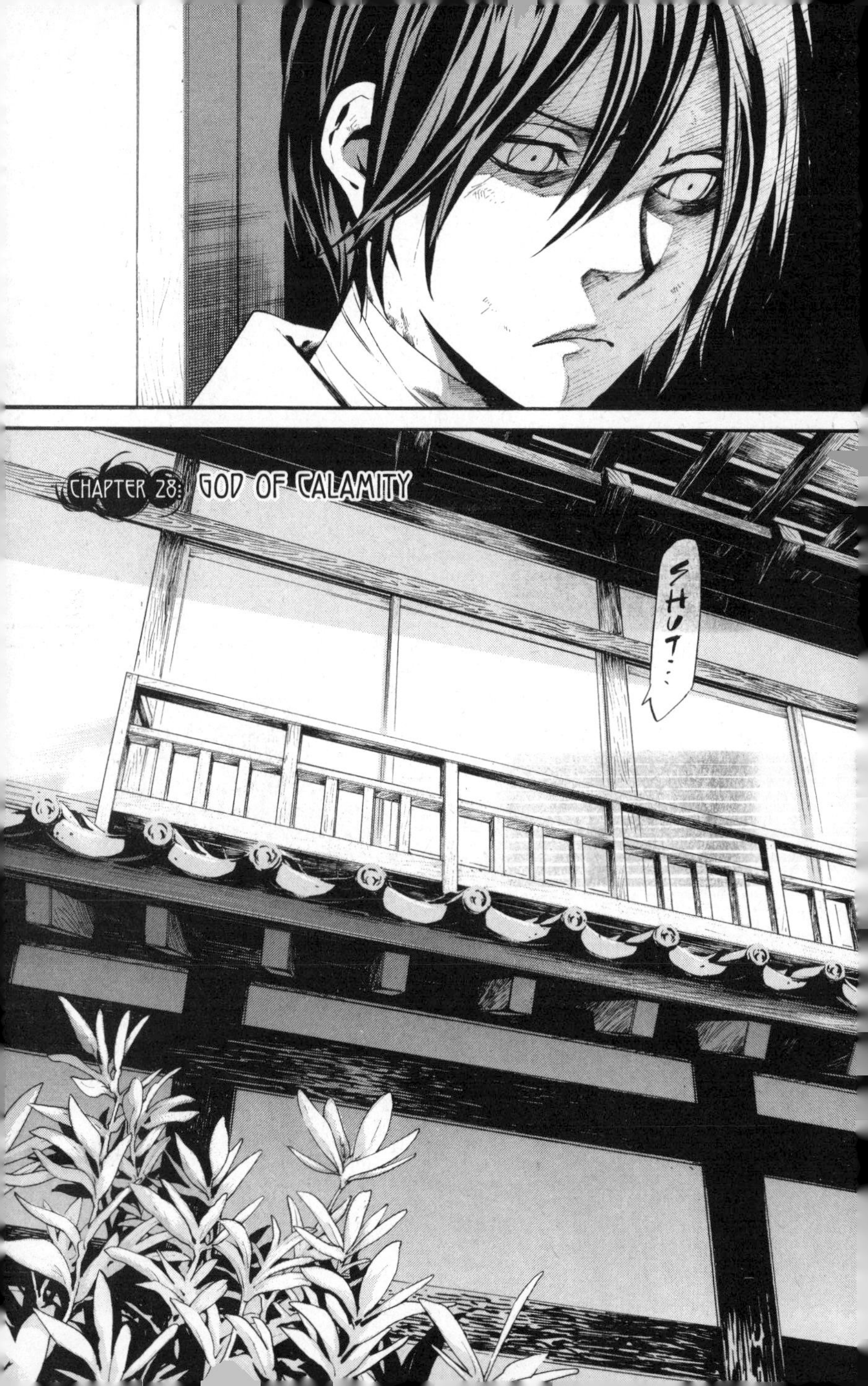
CHAPTER 28: GOD OF CALAMITY
SHUT...

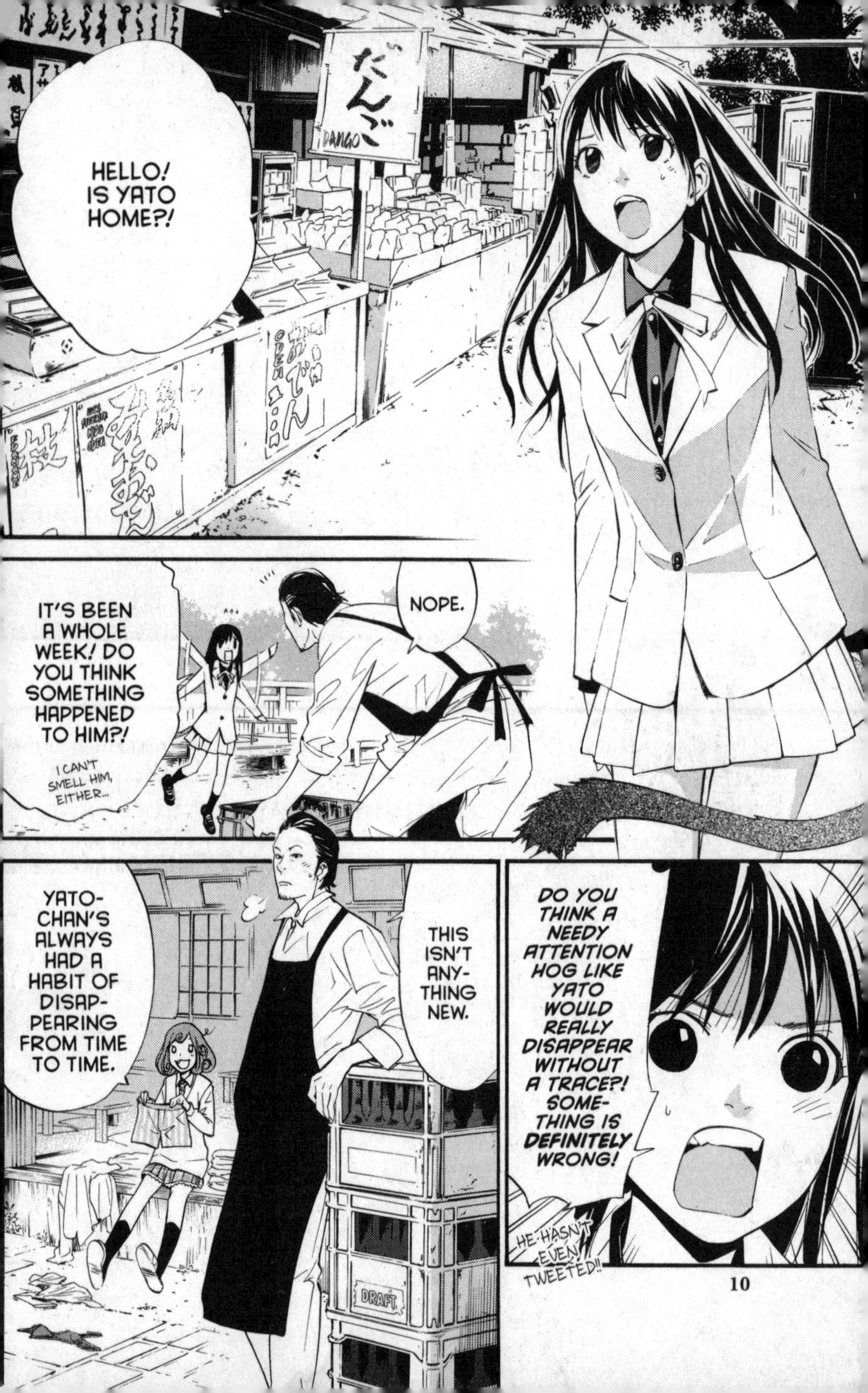

だんご
DANGO
HELLO! IS YATO HOME?!
おでん
ODEN
NOPE.
IT'S BEEN A WHOLE WEEK! DO YOU THINK SOMETHING HAPPENED TO HIM?!
I CAN'T SMELL HIM, EITHER...
DO YOU THINK A NEEDY ATTENTION HOG LIKE YATO WOULD REALLY DISAPPEAR WITHOUT A TRACE?! SOMETHING IS **DEFINITELY** WRONG!
HE HASN'T EVEN TWEETED!!
THIS ISN'T ANYTHING NEW.
YATO-CHAN'S ALWAYS HAD A HABIT OF DISAPPEARING FROM TIME TO TIME.
DRAFT

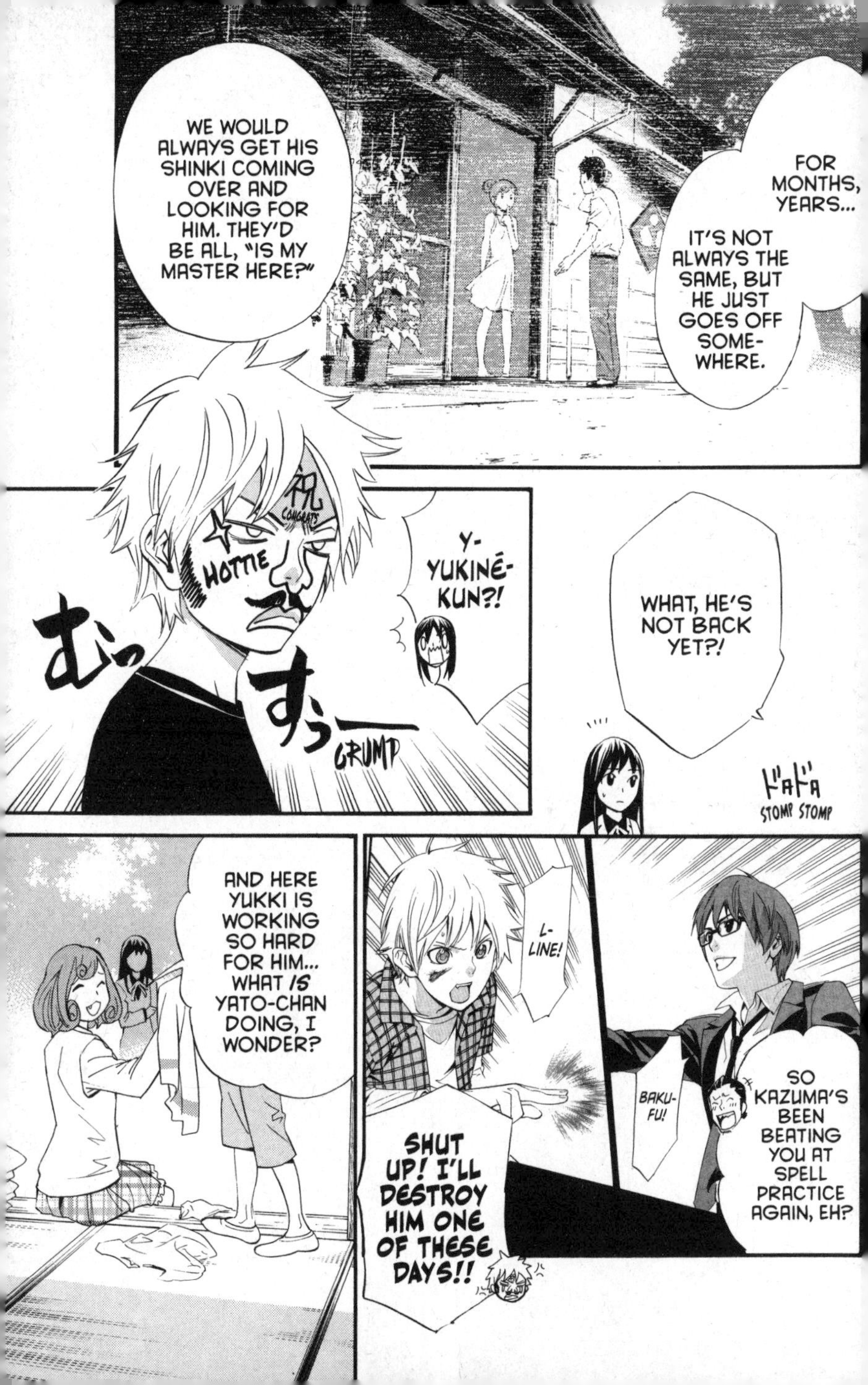
FOR MONTHS, YEARS...
IT'S NOT ALWAYS THE SAME, BUT HE JUST GOES OFF SOME-WHERE.
WE WOULD ALWAYS GET HIS SHINKI COMING OVER AND LOOKING FOR HIM. THEY'D BE ALL, "IS MY MASTER HERE?"
WHAT, HE'S NOT BACK YET?!
ドタドタ
STOMP STOMP
Y-YUKINĒ-KUN?!
祝
CONGRATS
HOTTIE
むっすぅー
GRUMP
SO KAZUMA'S BEEN BEATING YOU AT SPELL PRACTICE AGAIN, EH?
BAKU-FU!
L-LINE!
SHUT UP! I'LL DESTROY HIM ONE OF THESE DAYS!!
AND HERE YUKKI IS WORKING SO HARD FOR HIM... WHAT *IS* YATO-CHAN DOING, I WONDER?

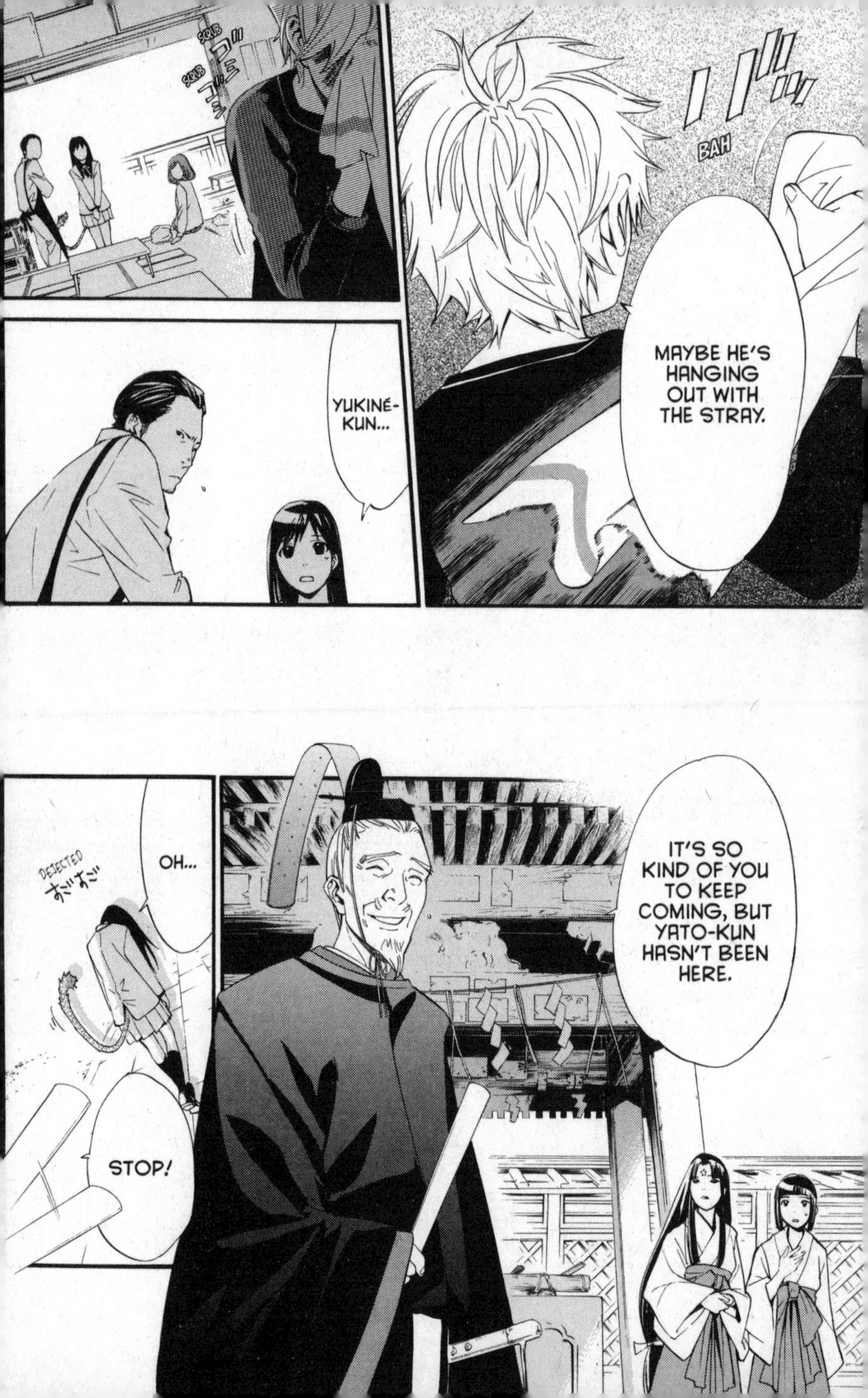
BAH
MAYBE HE'S HANGING OUT WITH THE STRAY.
SCRUB
SCRUB
YUKINÉ-KUN...
IT'S SO KIND OF YOU TO KEEP COMING, BUT YATO-KUN HASN'T BEEN HERE.
OH...
DEJECTED
STOP!

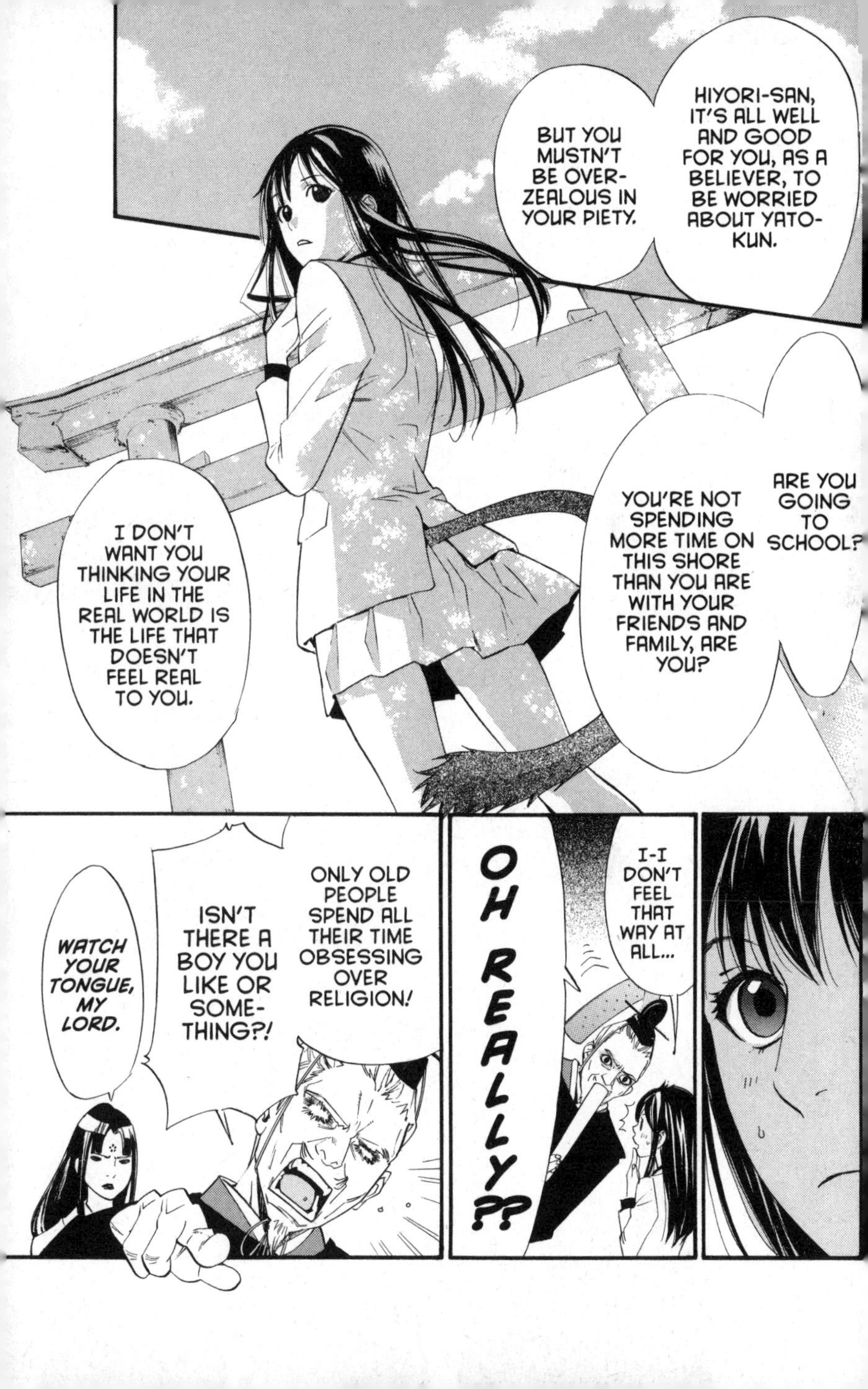
HIYORI-SAN, IT'S ALL WELL AND GOOD FOR YOU, AS A BELIEVER, TO BE WORRIED ABOUT YATO-KUN.
BUT YOU MUSTN'T BE OVER-ZEALOUS IN YOUR PIETY.
ARE YOU GOING TO SCHOOL?
YOU'RE NOT SPENDING MORE TIME ON THIS SHORE THAN YOU ARE WITH YOUR FRIENDS AND FAMILY, ARE YOU?
I DON'T WANT YOU THINKING YOUR LIFE IN THE REAL WORLD IS THE LIFE THAT DOESN'T FEEL REAL TO YOU.
I-I DON'T FEEL THAT WAY AT ALL...
OH REALLY??
ONLY OLD PEOPLE SPEND ALL THEIR TIME OBSESSING OVER RELIGION!
ISN'T THERE A BOY YOU LIKE OR SOME-THING?!
WATCH YOUR TONGUE, MY LORD.

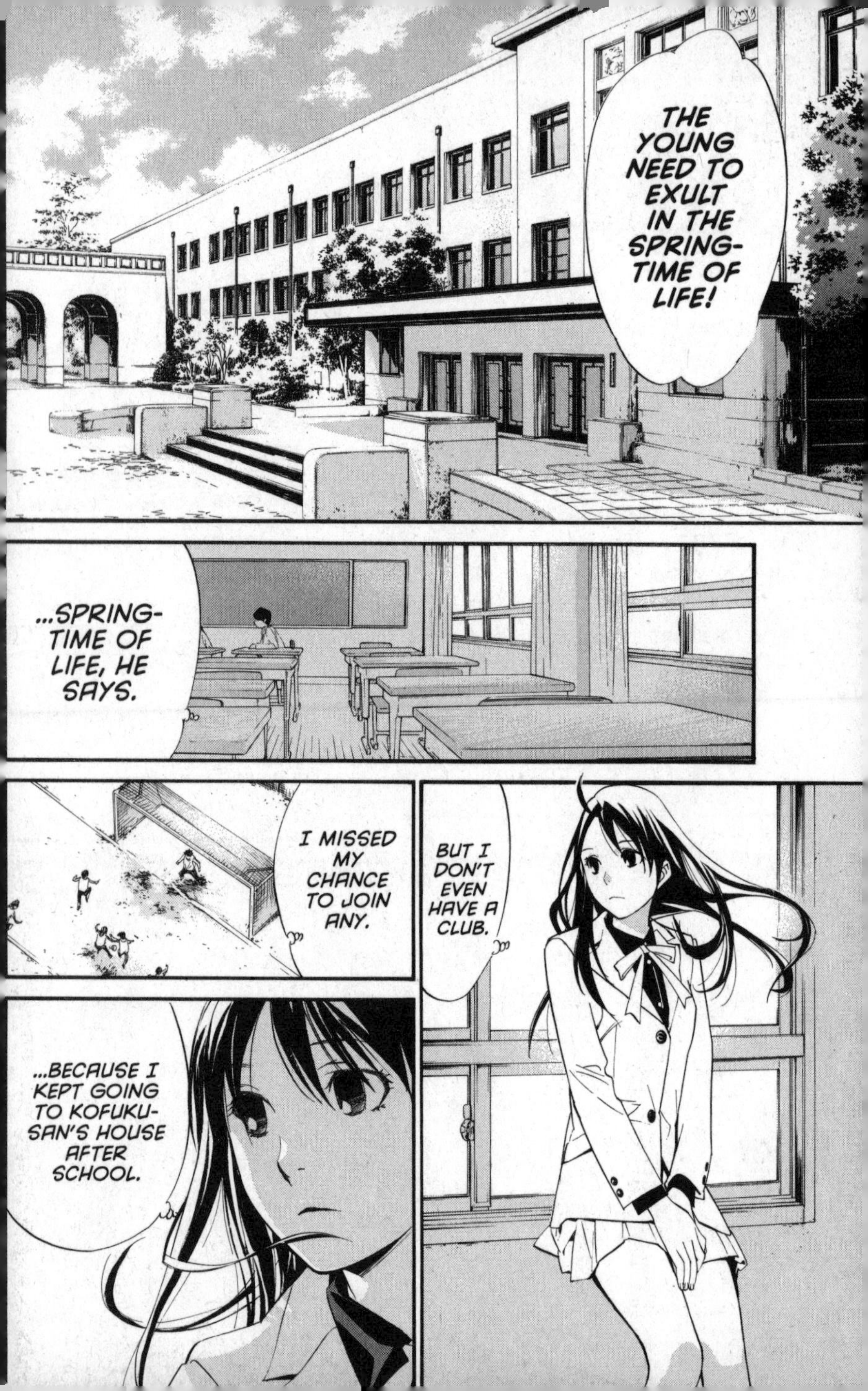
THE YOUNG NEED TO EXULT IN THE SPRING-TIME OF LIFE!
...SPRING-TIME OF LIFE, HE SAYS.
BUT I DON'T EVEN HAVE A CLUB.
I MISSED MY CHANCE TO JOIN ANY.
...BECAUSE I KEPT GOING TO KOFUKU-SAN'S HOUSE AFTER SCHOOL.

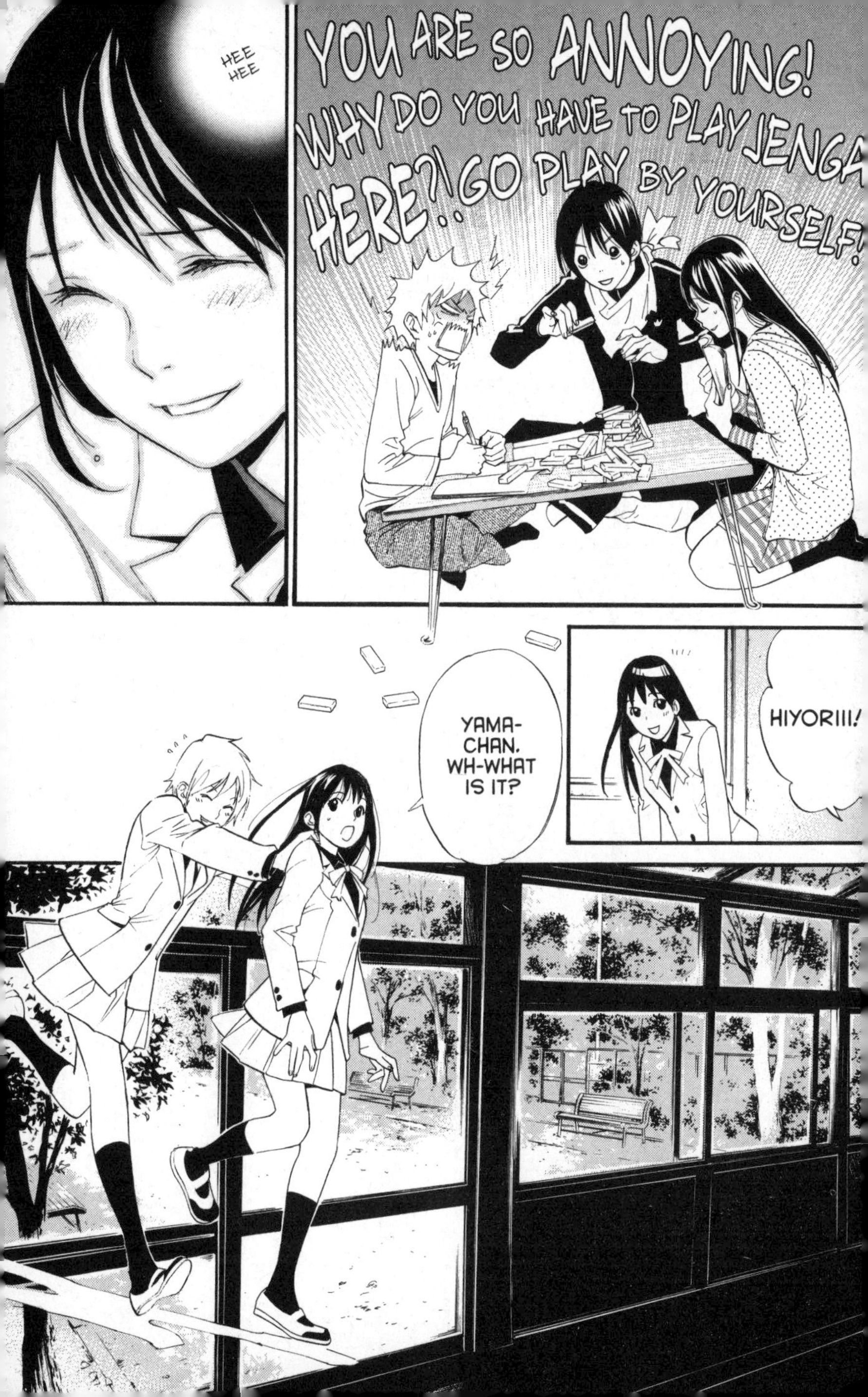
YOU ARE SO ANNOYING! WHY DO YOU HAVE TO PLAY JENGA HERE?! GO PLAY BY YOURSELF!
HEE HEE
HIYORIII!
YAMA-CHAN. WH-WHAT IS IT?

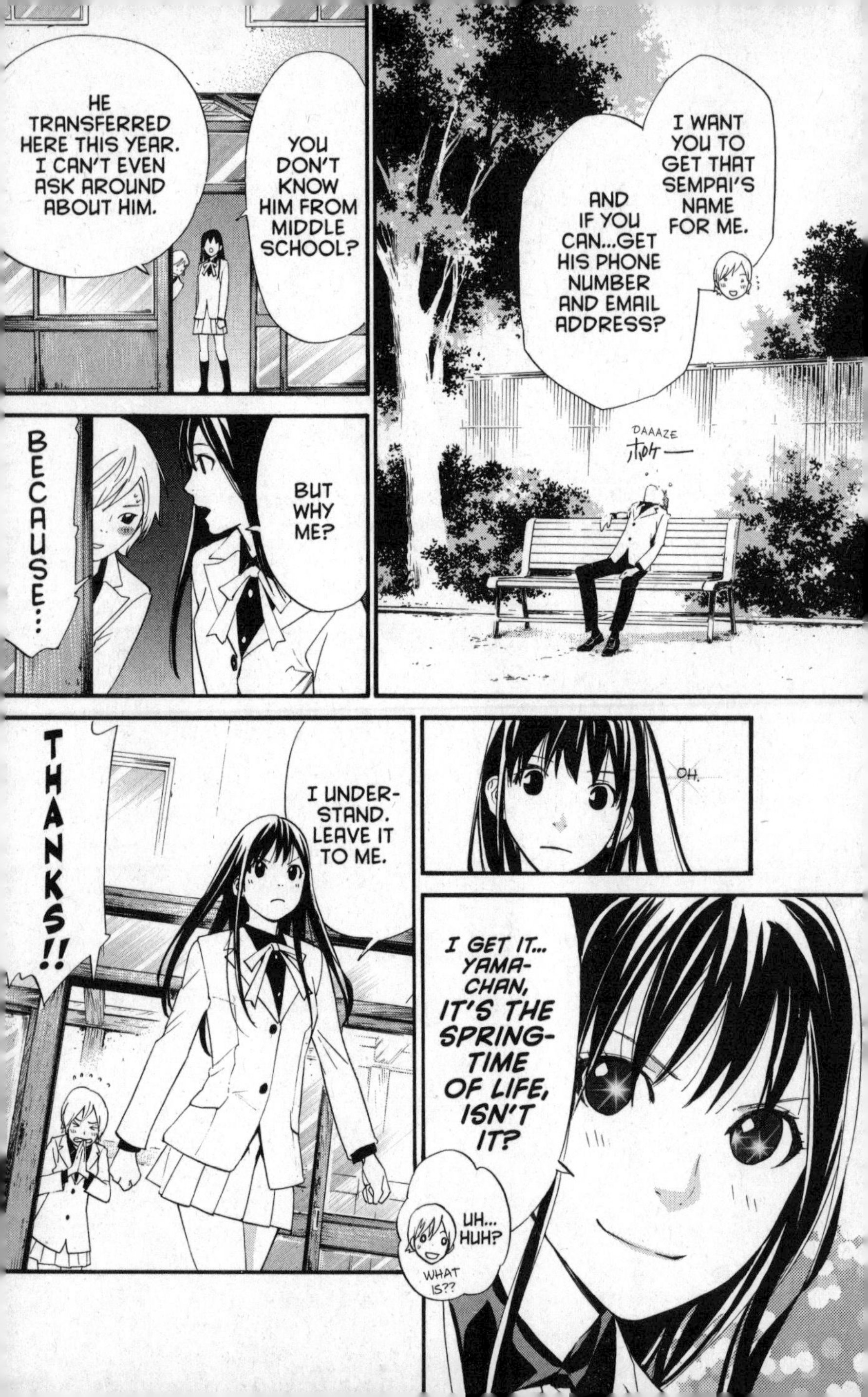
I WANT YOU TO GET THAT SEMPAI'S NAME FOR ME.
AND IF YOU CAN...GET HIS PHONE NUMBER AND EMAIL ADDRESS?
DAAAZE
YOU DON'T KNOW HIM FROM MIDDLE SCHOOL?
HE TRANSFERRED HERE THIS YEAR. I CAN'T EVEN ASK AROUND ABOUT HIM.
BUT WHY ME?
BECAUSE...
OH.
I GET IT... YAMA-CHAN, IT'S THE SPRING-TIME OF LIFE, ISN'T IT?
UH... HUH?
WHAT IS??
I UNDER-STAND. LEAVE IT TO ME.
THANKS!!

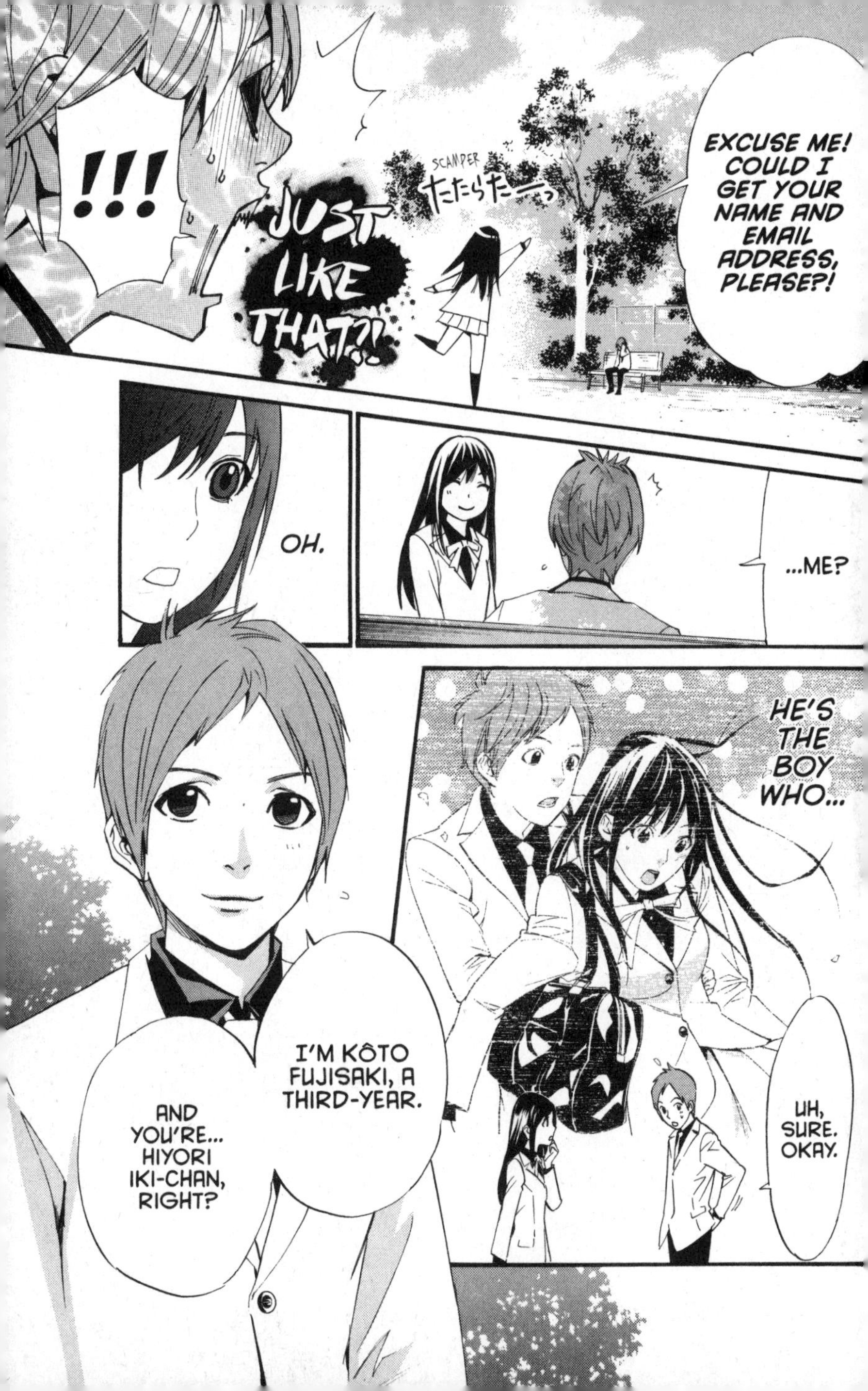
EXCUSE ME! COULD I GET YOUR NAME AND EMAIL ADDRESS, PLEASE?!
SCAMPER
たたらたーっ
JUST LIKE THAT?!
!!!
...ME?
OH.
HE'S THE BOY WHO...
UH, SURE. OKAY.
I'M KÔTO FUJISAKI, A THIRD-YEAR.
AND YOU'RE... HIYORI IKI-CHAN, RIGHT?

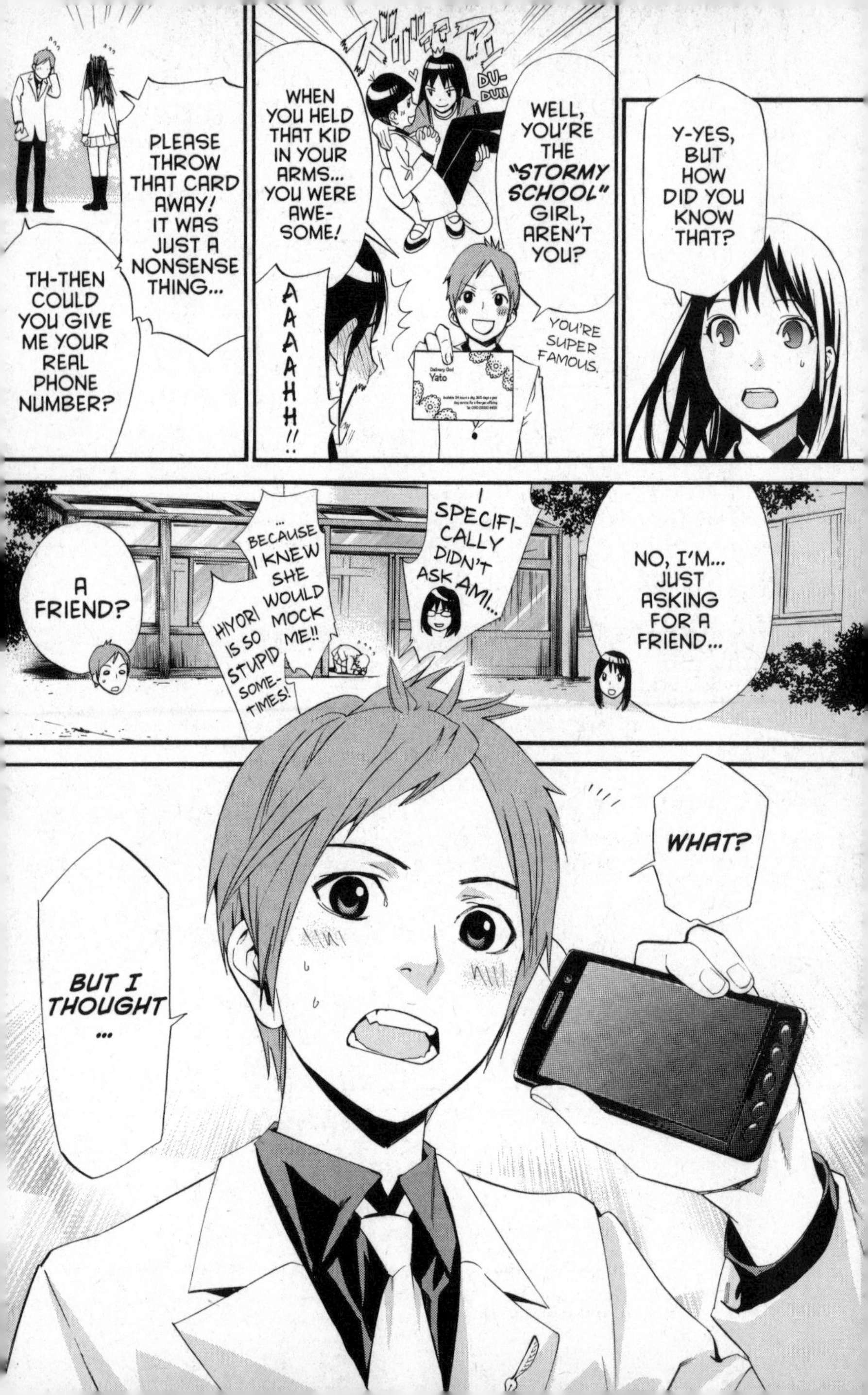
Y-YES, BUT HOW DID YOU KNOW THAT?
WELL, YOU'RE THE "STORMY SCHOOL" GIRL, AREN'T YOU?
DU-DUN
YOU'RE SUPER FAMOUS.
WHEN YOU HELD THAT KID IN YOUR ARMS... YOU WERE AWESOME!
Delivery God Yato
AAAAAHH!!
PLEASE THROW THAT CARD AWAY! IT WAS JUST A NONSENSE THING...
TH-THEN COULD YOU GIVE ME YOUR REAL PHONE NUMBER?
NO, I'M... JUST ASKING FOR A FRIEND...
I SPECIFICALLY DIDN'T ASK AMI...
...BECAUSE I KNEW SHE WOULD MOCK ME!!
HIYORI IS SO STUPID SOMETIMES!
A FRIEND?
WHAT?
BUT I THOUGHT ...

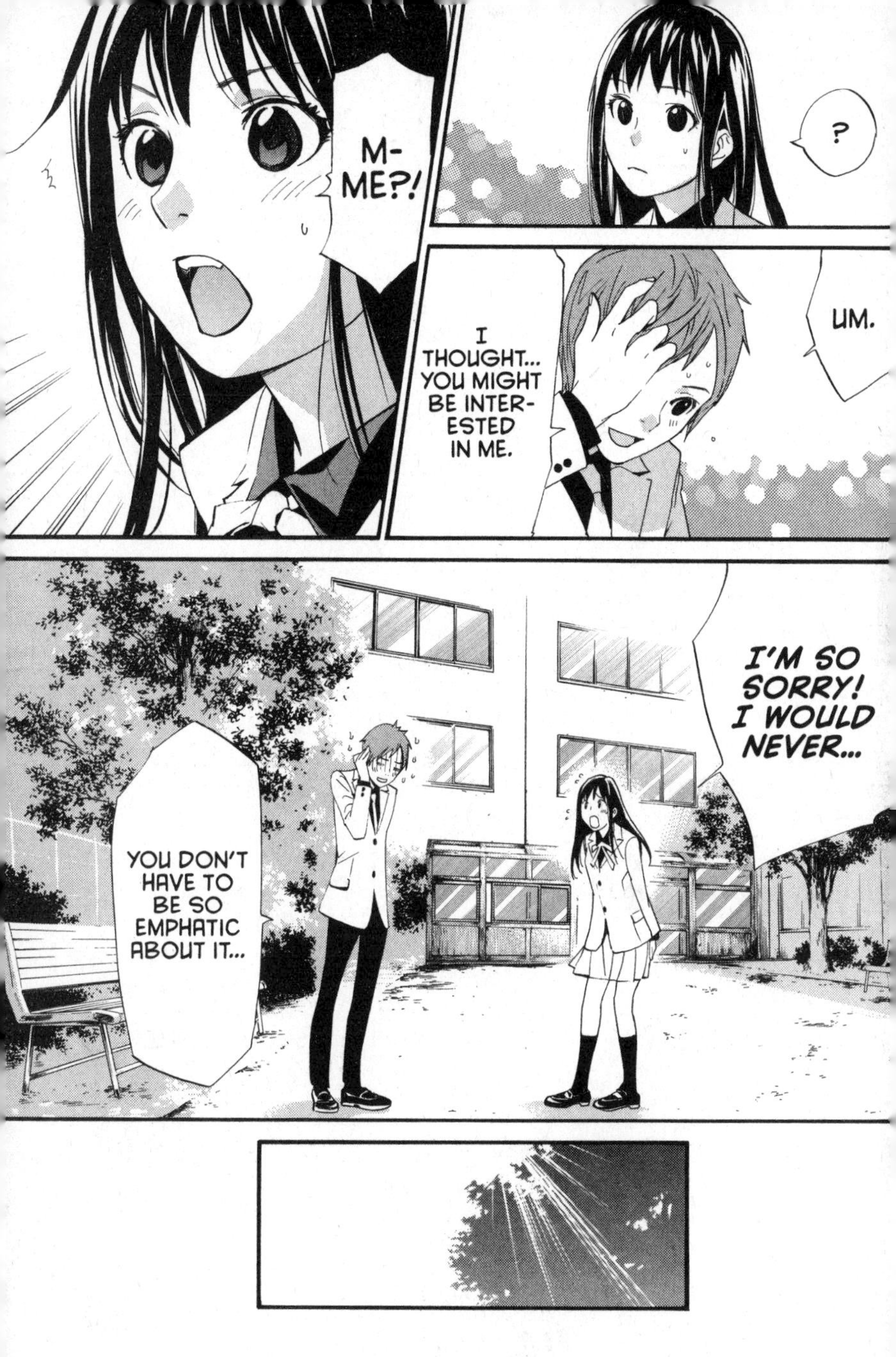
?
UM.
I THOUGHT... YOU MIGHT BE INTER-ESTED IN ME.
M-ME?!
I'M SO SORRY! I WOULD NEVER...
YOU DON'T HAVE TO BE SO EMPHATIC ABOUT IT...

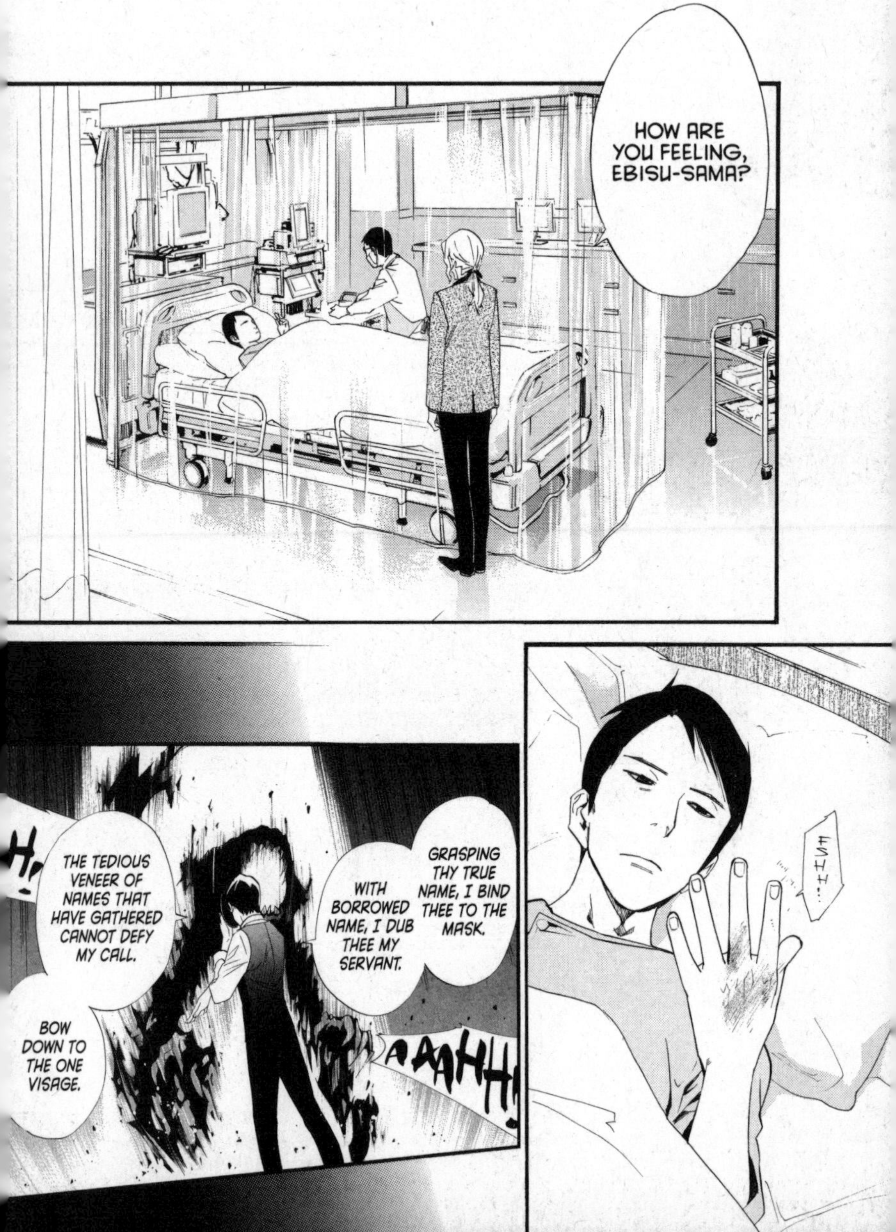
HOW ARE YOU FEELING, EBISU-SAMA?
FSHH...
GRASPING THY TRUE NAME, I BIND THEE TO THE MASK.
WITH BORROWED NAME, I DUB THEE MY SERVANT.
THE TEDIOUS VENEER OF NAMES THAT HAVE GATHERED CANNOT DEFY MY CALL.
AAHH!
BOW DOWN TO THE ONE VISAGE.

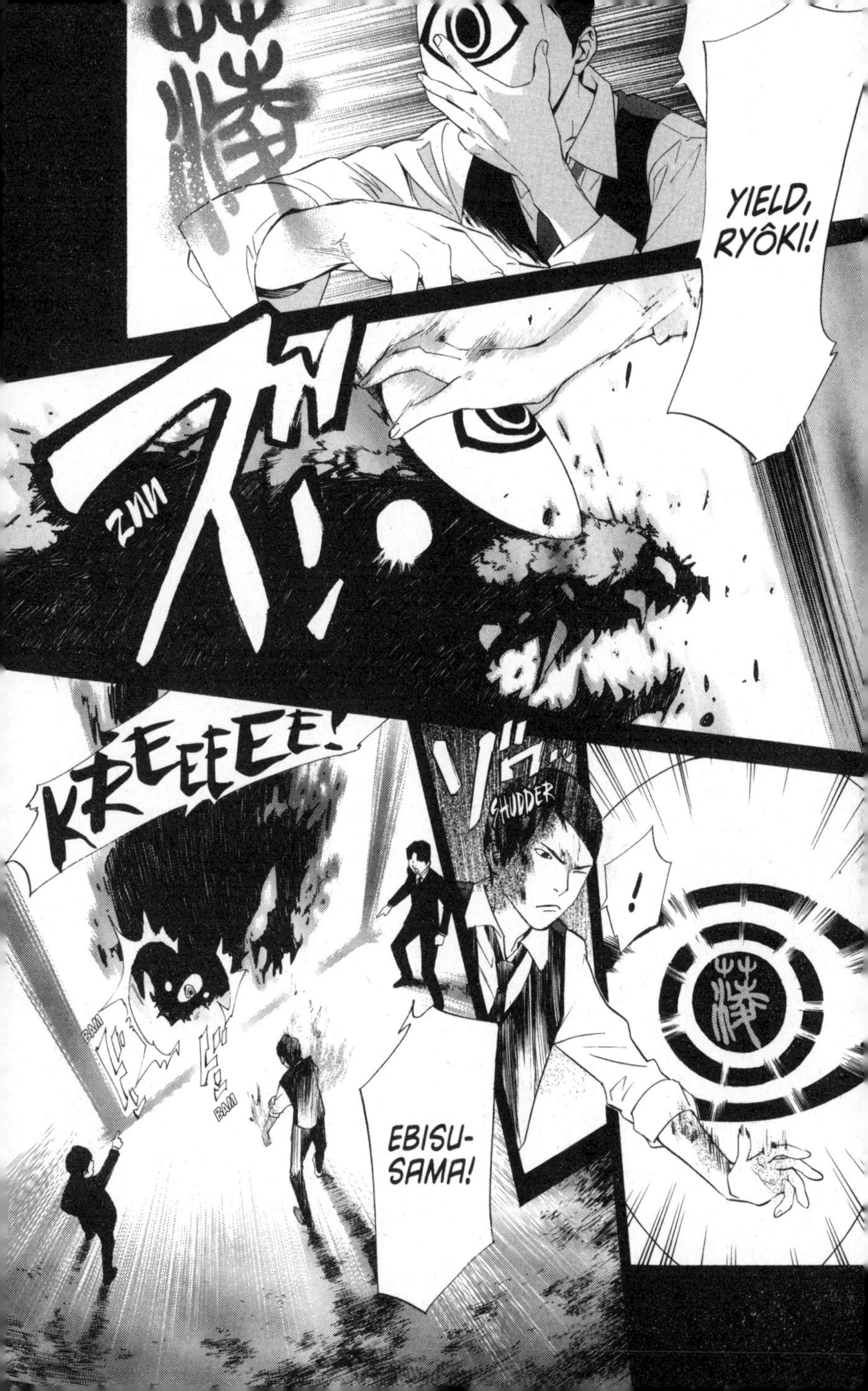
YIELD, RYÔKI!
ZNN
SHUDDER
!
EBISU-SAMA!
KREEEEE!
BAM
BAM

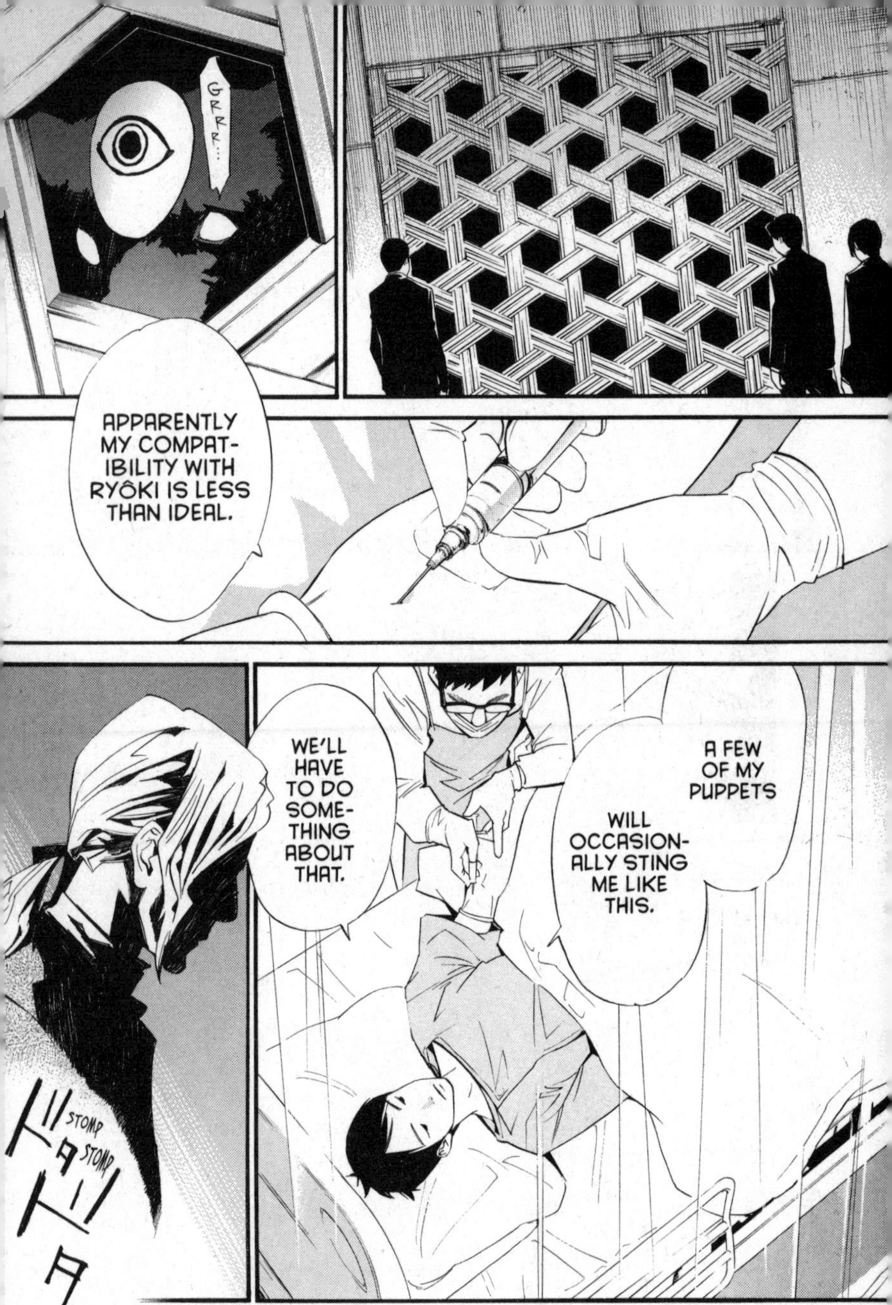
GRRR...
APPARENTLY MY COMPAT-IBILITY WITH RYÔKI IS LESS THAN IDEAL.
A FEW OF MY PUPPETS
WILL OCCASION-ALLY STING ME LIKE THIS.
WE'LL HAVE TO DO SOME-THING ABOUT THAT.
STOMP STOMP

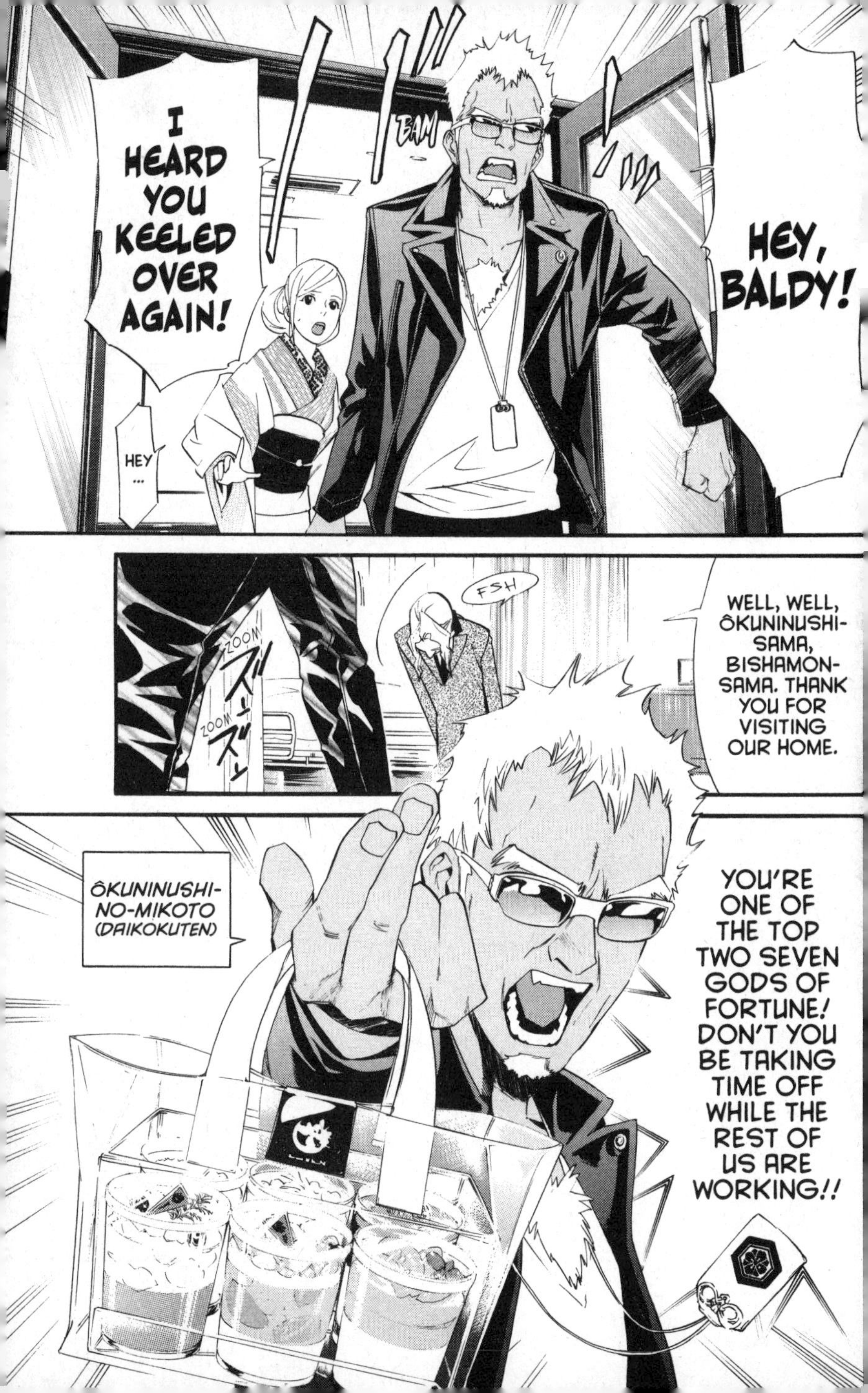
HEY, BALDY!
BAM
I HEARD YOU KEELED OVER AGAIN!
HEY ...
WELL, WELL, ÔKUNINUSHI-SAMA, BISHAMON-SAMA. THANK YOU FOR VISITING OUR HOME.
FSH
ZOOM
ZOOM
YOU'RE ONE OF THE TOP TWO SEVEN GODS OF FORTUNE! DON'T YOU BE TAKING TIME OFF WHILE THE REST OF US ARE WORKING!!
ÔKUNINUSHI-NO-MIKOTO (DAIKOKUTEN)

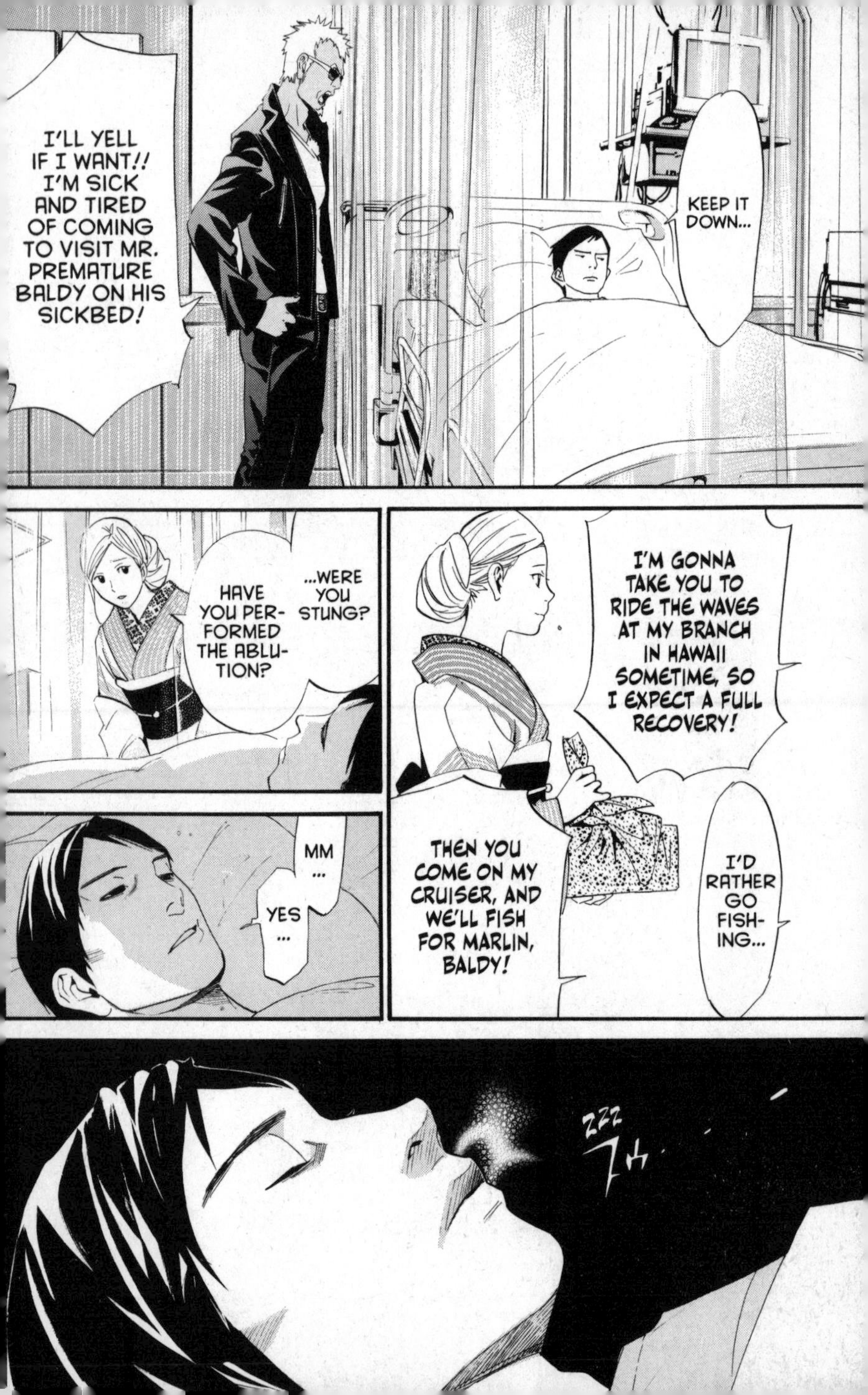
KEEP IT DOWN...
I'LL YELL IF I WANT!! I'M SICK AND TIRED OF COMING TO VISIT MR. PREMATURE BALDY ON HIS SICKBED!
I'M GONNA TAKE YOU TO RIDE THE WAVES AT MY BRANCH IN HAWAII SOMETIME, SO I EXPECT A FULL RECOVERY!
I'D RATHER GO FISH-ING...
THEN YOU COME ON MY CRUISER, AND WE'LL FISH FOR MARLIN, BALDY!
...WERE YOU STUNG?
HAVE YOU PER-FORMED THE ABLU-TION?
MM...
YES...
ZZZ

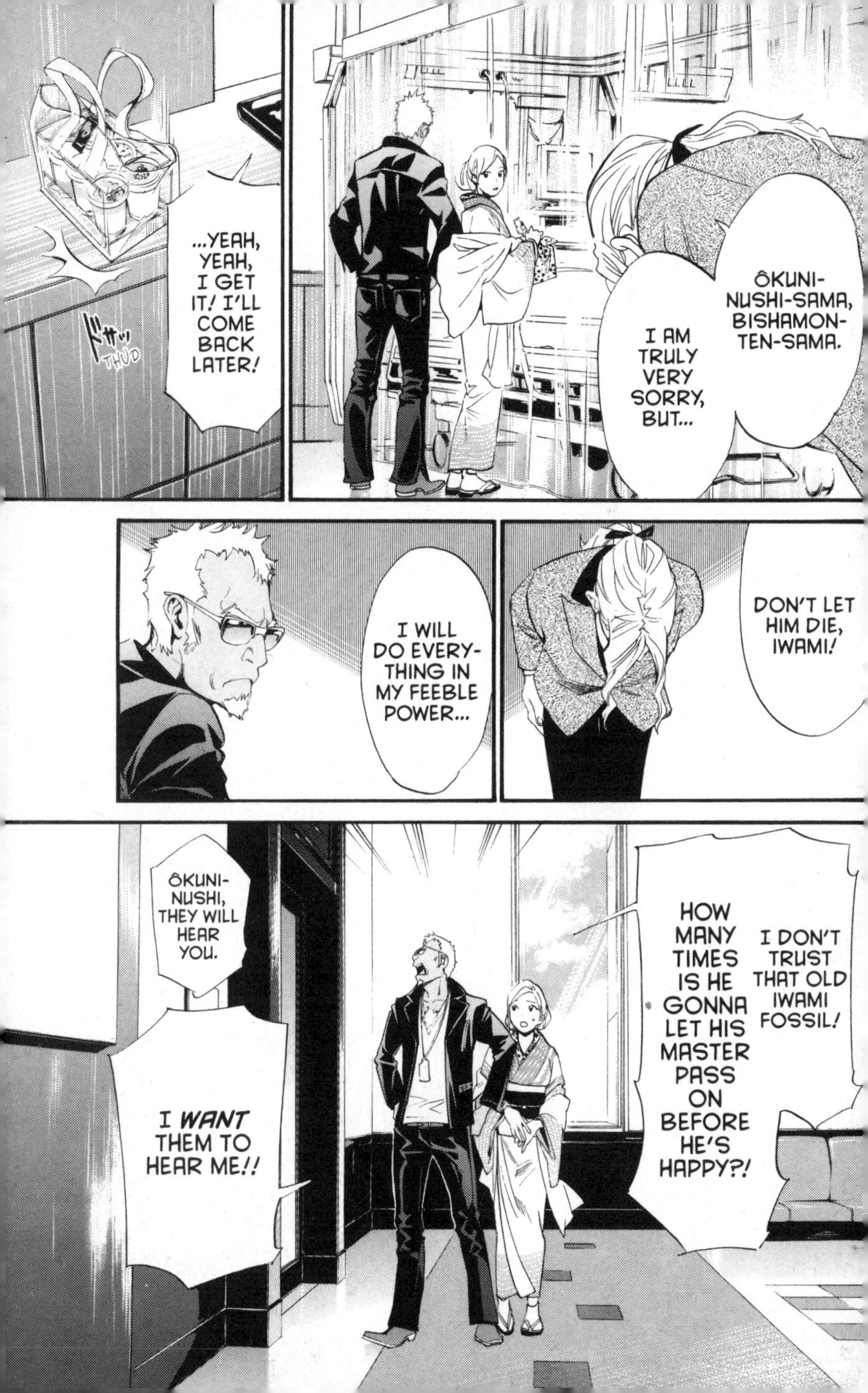
ÔKUNI-NUSHI-SAMA, BISHAMON-TEN-SAMA.
I AM TRULY VERY SORRY, BUT...
...YEAH, YEAH, I GET IT! I'LL COME BACK LATER!
ドサッ THUD
DON'T LET HIM DIE, IWAMI!
I WILL DO EVERY-THING IN MY FEEBLE POWER...
I DON'T TRUST THAT OLD IWAMI FOSSIL!
HOW MANY TIMES IS HE GONNA LET HIS MASTER PASS ON BEFORE HE'S HAPPY?!
ÔKUNI-NUSHI, THEY WILL HEAR YOU.
I *WANT* THEM TO HEAR ME!!

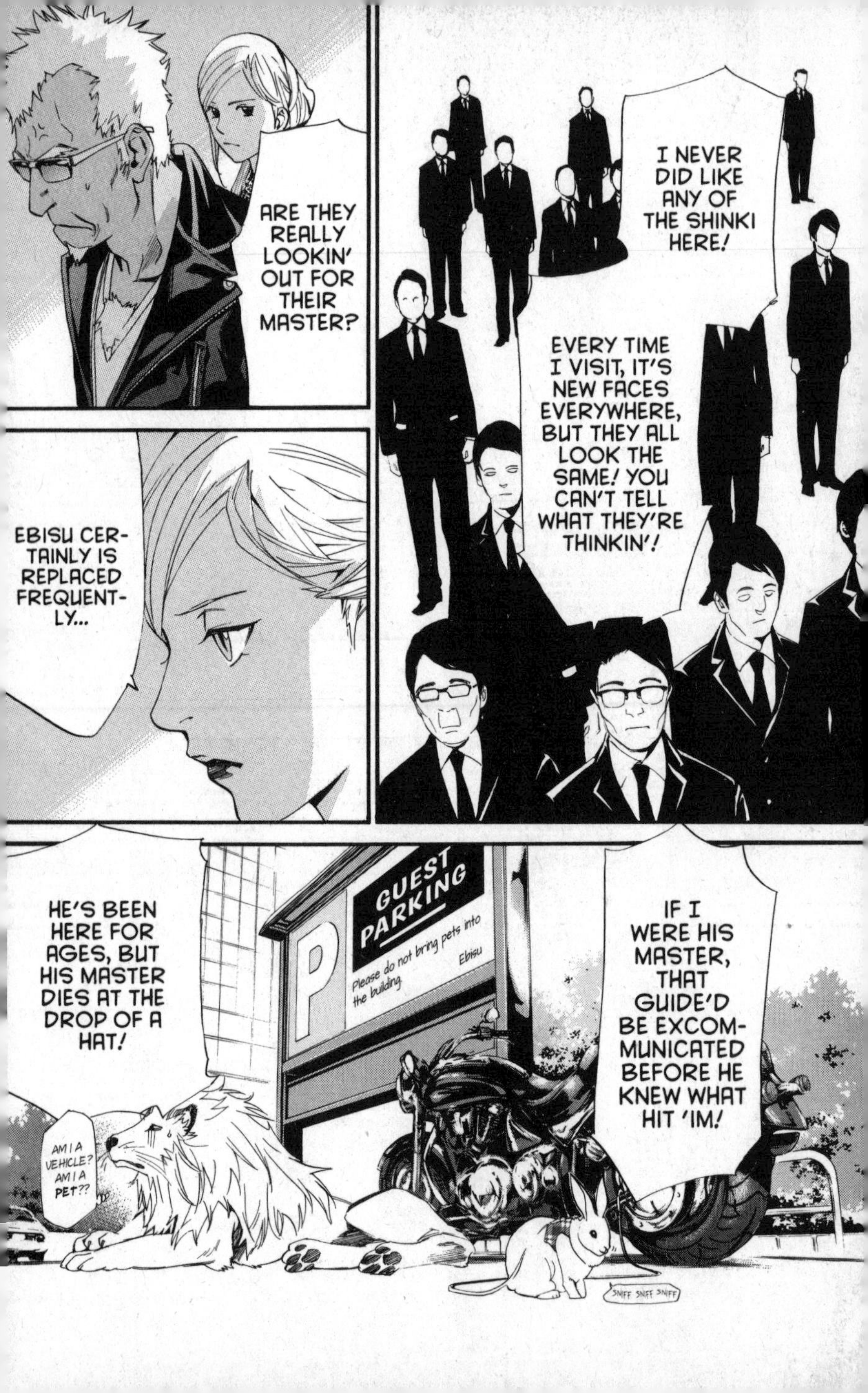
I NEVER DID LIKE ANY OF THE SHINKI HERE!
EVERY TIME I VISIT, IT'S NEW FACES EVERYWHERE, BUT THEY ALL LOOK THE SAME! YOU CAN'T TELL WHAT THEY'RE THINKIN'!
ARE THEY REALLY LOOKIN' OUT FOR THEIR MASTER?
EBISU CERTAINLY IS REPLACED FREQUENTLY...
IF I WERE HIS MASTER, THAT GUIDE'D BE EXCOMMUNICATED BEFORE HE KNEW WHAT HIT 'IM!
HE'S BEEN HERE FOR AGES, BUT HIS MASTER DIES AT THE DROP OF A HAT!
GUEST PARKING
P
Please do not bring pets into the building.
Ebisu
AM I A VEHICLE? AM I A PET??
SNIFF SNIFF SNIFF

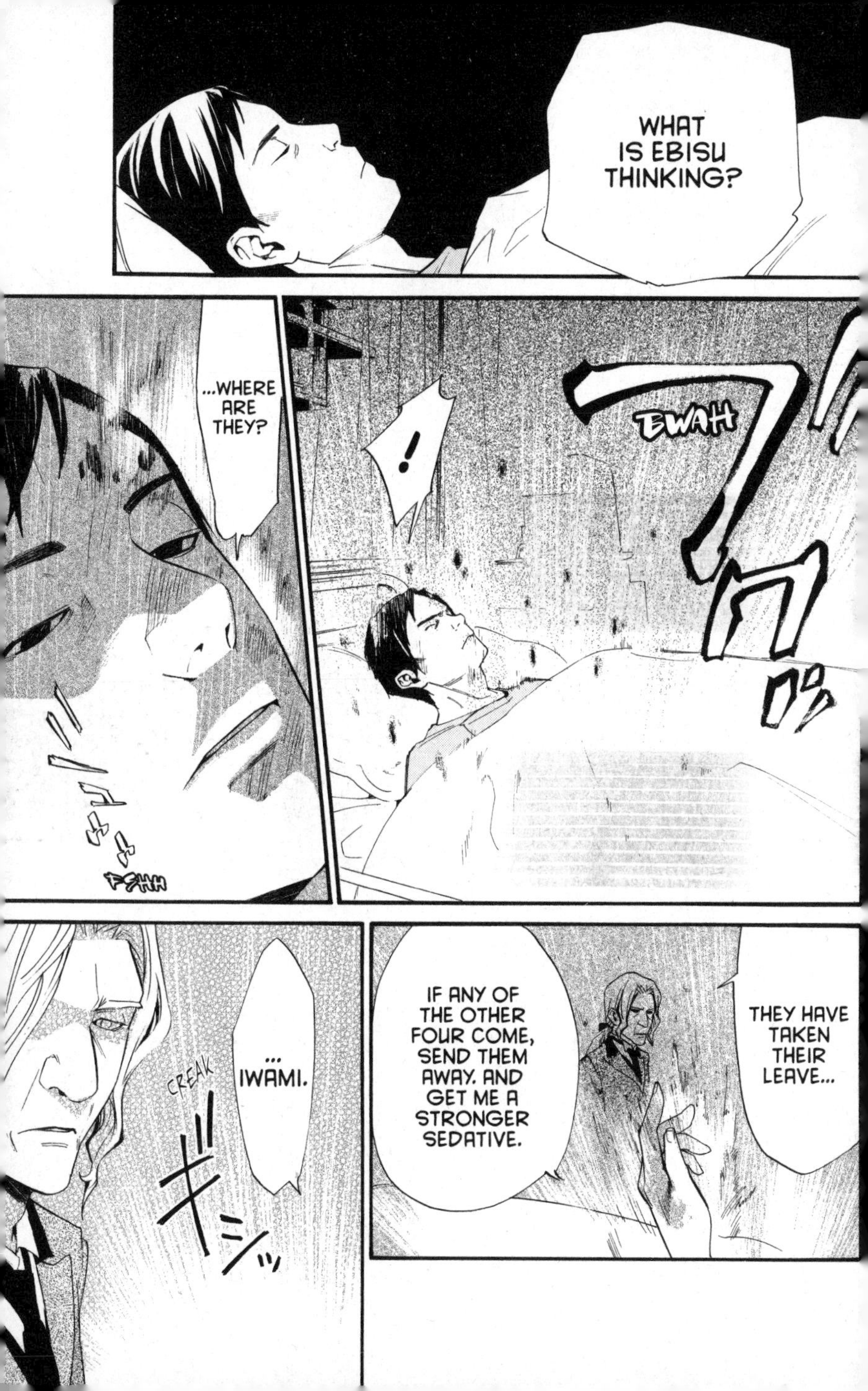
WHAT IS EBISU THINKING?
TWAH
!
...WHERE ARE THEY?
FSHH
THEY HAVE TAKEN THEIR LEAVE...
IF ANY OF THE OTHER FOUR COME, SEND THEM AWAY. AND GET ME A STRONGER SEDATIVE.
... IWAMI.
CREAK

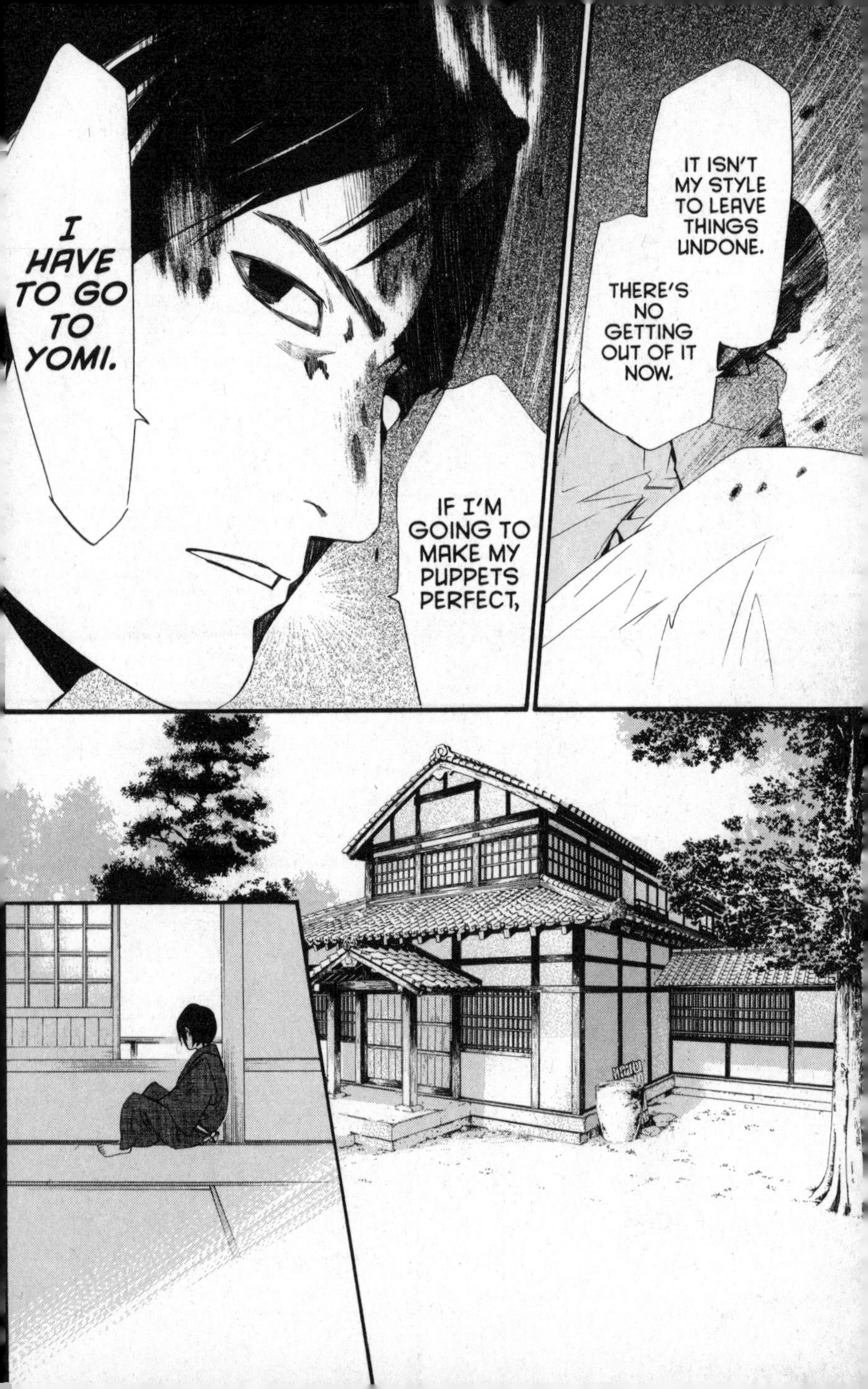
IT ISN'T MY STYLE TO LEAVE THINGS UNDONE.
THERE'S NO GETTING OUT OF IT NOW.
IF I'M GOING TO MAKE MY PUPPETS PERFECT,
I HAVE TO GO TO YOMI.

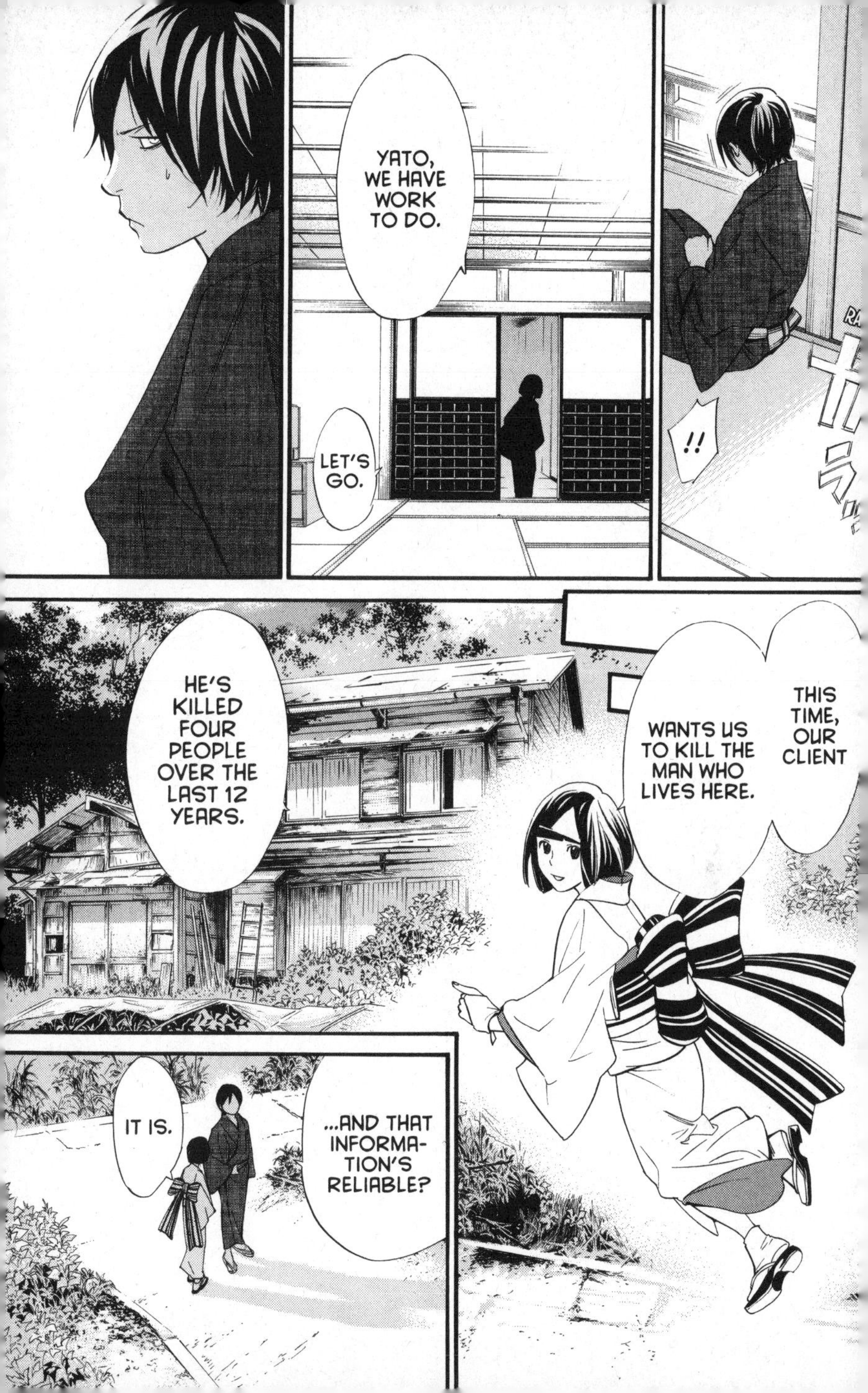
!!
YATO, WE HAVE WORK TO DO.
LET'S GO.
THIS TIME, OUR CLIENT
WANTS US TO KILL THE MAN WHO LIVES HERE.
HE'S KILLED FOUR PEOPLE OVER THE LAST 12 YEARS.
...AND THAT INFORMA-TION'S RELIABLE?
IT IS.

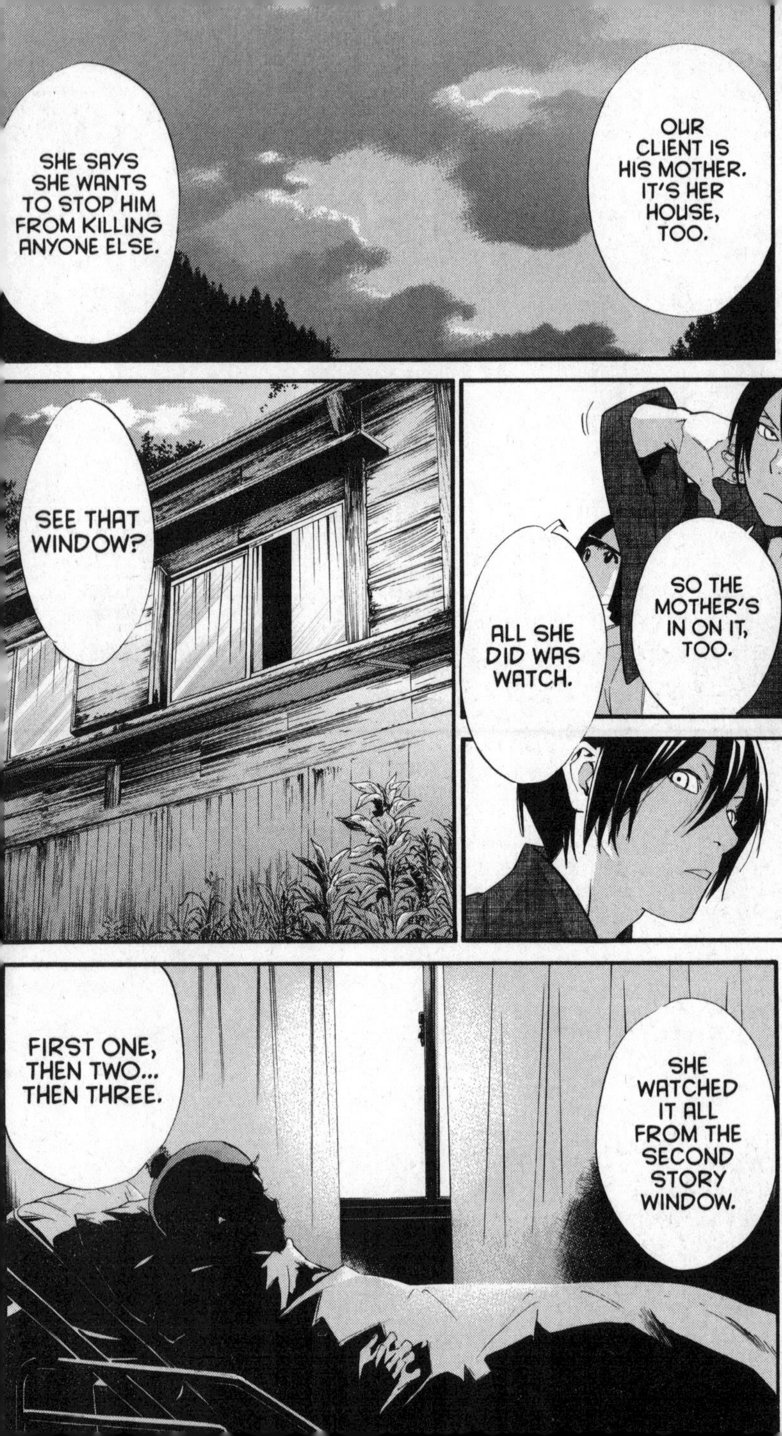
OUR CLIENT IS HIS MOTHER. IT'S HER HOUSE, TOO.
SHE SAYS SHE WANTS TO STOP HIM FROM KILLING ANYONE ELSE.
SO THE MOTHER'S IN ON IT, TOO.
ALL SHE DID WAS WATCH.
SEE THAT WINDOW?
SHE WATCHED IT ALL FROM THE SECOND STORY WINDOW.
FIRST ONE, THEN TWO... THEN THREE.

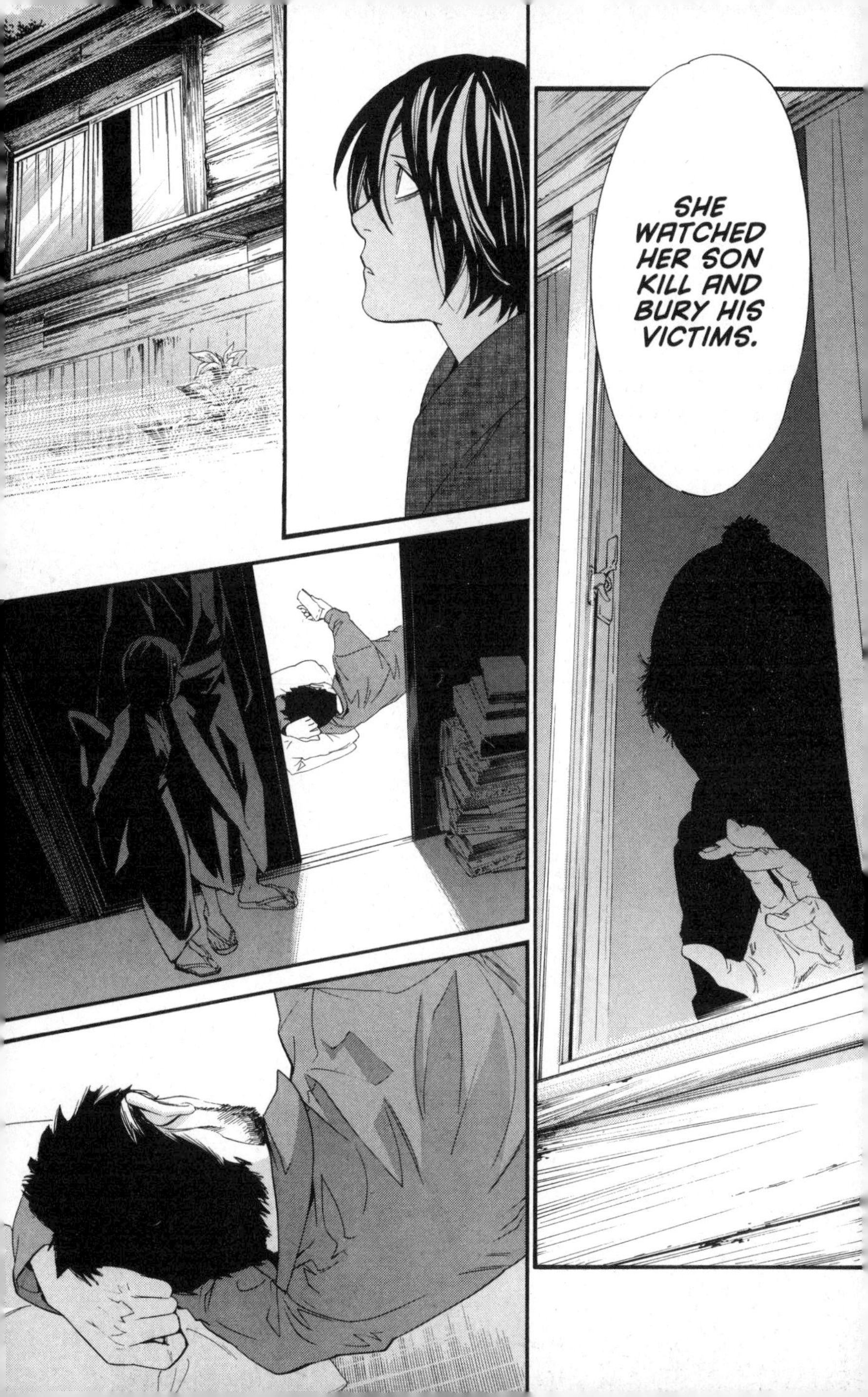
SHE WATCHED HER SON KILL AND BURY HIS VICTIMS.

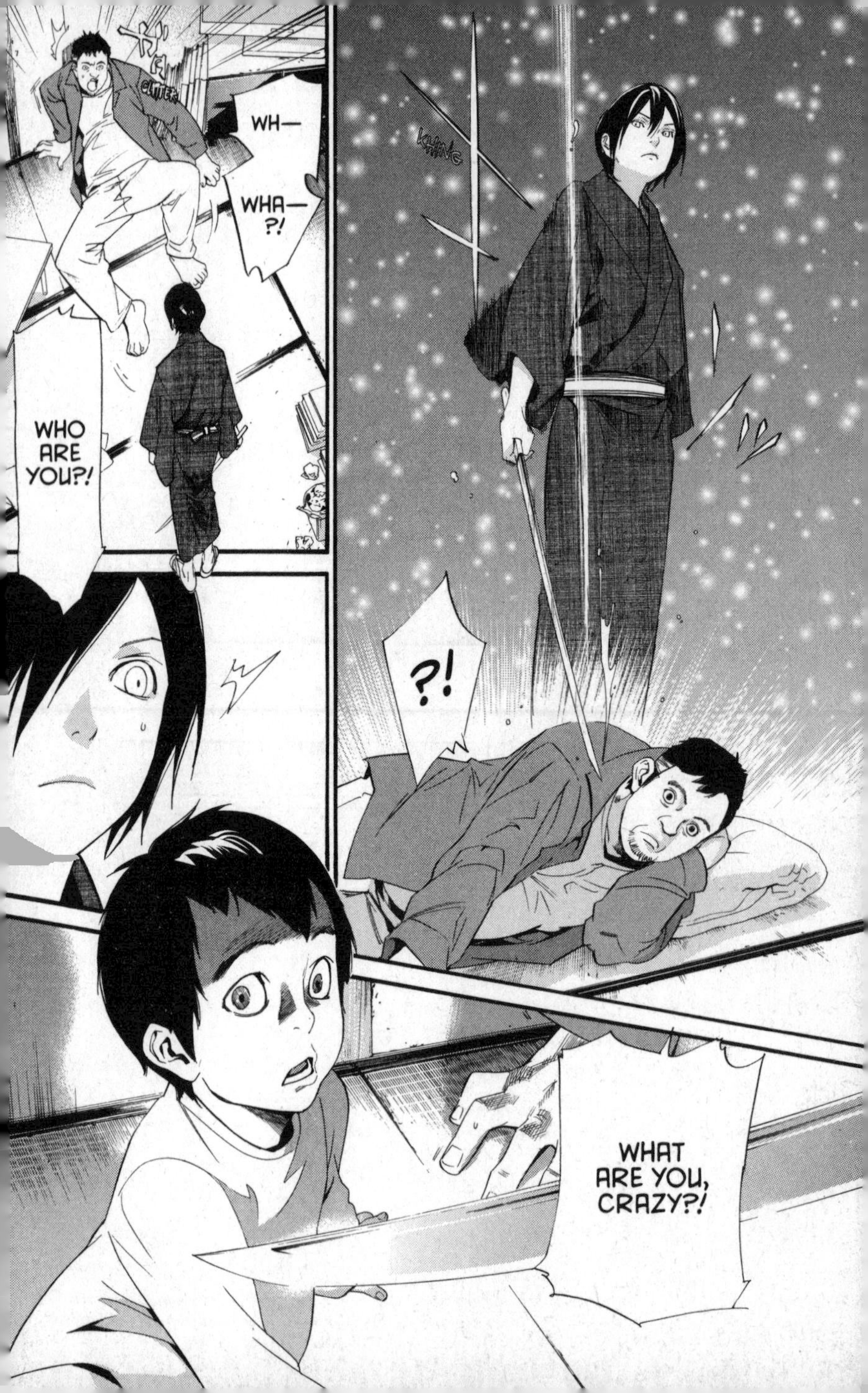
KHANG
?!
GLITTER
WH—
WHA—?!
WHO ARE YOU?!
WHAT ARE YOU, CRAZY?!

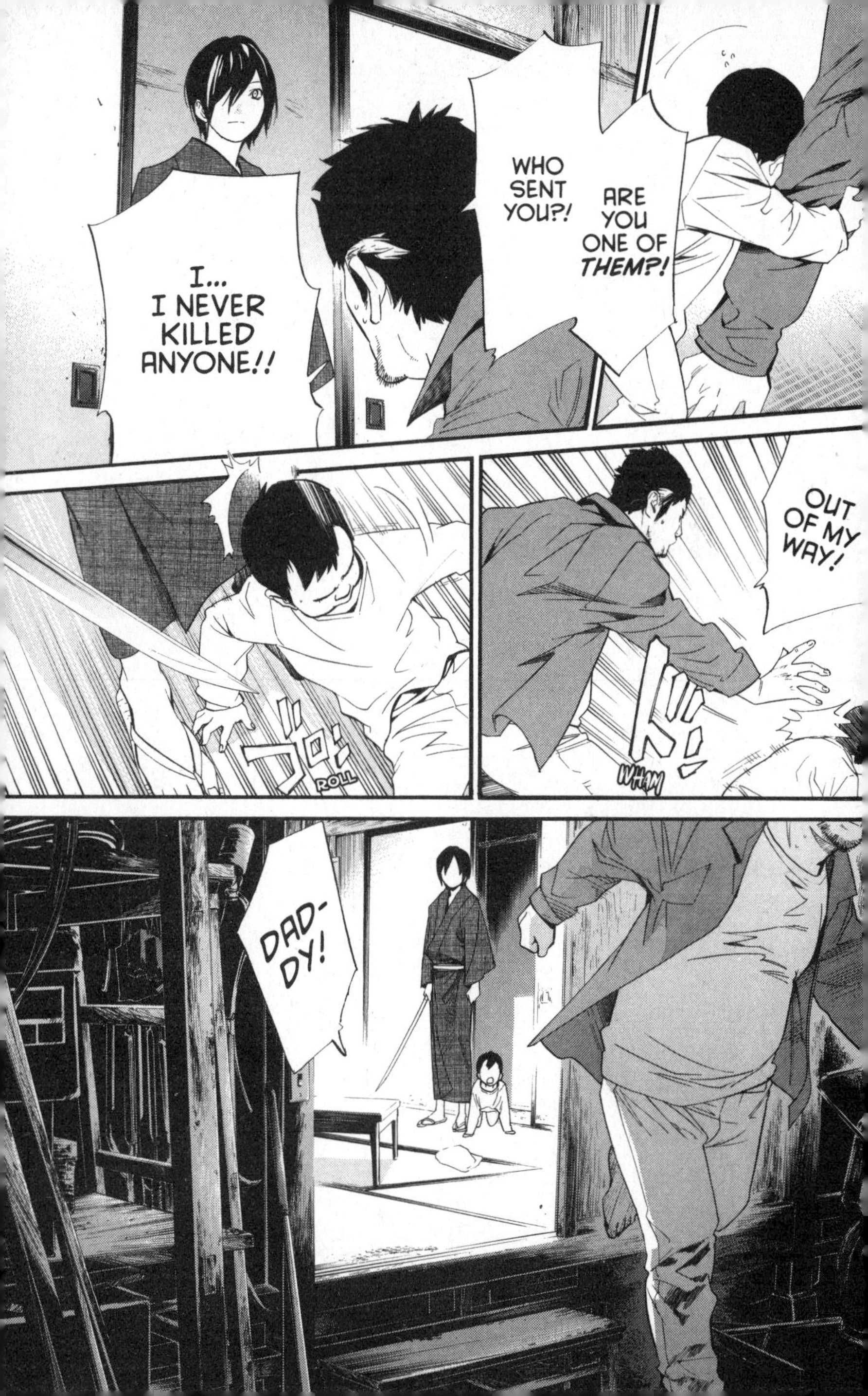

ARE YOU ONE OF THEM?!
WHO SENT YOU?!
I... I NEVER KILLED ANYONE!!
OUT OF MY WAY!
WHAM
ROLL
DAD-DY!

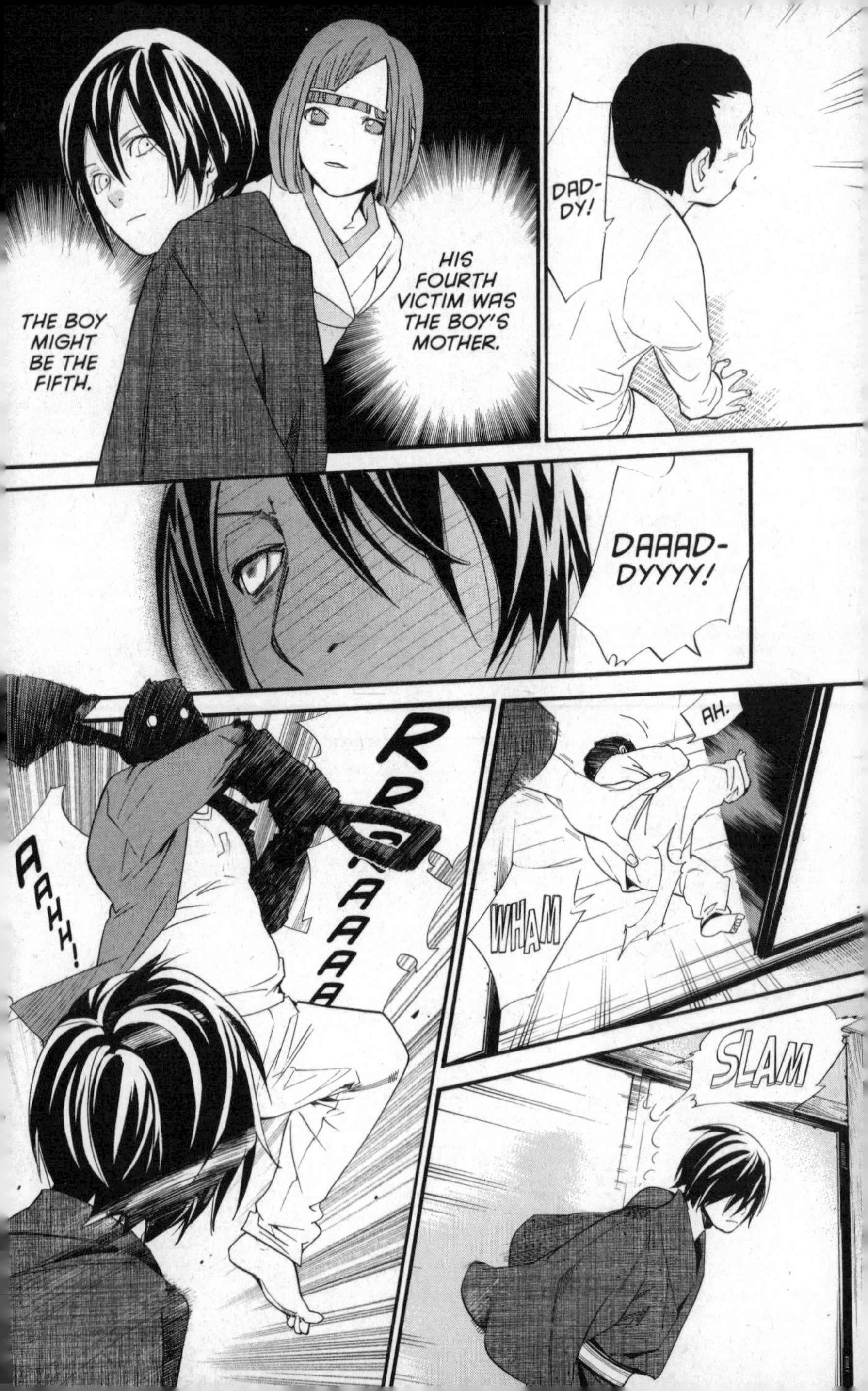
DAD-DY!
HIS FOURTH VICTIM WAS THE BOY'S MOTHER.
THE BOY MIGHT BE THE FIFTH.
DAAAD-DYYYY!
AH.
WHAM
SLAM
RRAAAAAAA
AAHH!

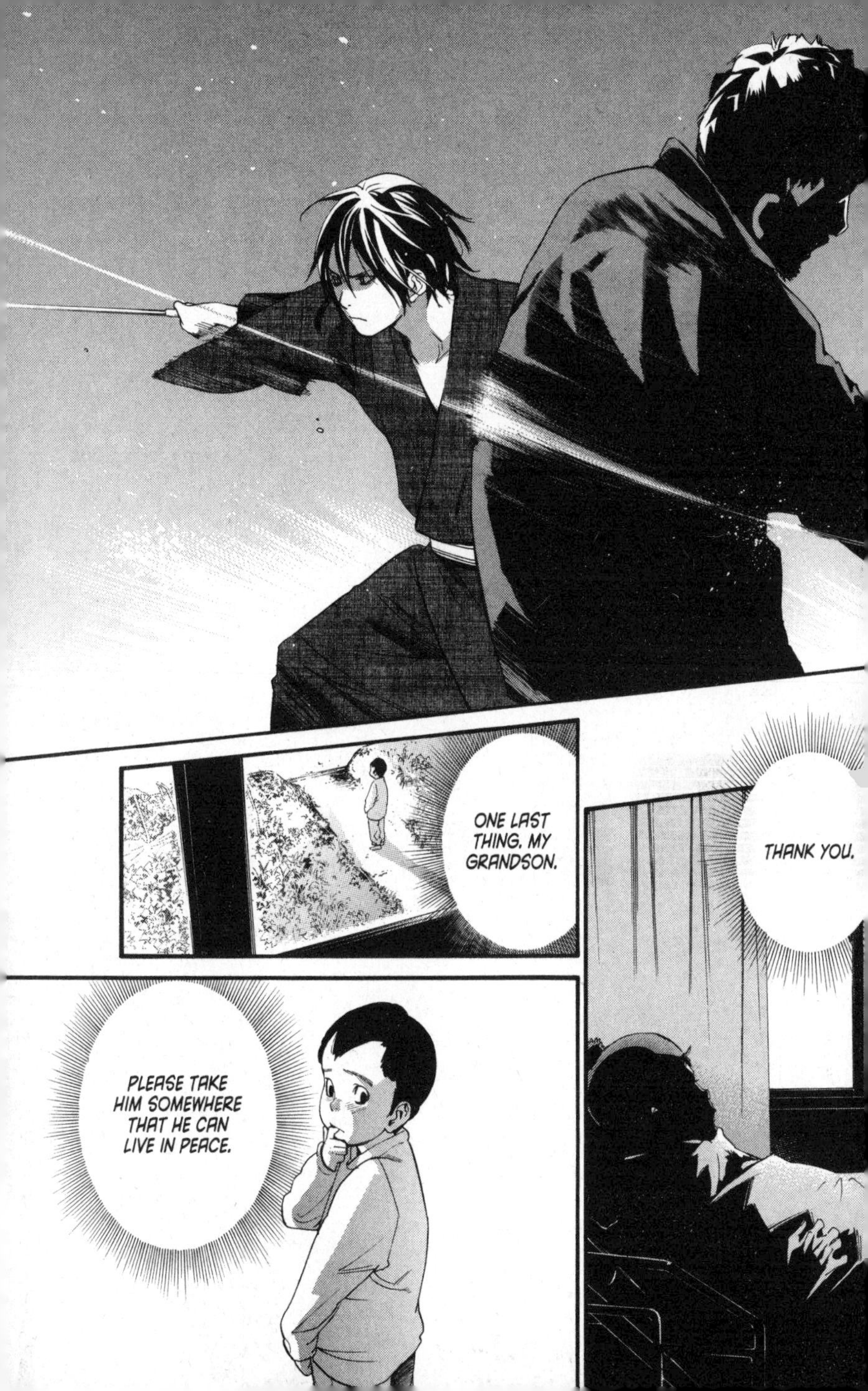
THANK YOU.
ONE LAST THING. MY GRANDSON.
PLEASE TAKE HIM SOMEWHERE THAT HE CAN LIVE IN PEACE.

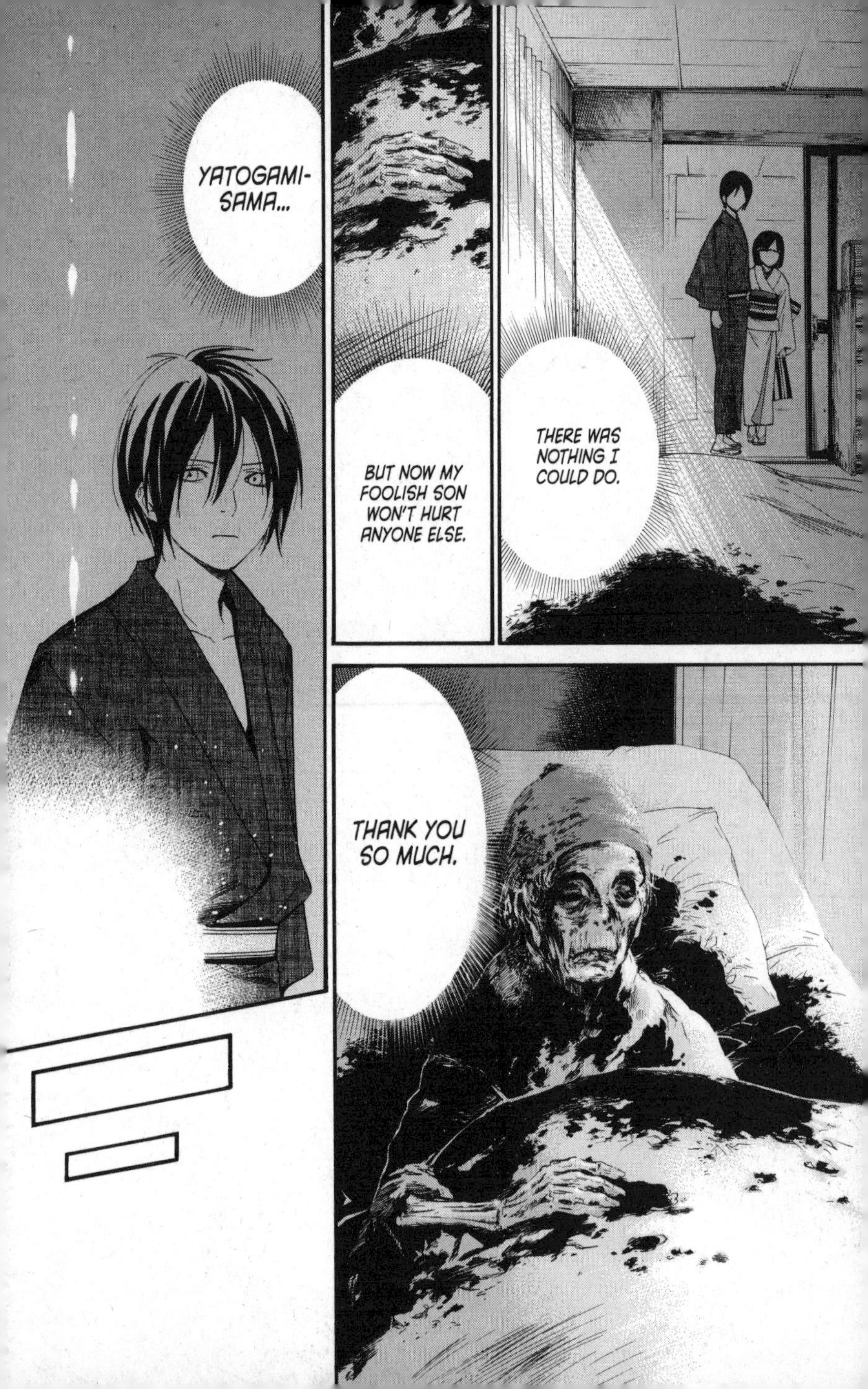
THERE WAS NOTHING I COULD DO.
BUT NOW MY FOOLISH SON WON'T HURT ANYONE ELSE.
THANK YOU SO MUCH.
YATOGAMI-SAMA...

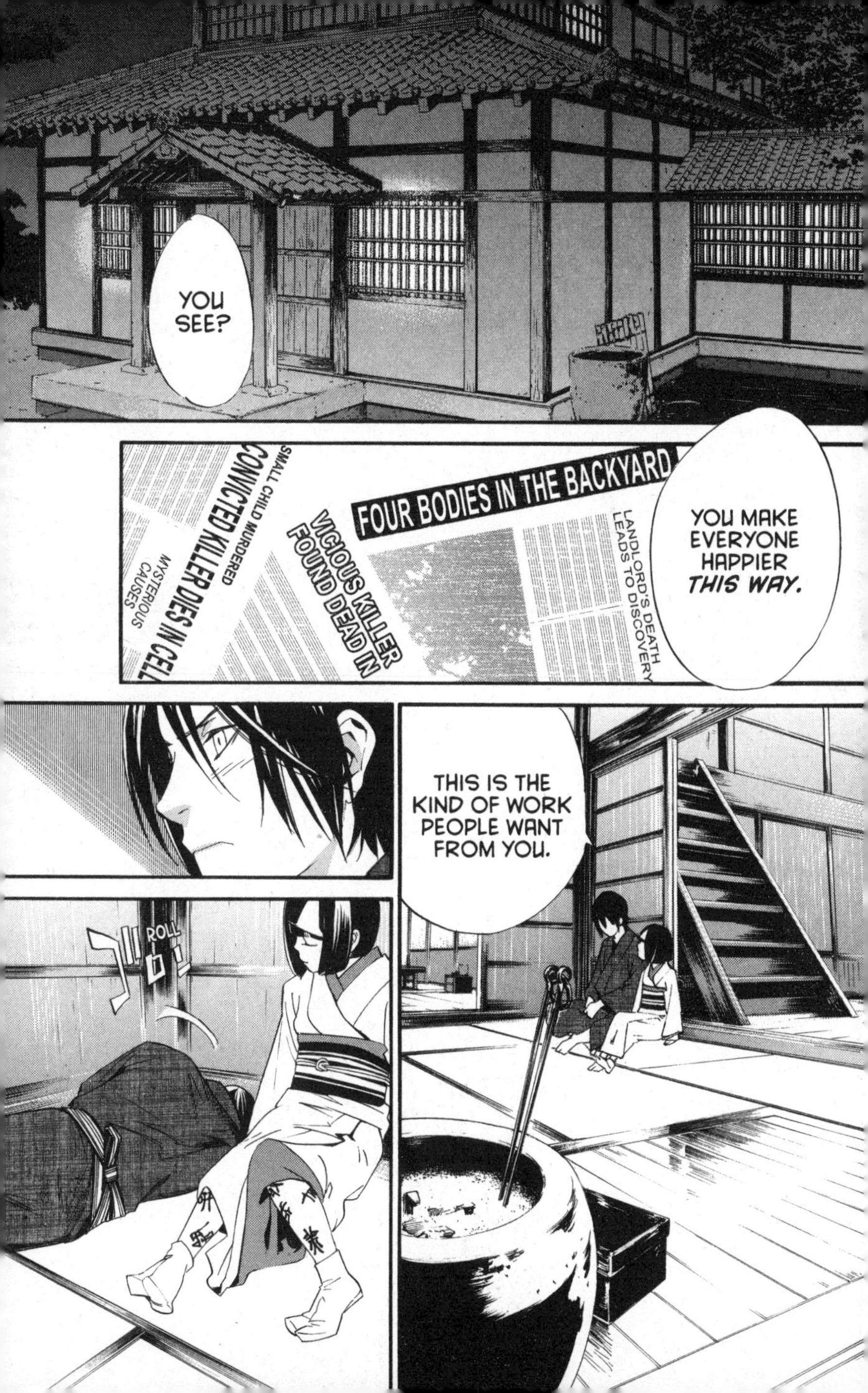
YOU SEE?
YOU MAKE EVERYONE HAPPIER *THIS WAY.*
FOUR BODIES IN THE BACKYARD
LANDLORD'S DEATH LEADS TO DISCOVERY
VICIOUS KILLER FOUND DEAD IN
SMALL CHILD MURDERED
CONVICTED KILLER DIES IN CEL
MYSTERIOUS CAUSES
THIS IS THE KIND OF WORK PEOPLE WANT FROM YOU.
ROLL

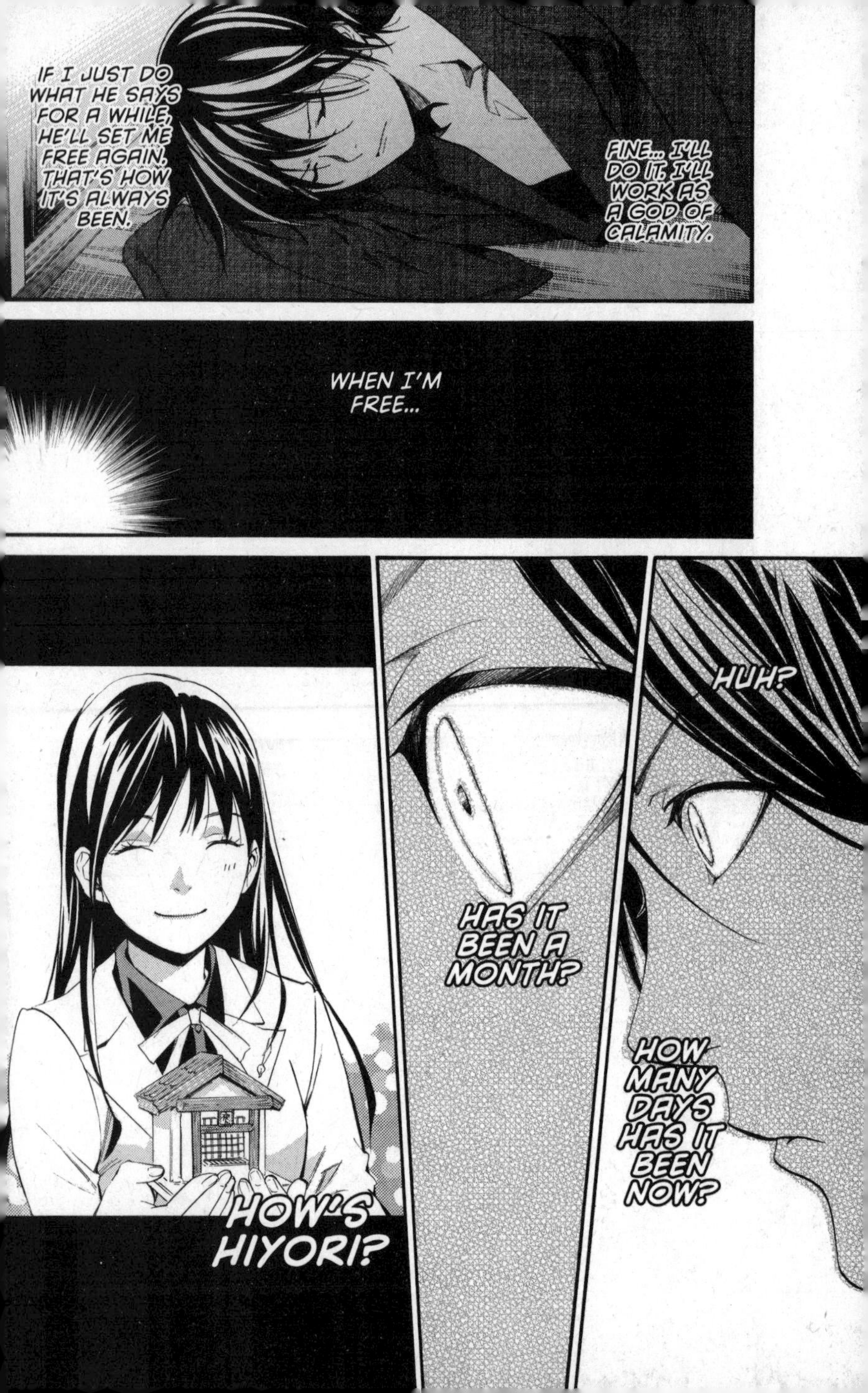
FINE... I'LL DO IT. I'LL WORK AS A GOD OF CALAMITY.
IF I JUST DO WHAT HE SAYS FOR A WHILE, HE'LL SET ME FREE AGAIN. THAT'S HOW IT'S ALWAYS BEEN.
WHEN I'M FREE...
HUH?
HOW MANY DAYS HAS IT BEEN NOW?
HAS IT BEEN A MONTH?
HOW'S HIYORI?

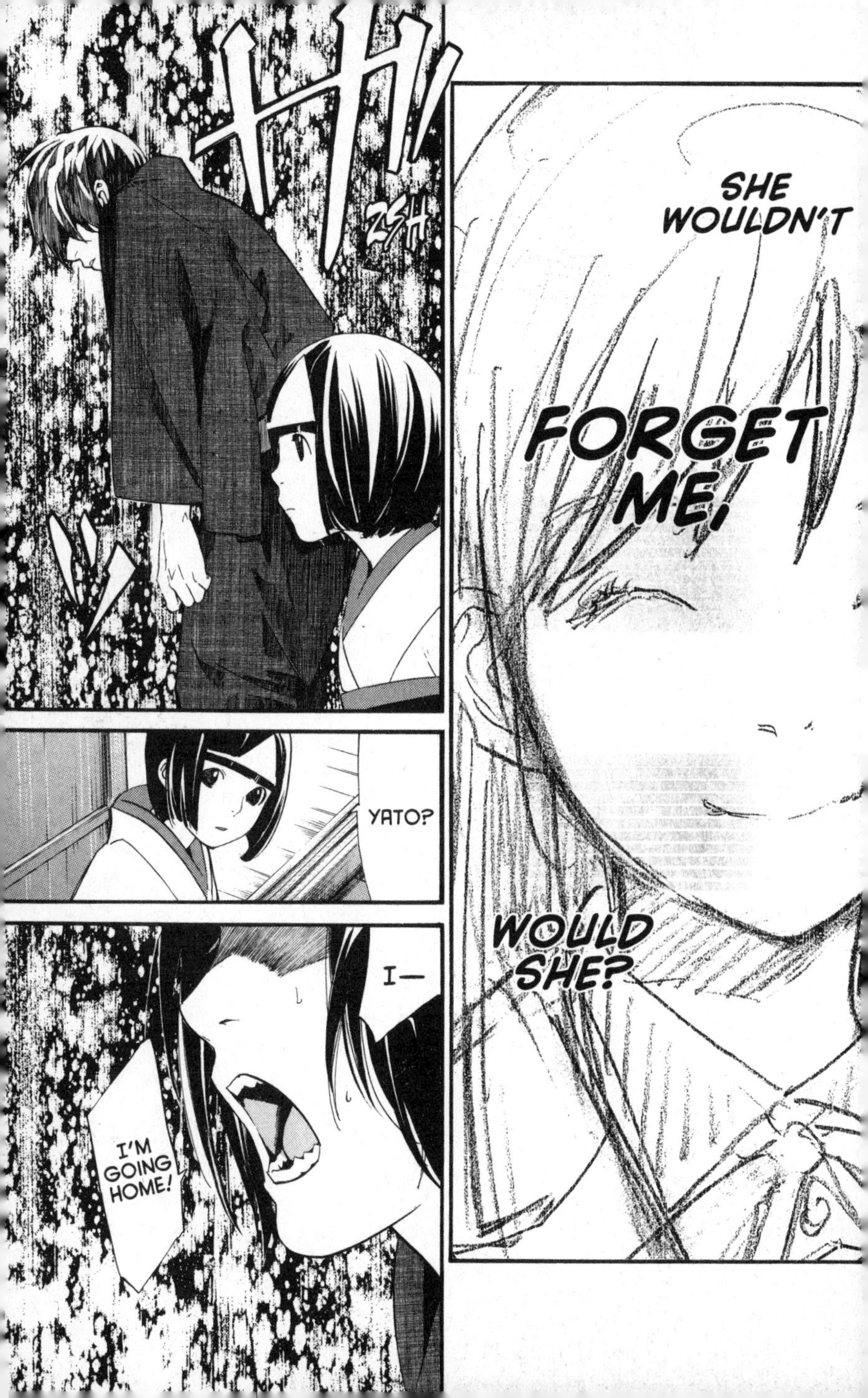
SHE WOULDN'T
FORGET ME.
WOULD SHE?
ZSH
YATO?
I—
I'M GOING HOME!

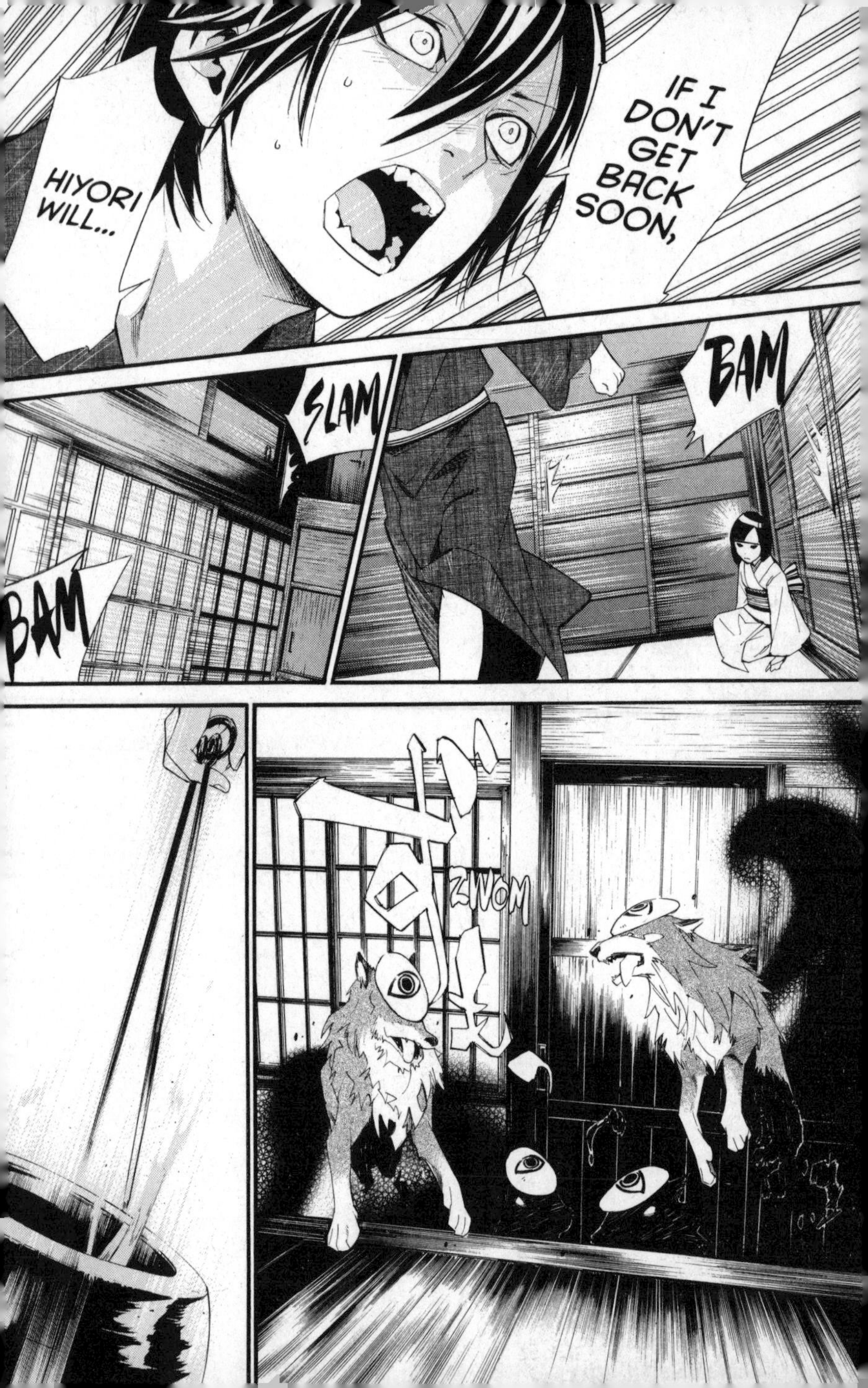
IF I DON'T GET BACK SOON,
HIYORI WILL...
BAM
SLAM
BAM
ZWOM

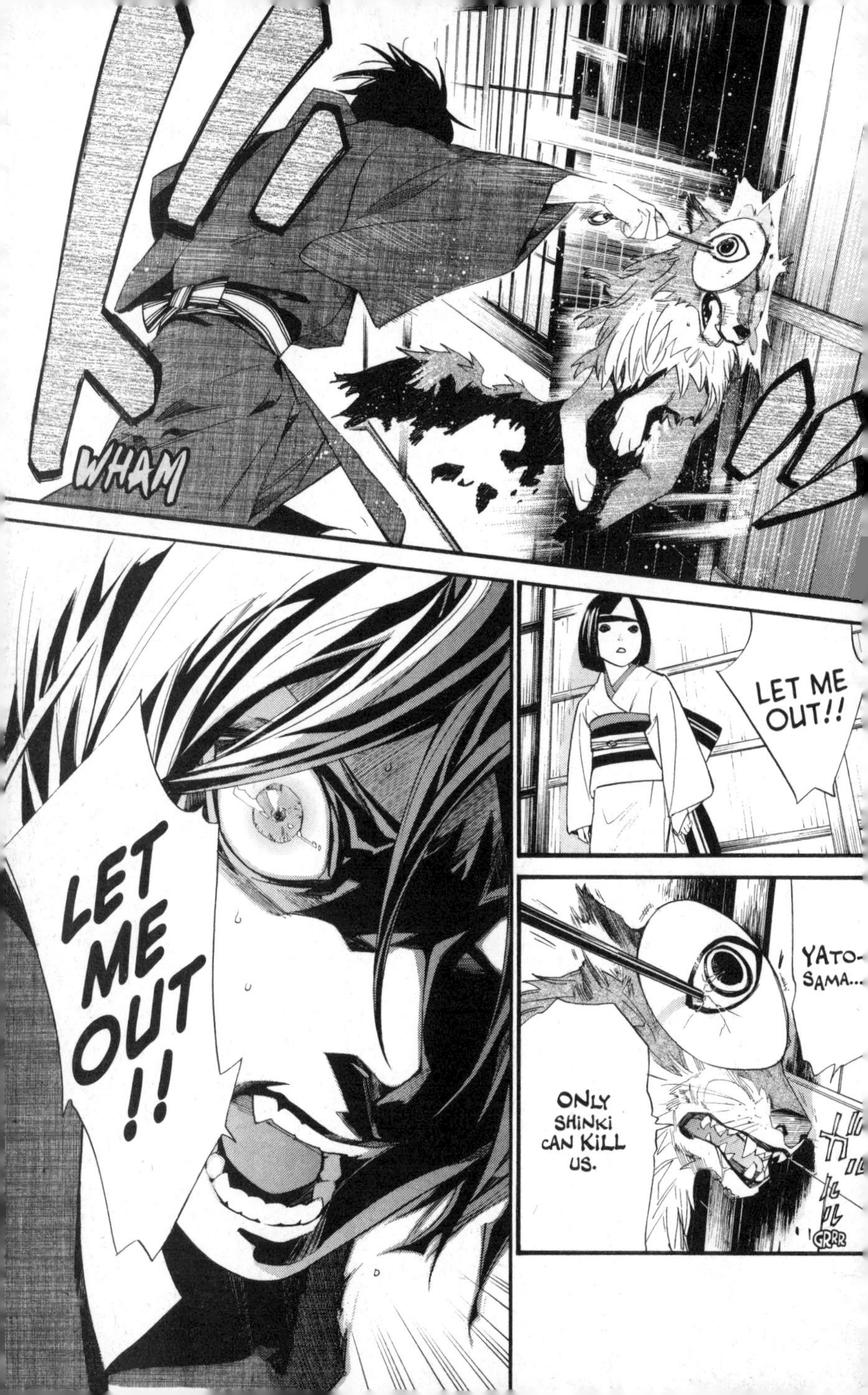
WHAM
LET ME OUT!!
YATO-SAMA...
ONLY SHINKI CAN KILL US.
GRRR
LET ME OUT!!

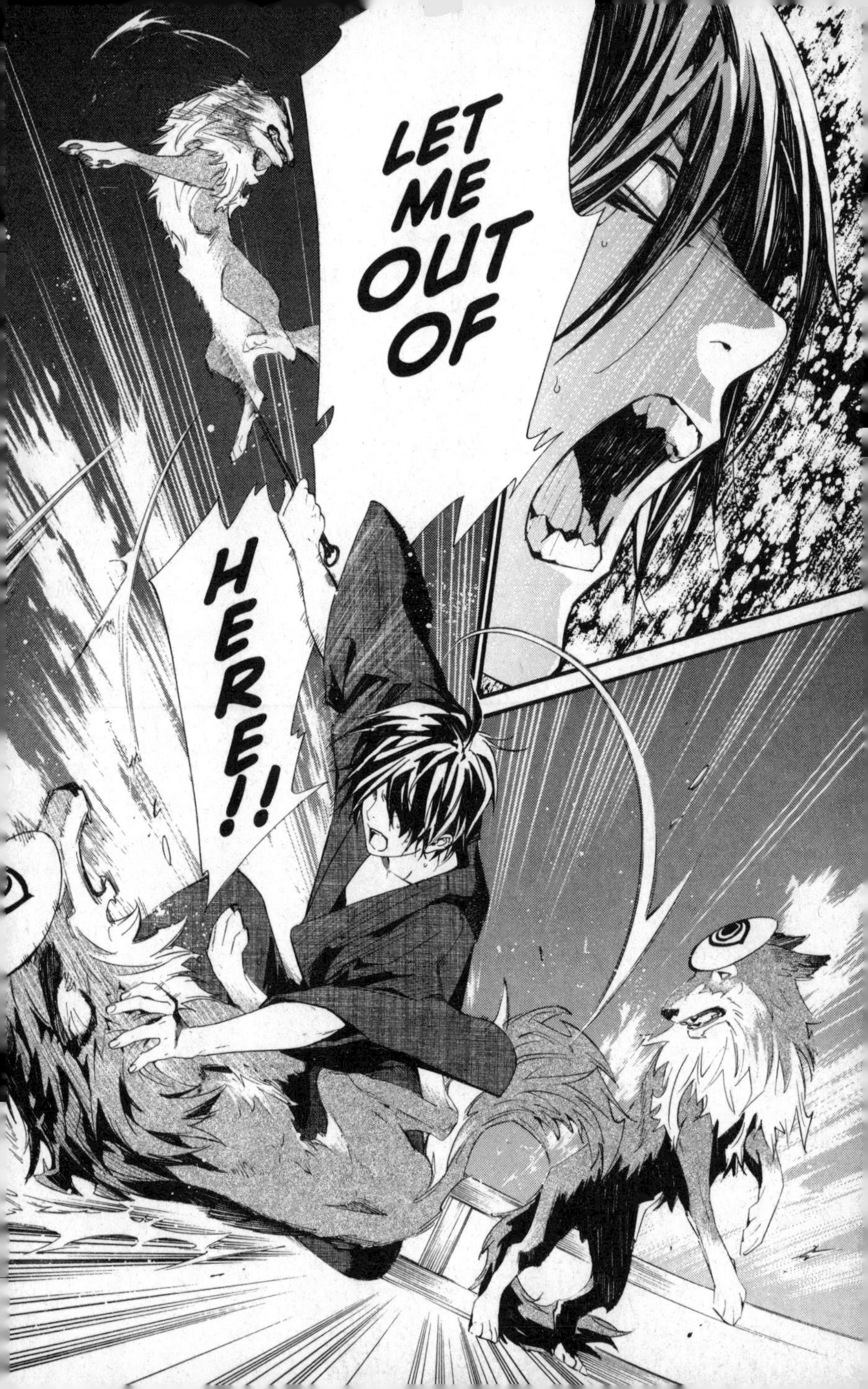
LET ME OUT OF
HERE!!

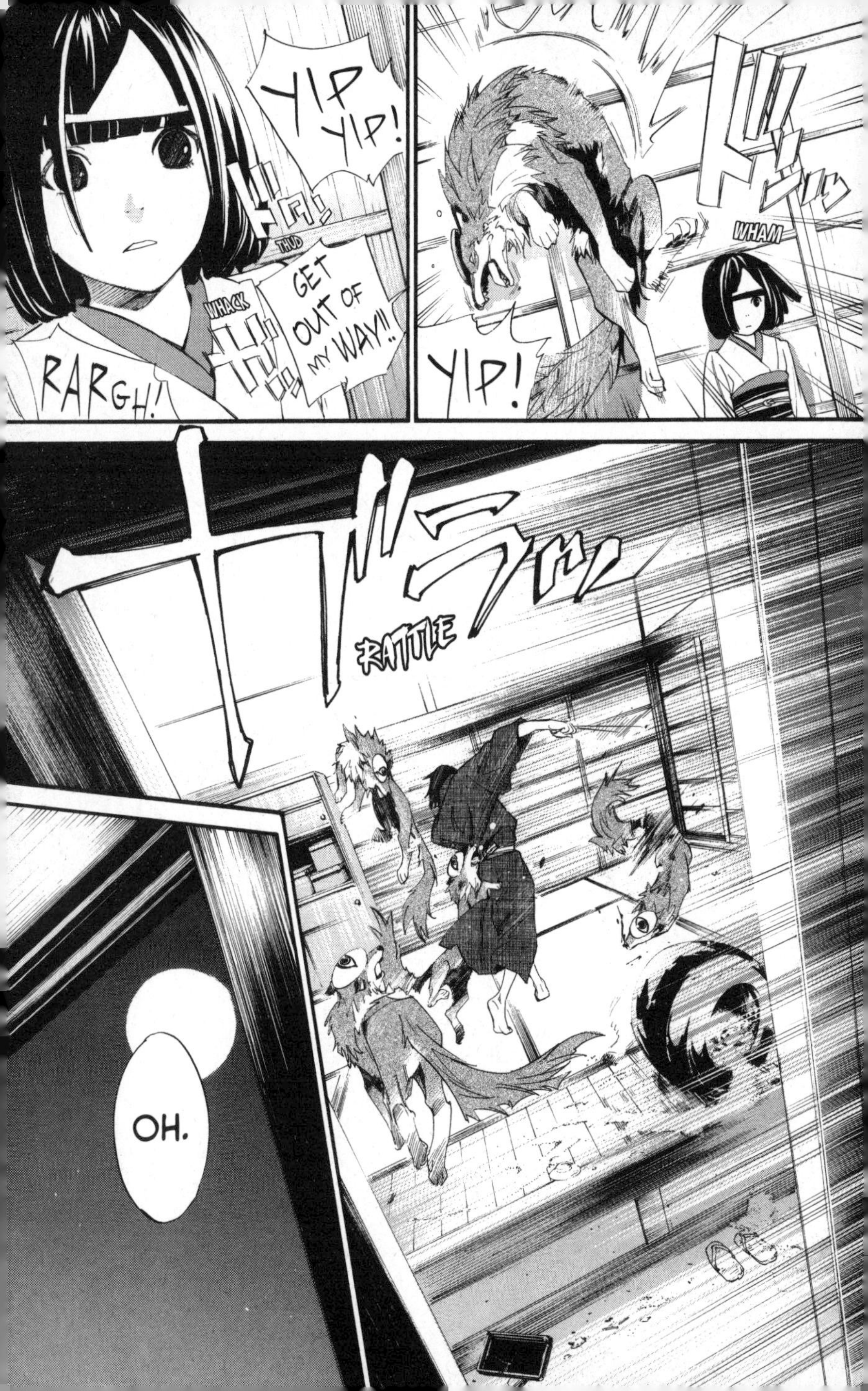

WHAM
YIP!
YIP YIP!
THUD
GET OUT OF MY WAY!!
WHACK
RARGH!
RATTLE
OH.

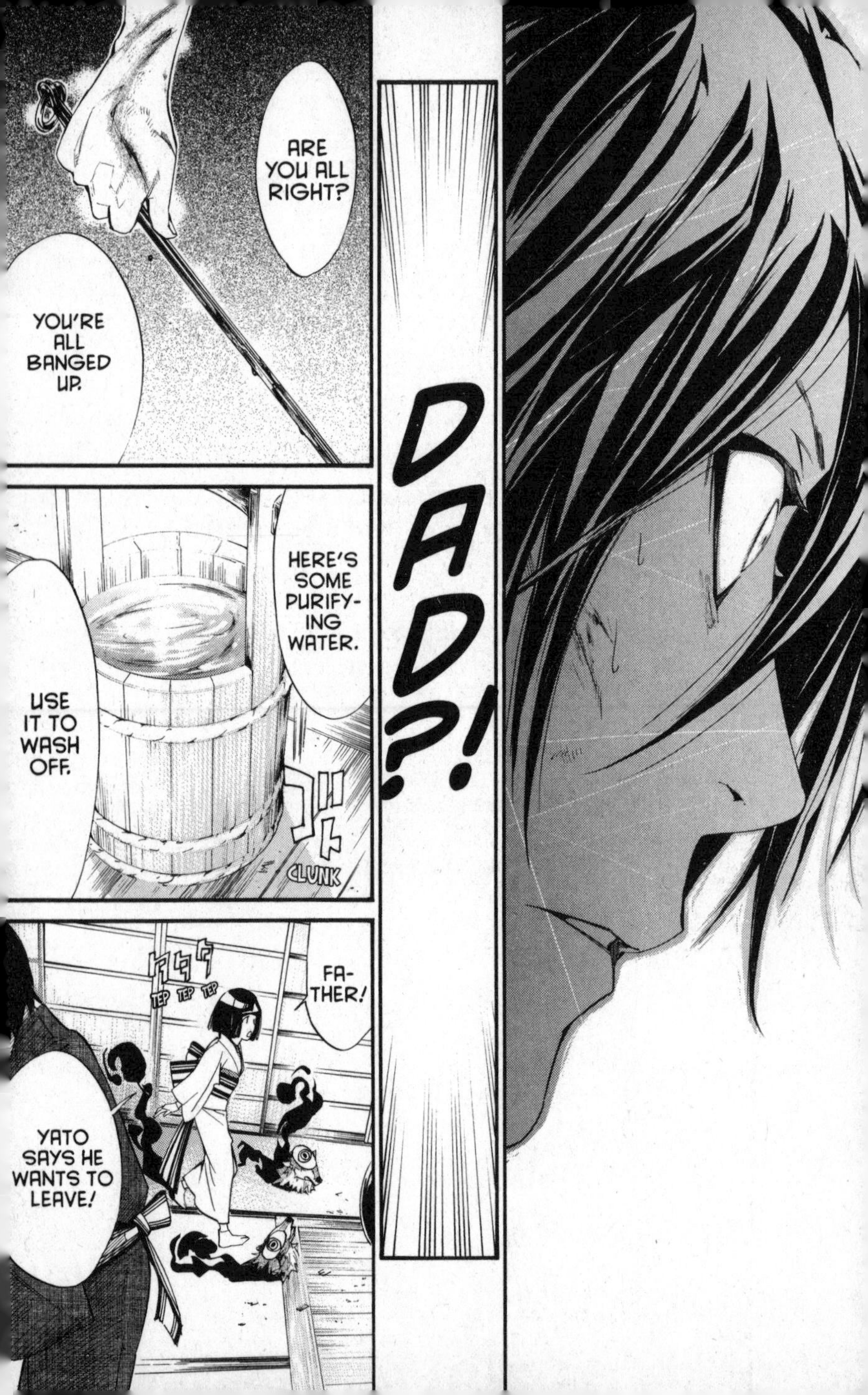
ARE YOU ALL RIGHT?
YOU'RE ALL BANGED UP.
HERE'S SOME PURIFY-ING WATER.
USE IT TO WASH OFF.
CLUNK
TEP TEP TEP
FA-THER!
YATO SAYS HE WANTS TO LEAVE!
DAD?!

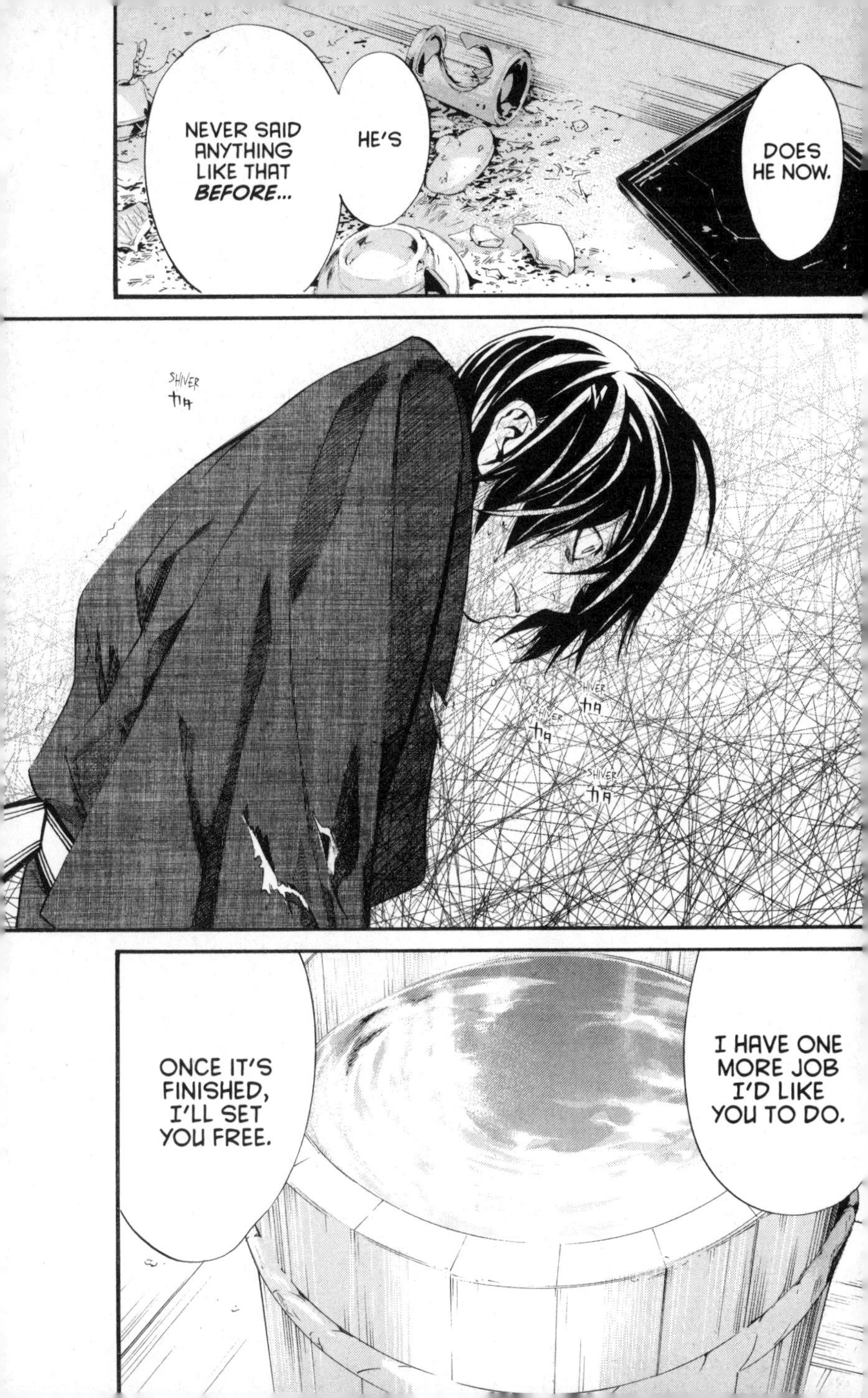
HE'S
NEVER SAID ANYTHING LIKE THAT *BEFORE*...
DOES HE NOW.
SHIVER
SHIVER
SHIVER
SHIVER
I HAVE ONE MORE JOB I'D LIKE YOU TO DO.
ONCE IT'S FINISHED, I'LL SET YOU FREE.

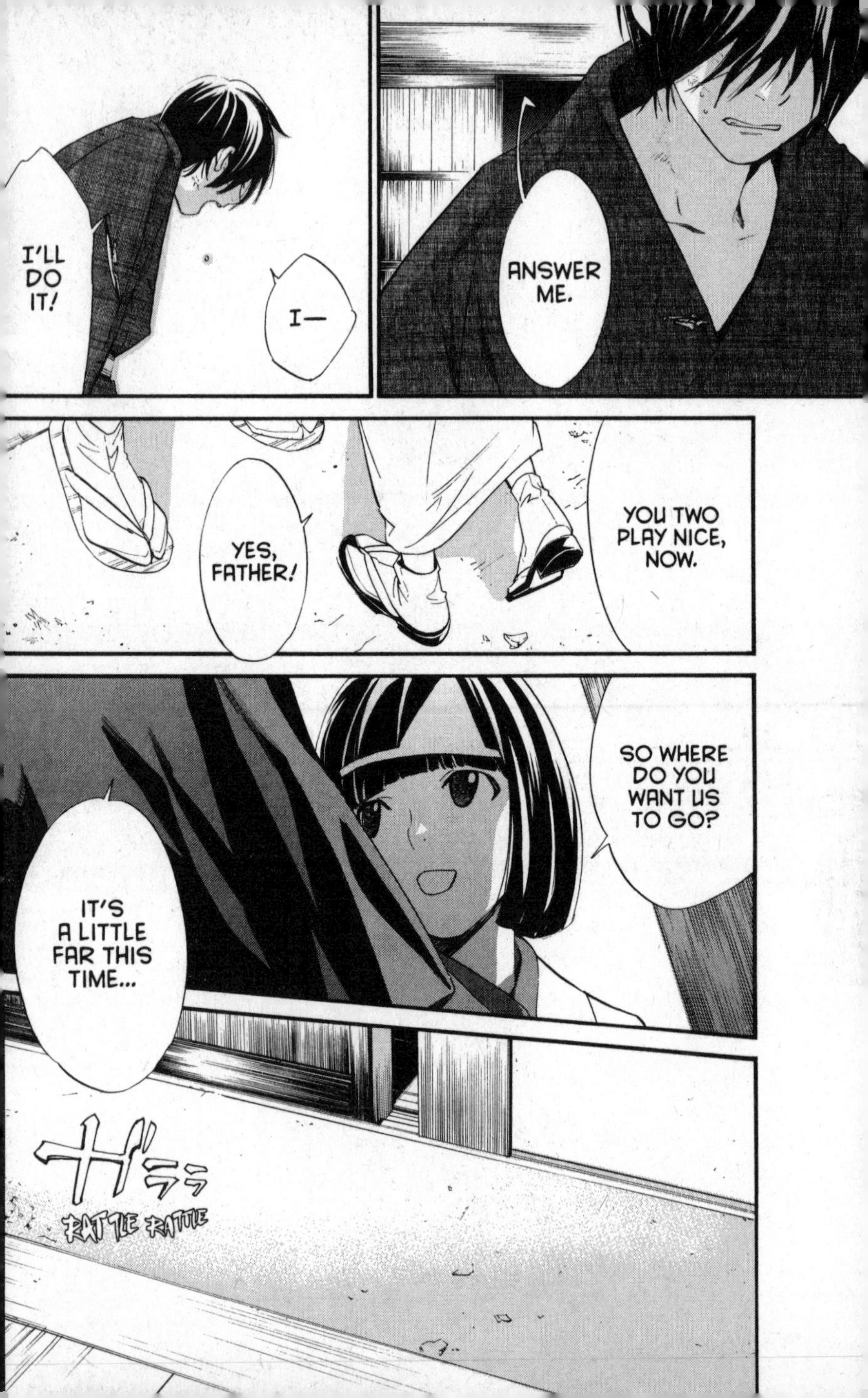
ANSWER ME.
I—
I'LL DO IT!
YOU TWO PLAY NICE, NOW.
YES, FATHER!
SO WHERE DO YOU WANT US TO GO?
IT'S A LITTLE FAR THIS TIME...
RATTLE RATTLE

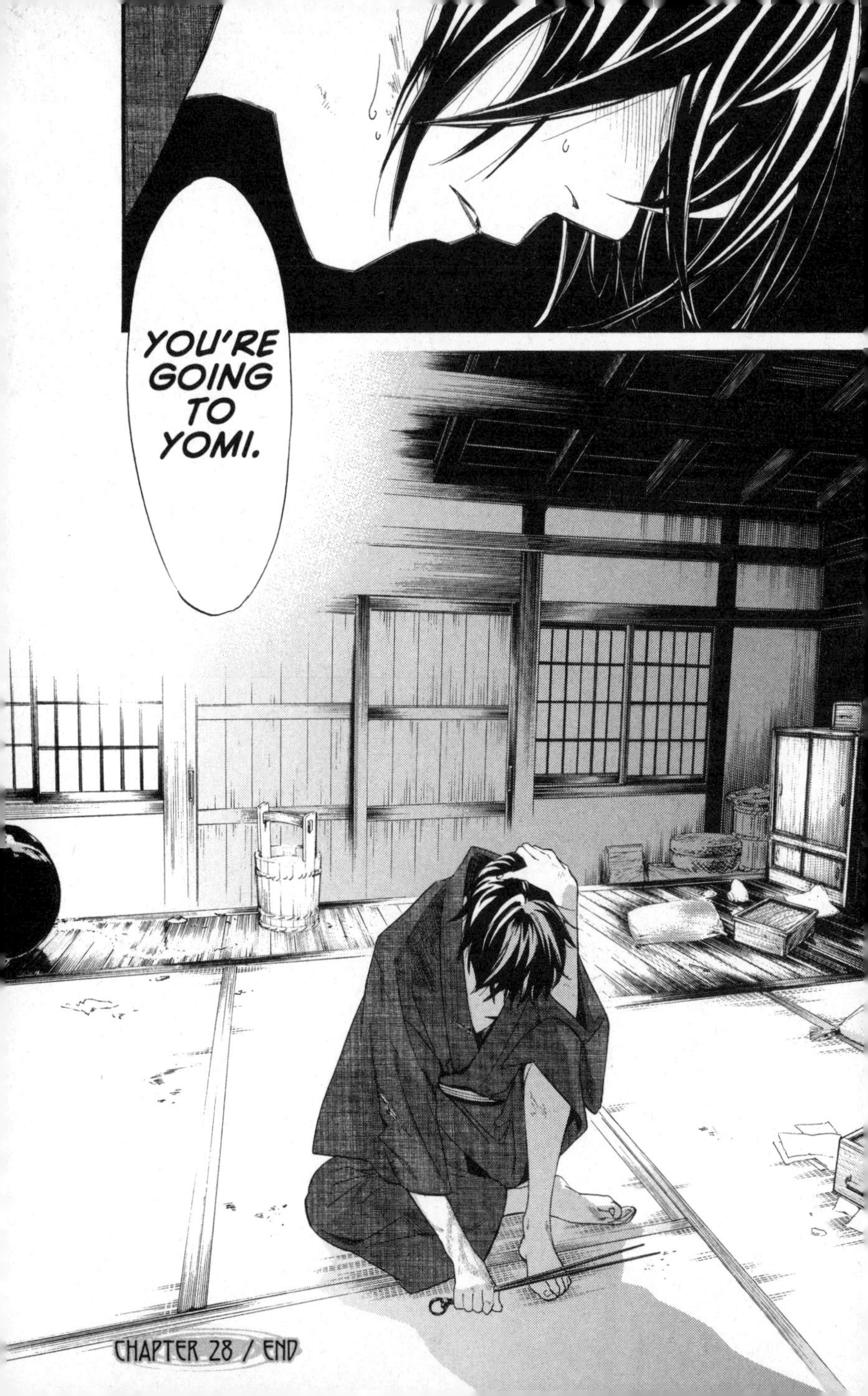
YOU'RE GOING TO YOMI.
CHAPTER 28 / END

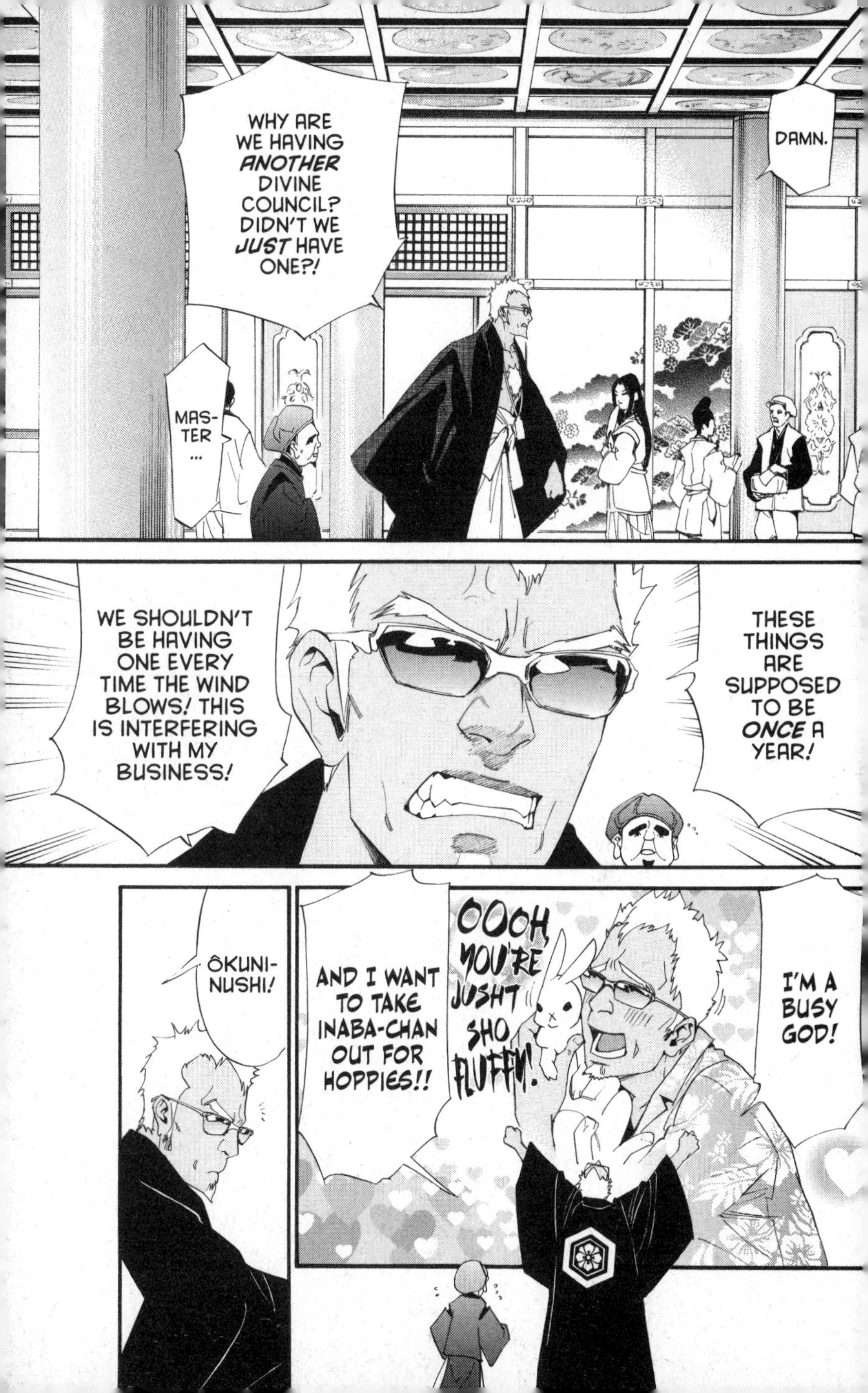
DAMN.
WHY ARE WE HAVING ANOTHER DIVINE COUNCIL? DIDN'T WE JUST HAVE ONE?!
MAS-TER ...
THESE THINGS ARE SUPPOSED TO BE ONCE A YEAR!
WE SHOULDN'T BE HAVING ONE EVERY TIME THE WIND BLOWS! THIS IS INTERFERING WITH MY BUSINESS!
I'M A BUSY GOD!
OOOH, YOU'RE JUSHT SHO FLUFFY!
AND I WANT TO TAKE INABA-CHAN OUT FOR HOPPIES!!
ÔKUNI-NUSHI!

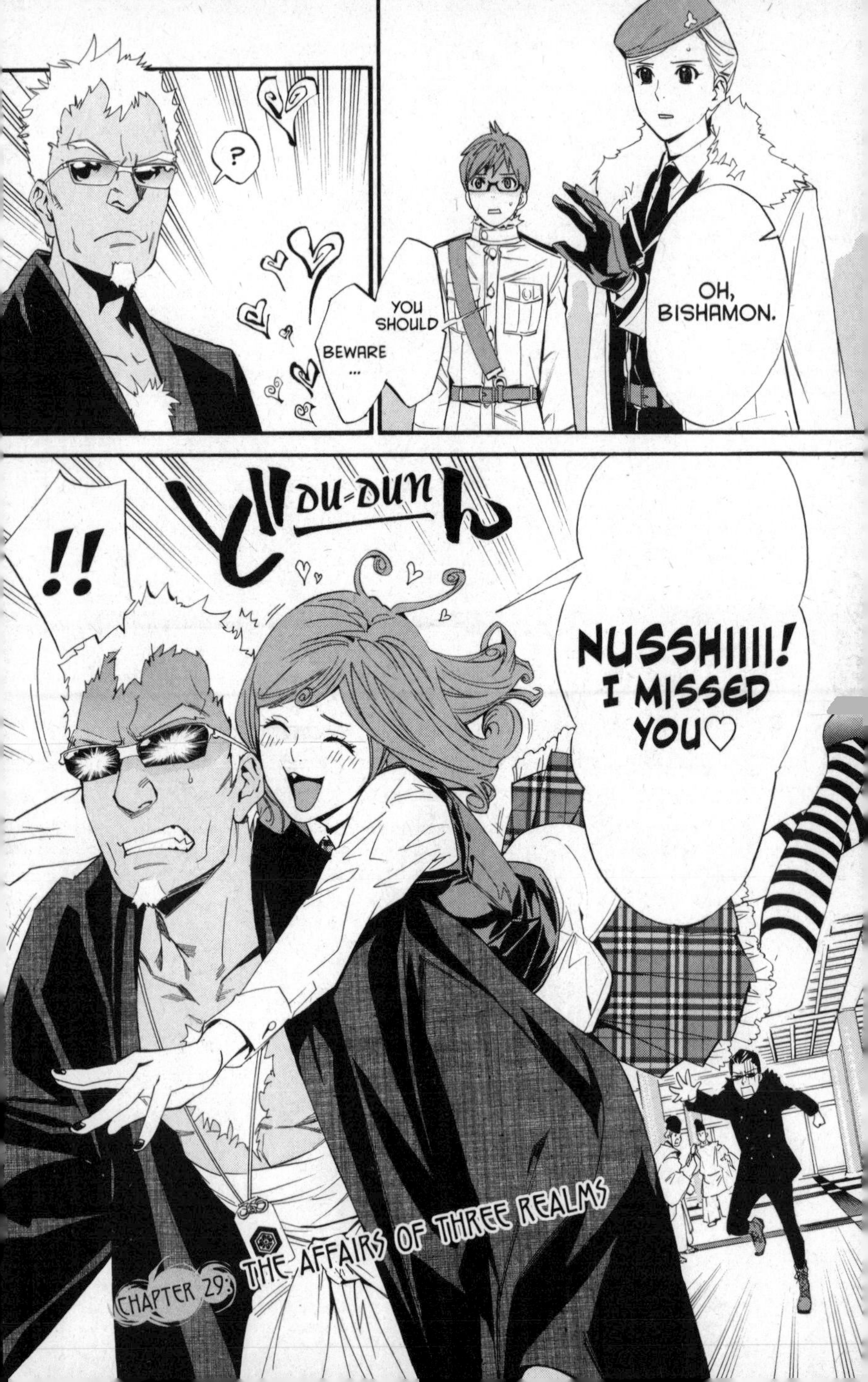
OH, BISHAMON.
YOU SHOULD BEWARE ...
?
NUSSHIIIII! I MISSED YOU♡
DU-DUN
!!
CHAPTER 29: THE AFFAIRS OF THREE REALMS

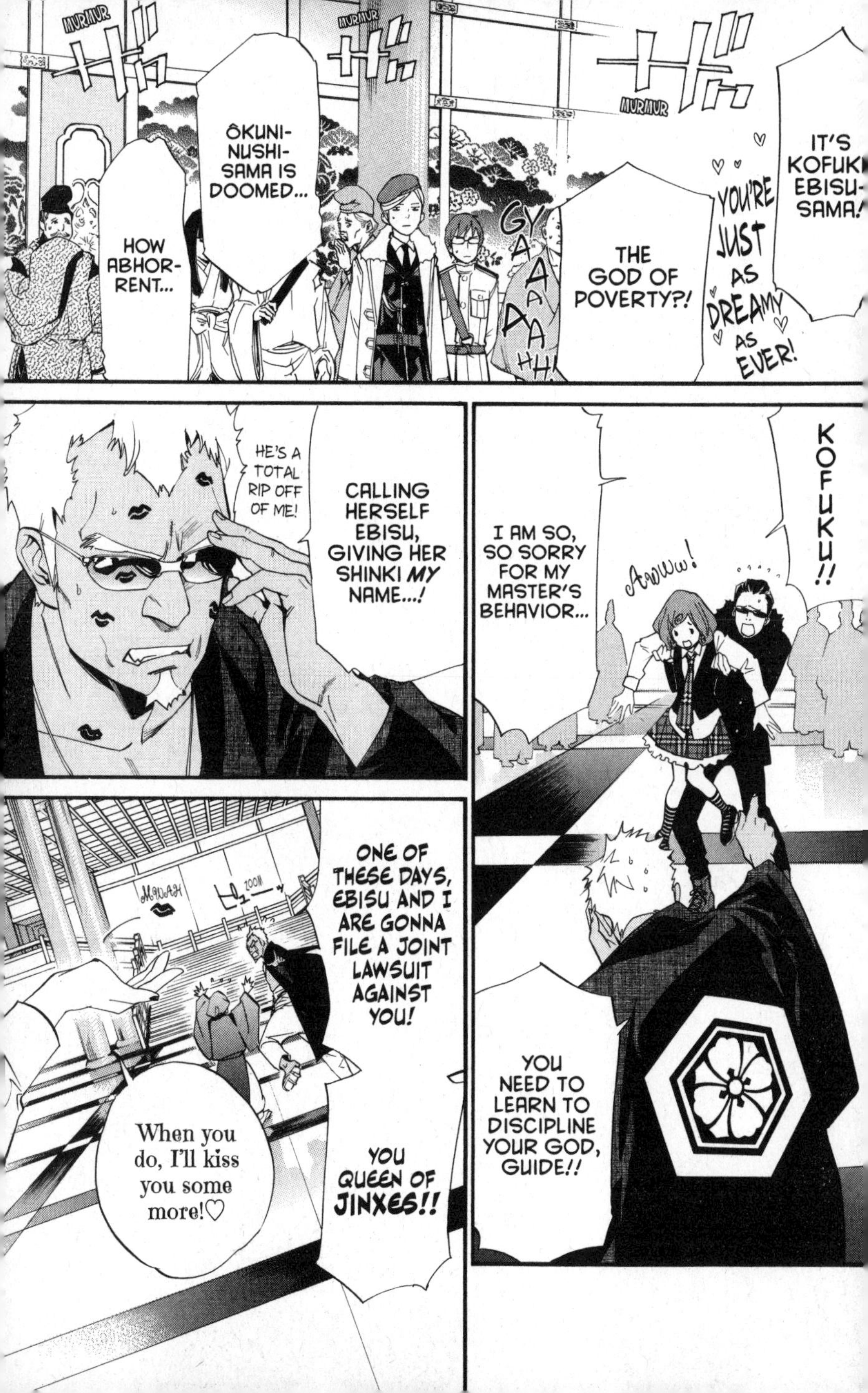
MURMUR
IT'S KOFUKU EBISU-SAMA!
YOU'RE JUST AS DREAMY AS EVER!
MURMUR
THE GOD OF POVERTY?!
GYAAAAHH
ŌKUNI-NUSHI-SAMA IS DOOMED...
MURMUR
HOW ABHOR-RENT...
KOFUKU!!
Awww!
I AM SO, SO SORRY FOR MY MASTER'S BEHAVIOR...
YOU NEED TO LEARN TO DISCIPLINE YOUR GOD, GUIDE!!
CALLING HERSELF EBISU, GIVING HER SHINKI MY NAME...!
HE'S A TOTAL RIP OFF OF ME!
ONE OF THESE DAYS, EBISU AND I ARE GONNA FILE A JOINT LAWSUIT AGAINST YOU!
YOU QUEEN OF JINXES!!
ZOOM
MWAH
When you do, I'll kiss you some more!♡

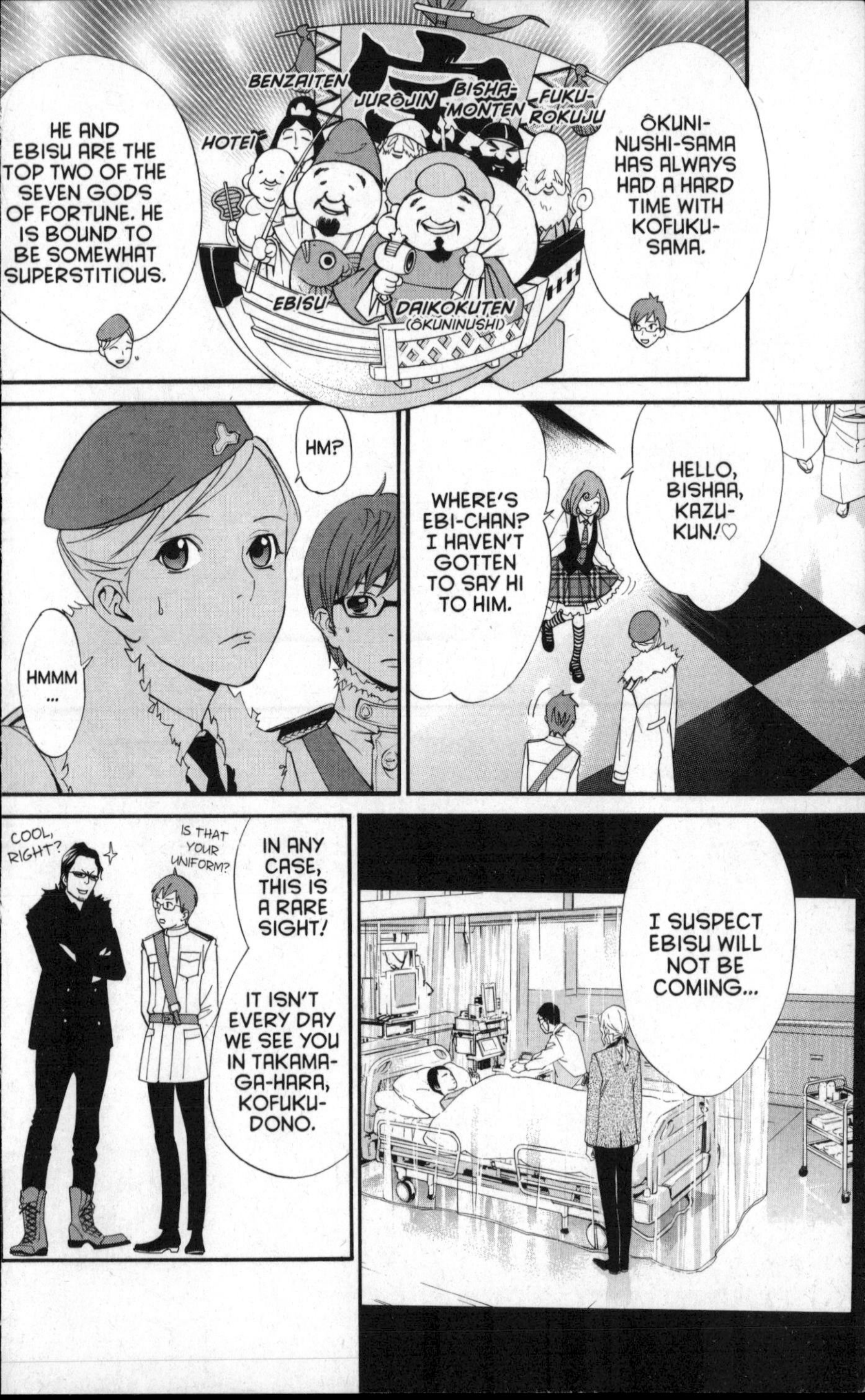
ÔKUNI-NUSHI-SAMA HAS ALWAYS HAD A HARD TIME WITH KOFUKU-SAMA.
FUKU-ROKUJU
BISHA-MONTEN
JURÔJIN
BENZAITEN
HOTEI
DAIKOKUTEN (ÔKUNINUSHI)
EBISU
HE AND EBISU ARE THE TOP TWO OF THE SEVEN GODS OF FORTUNE. HE IS BOUND TO BE SOMEWHAT SUPERSTITIOUS.
HELLO, BISHAA, KAZU-KUN!♡
WHERE'S EBI-CHAN? I HAVEN'T GOTTEN TO SAY HI TO HIM.
HM?
HMMM ...
I SUSPECT EBISU WILL NOT BE COMING...
IN ANY CASE, THIS IS A RARE SIGHT!
IT ISN'T EVERY DAY WE SEE YOU IN TAKAMA-GA-HARA, KOFUKU-DONO.
IS THAT YOUR UNIFORM?
COOL, RIGHT?

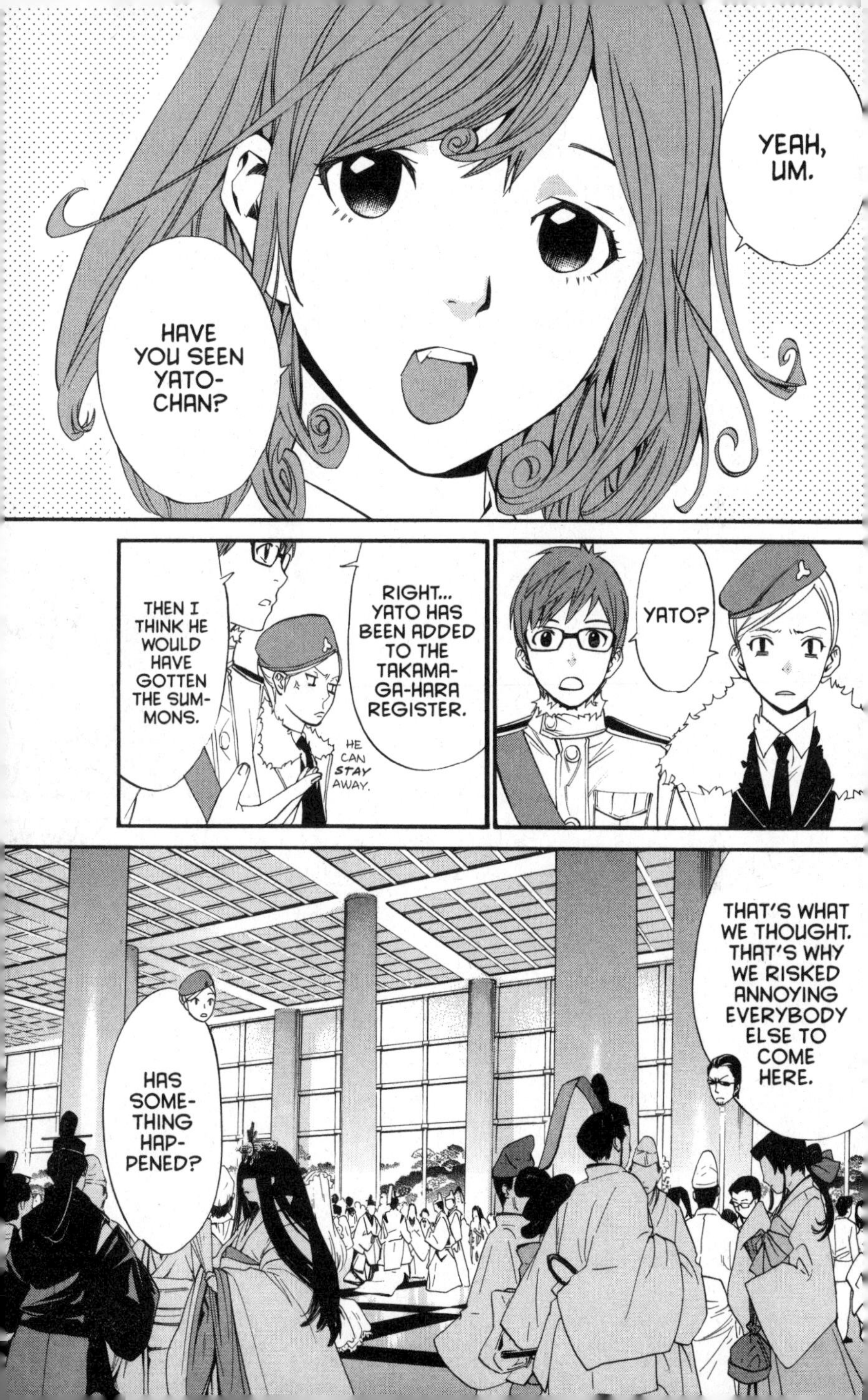
YEAH, UM.
HAVE YOU SEEN YATO-CHAN?
YATO?
RIGHT... YATO HAS BEEN ADDED TO THE TAKAMA-GA-HARA REGISTER.
THEN I THINK HE WOULD HAVE GOTTEN THE SUMMONS.
HE CAN STAY AWAY.
THAT'S WHAT WE THOUGHT. THAT'S WHY WE RISKED ANNOYING EVERYBODY ELSE TO COME HERE.
HAS SOMETHING HAPPENED?

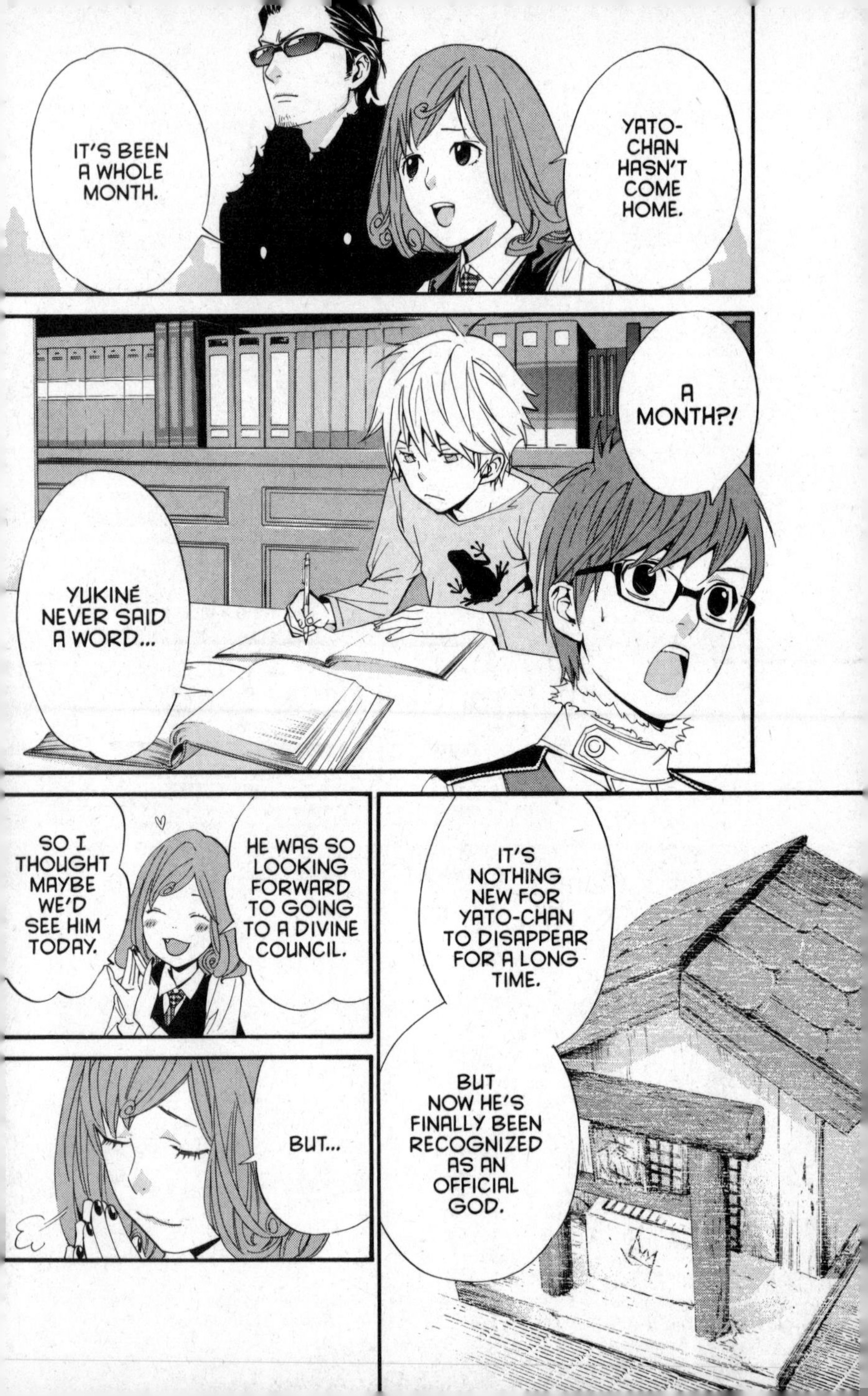
YATO-CHAN HASN'T COME HOME.
IT'S BEEN A WHOLE MONTH.
A MONTH?!
YUKINÉ NEVER SAID A WORD...
IT'S NOTHING NEW FOR YATO-CHAN TO DISAPPEAR FOR A LONG TIME.
BUT NOW HE'S FINALLY BEEN RECOGNIZED AS AN OFFICIAL GOD.
HE WAS SO LOOKING FORWARD TO GOING TO A DIVINE COUNCIL.
SO I THOUGHT MAYBE WE'D SEE HIM TODAY.
BUT...

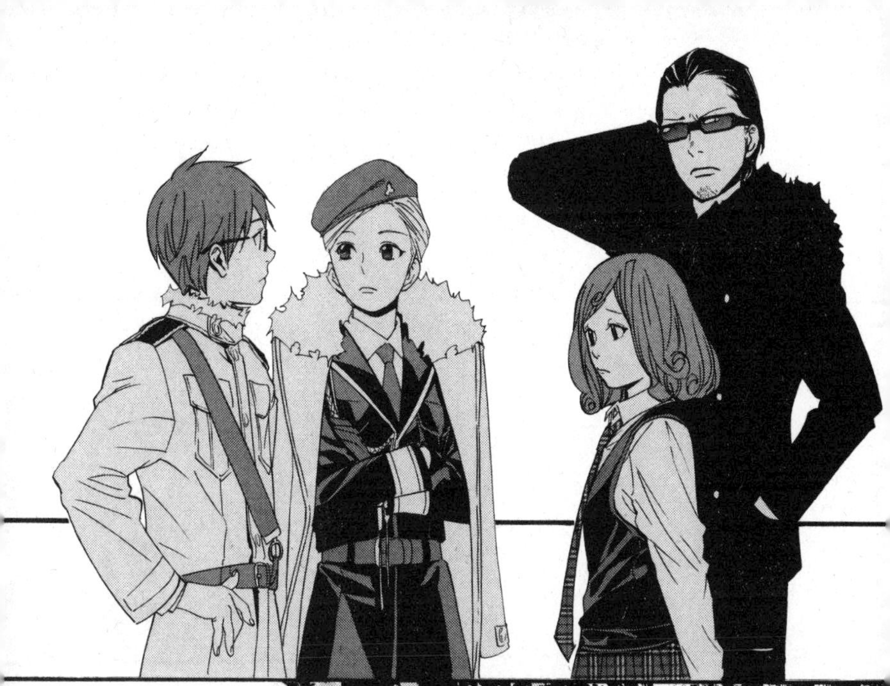
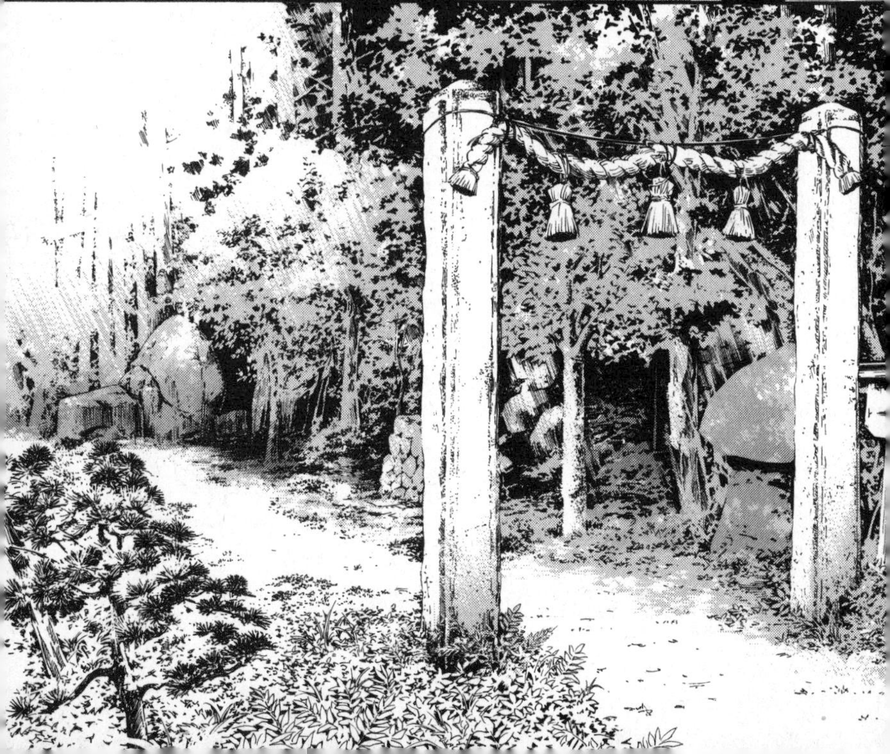

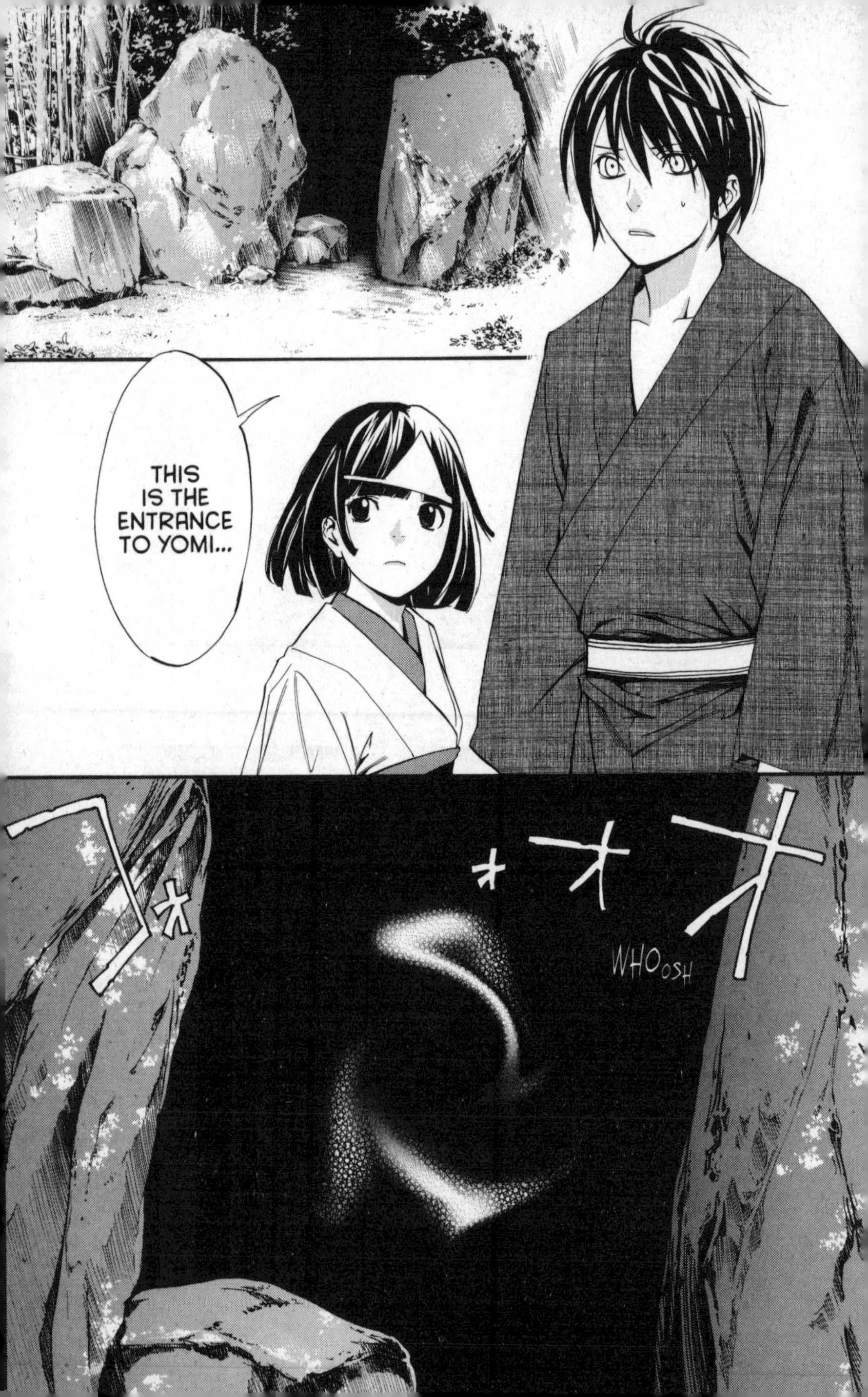
THIS IS THE ENTRANCE TO YOMI...
WHOOSH

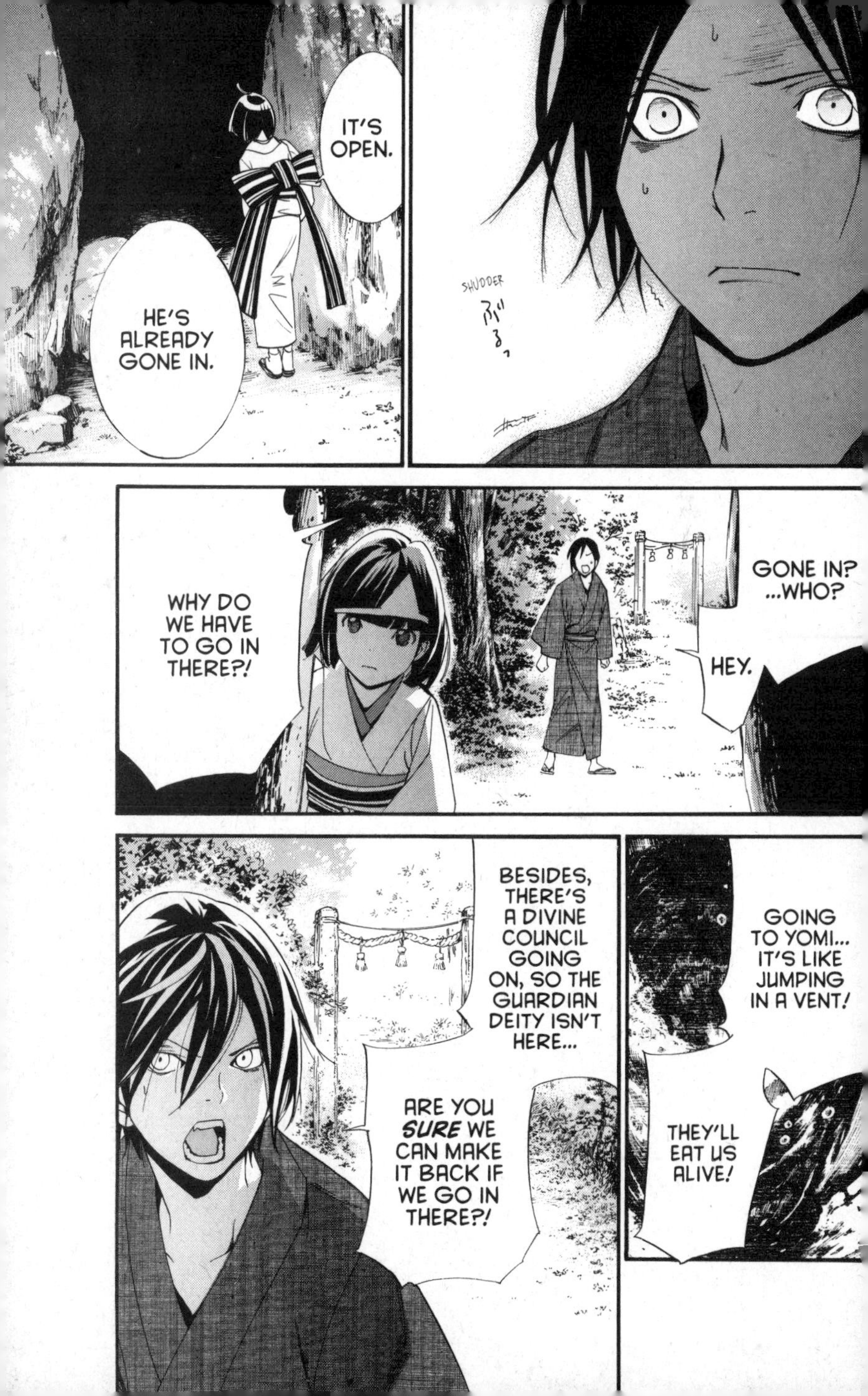
SHUDDER
ぶるっ
IT'S OPEN.
HE'S ALREADY GONE IN.
GONE IN? ...WHO?
HEY.
WHY DO WE HAVE TO GO IN THERE?!
GOING TO YOMI... IT'S LIKE JUMPING IN A VENT!
THEY'LL EAT US ALIVE!
BESIDES, THERE'S A DIVINE COUNCIL GOING ON, SO THE GUARDIAN DEITY ISN'T HERE...
ARE YOU *SURE* WE CAN MAKE IT BACK IF WE GO IN THERE?!

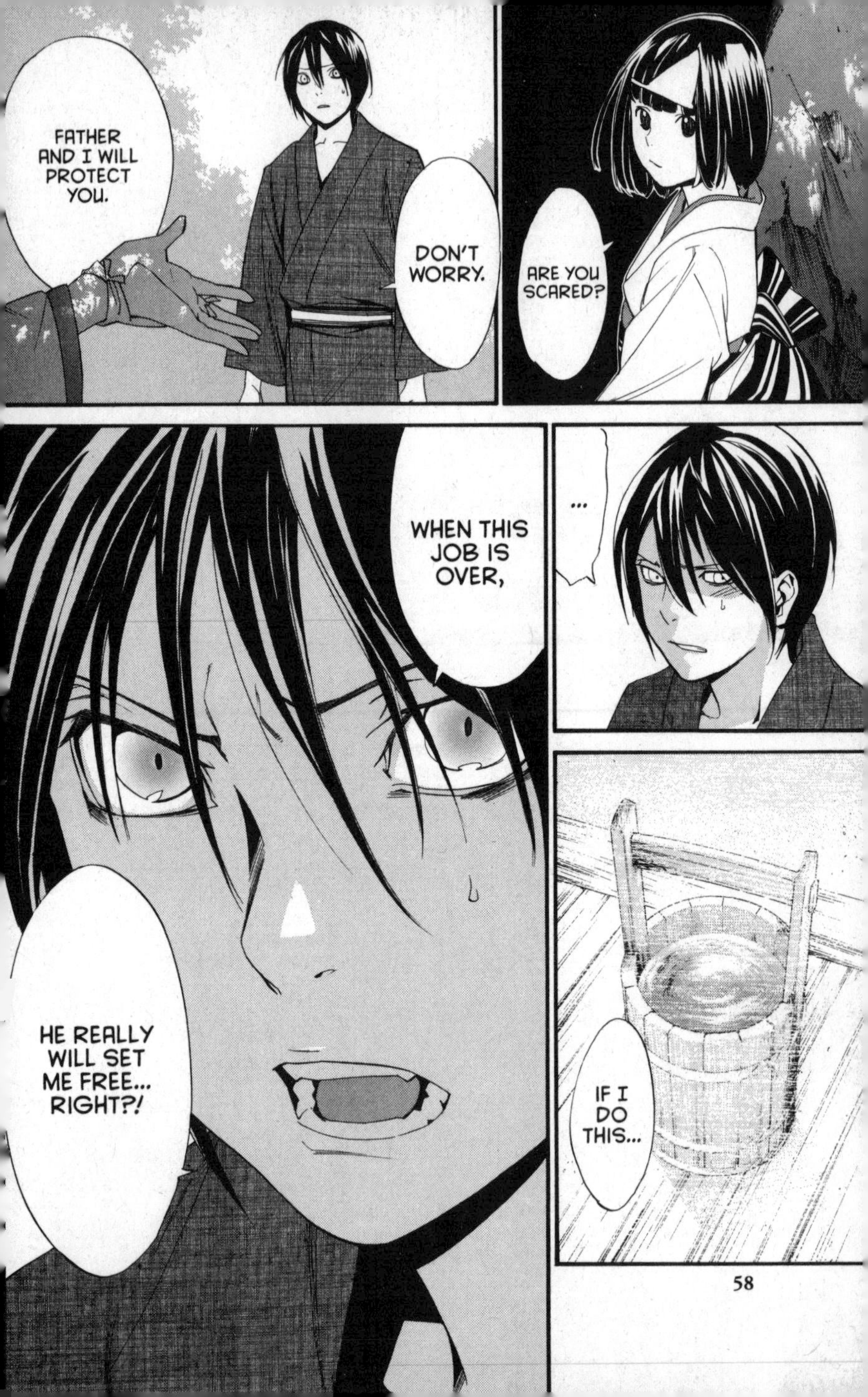
ARE YOU SCARED?
DON'T WORRY.
FATHER AND I WILL PROTECT YOU.
...
IF I DO THIS...
WHEN THIS JOB IS OVER,
HE REALLY WILL SET ME FREE... RIGHT?!

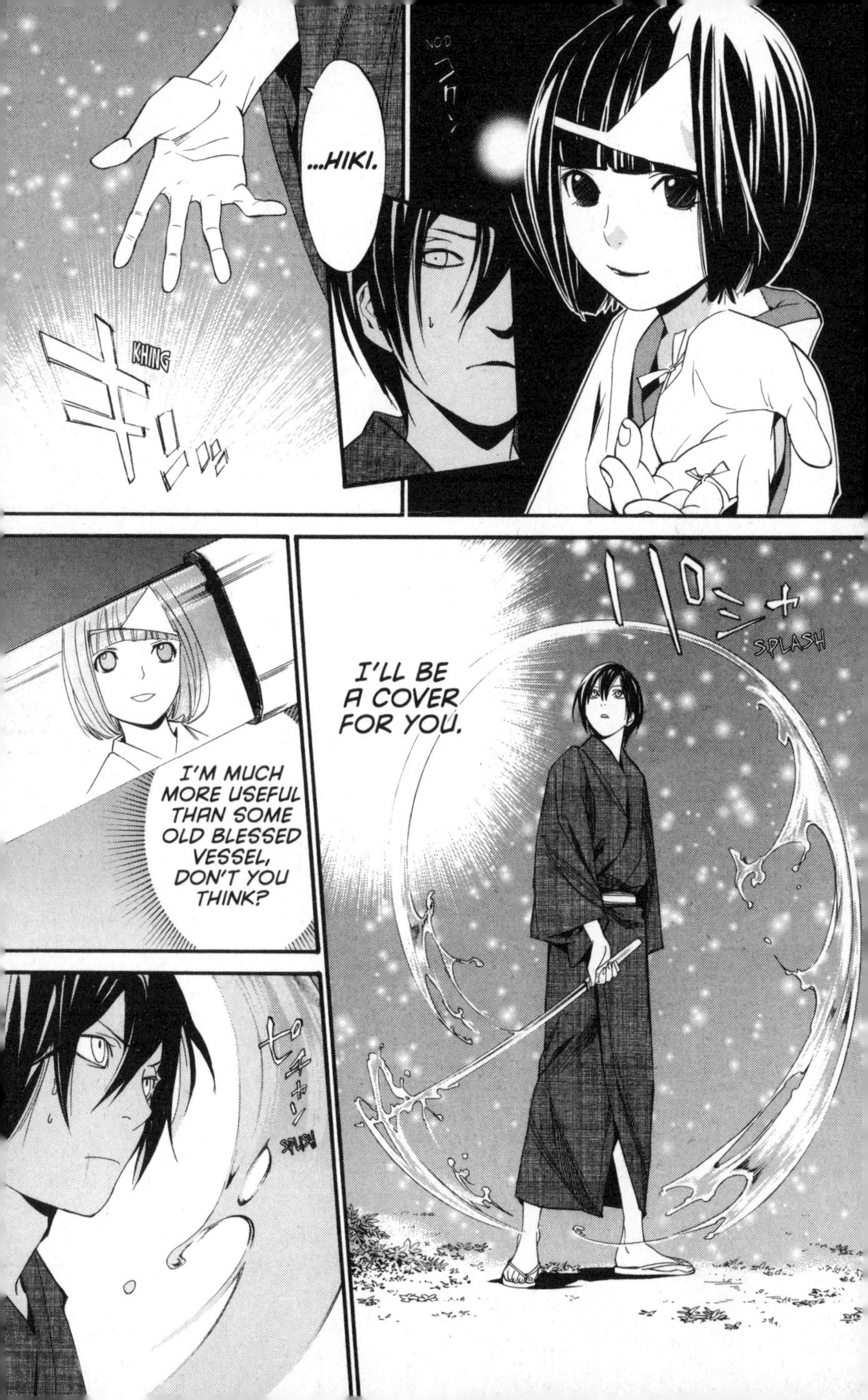
NOD
...HIKI.
KHING
SPLASH
I'LL BE A COVER FOR YOU.
I'M MUCH MORE USEFUL THAN SOME OLD BLESSED VESSEL, DON'T YOU THINK?
SPLASH

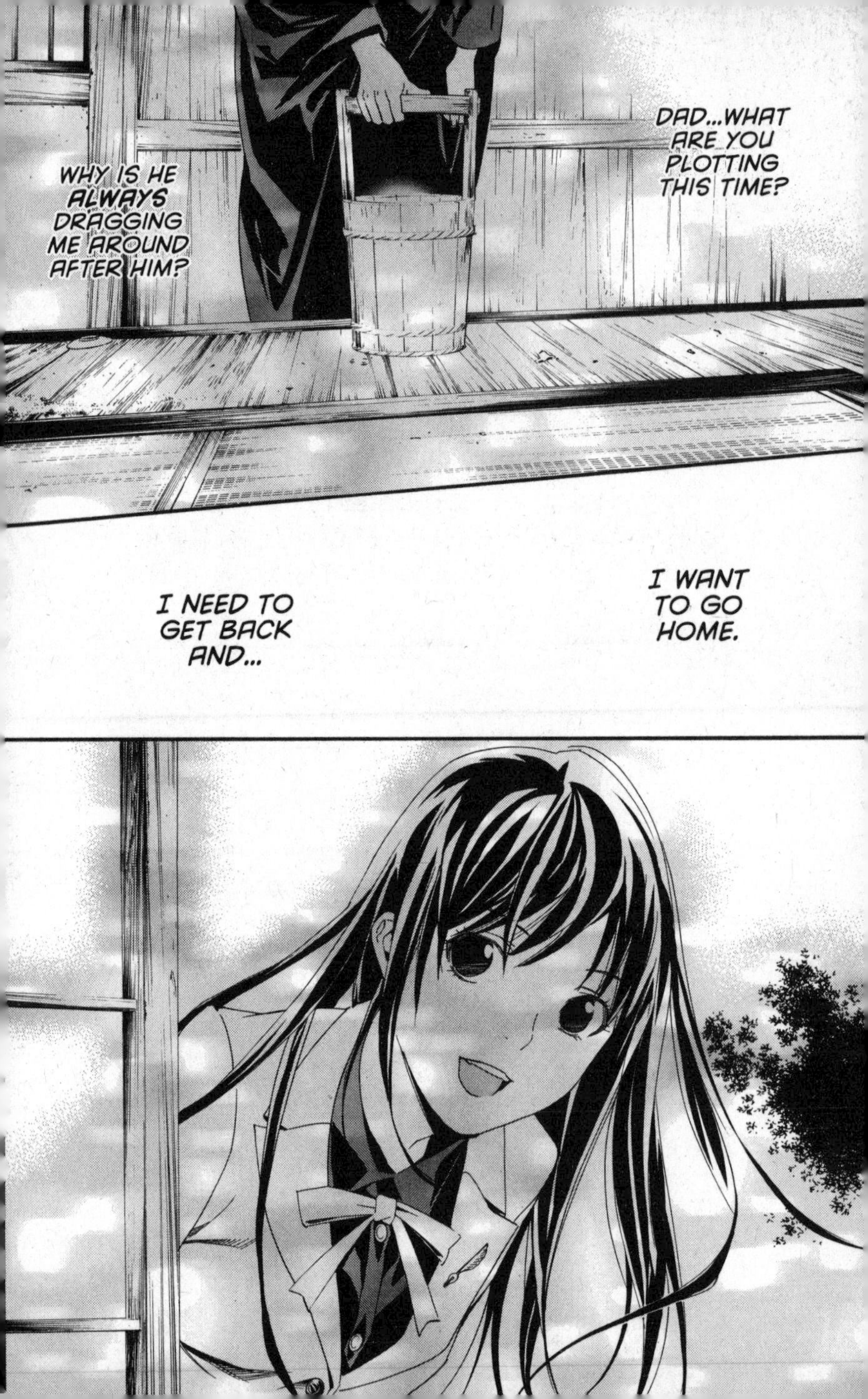
DAD...WHAT ARE YOU PLOTTING THIS TIME?
WHY IS HE ALWAYS DRAGGING ME AROUND AFTER HIM?
I WANT TO GO HOME.
I NEED TO GET BACK AND...

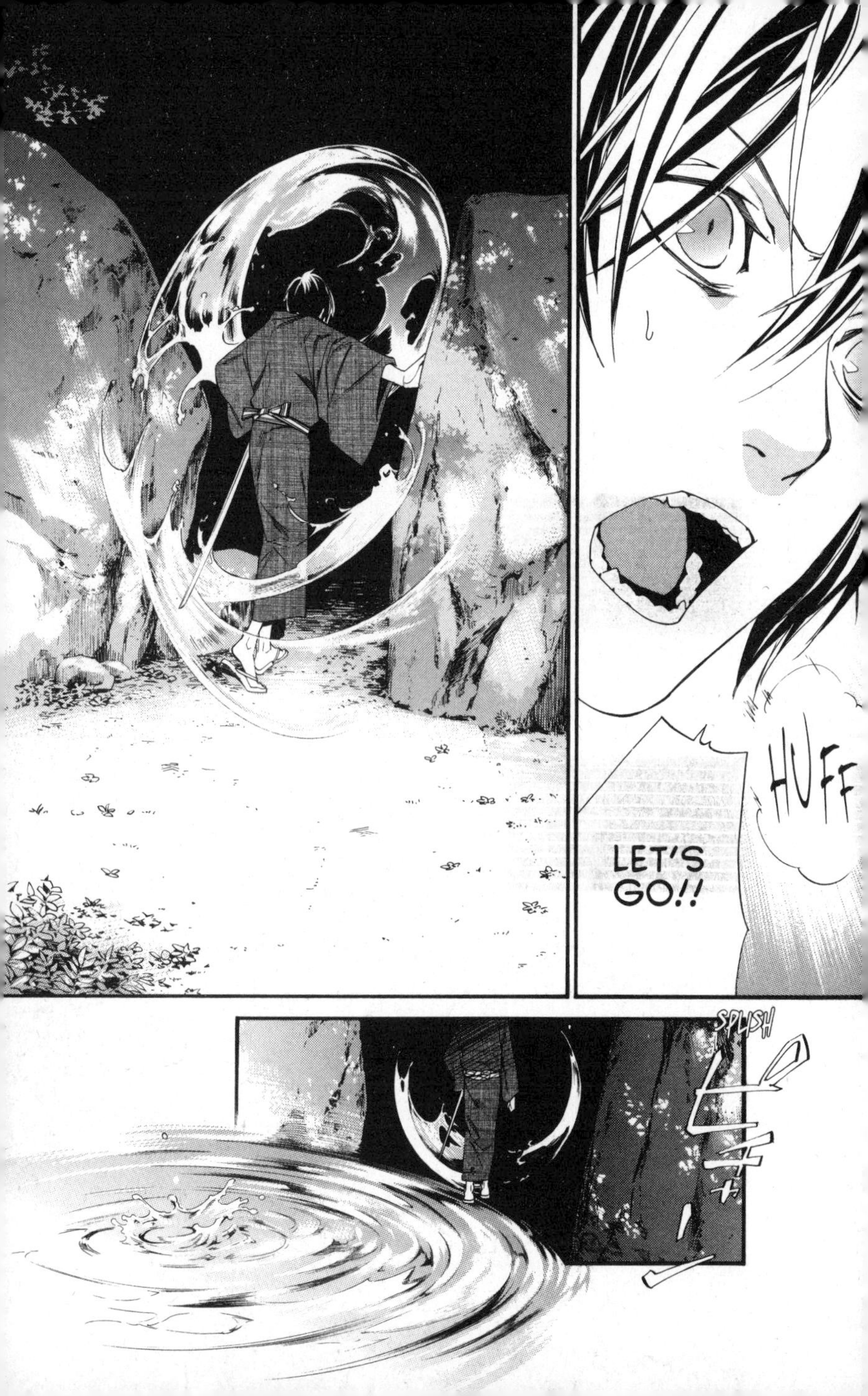
HUFF
LET'S GO!!
SPLISH

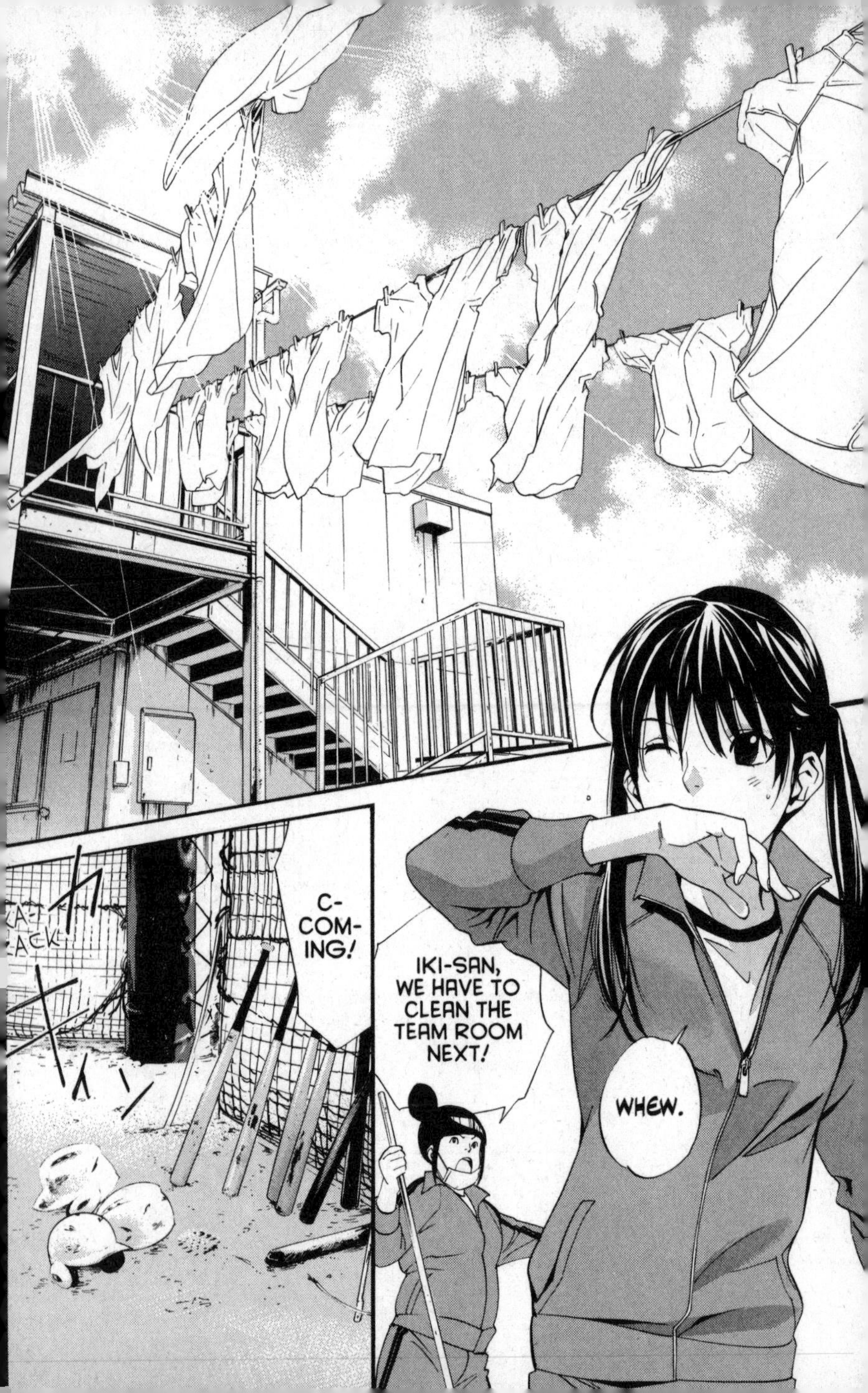
WHEW.
IKI-SAN, WE HAVE TO CLEAN THE TEAM ROOM NEXT!
C-COMING!

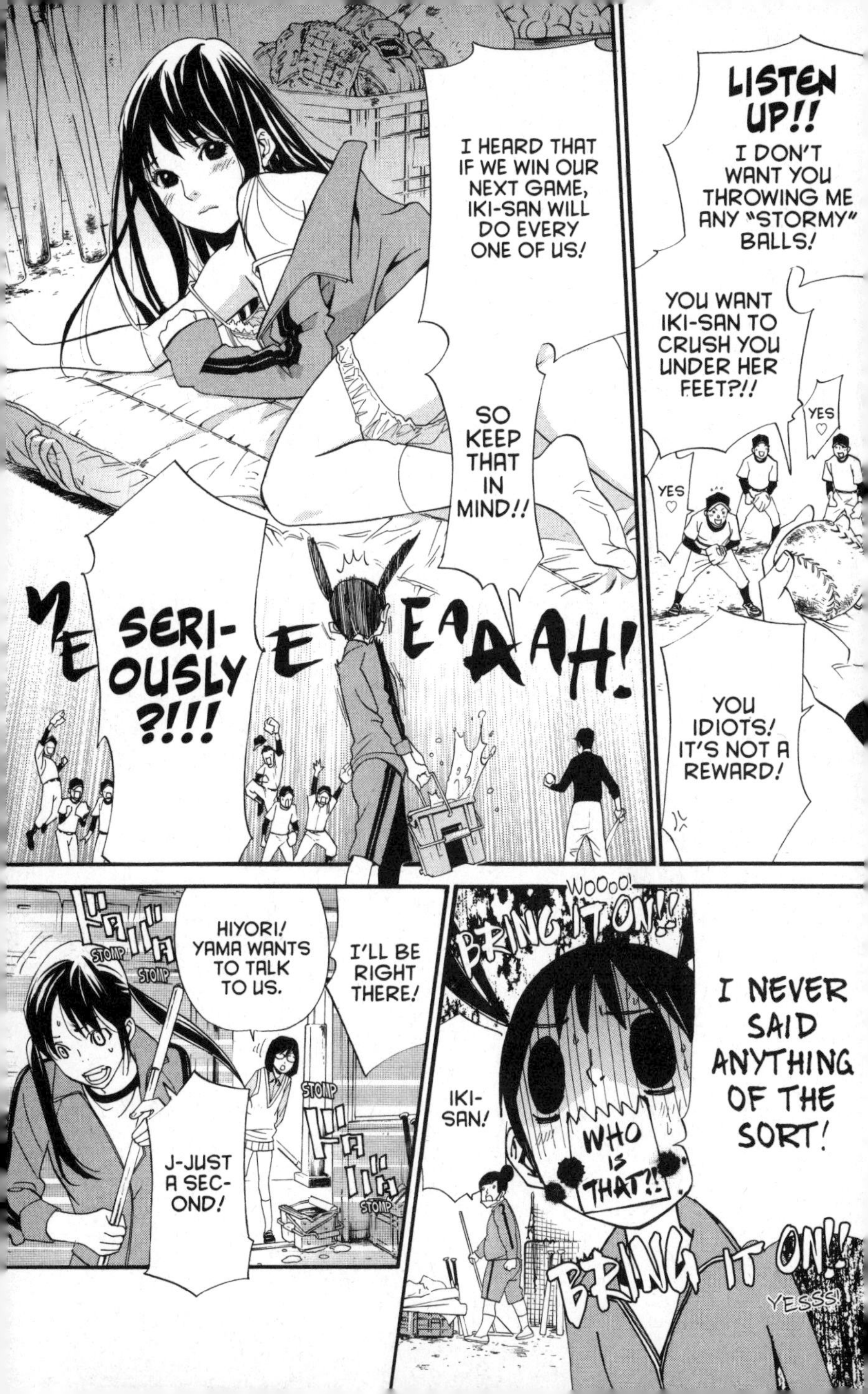
LISTEN UP!! I DON'T WANT YOU THROWING ME ANY "STORMY" BALLS!
YOU WANT IKI-SAN TO CRUSH YOU UNDER HER FEET?!!
YES ♡
YES ♡
YOU IDIOTS! IT'S NOT A REWARD!
I HEARD THAT IF WE WIN OUR NEXT GAME, IKI-SAN WILL DO EVERY ONE OF US!
SO KEEP THAT IN MIND!!
MEEEAAAH!
SERI-OUSLY?!!!
WOOOO!
BRING IT ON!!
I NEVER SAID ANYTHING OF THE SORT!
IKI-SAN!
WHO IS THAT?!
BRING IT ON!!
YESSS!
HIYORI! YAMA WANTS TO TALK TO US.
I'LL BE RIGHT THERE!
STOMP
STOMP
J-JUST A SEC-OND!
STOMP
STOMP

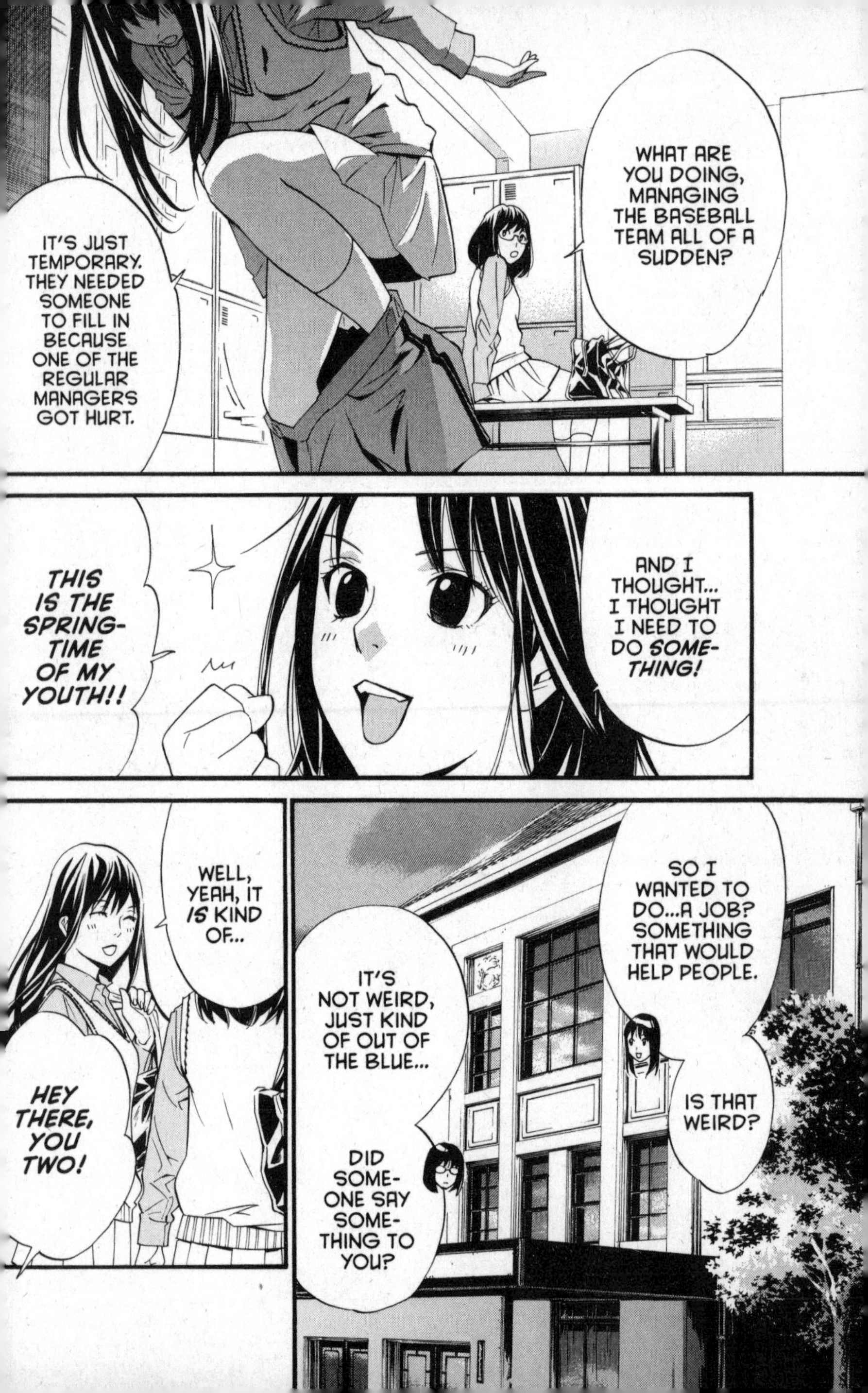
WHAT ARE YOU DOING, MANAGING THE BASEBALL TEAM ALL OF A SUDDEN?
IT'S JUST TEMPORARY. THEY NEEDED SOMEONE TO FILL IN BECAUSE ONE OF THE REGULAR MANAGERS GOT HURT.
AND I THOUGHT... I THOUGHT I NEED TO DO *SOMETHING!*
THIS IS THE SPRINGTIME OF MY YOUTH!!
SO I WANTED TO DO...A JOB? SOMETHING THAT WOULD HELP PEOPLE.
IS THAT WEIRD?
IT'S NOT WEIRD, JUST KIND OF OUT OF THE BLUE...
DID SOMEONE SAY SOMETHING TO YOU?
WELL, YEAH, IT *IS* KIND OF...
HEY THERE, YOU TWO!

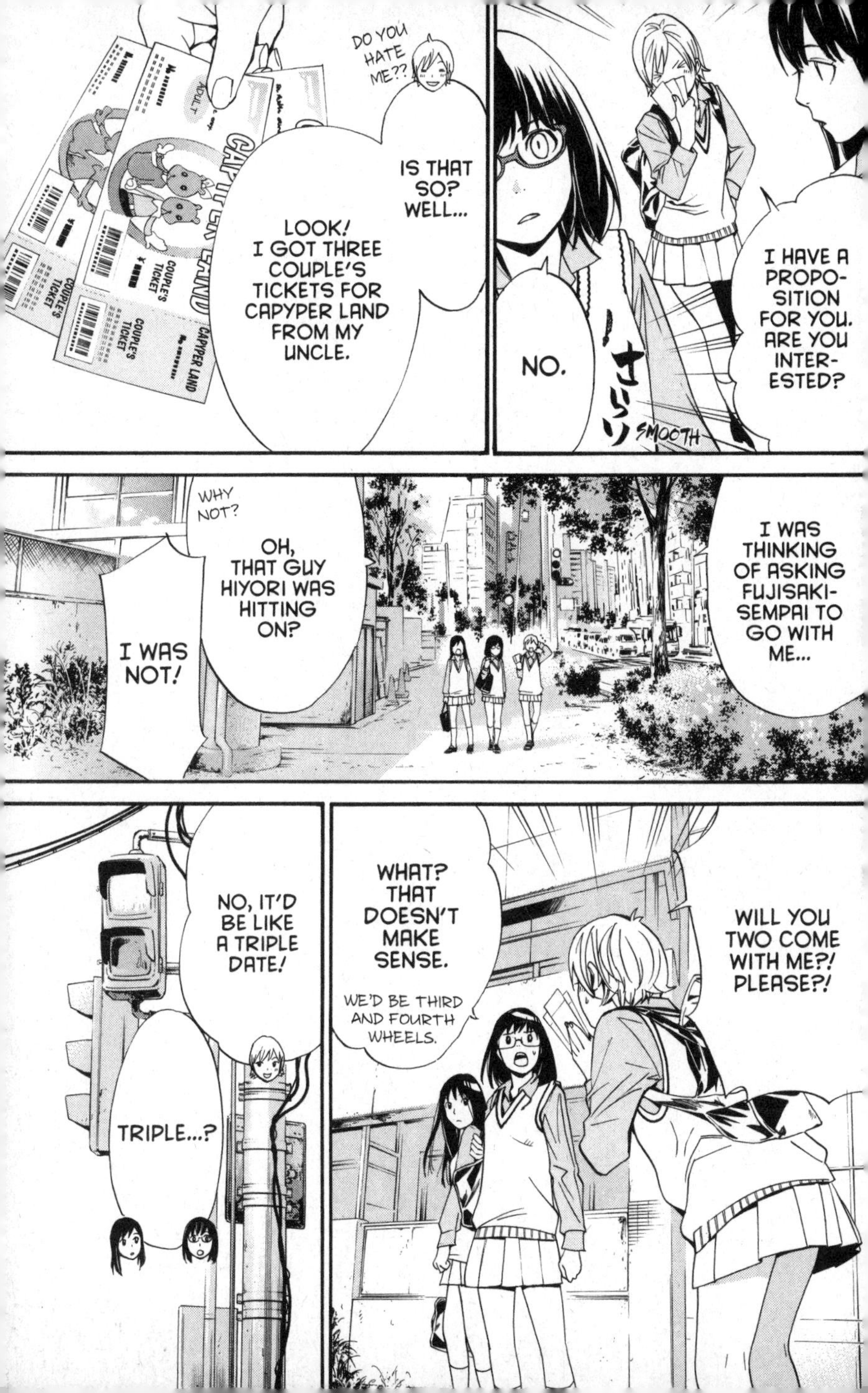
I HAVE A PROPOSITION FOR YOU. ARE YOU INTERESTED?
NO.
さらり
SMOOTH
IS THAT SO? WELL...
LOOK! I GOT THREE COUPLE'S TICKETS FOR CAPYPER LAND FROM MY UNCLE.
DO YOU HATE ME??
CAPYPER LAND
COUPLE'S TICKET
ADULT
I WAS THINKING OF ASKING FUJISAKI-SEMPAI TO GO WITH ME...
OH, THAT GUY HIYORI WAS HITTING ON?
WHY NOT?
I WAS NOT!
WILL YOU TWO COME WITH ME?! PLEASE?!
WHAT? THAT DOESN'T MAKE SENSE.
WE'D BE THIRD AND FOURTH WHEELS.
NO, IT'D BE LIKE A TRIPLE DATE!
TRIPLE...?

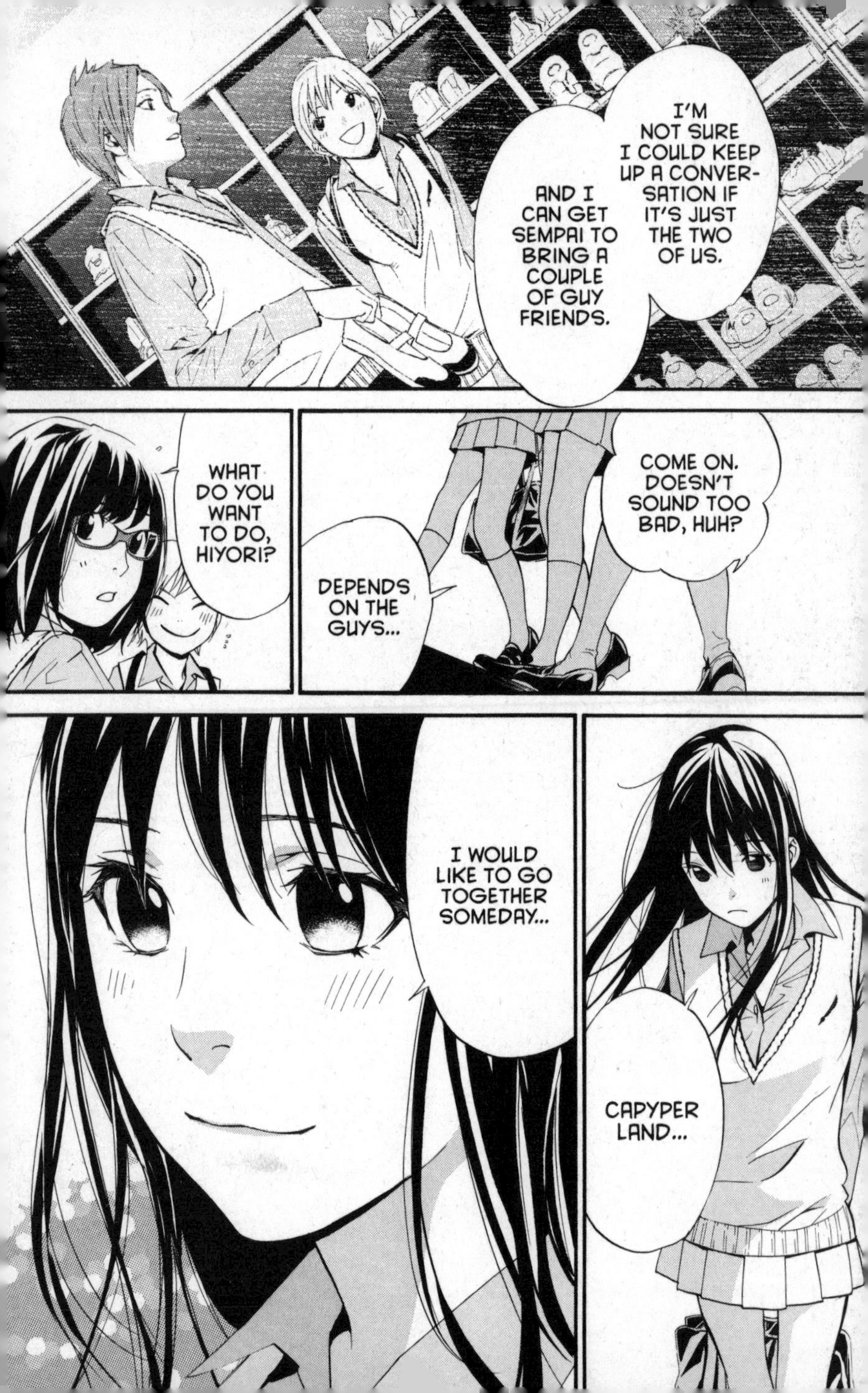
I'M NOT SURE I COULD KEEP UP A CONVERSATION IF IT'S JUST THE TWO OF US.
AND I CAN GET SEMPAI TO BRING A COUPLE OF GUY FRIENDS.
COME ON. DOESN'T SOUND TOO BAD, HUH?
DEPENDS ON THE GUYS...
WHAT DO YOU WANT TO DO, HIYORI?
CAPYPER LAND...
I WOULD LIKE TO GO TOGETHER SOMEDAY...

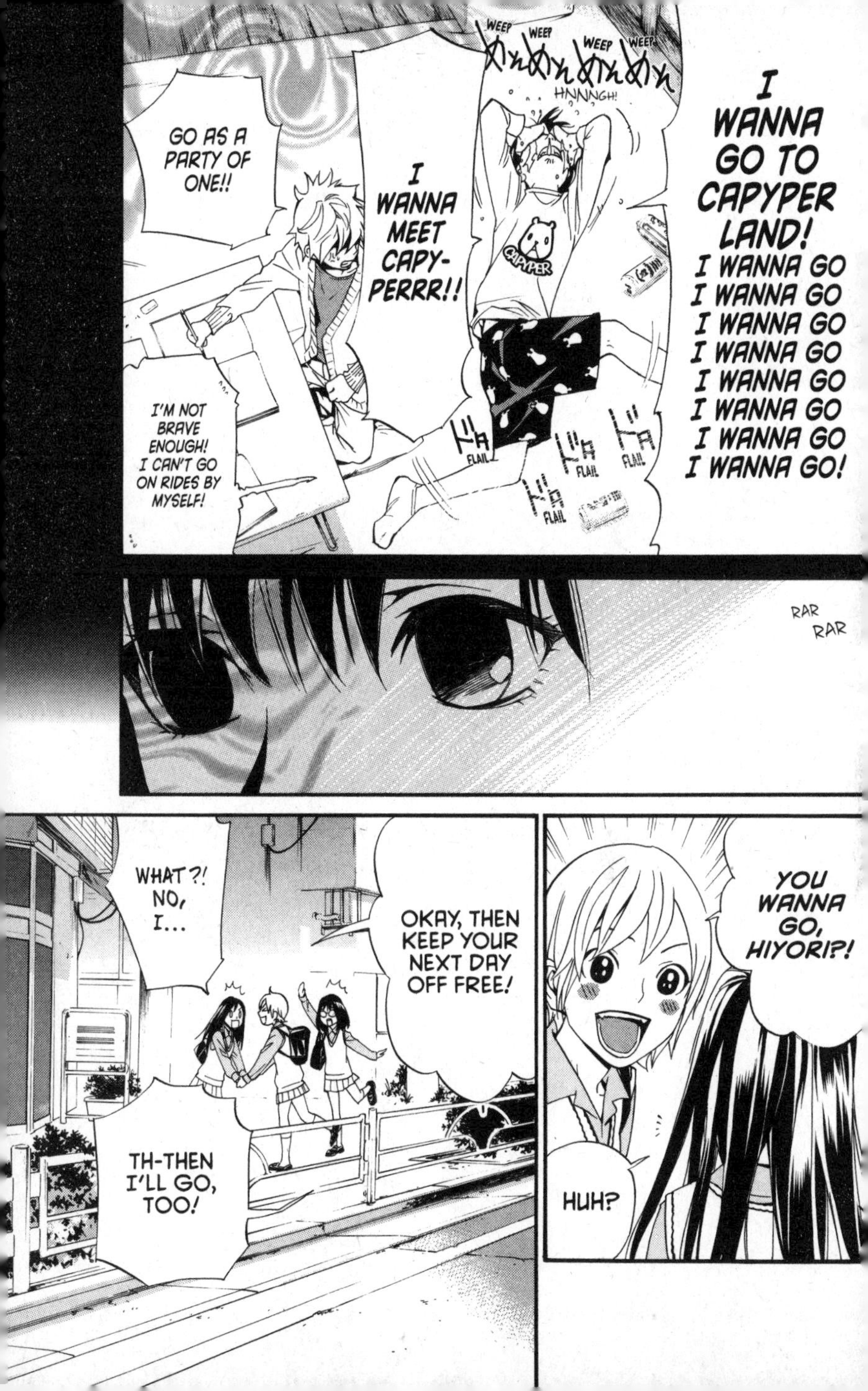
I WANNA GO TO CAPYPER LAND! I WANNA GO I WANNA GO I WANNA GO I WANNA GO I WANNA GO I WANNA GO I WANNA GO I WANNA GO!
WEEP WEEP WEEP WEEP
HNNNGH!
CAPYPER
I WANNA MEET CAPY-PERRR!!
FLAIL
FLAIL
FLAIL
FLAIL
GO AS A PARTY OF ONE!!
I'M NOT BRAVE ENOUGH! I CAN'T GO ON RIDES BY MYSELF!
RAR RAR
YOU WANNA GO, HIYORI?!
HUH?
OKAY, THEN KEEP YOUR NEXT DAY OFF FREE!
WHAT?! NO, I...
TH-THEN I'LL GO, TOO!

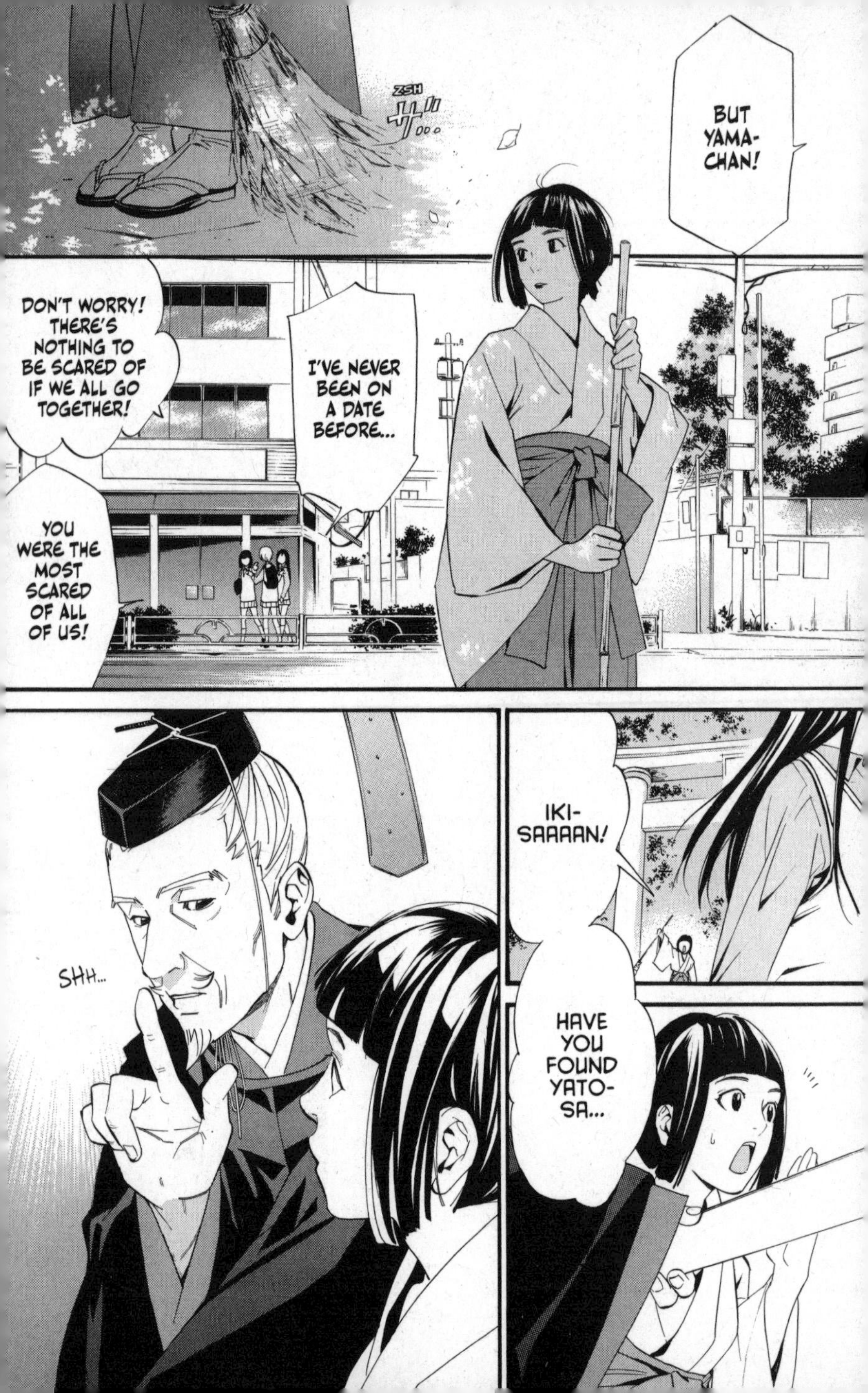
ZSH
BUT YAMA-CHAN!
I'VE NEVER BEEN ON A DATE BEFORE...
DON'T WORRY! THERE'S NOTHING TO BE SCARED OF IF WE ALL GO TOGETHER!
YOU WERE THE MOST SCARED OF ALL OF US!
IKI-SAAAAN!
HAVE YOU FOUND YATO-SA...
SHH...

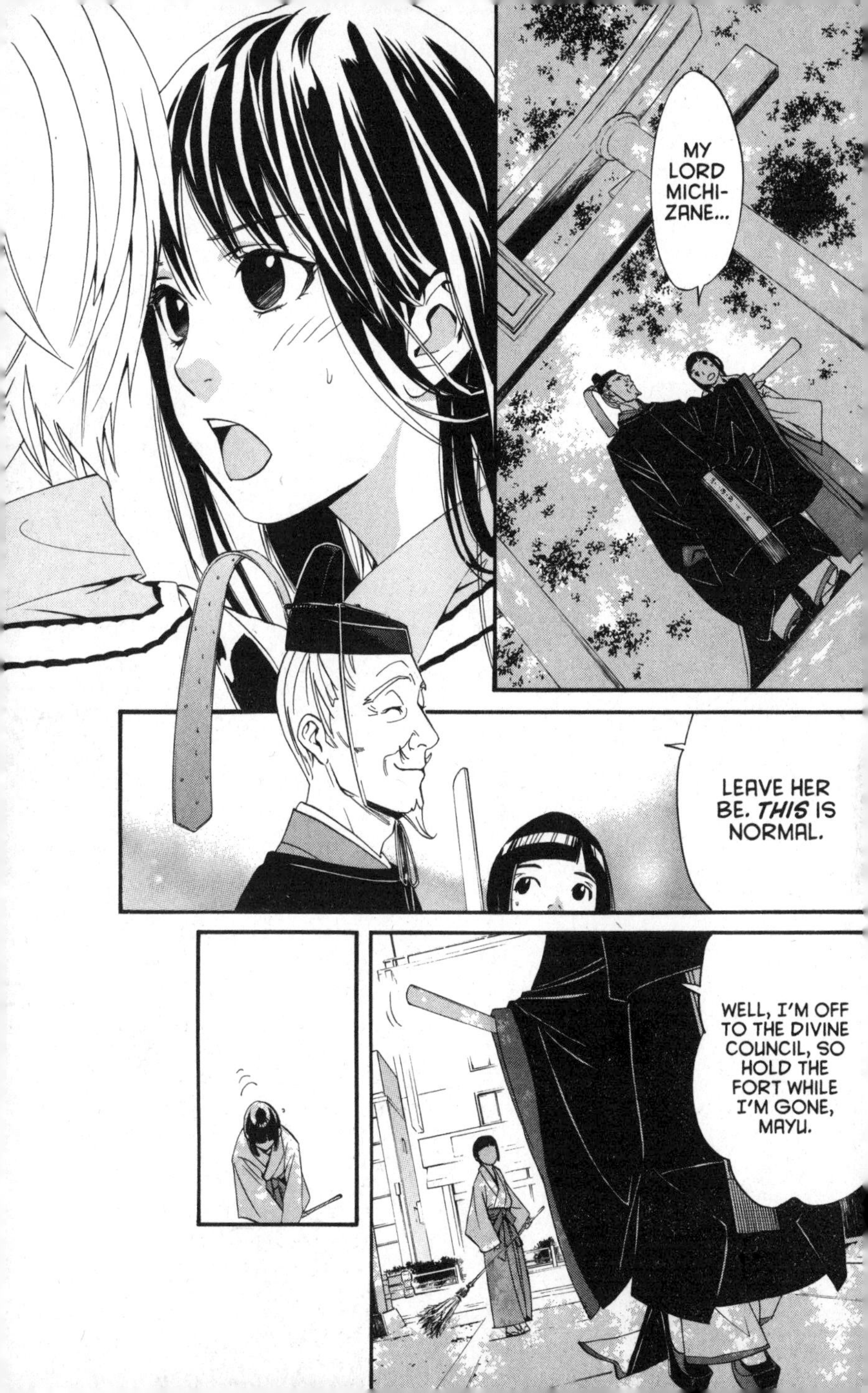
MY LORD MICHI-ZANE...
LEAVE HER BE. *THIS* IS NORMAL.
WELL, I'M OFF TO THE DIVINE COUNCIL, SO HOLD THE FORT WHILE I'M GONE, MAYU.

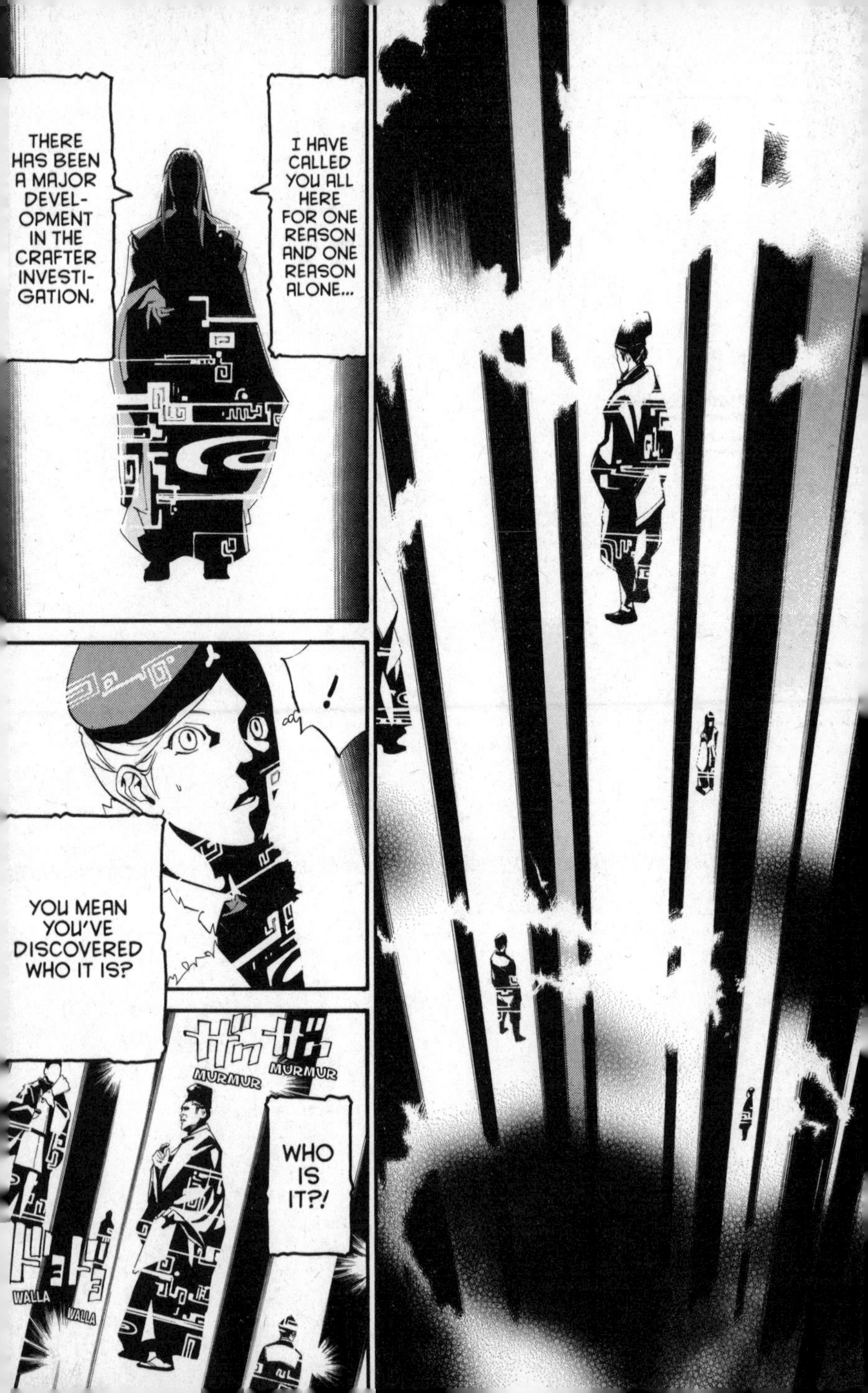
I HAVE CALLED YOU ALL HERE FOR ONE REASON AND ONE REASON ALONE...
THERE HAS BEEN A MAJOR DEVEL-OPMENT IN THE CRAFTER INVESTI-GATION.
!
YOU MEAN YOU'VE DISCOVERED WHO IT IS?
MURMUR
MURMUR
WHO IS IT?!
WALLA
WALLA

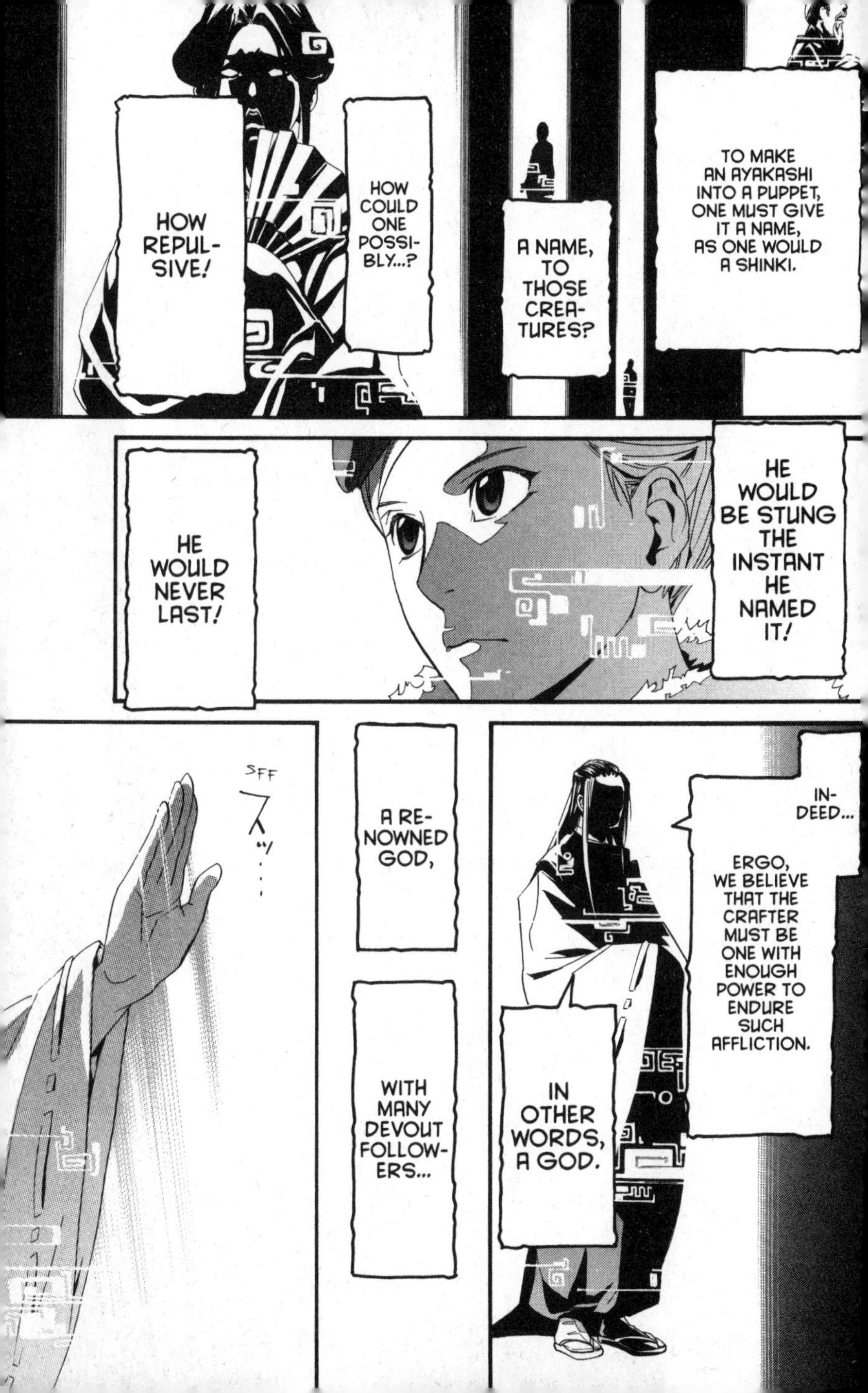
TO MAKE AN AYAKASHI INTO A PUPPET, ONE MUST GIVE IT A NAME, AS ONE WOULD A SHINKI.
A NAME, TO THOSE CREATURES?
HOW COULD ONE POSSIBLY...?
HOW REPULSIVE!
HE WOULD BE STUNG THE INSTANT HE NAMED IT!
HE WOULD NEVER LAST!
INDEED...
ERGO, WE BELIEVE THAT THE CRAFTER MUST BE ONE WITH ENOUGH POWER TO ENDURE SUCH AFFLICTION.
IN OTHER WORDS, A GOD.
A RENOWNED GOD,
WITH MANY DEVOUT FOLLOWERS...
SFF

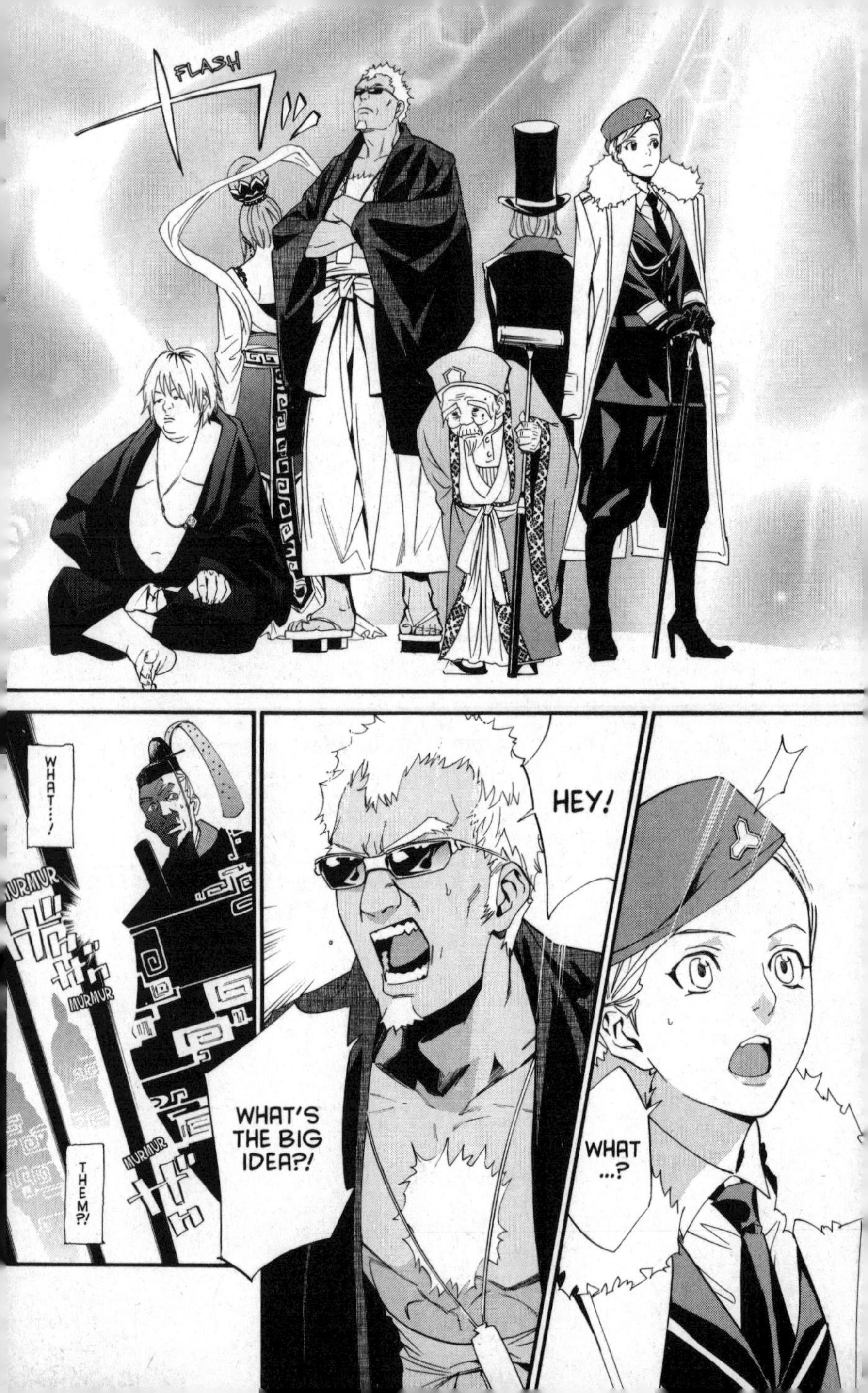
FLASH
WHAT ...?
HEY!
WHAT'S THE BIG IDEA?!
WHAT...!
MURMUR
MURMUR
MURMUR
THEM?!

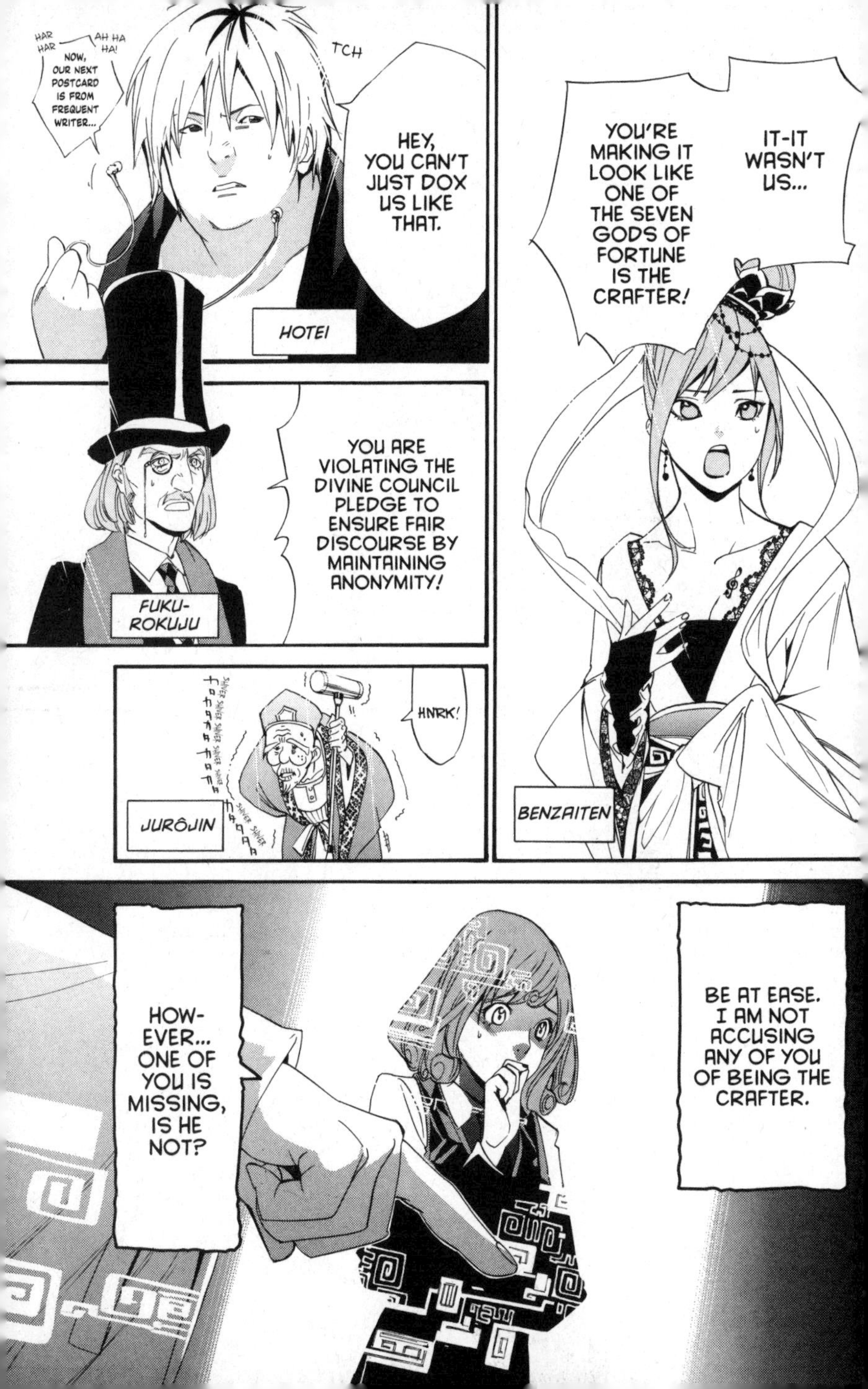
IT-IT WASN'T US...
YOU'RE MAKING IT LOOK LIKE ONE OF THE SEVEN GODS OF FORTUNE IS THE CRAFTER!
BENZAITEN
TCH
HEY, YOU CAN'T JUST DOX US LIKE THAT.
AH HA HA!
HAR HAR
NOW, OUR NEXT POSTCARD IS FROM FREQUENT WRITER...
HOTEI
YOU ARE VIOLATING THE DIVINE COUNCIL PLEDGE TO ENSURE FAIR DISCOURSE BY MAINTAINING ANONYMITY!
FUKU-ROKUJU
HNRK!
SHIVER SHIVER
JURÔJIN
BE AT EASE. I AM NOT ACCUSING ANY OF YOU OF BEING THE CRAFTER.
HOW-EVER... ONE OF YOU IS MISSING, IS HE NOT?

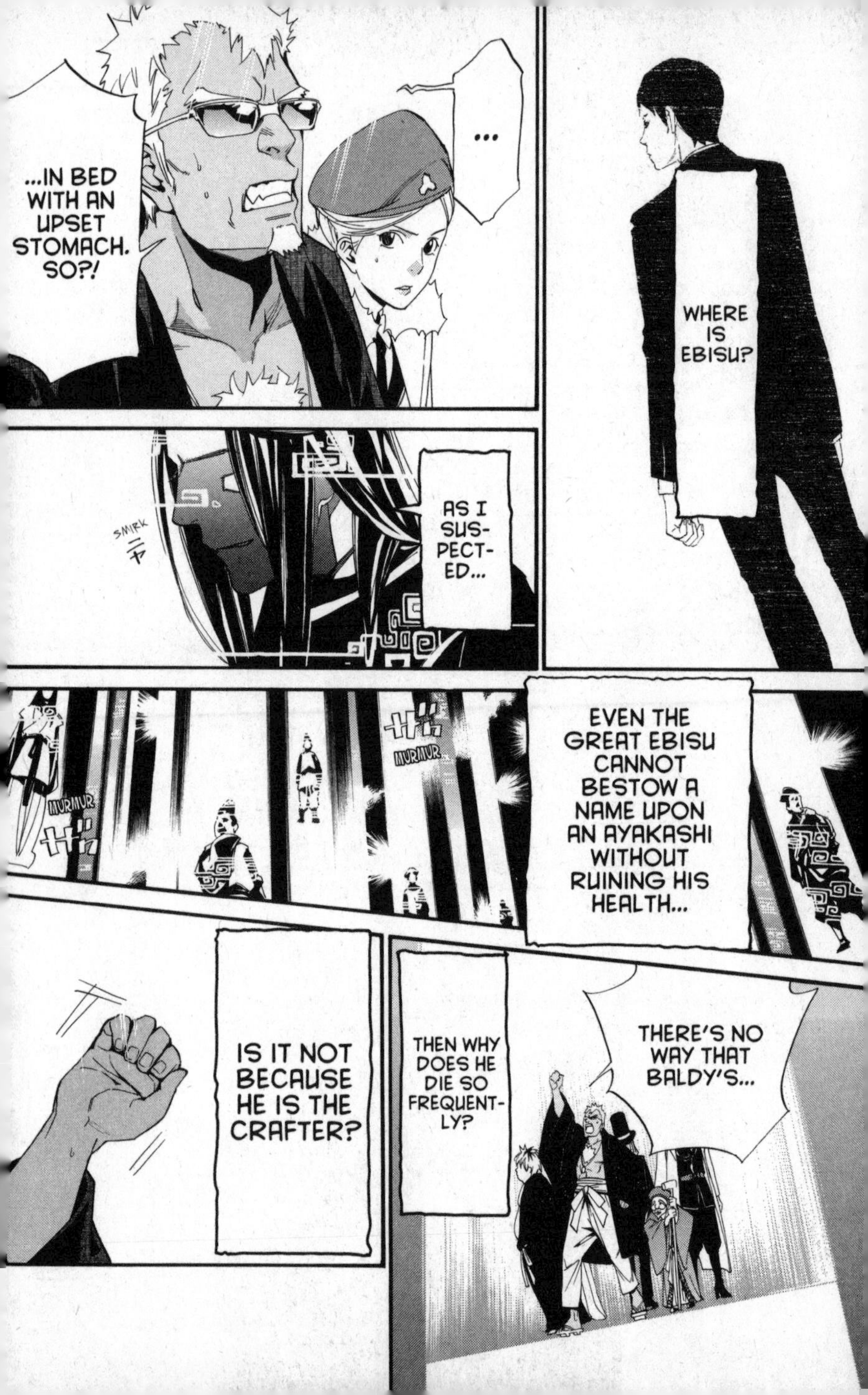
WHERE IS EBISU?
...
...IN BED WITH AN UPSET STOMACH. SO?!
AS I SUSPECTED...
SMIRK
EVEN THE GREAT EBISU CANNOT BESTOW A NAME UPON AN AYAKASHI WITHOUT RUINING HIS HEALTH...
MURMUR
MURMUR
THERE'S NO WAY THAT BALDY'S...
THEN WHY DOES HE DIE SO FREQUENTLY?
IS IT NOT BECAUSE HE IS THE CRAFTER?

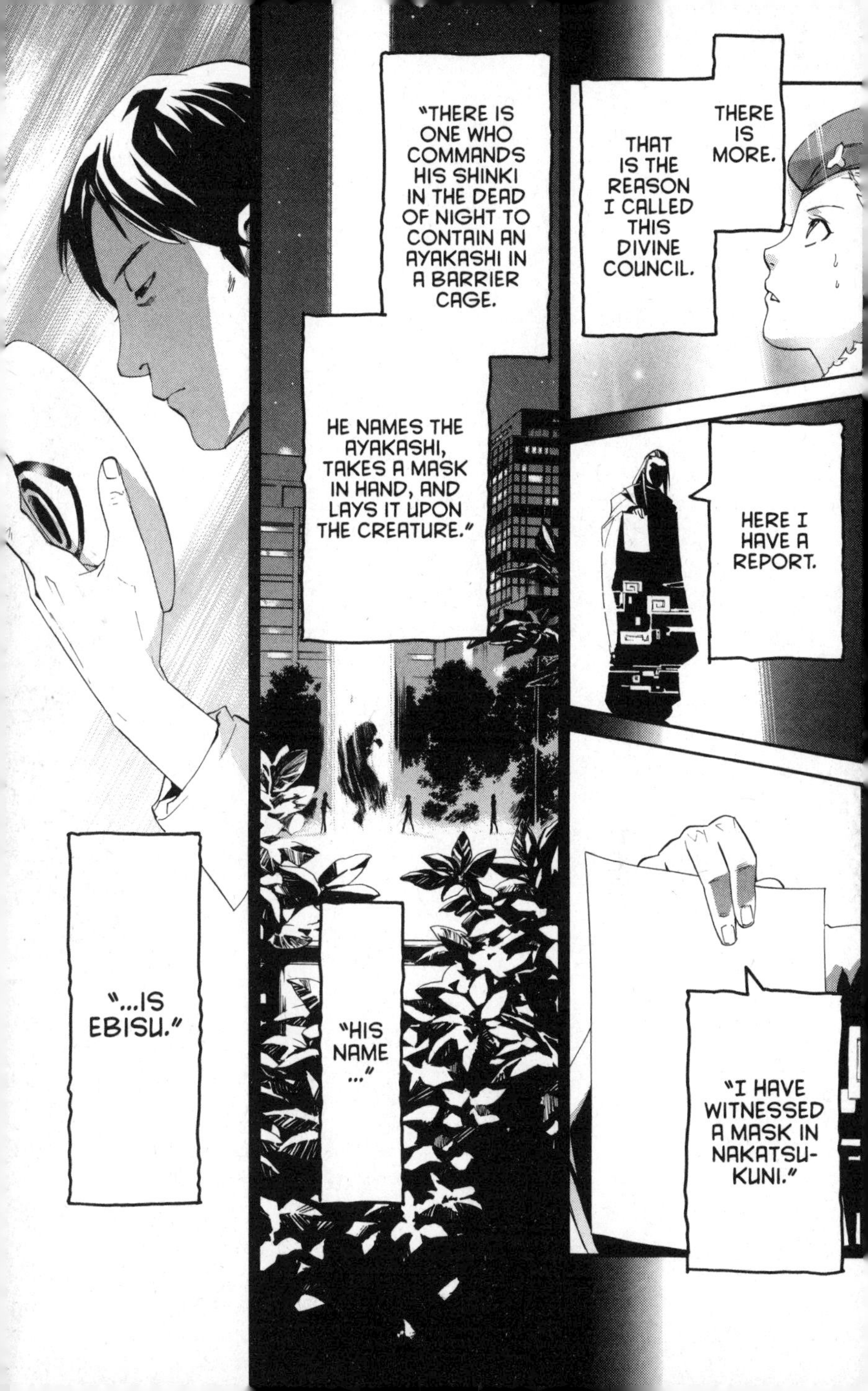
THERE IS MORE.
THAT IS THE REASON I CALLED THIS DIVINE COUNCIL.
HERE I HAVE A REPORT.
"I HAVE WITNESSED A MASK IN NAKATSU-KUNI."
"THERE IS ONE WHO COMMANDS HIS SHINKI IN THE DEAD OF NIGHT TO CONTAIN AN AYAKASHI IN A BARRIER CAGE.
HE NAMES THE AYAKASHI, TAKES A MASK IN HAND, AND LAYS IT UPON THE CREATURE."
"HIS NAME ..."
"...IS EBISU."

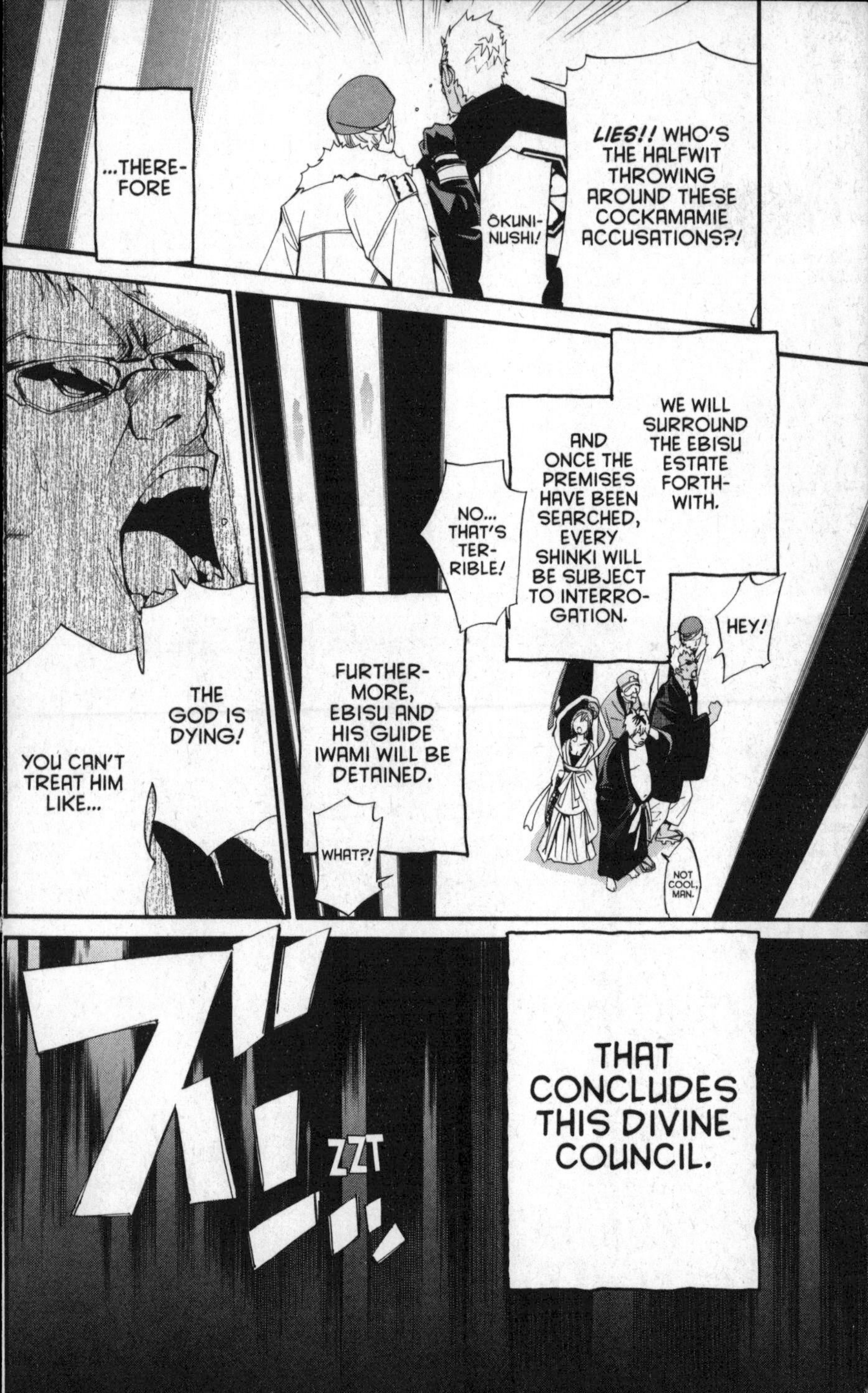

LIES!! WHO'S THE HALFWIT THROWING AROUND THESE COCKAMAMIE ACCUSATIONS?!
ŌKUNI-NUSHI!
...THERE-FORE
WE WILL SURROUND THE EBISU ESTATE FORTH-WITH.
AND ONCE THE PREMISES HAVE BEEN SEARCHED, EVERY SHINKI WILL BE SUBJECT TO INTERRO-GATION.
HEY!
NO... THAT'S TER-RIBLE!
NOT COOL, MAN.
FURTHER-MORE, EBISU AND HIS GUIDE IWAMI WILL BE DETAINED.
WHAT?!
THE GOD IS DYING!
YOU CAN'T TREAT HIM LIKE...
THAT CONCLUDES THIS DIVINE COUNCIL.
ZZT

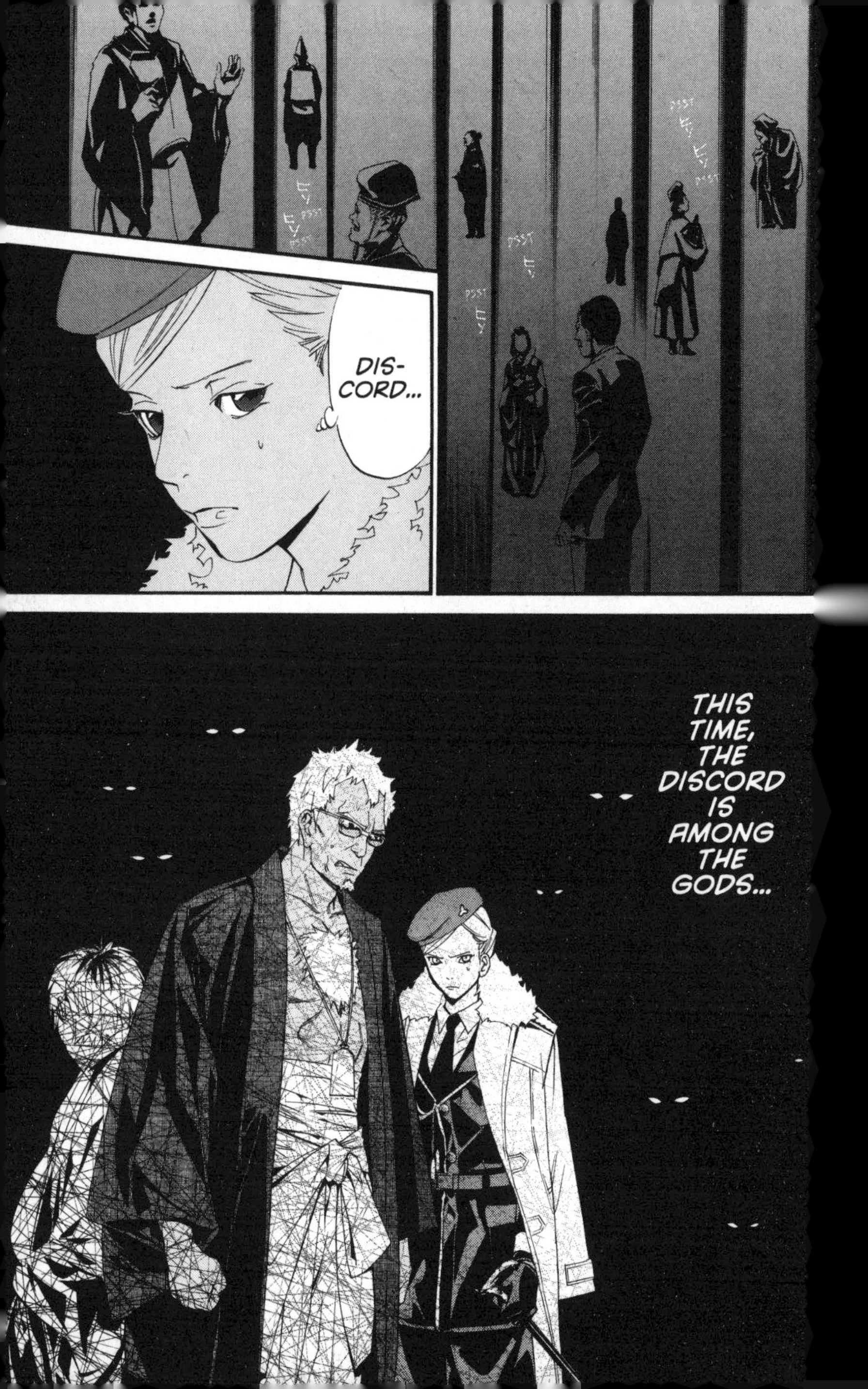
PSST
PSST
PSST
PSST
PSST
DIS-CORD...
THIS TIME, THE DISCORD IS AMONG THE GODS...

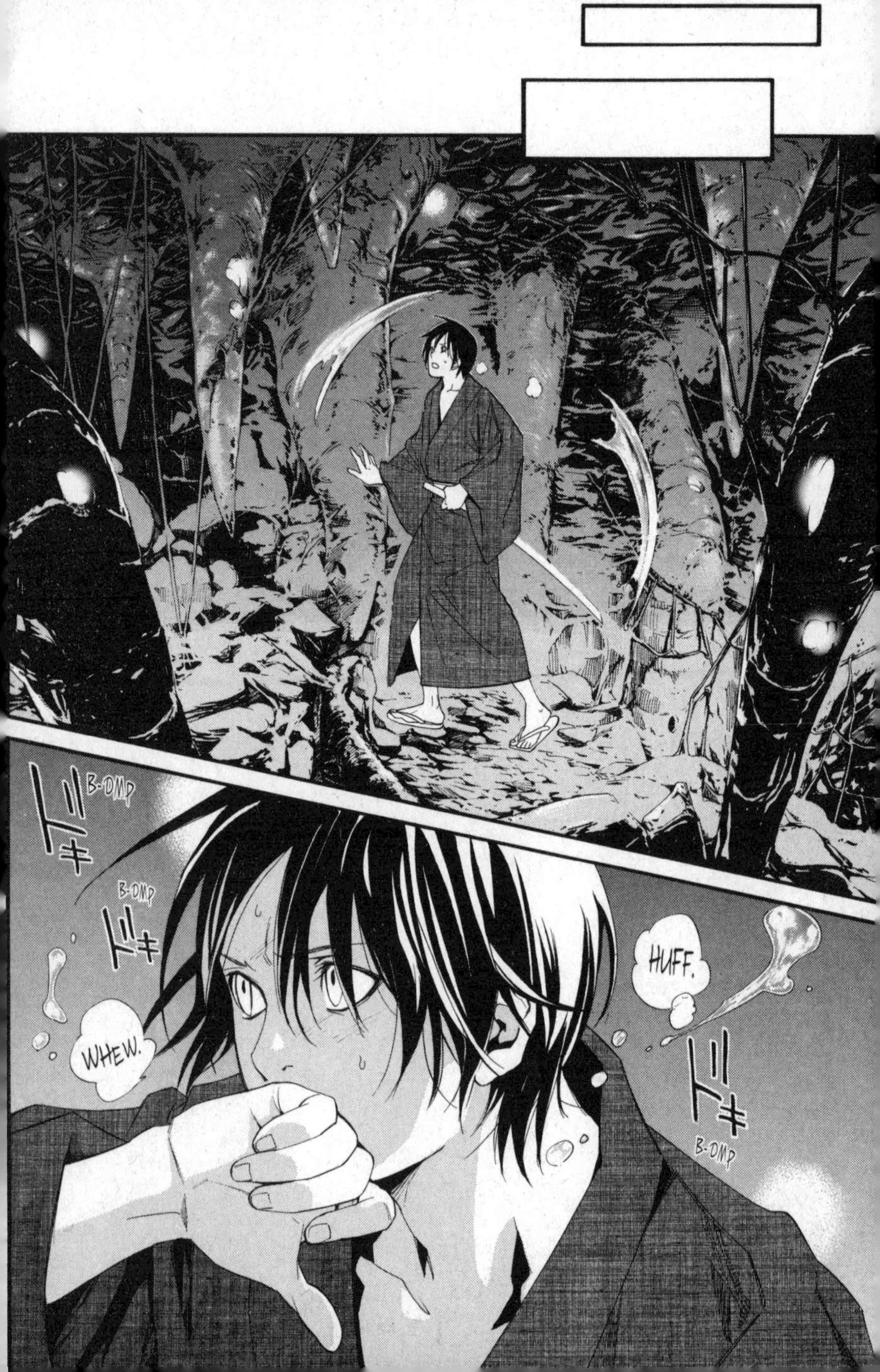
HUFF.
ドキ
B-DMP
ドキ
B-DMP
ドキ
B-DMP
WHEW.

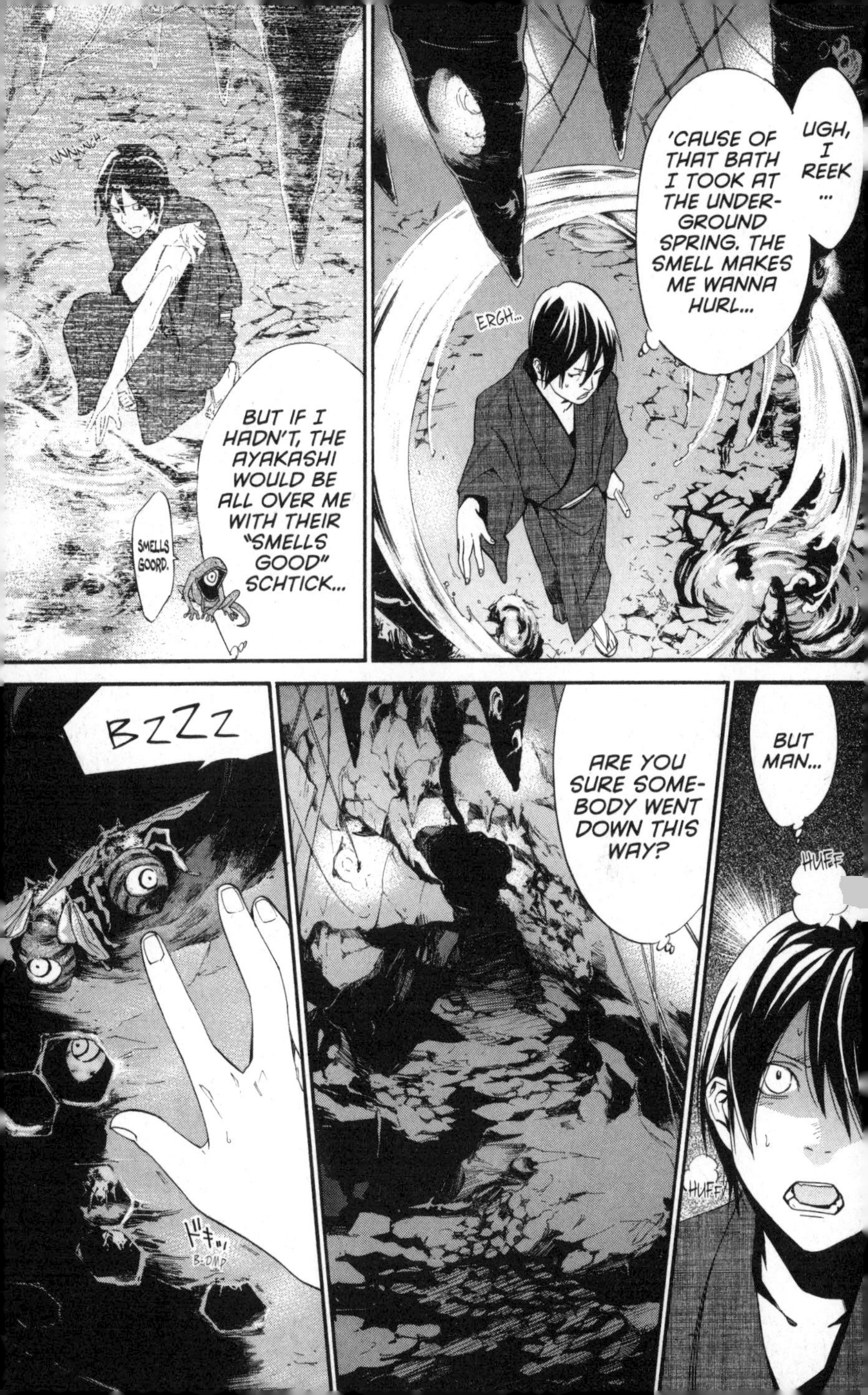
UGH, I REEK ...
'CAUSE OF THAT BATH I TOOK AT THE UNDERGROUND SPRING. THE SMELL MAKES ME WANNA HURL...
ERGH...
NNNNNGH...
BUT IF I HADN'T, THE AYAKASHI WOULD BE ALL OVER ME WITH THEIR "SMELLS GOOD" SCHTICK...
SMELLS GOORD.
BUT MAN...
HUFF
HUFF
ARE YOU SURE SOMEBODY WENT DOWN THIS WAY?
BZZZ
ドキッ
B-DMP

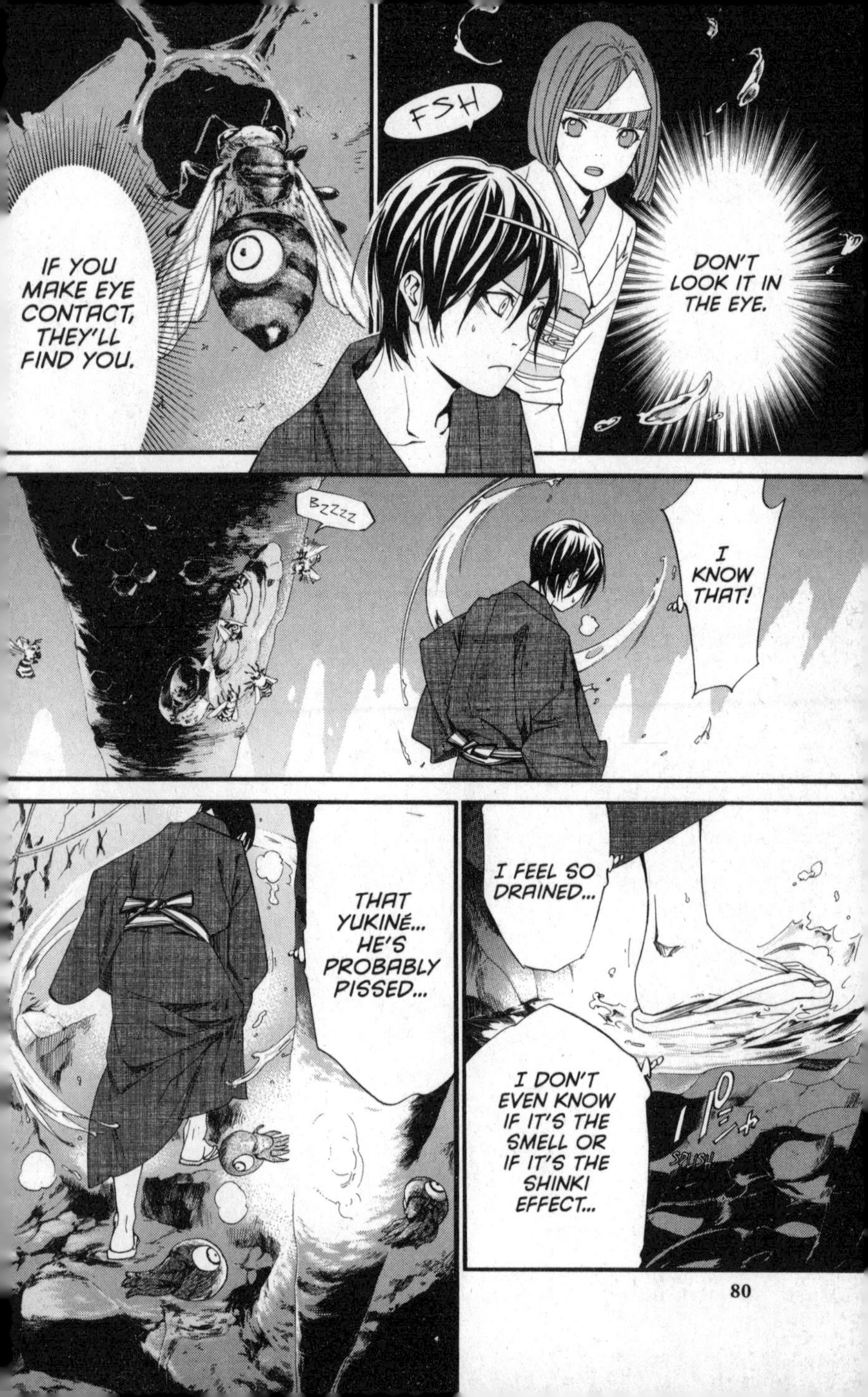
FSH
DON'T LOOK IT IN THE EYE.
IF YOU MAKE EYE CONTACT, THEY'LL FIND YOU.
I KNOW THAT!
BZZZZ
I FEEL SO DRAINED...
I DON'T EVEN KNOW IF IT'S THE SMELL OR IF IT'S THE SHINKI EFFECT...
SPLISH
THAT YUKINÉ... HE'S PROBABLY PISSED...

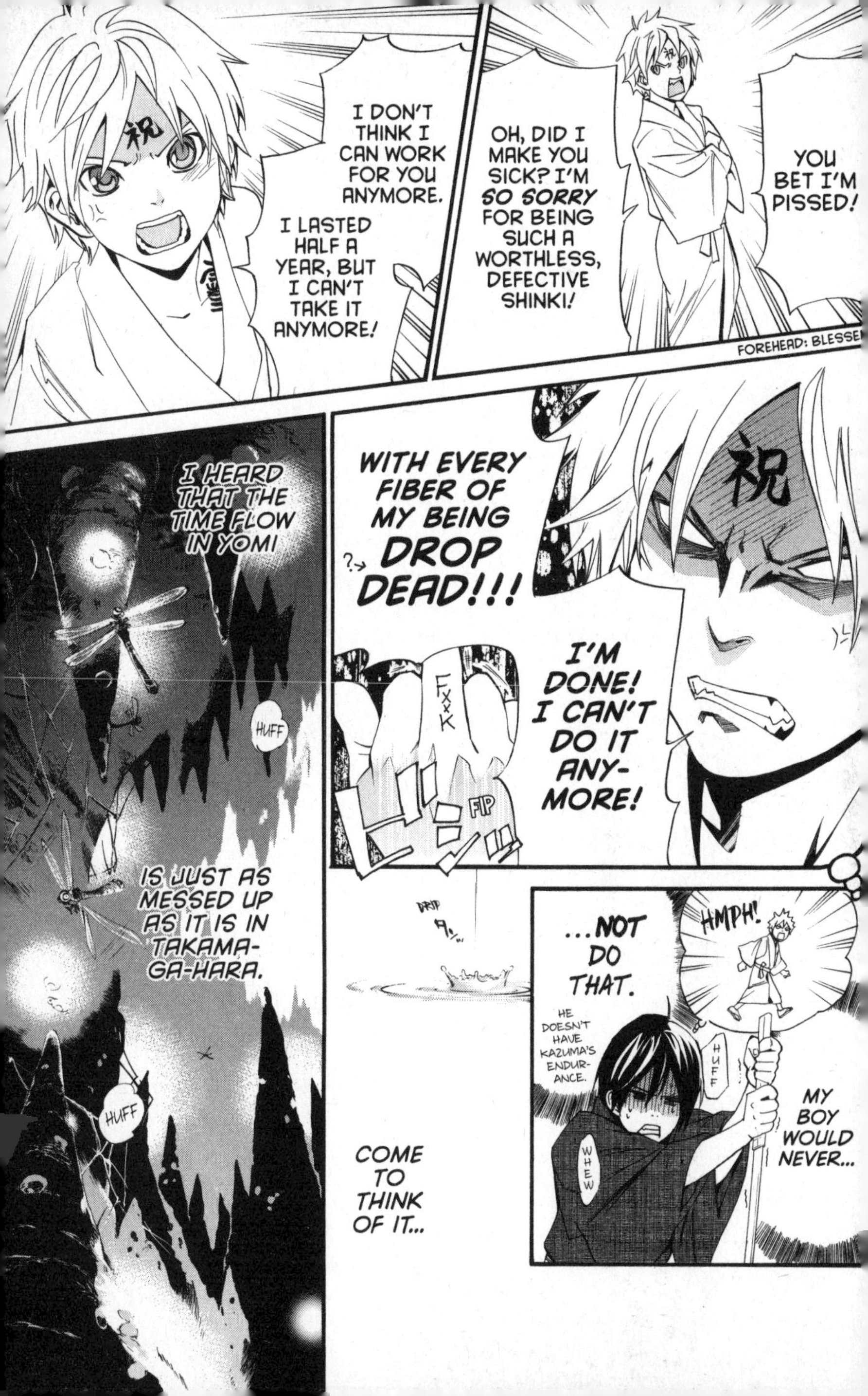
YOU BET I'M PISSED!
OH, DID I MAKE YOU SICK? I'M *SO SORRY* FOR BEING SUCH A WORTHLESS, DEFECTIVE SHINKI!
FOREHEAD: BLESSED
I DON'T THINK I CAN WORK FOR YOU ANYMORE.
I LASTED HALF A YEAR, BUT I CAN'T TAKE IT ANYMORE!
WITH EVERY FIBER OF MY BEING DROP DEAD!!!
?→
F××K
I'M DONE! I CAN'T DO IT ANY-MORE!
FIP
MY BOY WOULD NEVER...
...NOT DO THAT.
HMPH!
HE DOESN'T HAVE KAZUMA'S ENDUR-ANCE.
HUFF
WHEW
DRIP
COME TO THINK OF IT...
I HEARD THAT THE TIME FLOW IN YOMI
HUFF
IS JUST AS MESSED UP AS IT IS IN TAKAMA-GA-HARA.
HUFF

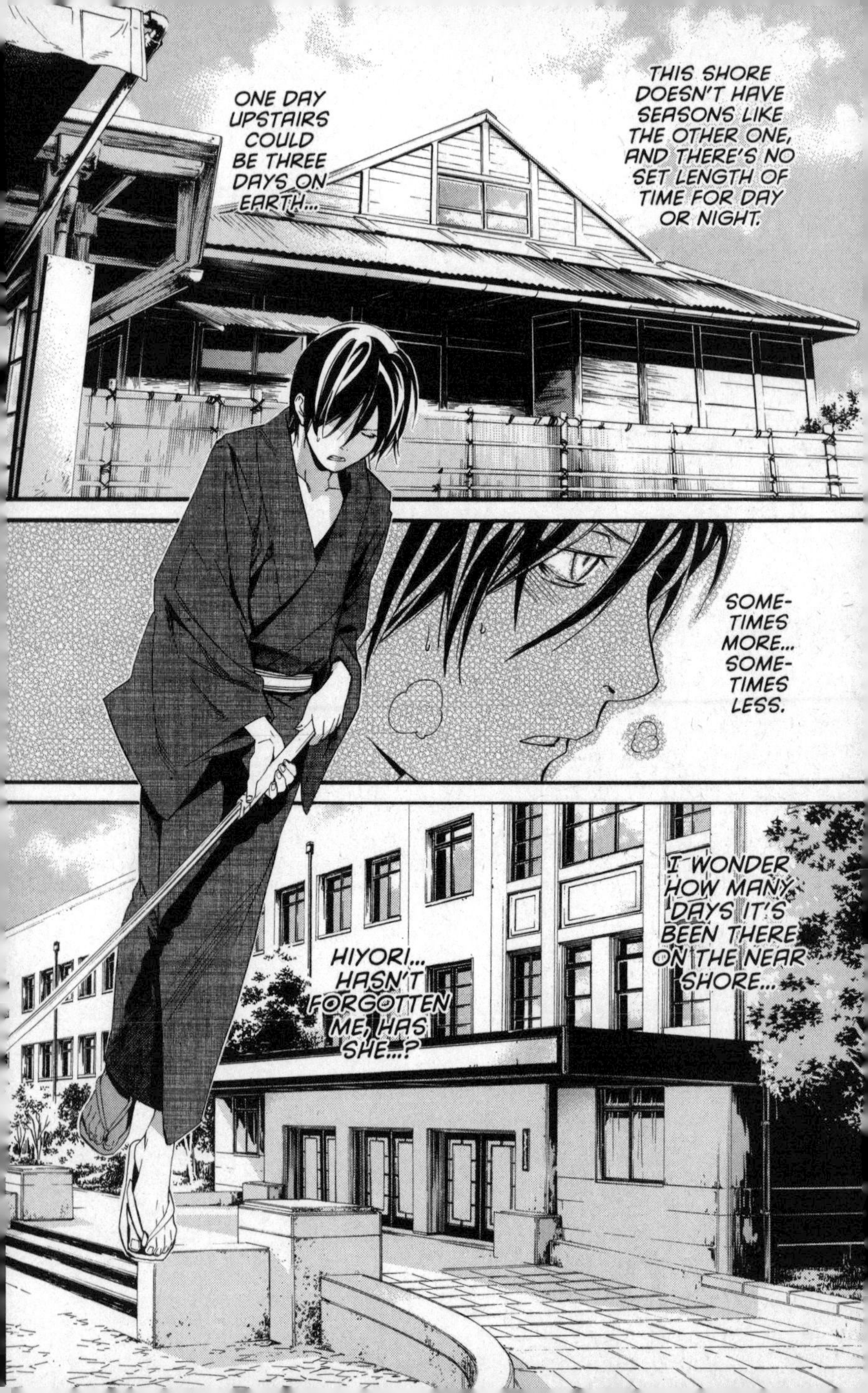
THIS SHORE DOESN'T HAVE SEASONS LIKE THE OTHER ONE, AND THERE'S NO SET LENGTH OF TIME FOR DAY OR NIGHT.
ONE DAY UPSTAIRS COULD BE THREE DAYS ON EARTH...
SOME-TIMES MORE... SOME-TIMES LESS.
I WONDER HOW MANY DAYS IT'S BEEN THERE ON THE NEAR SHORE...
HIYORI... HASN'T FORGOTTEN ME, HAS SHE...?

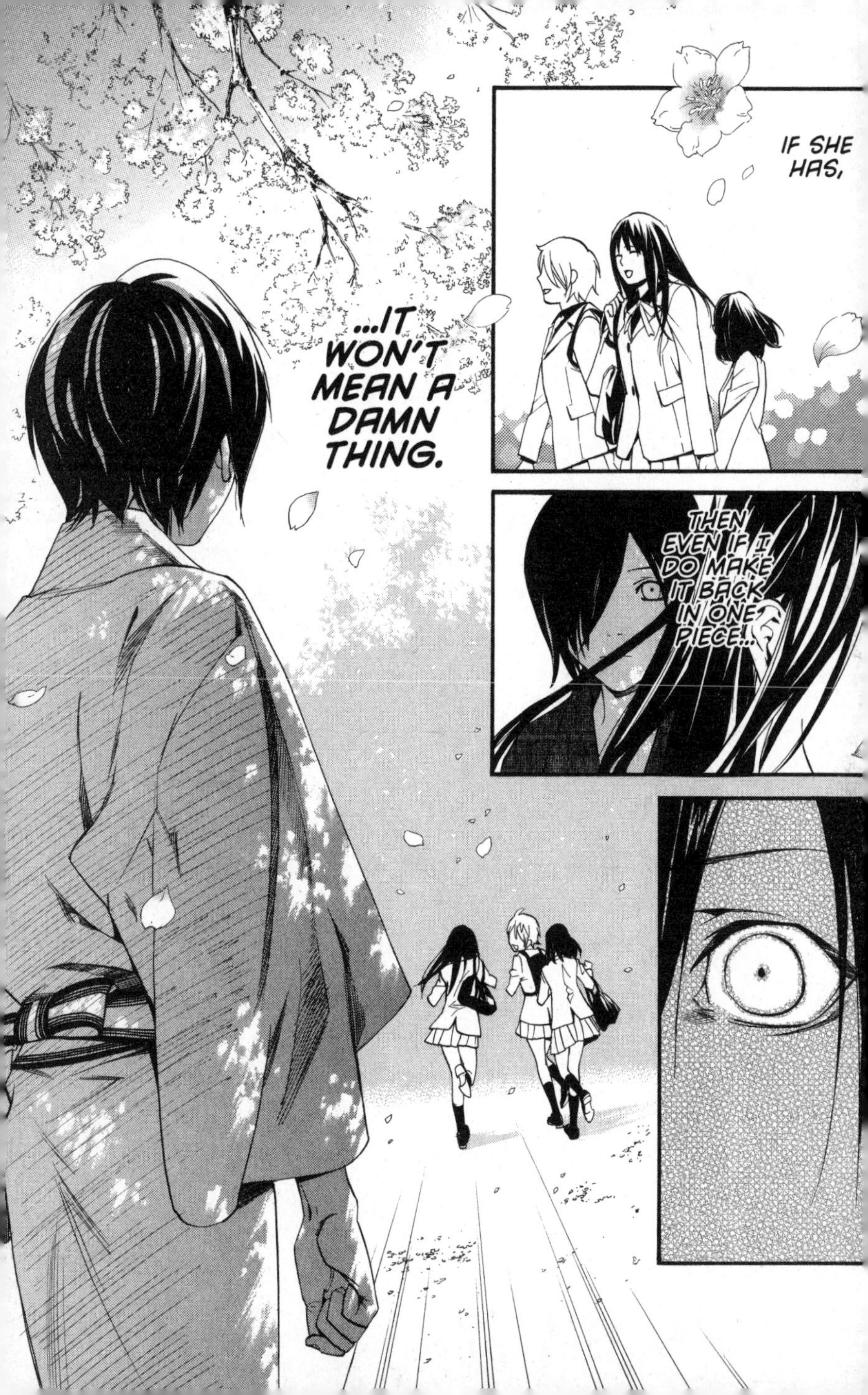
IF SHE HAS,
THEN EVEN IF I DO MAKE IT BACK IN ONE PIECE...
...IT WON'T MEAN A DAMN THING.

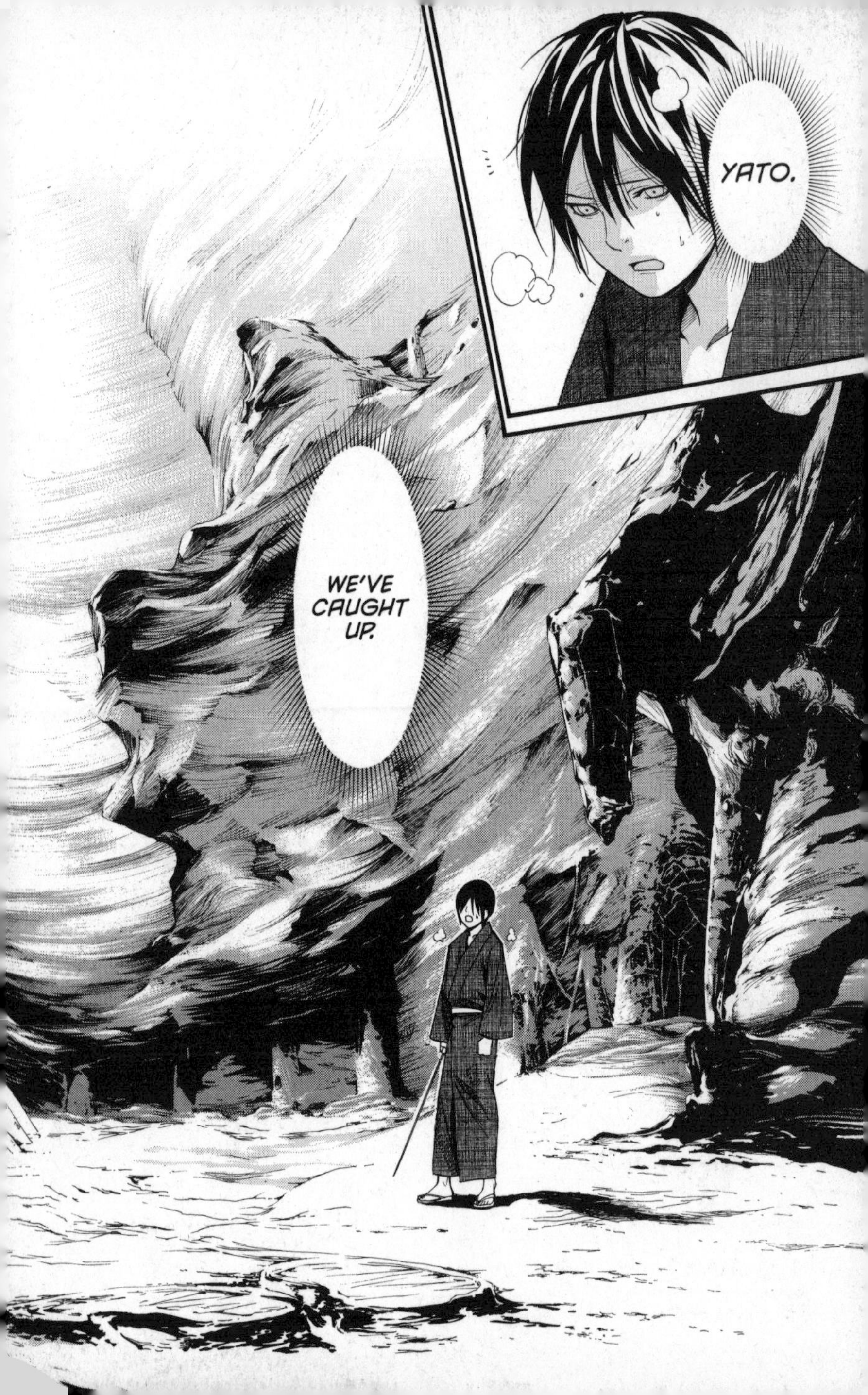
YATO.
WE'VE CAUGHT UP.

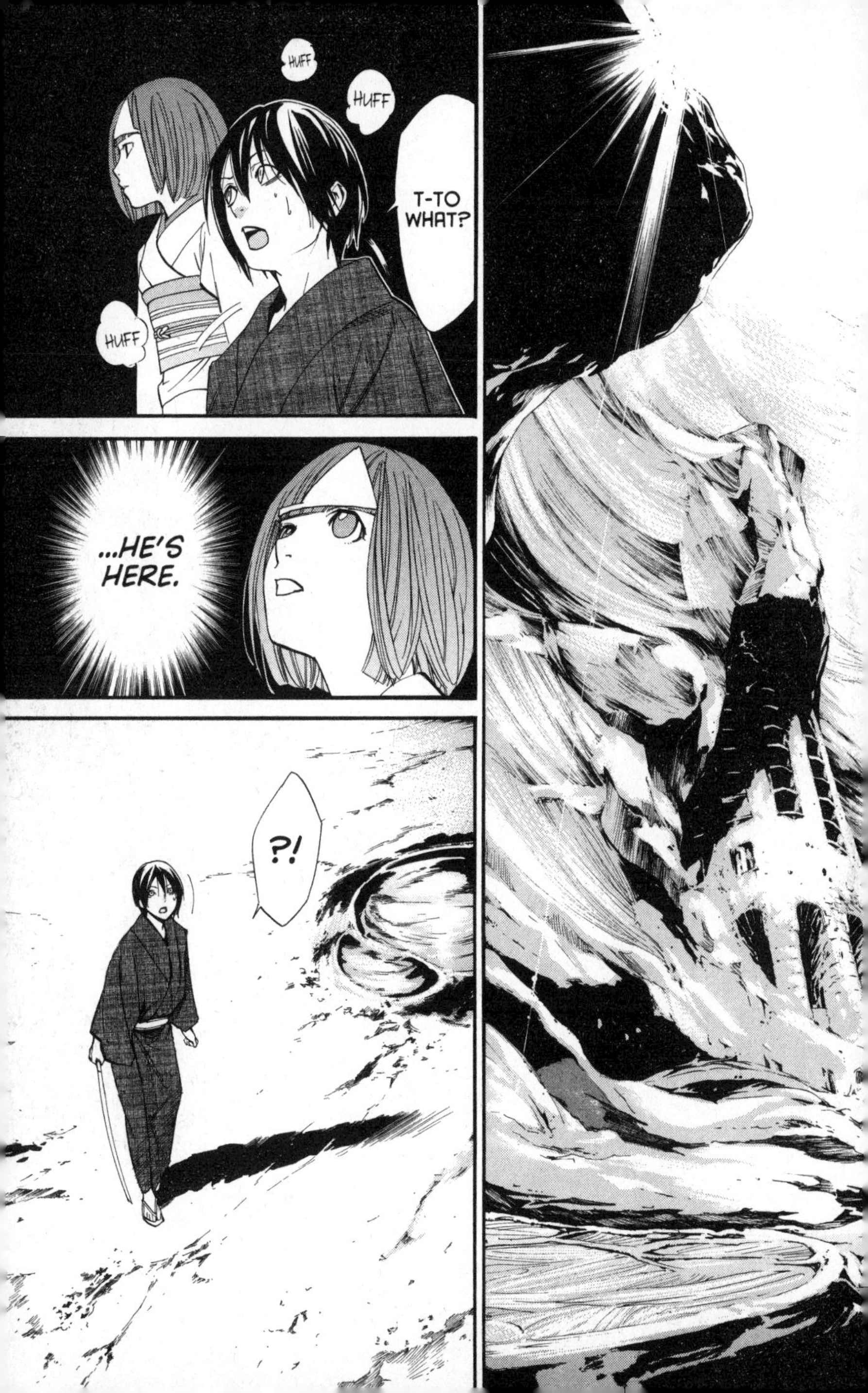
HUFF
HUFF
T-TO WHAT?
HUFF
...HE'S HERE.
?!

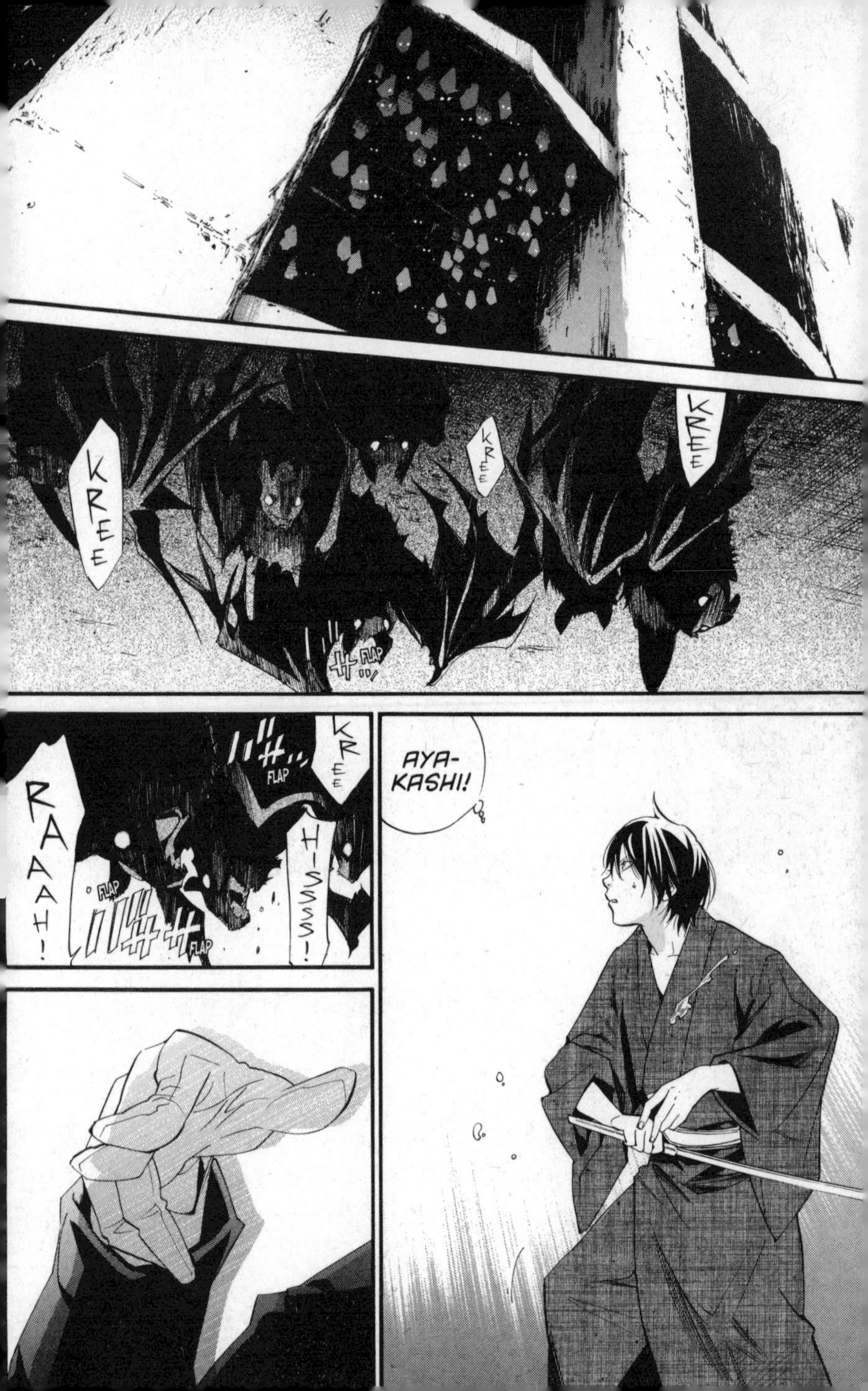
KREE
KREE
KREE
FLAP
AYA-KASHI!
KREE
FLAP
HISSSS!
RAAAH!
FLAP
FLAP

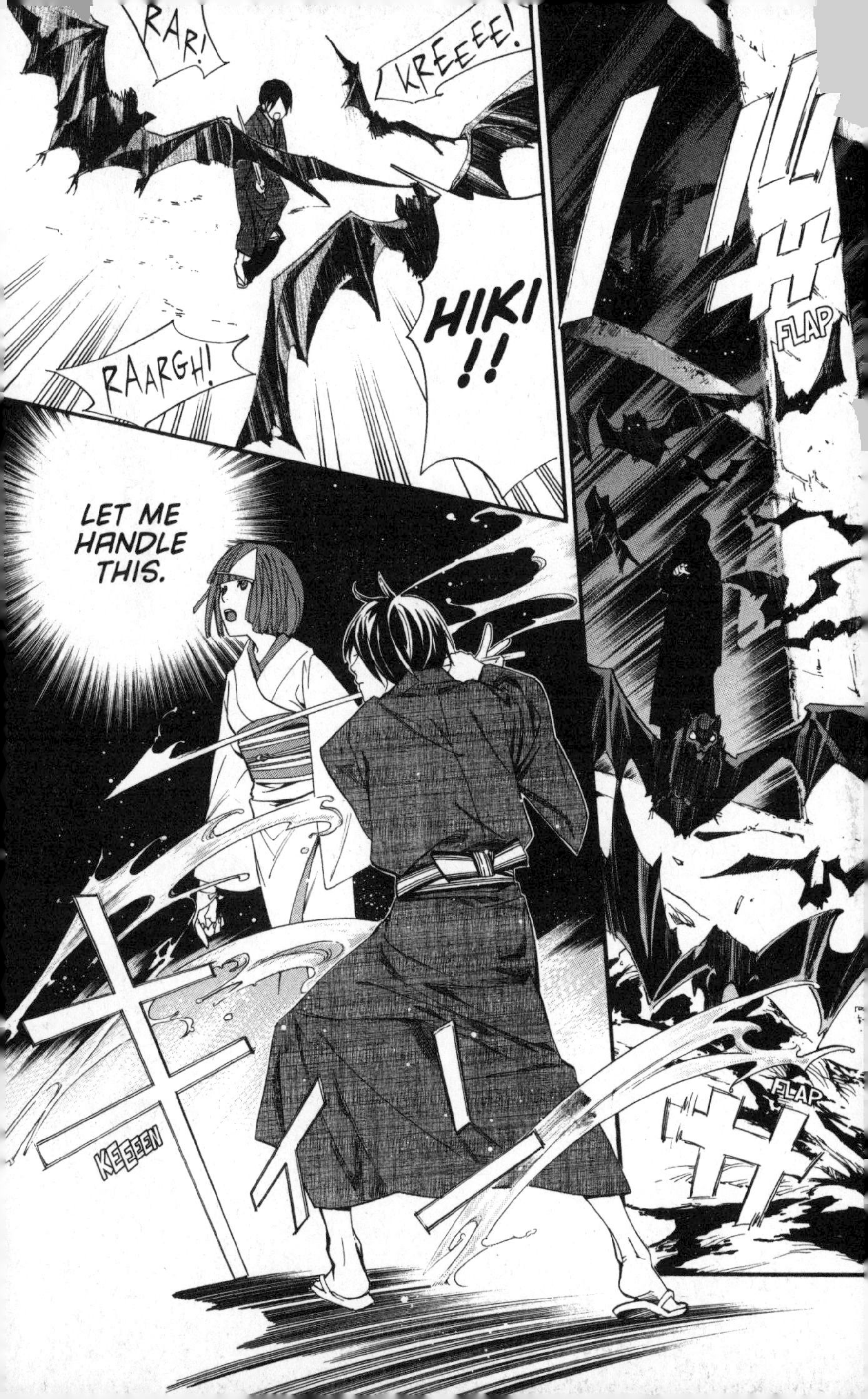
FLAP
FLAP
KREEEE!
RAR!
HIKI !!
RAARGH!
LET ME HANDLE THIS.
KEEEEN

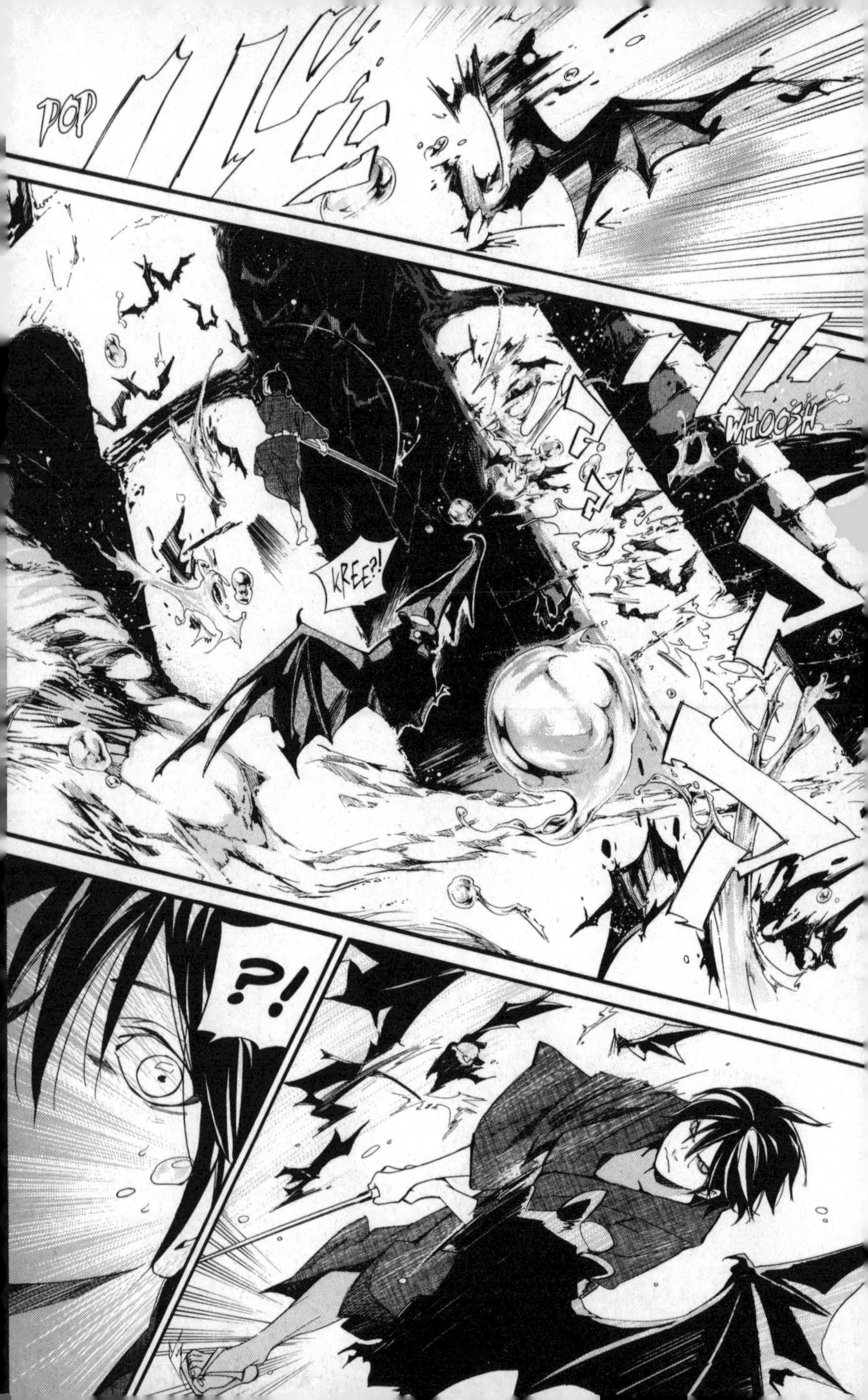
POP
WHOOSH
KREE?!
?!

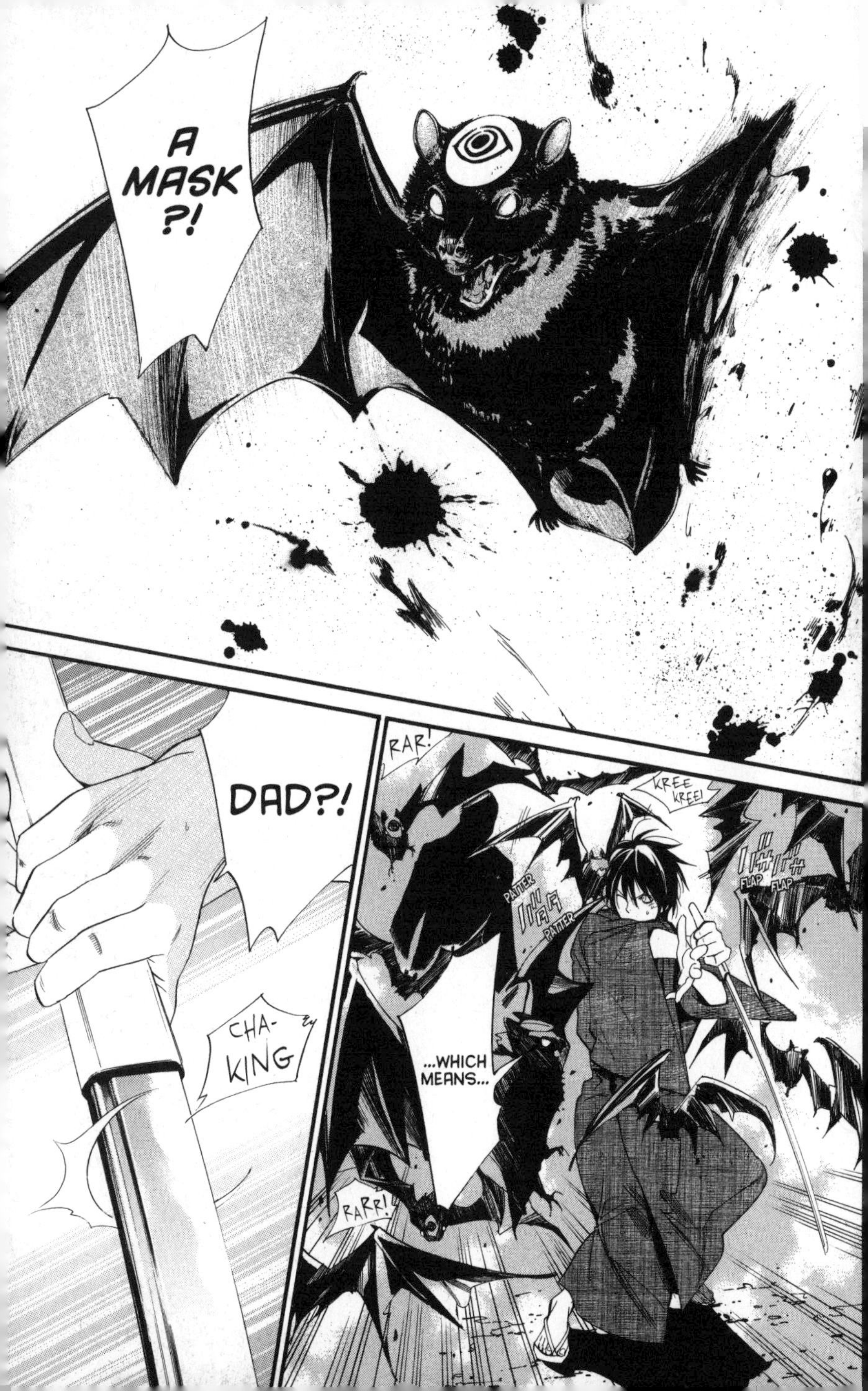
A MASK?!
KREE KREE!
FLAP FLAP
RAR!
PATTER PATTER
...WHICH MEANS...
RARR!
DAD?!
CHA-KING

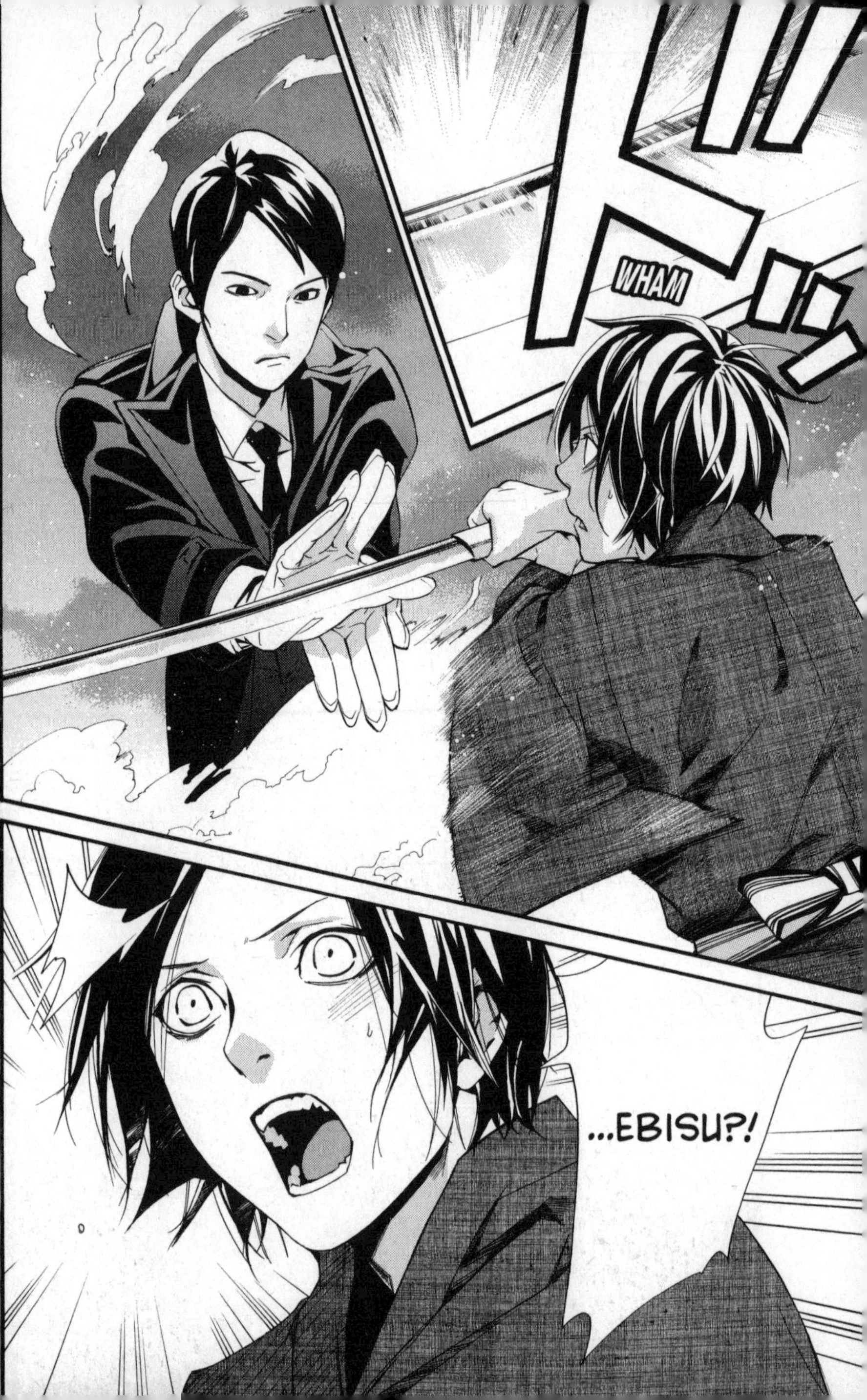
WHAM
...EBISU?!

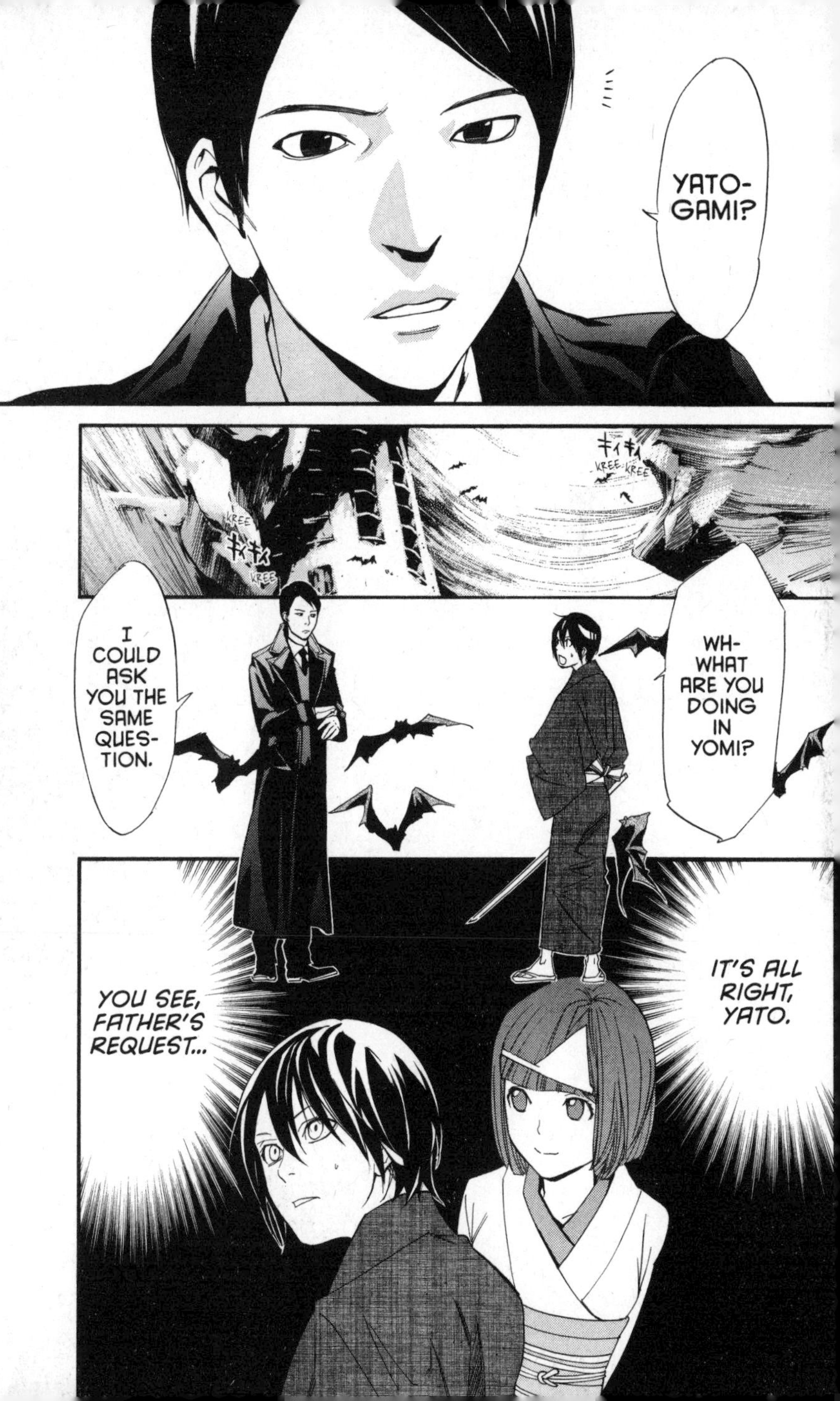
YATO-GAMI?
キィキィ
KREE KREE
キィキィ
KREE KREE
WH-WHAT ARE YOU DOING IN YOMI?
I COULD ASK YOU THE SAME QUES-TION.
IT'S ALL RIGHT, YATO.
YOU SEE, FATHER'S REQUEST...

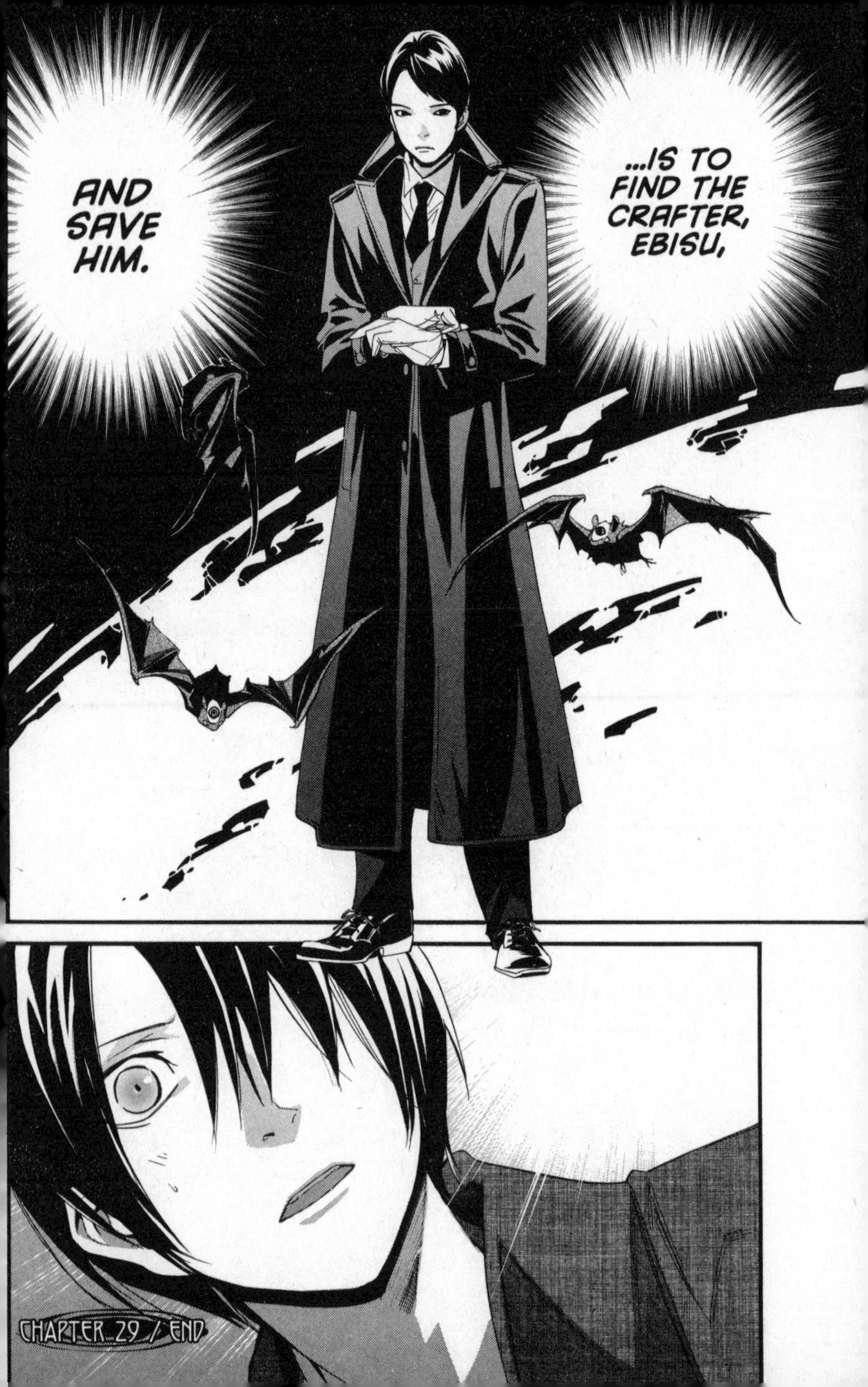
...IS TO FIND THE CRAFTER, EBISU,
AND SAVE HIM.
CHAPTER 29 / END

野

皀

神

YATO-
GAMI?

...EBISU?!

IT'S ALL
RIGHT,
YATO.
YOU SEE,
FATHER'S
REQUEST...

I
COULD
ASK
YOU
THE
SAME
QUES-
TION.

WH-WHAT
ARE YOU
DOING IN
YOMI?

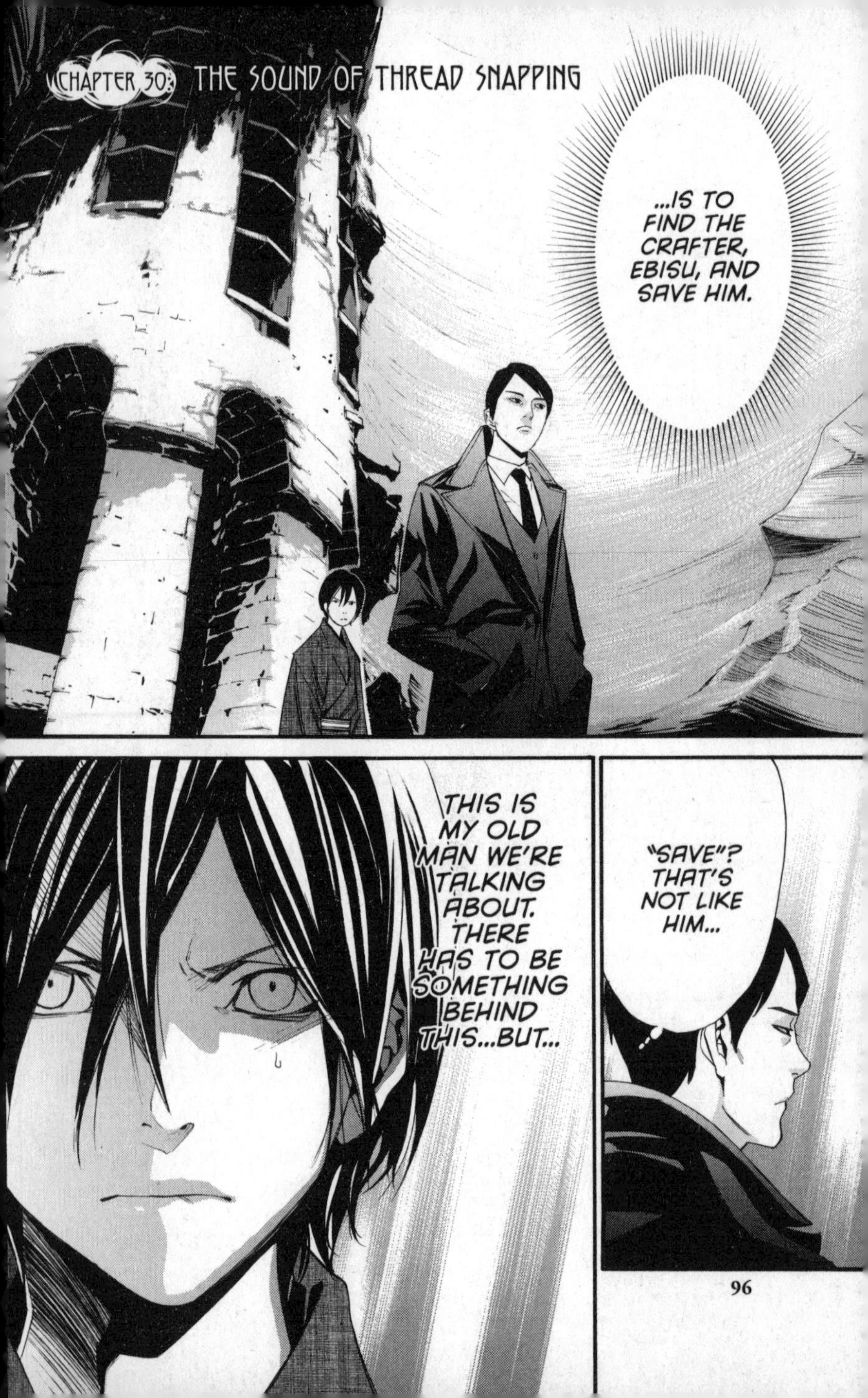
CHAPTER 30: THE SOUND OF THREAD SNAPPING
...IS TO FIND THE CRAFTER, EBISU, AND SAVE HIM.
"SAVE"? THAT'S NOT LIKE HIM...
THIS IS MY OLD MAN WE'RE TALKING ABOUT. THERE HAS TO BE SOMETHING BEHIND THIS...BUT...

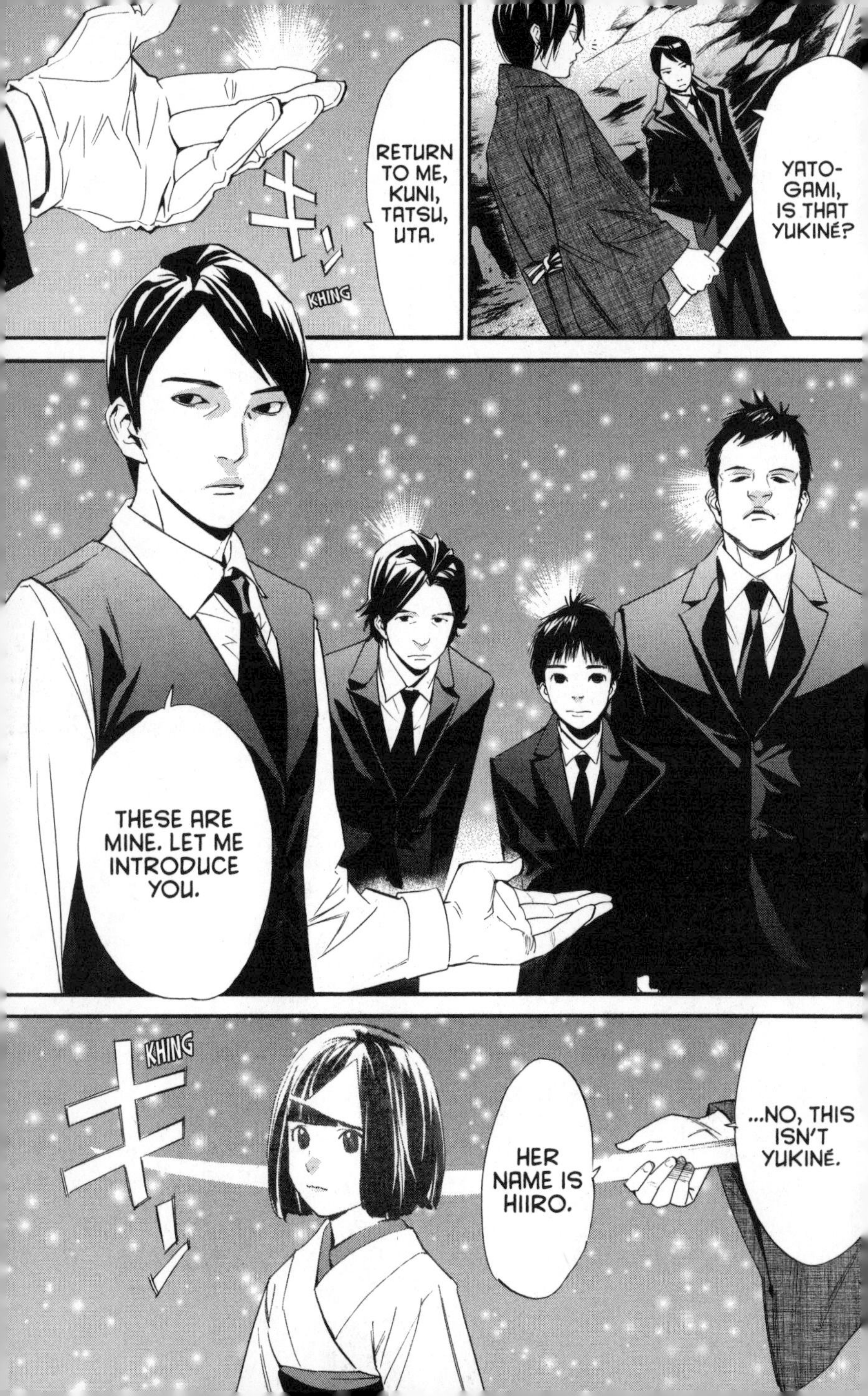

YATO-GAMI, IS THAT YUKINÉ?
RETURN TO ME, KUNI, TATSU, UTA.
キン
KHING
THESE ARE MINE. LET ME INTRODUCE YOU.
...NO, THIS ISN'T YUKINÉ.
HER NAME IS HIIRO.
キーン
KHING

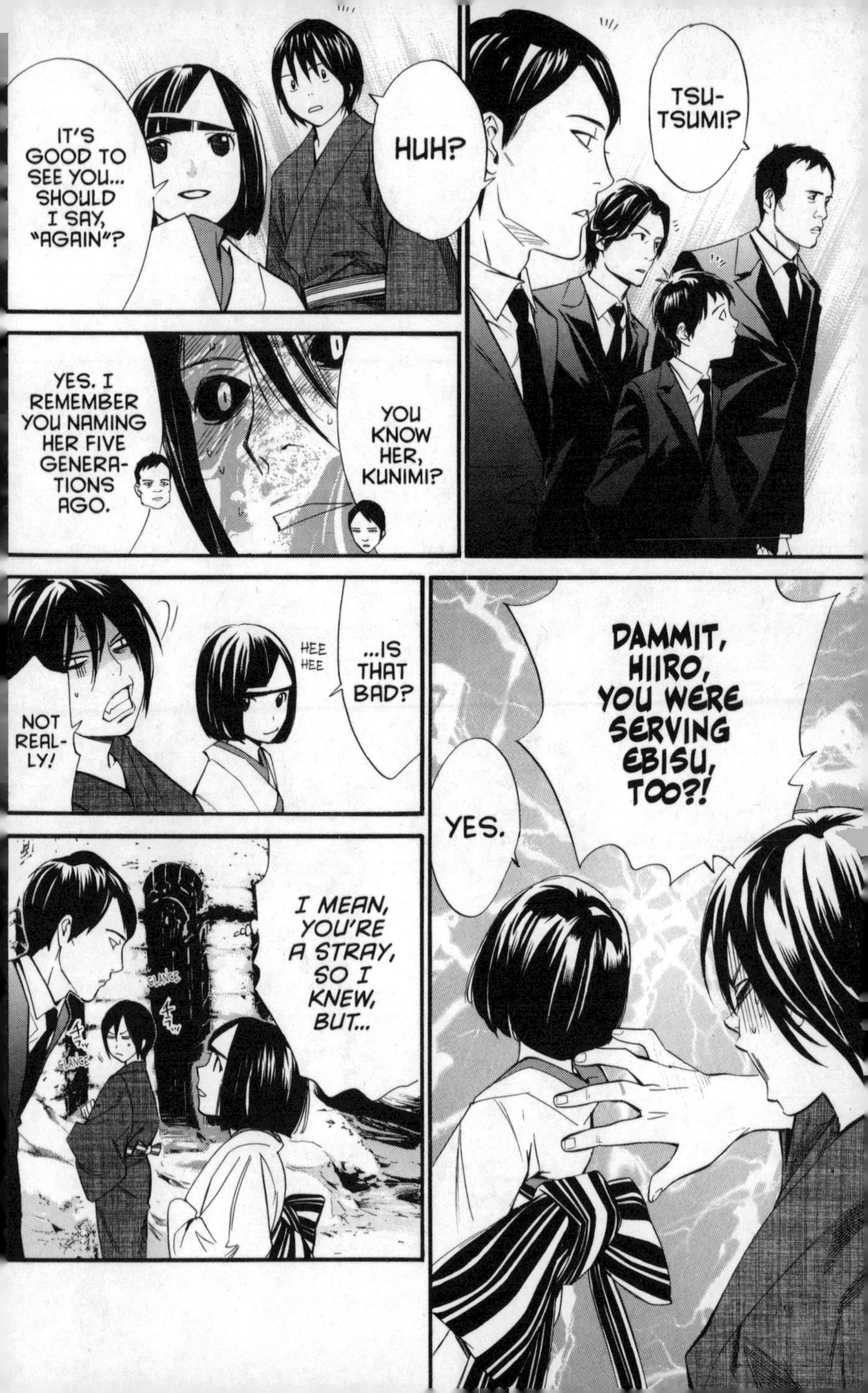
TSU-TSUMI?
HUH?
IT'S GOOD TO SEE YOU... SHOULD I SAY, "AGAIN"?
YOU KNOW HER, KUNIMI?
YES. I REMEMBER YOU NAMING HER FIVE GENERATIONS AGO.
DAMMIT, HIIRO, YOU WERE SERVING EBISU, TOO?!
YES.
...IS THAT BAD?
HEE HEE
NOT REALLY!
I MEAN, YOU'RE A STRAY, SO I KNEW, BUT...
GLANCE
GLANCE

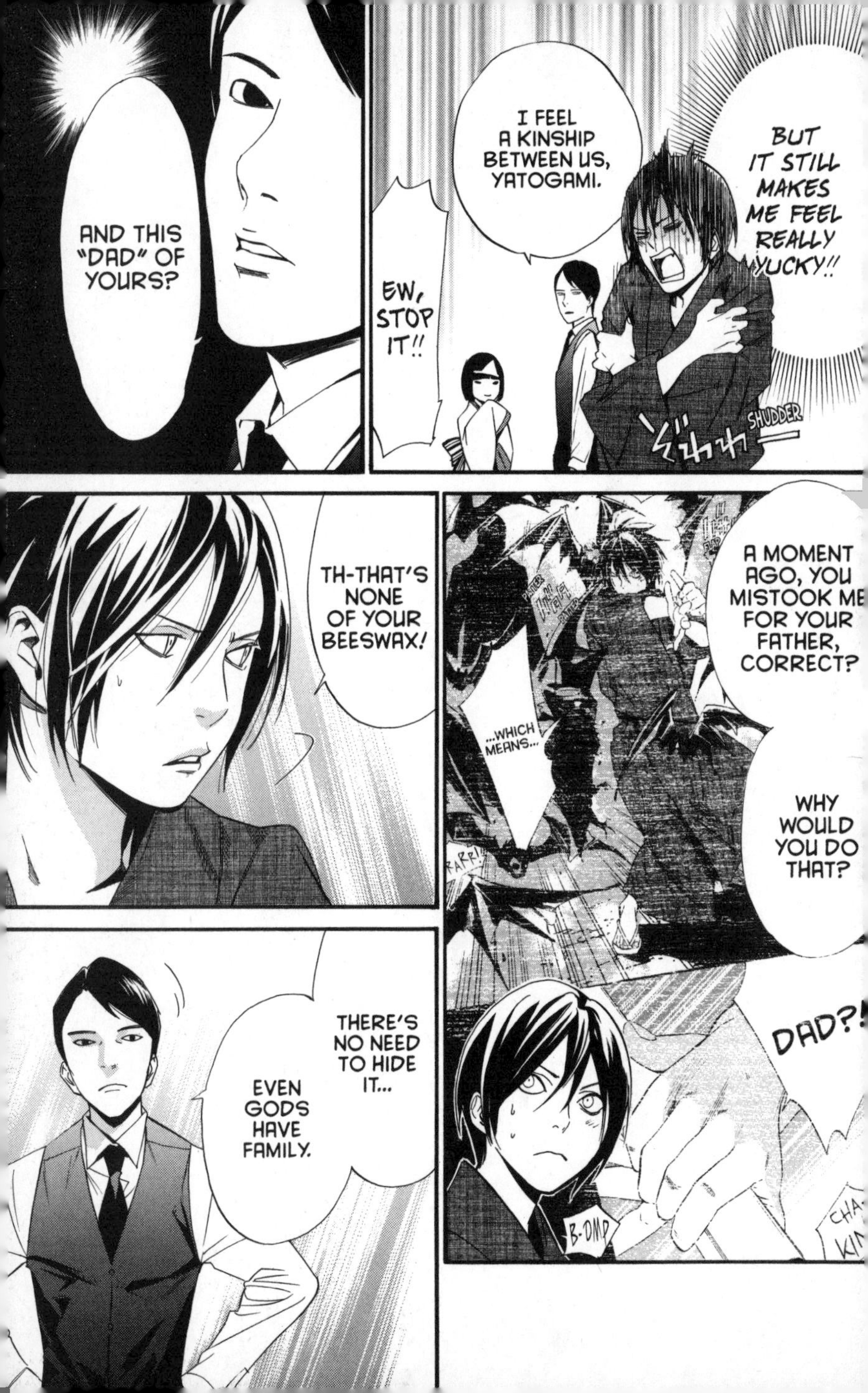
I FEEL A KINSHIP BETWEEN US, YATOGAMI.
EW, STOP IT!!
BUT IT STILL MAKES ME FEEL REALLY YUCKY!!
SHUDDER
AND THIS "DAD" OF YOURS?
A MOMENT AGO, YOU MISTOOK ME FOR YOUR FATHER, CORRECT?
...WHICH MEANS...
WHY WOULD YOU DO THAT?
DAD?!
B-DMP
TH-THAT'S NONE OF YOUR BEESWAX!
THERE'S NO NEED TO HIDE IT...
EVEN GODS HAVE FAMILY.

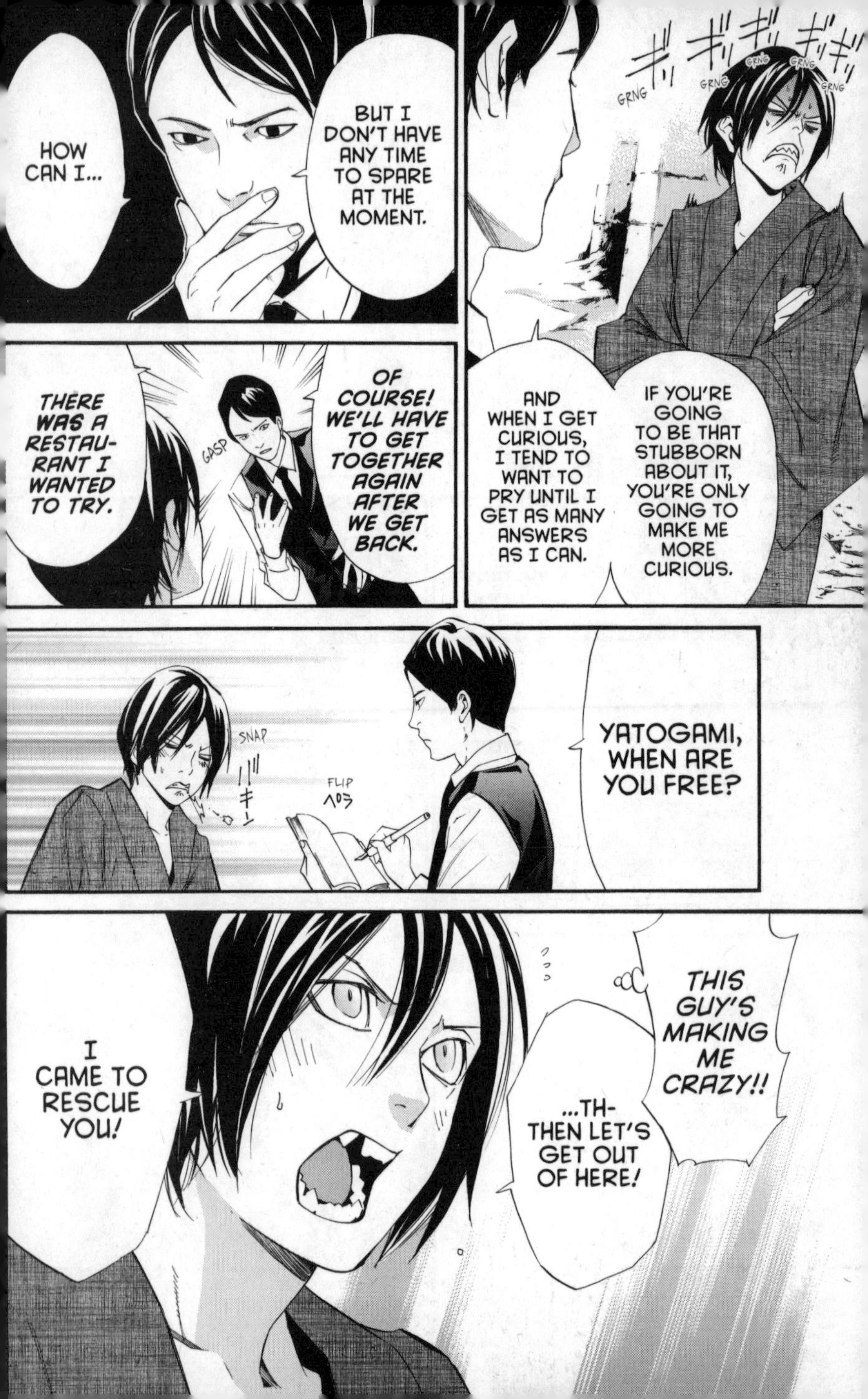
GRNG GRNG GRNG GRNG GRNG
IF YOU'RE GOING TO BE THAT STUBBORN ABOUT IT, YOU'RE ONLY GOING TO MAKE ME MORE CURIOUS.
AND WHEN I GET CURIOUS, I TEND TO WANT TO PRY UNTIL I GET AS MANY ANSWERS AS I CAN.
BUT I DON'T HAVE ANY TIME TO SPARE AT THE MOMENT.
HOW CAN I...
OF COURSE! WE'LL HAVE TO GET TOGETHER AGAIN AFTER WE GET BACK.
GASP
THERE WAS A RESTAU-RANT I WANTED TO TRY.
YATOGAMI, WHEN ARE YOU FREE?
FLIP
SNAP
THIS GUY'S MAKING ME CRAZY!!
...TH-THEN LET'S GET OUT OF HERE!
I CAME TO RESCUE YOU!

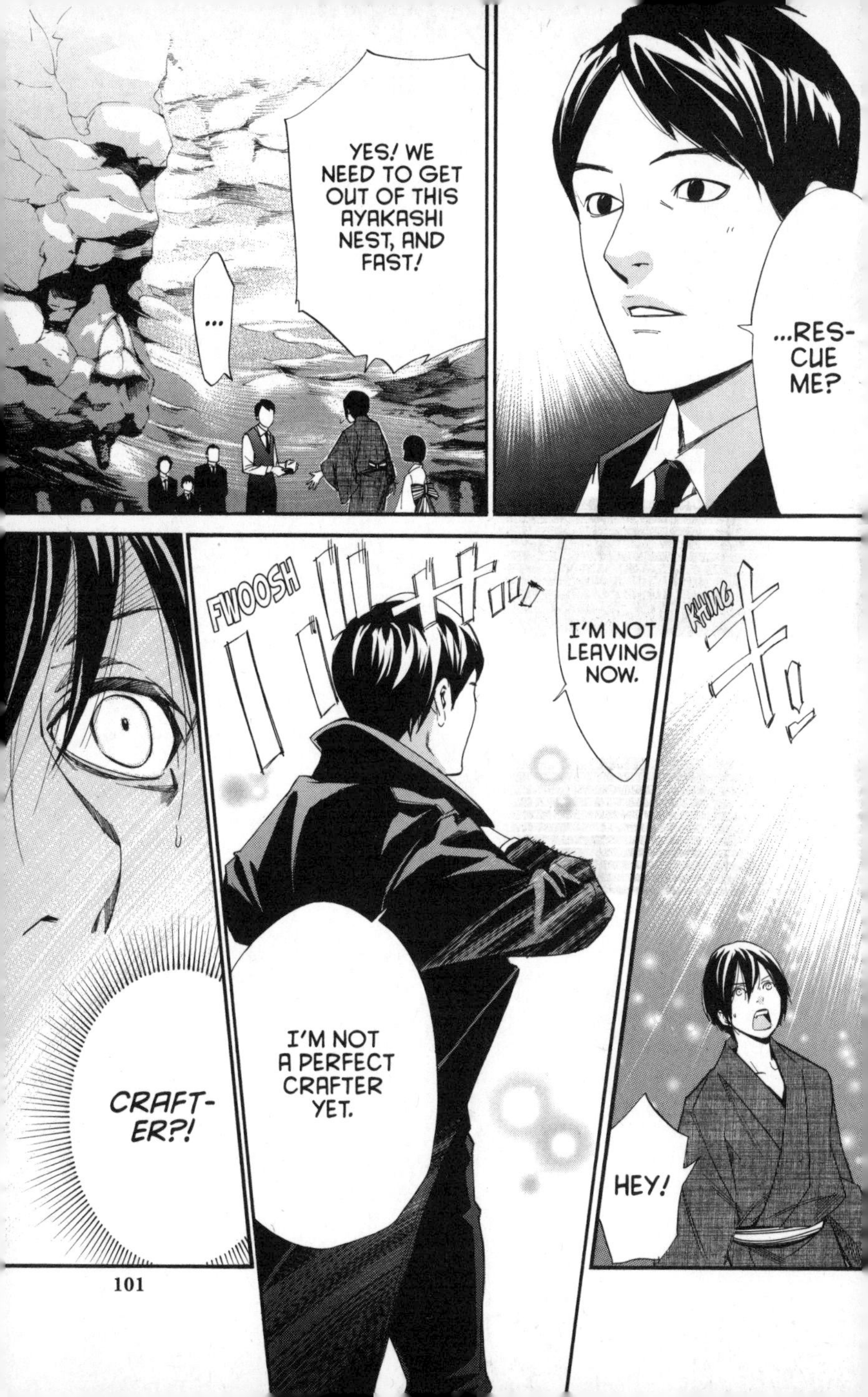
...RES-
CUE
ME?
YES! WE NEED TO GET OUT OF THIS AYAKASHI NEST, AND FAST!
...
KHING
HEY!
I'M NOT LEAVING NOW.
FWOOSH
I'M NOT A PERFECT CRAFTER YET.
CRAFT-
ER?!

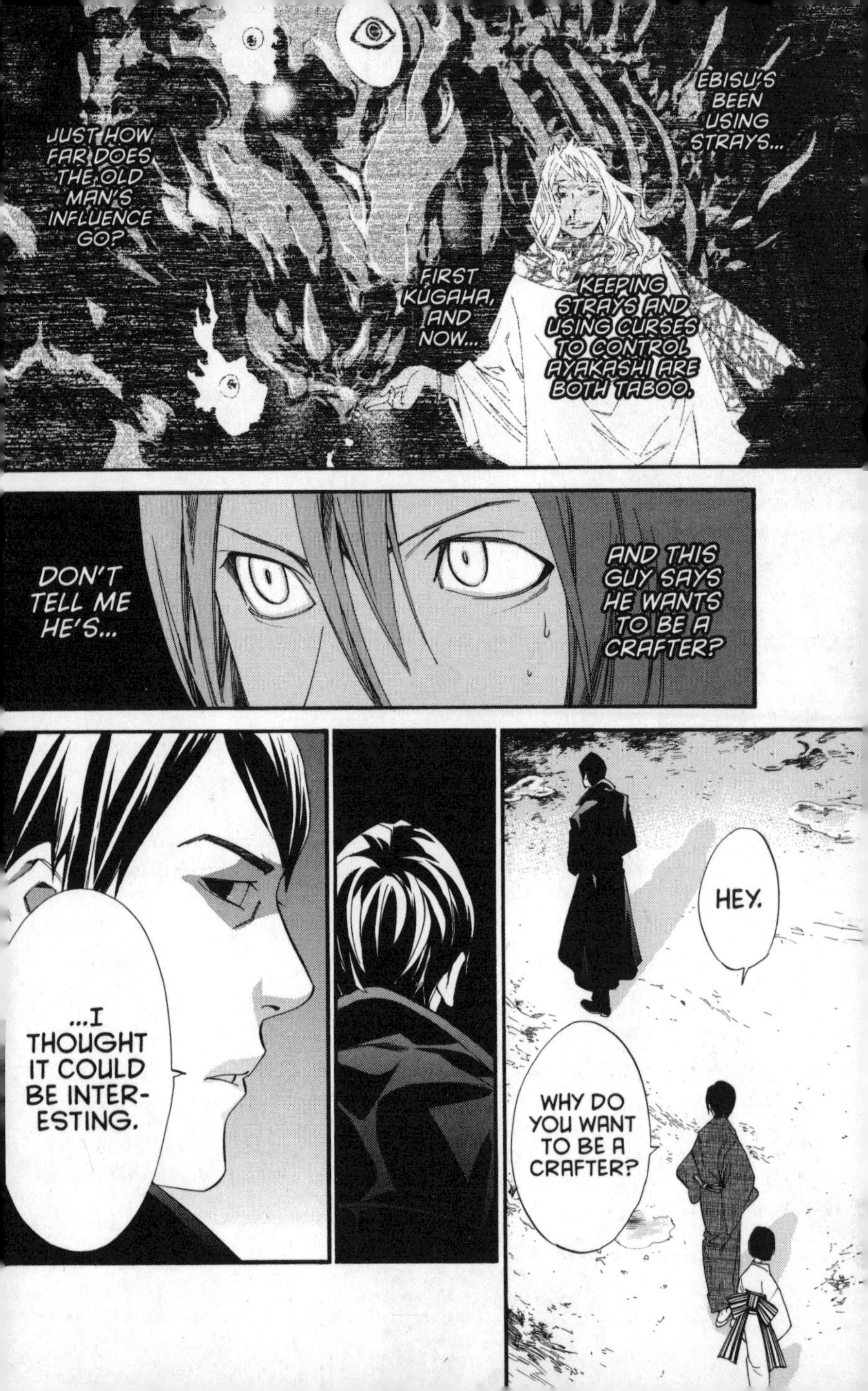
EBISU'S BEEN USING STRAYS...
KEEPING STRAYS AND USING CURSES TO CONTROL AYAKASHI ARE BOTH TABOO.
FIRST KŪGAHA, AND NOW...
JUST HOW FAR DOES THE OLD MAN'S INFLUENCE GO?
AND THIS GUY SAYS HE WANTS TO BE A CRAFTER?
DON'T TELL ME HE'S...
HEY.
WHY DO YOU WANT TO BE A CRAFTER?
...I THOUGHT IT COULD BE INTER-ESTING.

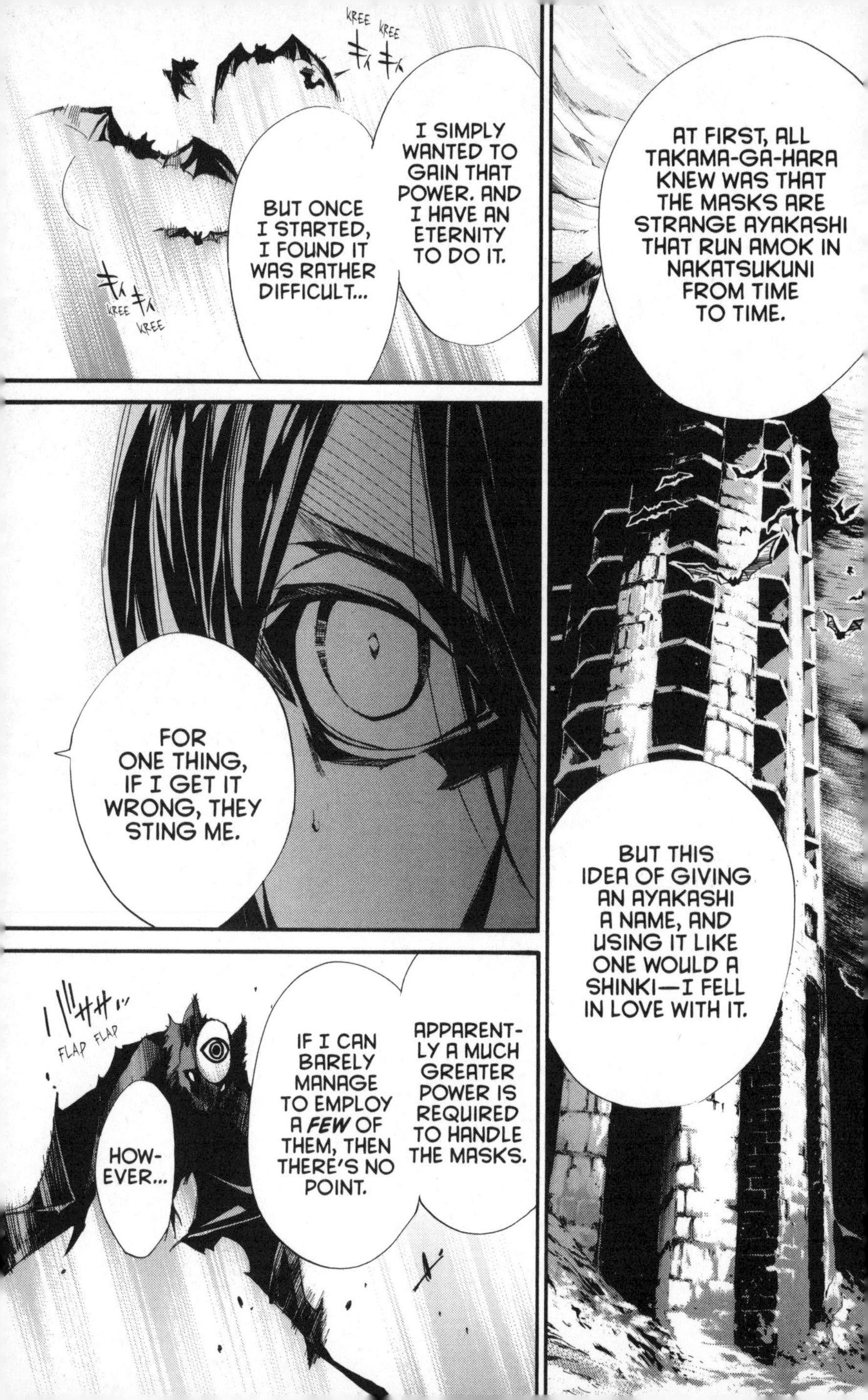
AT FIRST, ALL TAKAMA-GA-HARA KNEW WAS THAT THE MASKS ARE STRANGE AYAKASHI THAT RUN AMOK IN NAKATSUKUNI FROM TIME TO TIME.
BUT THIS IDEA OF GIVING AN AYAKASHI A NAME, AND USING IT LIKE ONE WOULD A SHINKI—I FELL IN LOVE WITH IT.
KREE KREE
I SIMPLY WANTED TO GAIN THAT POWER. AND I HAVE AN ETERNITY TO DO IT.
BUT ONCE I STARTED, I FOUND IT WAS RATHER DIFFICULT...
KREE KREE KREE
FOR ONE THING, IF I GET IT WRONG, THEY STING ME.
APPARENTLY A MUCH GREATER POWER IS REQUIRED TO HANDLE THE MASKS.
IF I CAN BARELY MANAGE TO EMPLOY A *FEW* OF THEM, THEN THERE'S NO POINT.
FLAP FLAP
HOW-EVER...

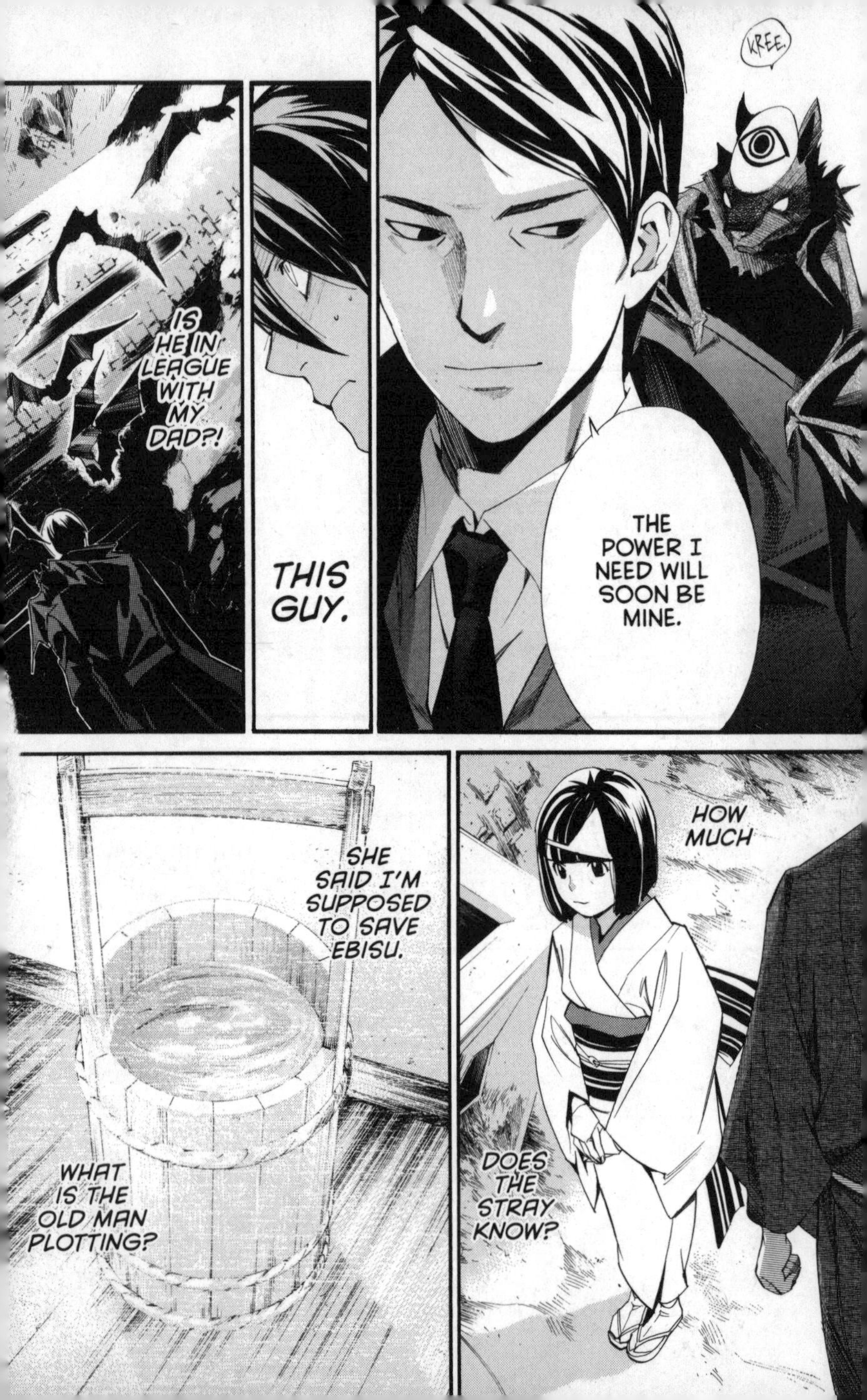
KREE.
THE POWER I NEED WILL SOON BE MINE.
THIS GUY.
IS HE IN LEAGUE WITH MY DAD?!
HOW MUCH
DOES THE STRAY KNOW?
SHE SAID I'M SUPPOSED TO SAVE EBISU.
WHAT IS THE OLD MAN PLOTTING?

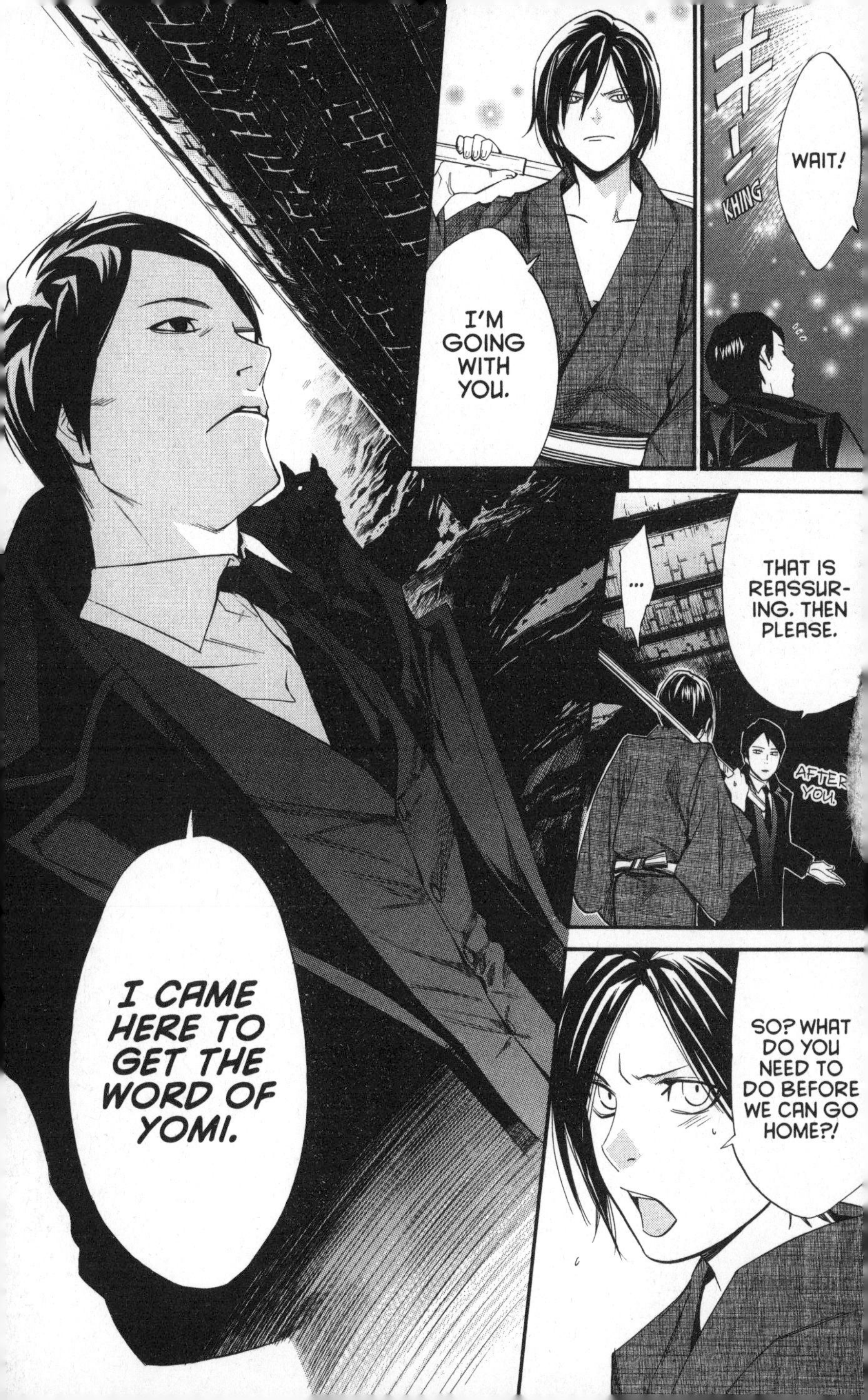
WAIT!
KHING
I'M GOING WITH YOU.
THAT IS REASSURING. THEN PLEASE.
...
AFTER YOU.
SO? WHAT DO YOU NEED TO DO BEFORE WE CAN GO HOME?!
I CAME HERE TO GET THE WORD OF YOMI.

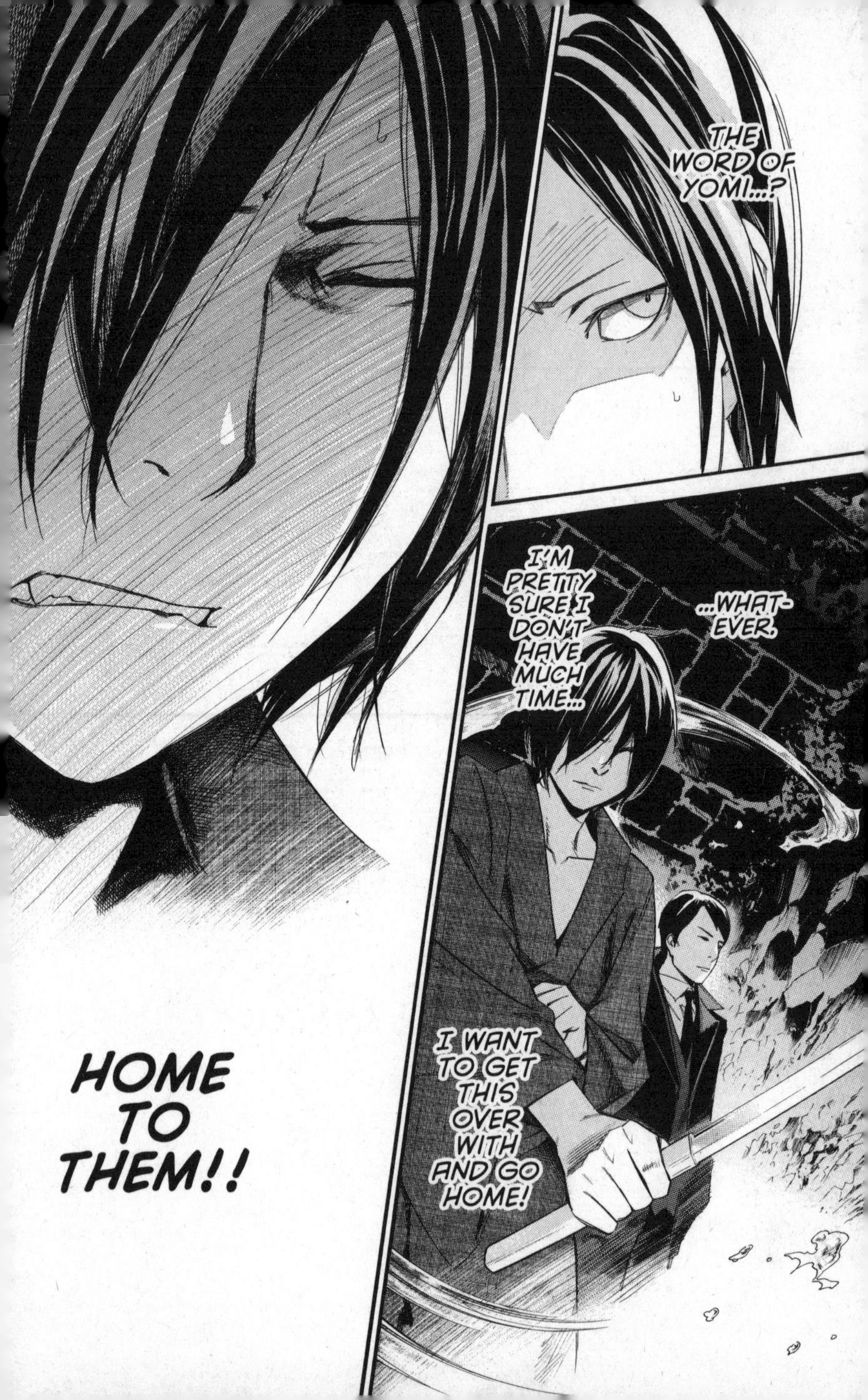
THE WORD OF YOMI...?
...WHAT-EVER.
I'M PRETTY SURE I DON'T HAVE MUCH TIME...
I WANT TO GET THIS OVER WITH AND GO HOME!
HOME TO THEM!!

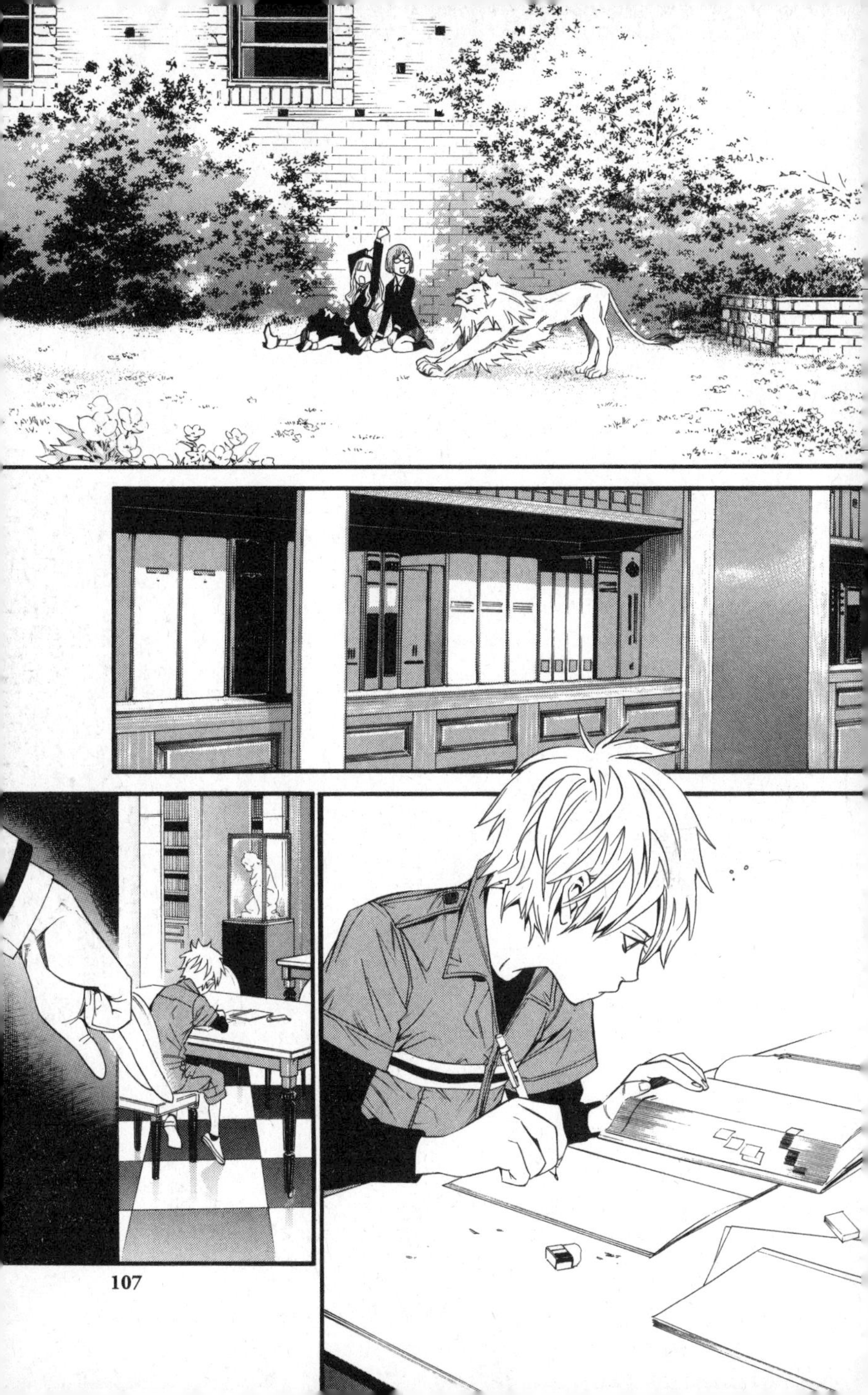

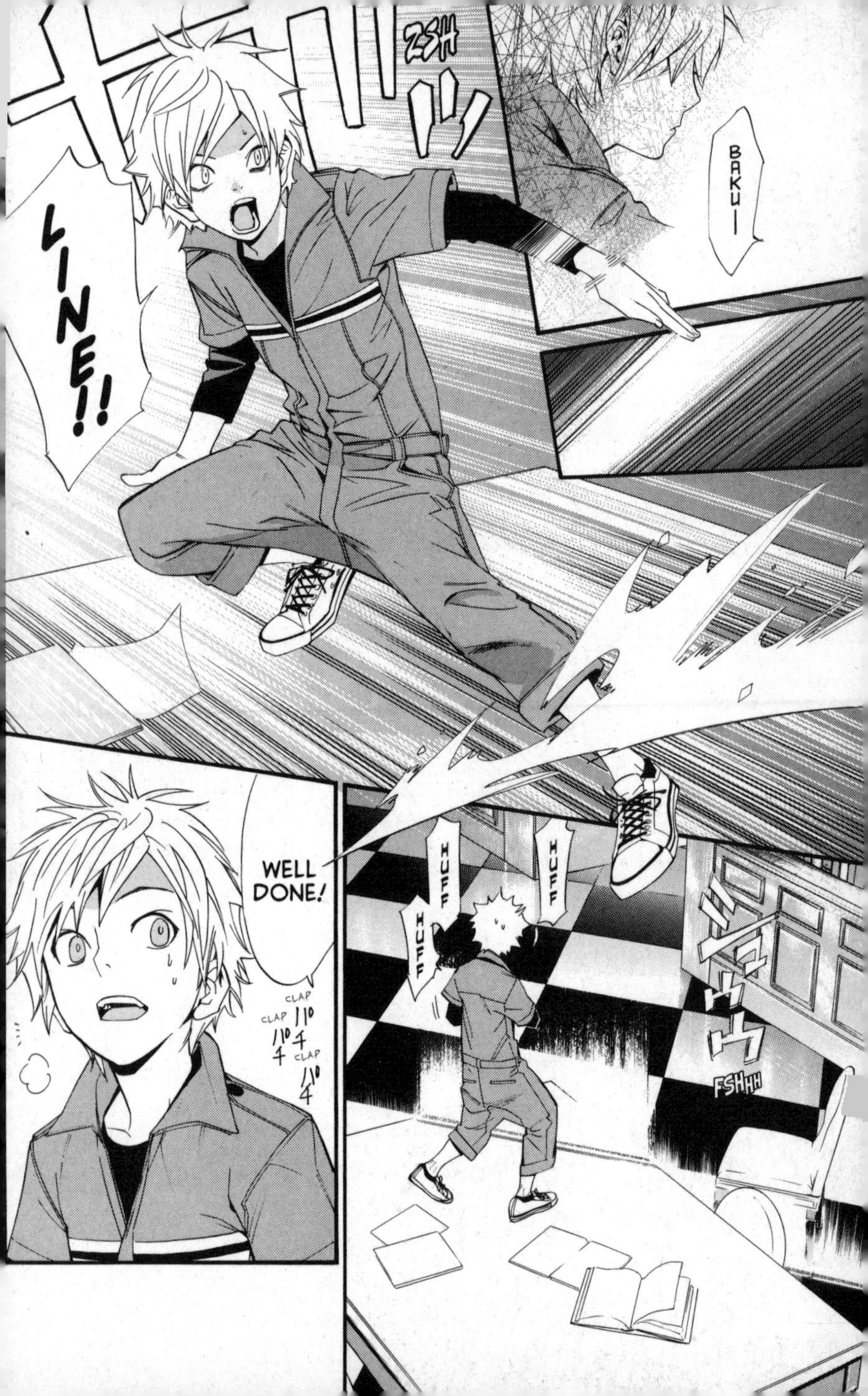
BAKU-!
ZSH
LINE!!
HUFF
HUFF
HUFF
FSHHH
WELL DONE!
CLAP
CLAP
CLAP

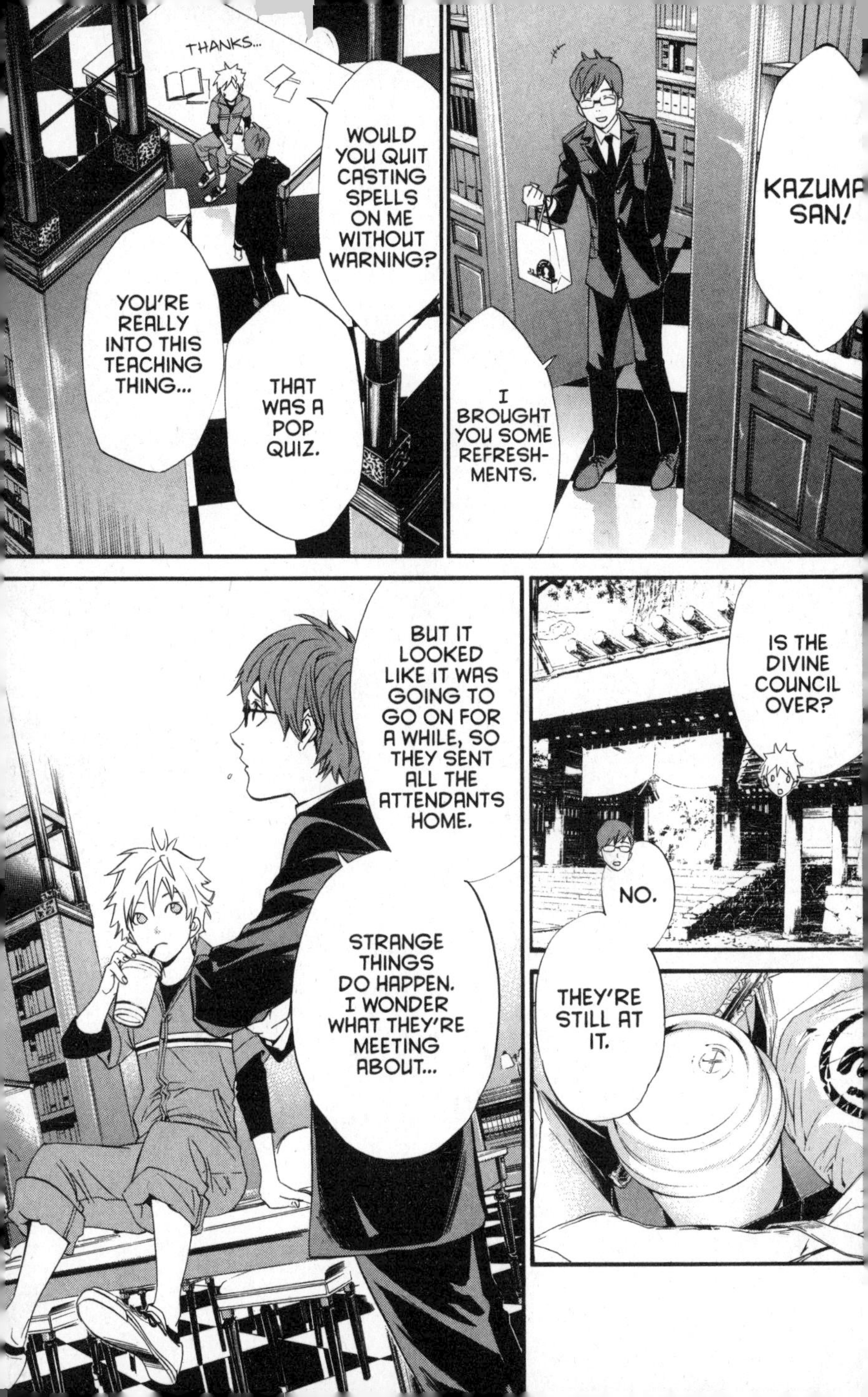
KAZUMA SAN!
I BROUGHT YOU SOME REFRESH-MENTS.
WOULD YOU QUIT CASTING SPELLS ON ME WITHOUT WARNING?
THAT WAS A POP QUIZ.
YOU'RE REALLY INTO THIS TEACHING THING...
THANKS...
IS THE DIVINE COUNCIL OVER?
NO.
THEY'RE STILL AT IT.
BUT IT LOOKED LIKE IT WAS GOING TO GO ON FOR A WHILE, SO THEY SENT ALL THE ATTENDANTS HOME.
STRANGE THINGS DO HAPPEN. I WONDER WHAT THEY'RE MEETING ABOUT...

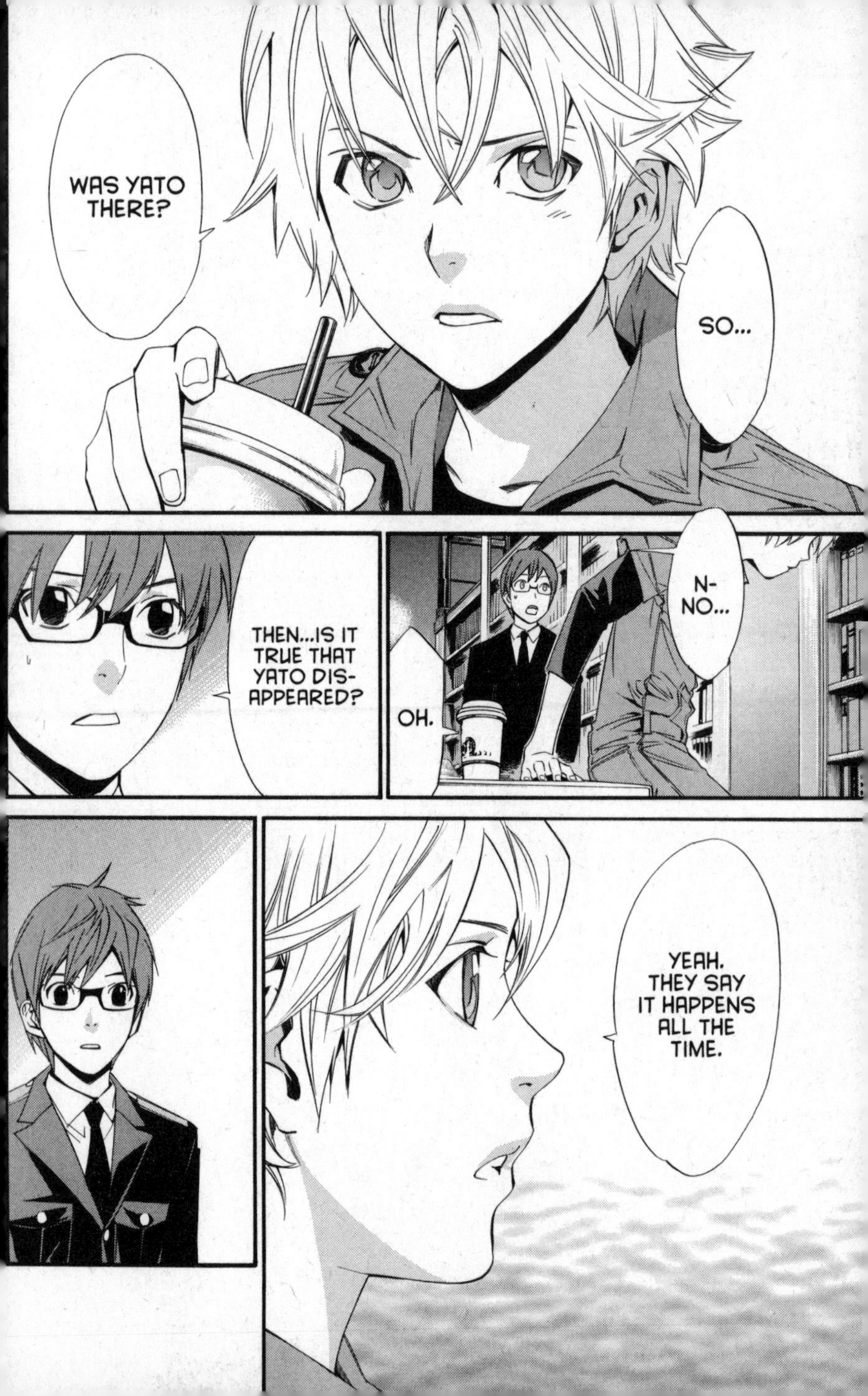
SO...
WAS YATO THERE?
N-NO...
OH.
THEN...IS IT TRUE THAT YATO DIS-APPEARED?
YEAH. THEY SAY IT HAPPENS ALL THE TIME.

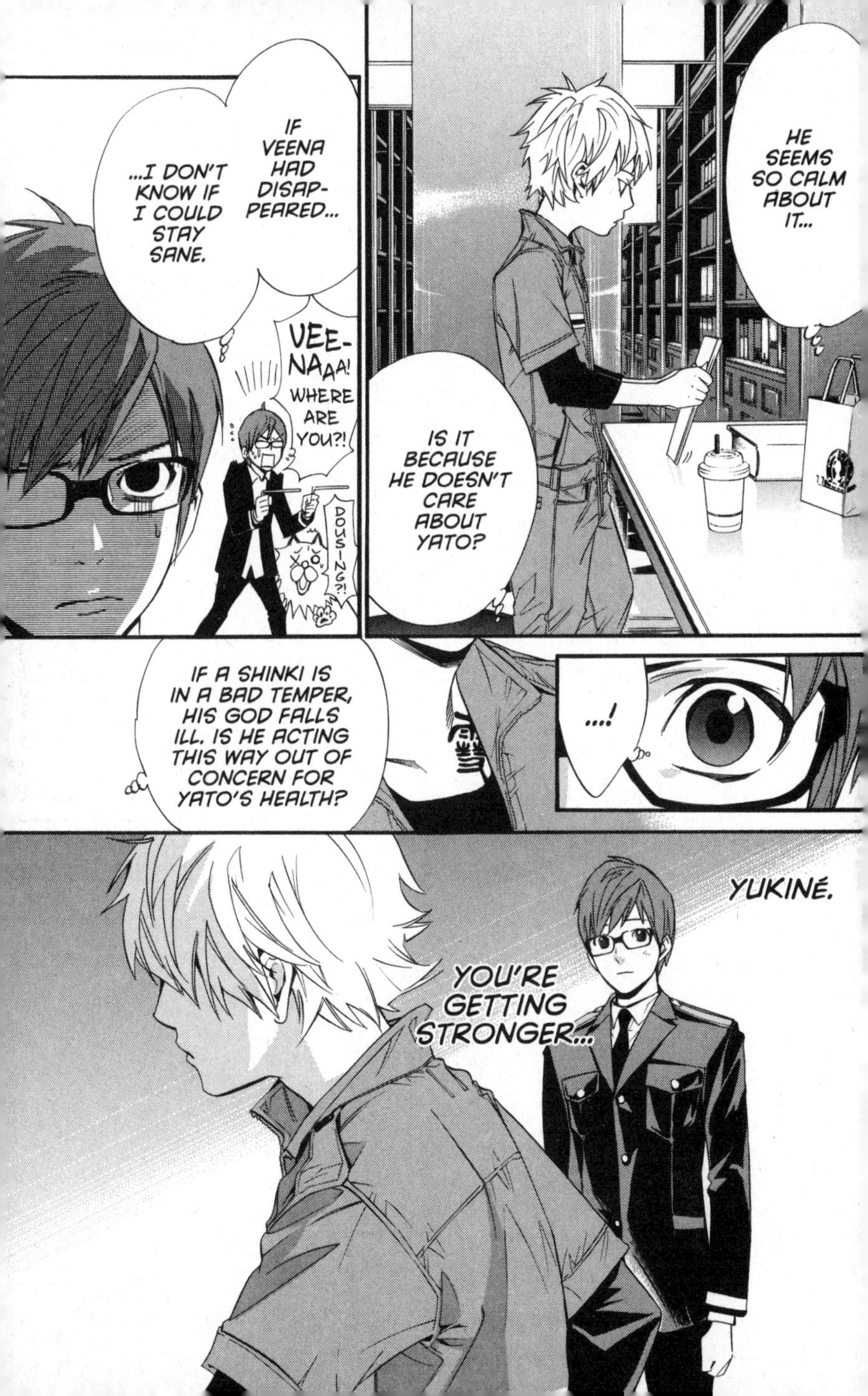
HE SEEMS SO CALM ABOUT IT...
IS IT BECAUSE HE DOESN'T CARE ABOUT YATO?
IF VEENA HAD DISAPPEARED...
...I DON'T KNOW IF I COULD STAY SANE.
VEE-NAAA! WHERE ARE YOU?!
DOUSING?!
...!
IF A SHINKI IS IN A BAD TEMPER, HIS GOD FALLS ILL. IS HE ACTING THIS WAY OUT OF CONCERN FOR YATO'S HEALTH?
YUKINÉ.
YOU'RE GETTING STRONGER...

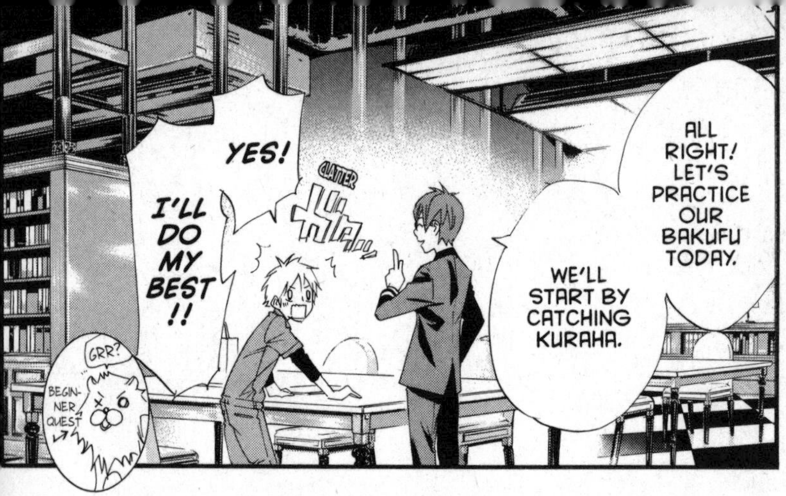
ALL RIGHT! LET'S PRACTICE OUR BAKUFU TODAY.
WE'LL START BY CATCHING KURAHA.
CLATTER
YES!
I'LL DO MY BEST!!
GRR?
BEGIN-NER QUEST

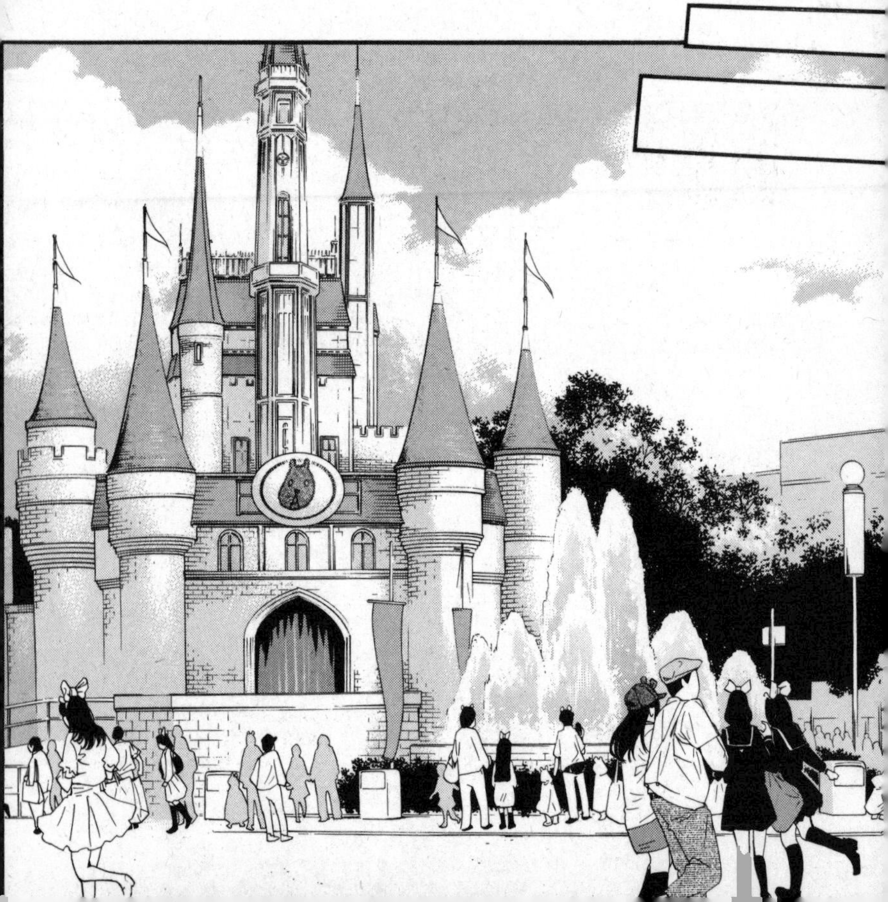

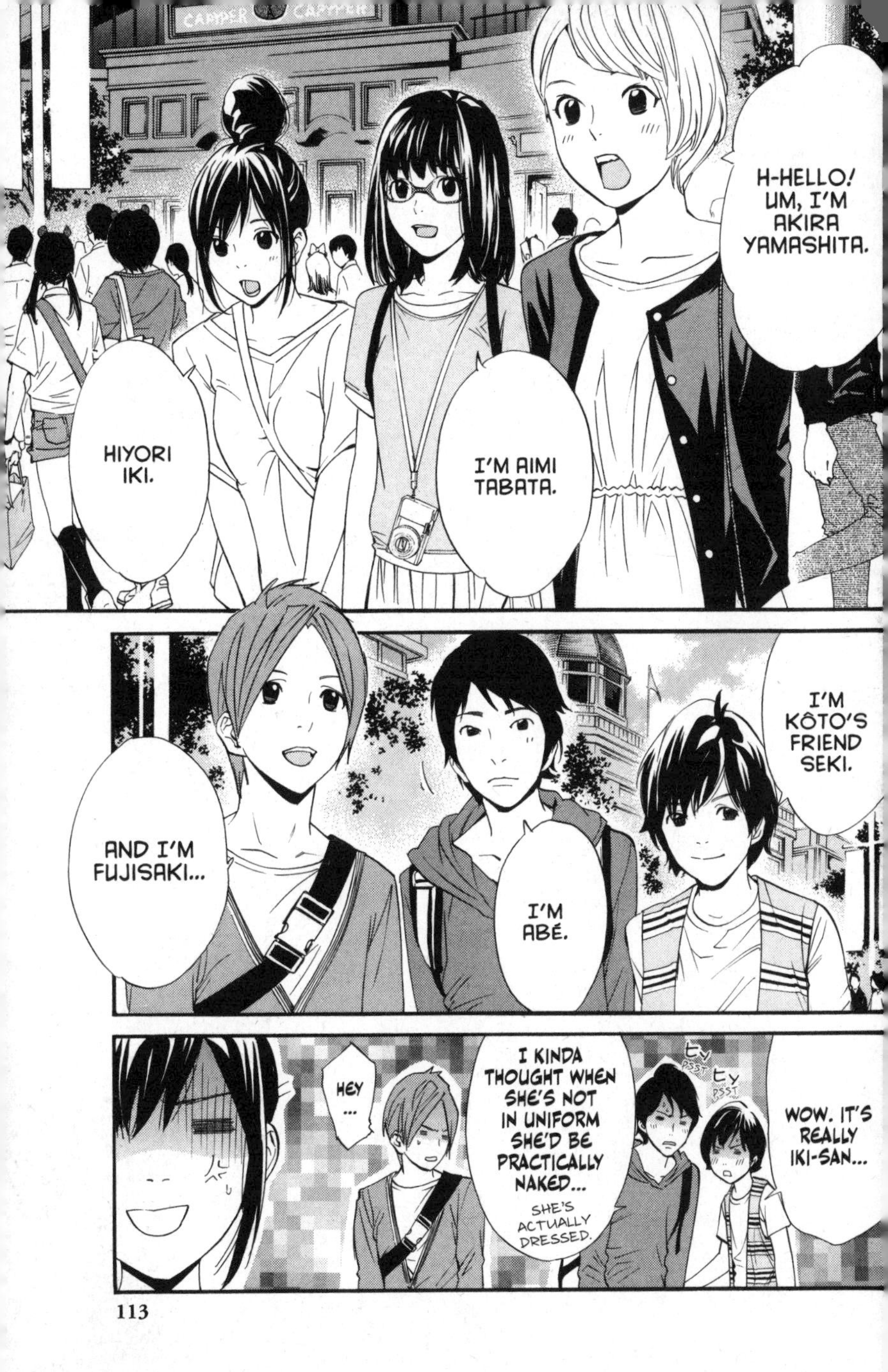
CAPPER CAPPER
H-HELLO! UM, I'M AKIRA YAMASHITA.
I'M AIMI TABATA.
HIYORI IKI.
I'M KÔTO'S FRIEND SEKI.
I'M ABÉ.
AND I'M FUJISAKI...
WOW. IT'S REALLY IKI-SAN...
PSST
PSST
I KINDA THOUGHT WHEN SHE'S NOT IN UNIFORM SHE'D BE PRACTICALLY NAKED...
SHE'S ACTUALLY DRESSED.
HEY ...

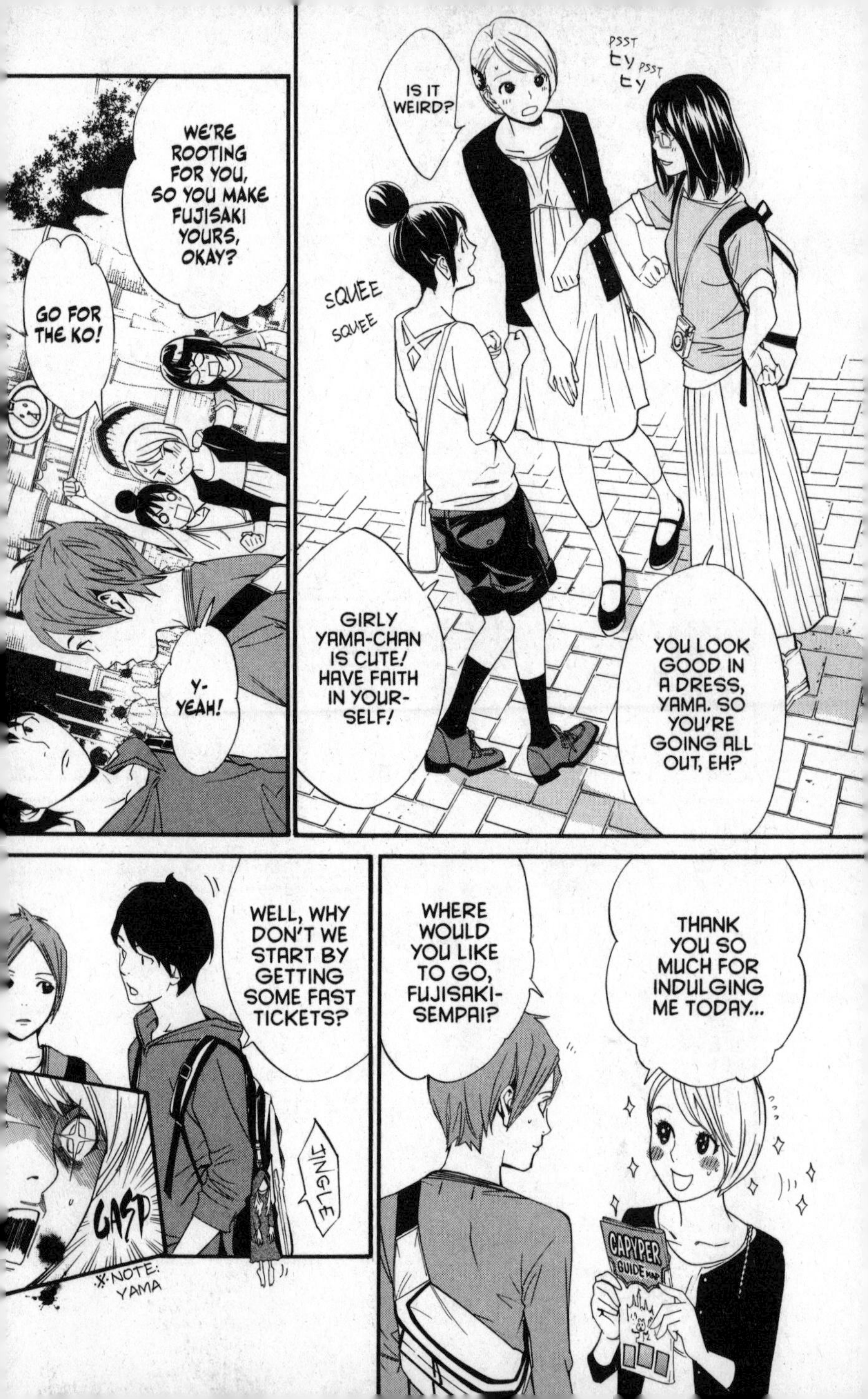
PSST
PSST
IS IT WEIRD?
SQUEE
SQUEE
YOU LOOK GOOD IN A DRESS, YAMA. SO YOU'RE GOING ALL OUT, EH?
GIRLY YAMA-CHAN IS CUTE! HAVE FAITH IN YOUR-SELF!
WE'RE ROOTING FOR YOU, SO YOU MAKE FUJISAKI YOURS, OKAY?
GO FOR THE KO!
Y-YEAH!
THANK YOU SO MUCH FOR INDULGING ME TODAY...
WHERE WOULD YOU LIKE TO GO, FUJISAKI-SEMPAI?
CAPYPER GUIDE MAP
WELL, WHY DON'T WE START BY GETTING SOME FAST TICKETS?
JINGLE
GASP
※NOTE: YAMA

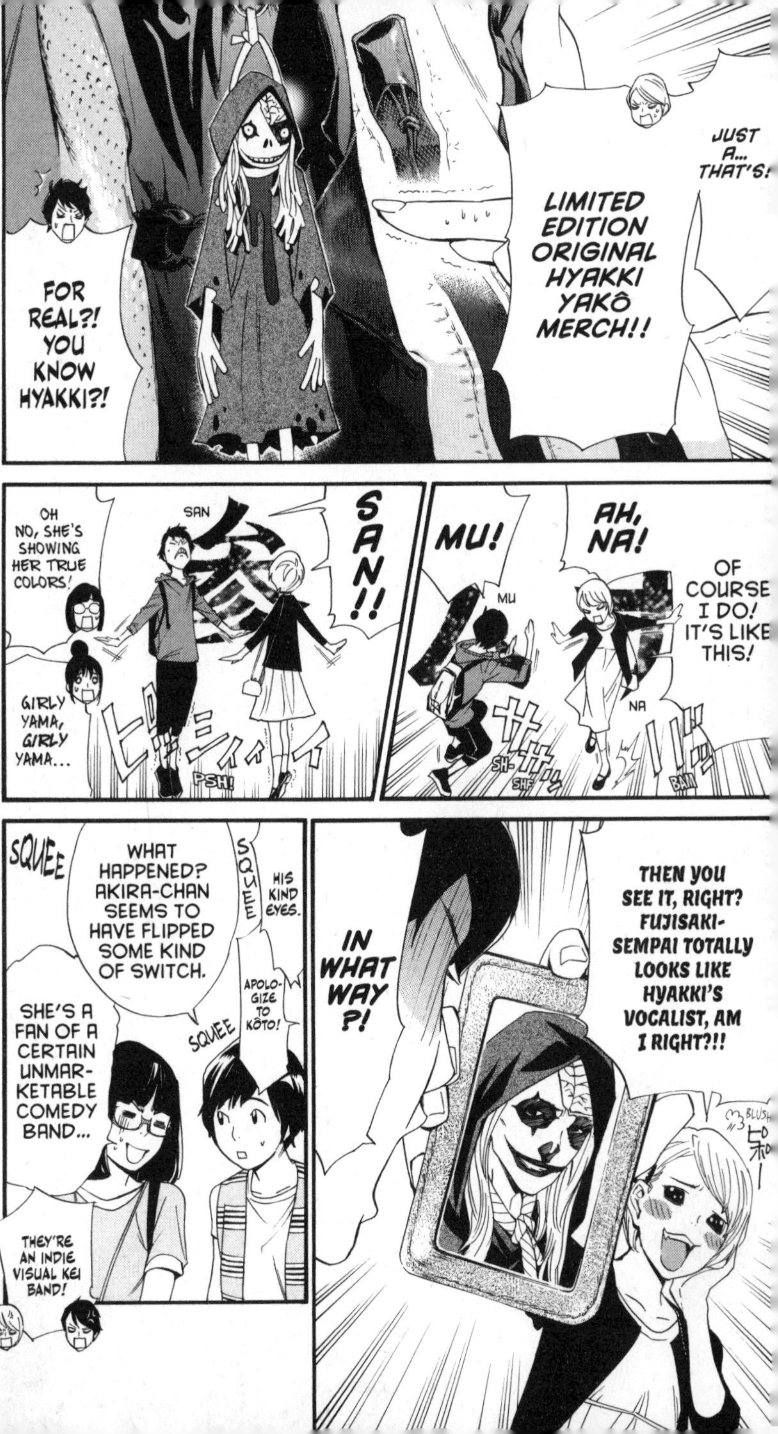
JUST A... THAT'S!
LIMITED EDITION ORIGINAL HYAKKI YAKÔ MERCH!!
FOR REAL?! YOU KNOW HYAKKI?!
AH, NA!
OF COURSE I DO! IT'S LIKE THIS!
MU!
MU
NA
SH-SHF
BAM
SAN!!
SAN
OH NO, SHE'S SHOWING HER TRUE COLORS!
GIRLY YAMA, GIRLY YAMA...
PSH!
THEN YOU SEE IT, RIGHT? FUJISAKI-SEMPAI TOTALLY LOOKS LIKE HYAKKI'S VOCALIST, AM I RIGHT?!!
BLUSH
IN WHAT WAY?!
SQUEE
HIS KIND EYES.
WHAT HAPPENED? AKIRA-CHAN SEEMS TO HAVE FLIPPED SOME KIND OF SWITCH.
SQUEE
APOLOGIZE TO KÔTO!
SQUEE
SQUEE
SHE'S A FAN OF A CERTAIN UNMARKETABLE COMEDY BAND...
THEY'RE AN INDIE VISUAL KEI BAND!

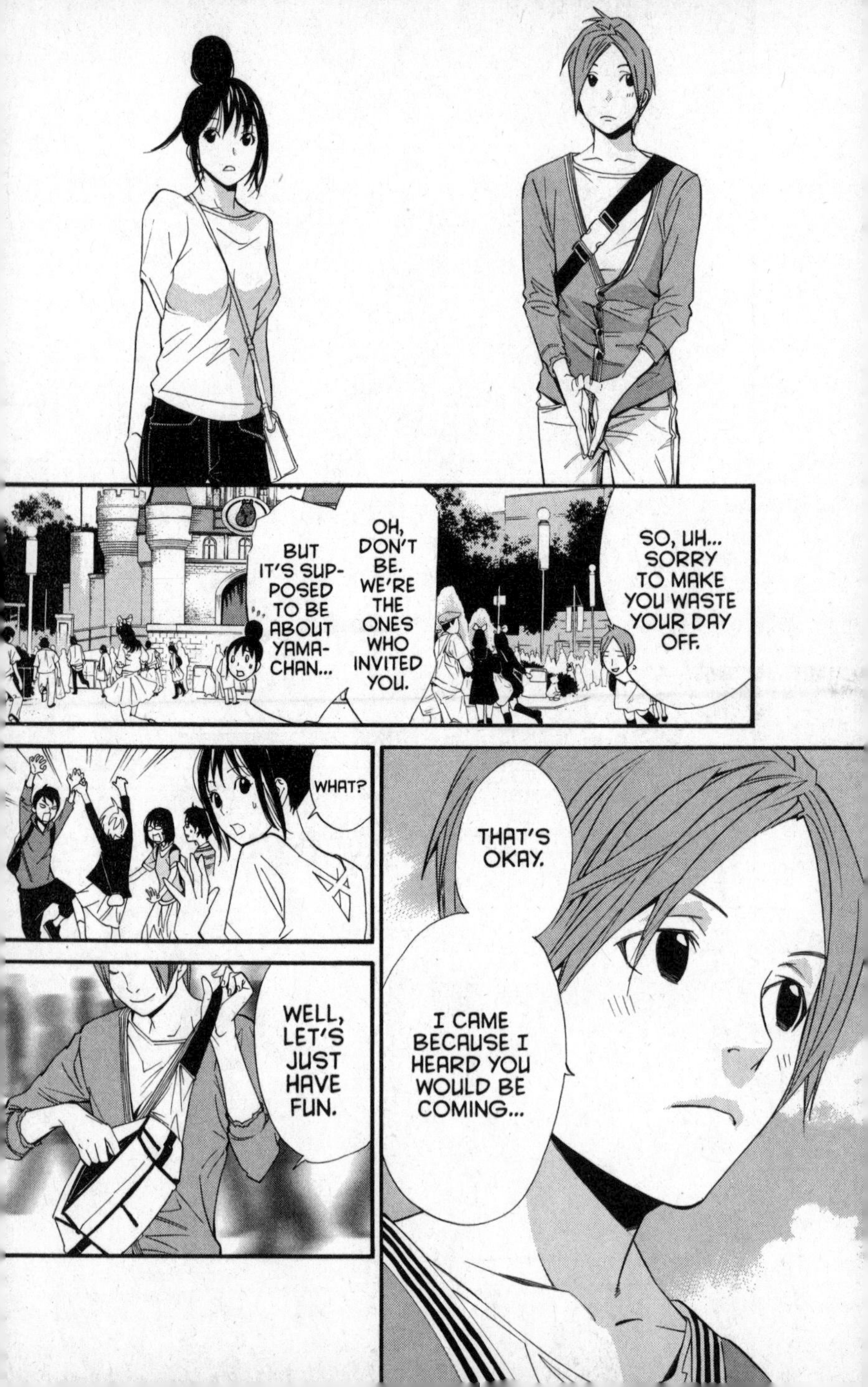
SO, UH... SORRY TO MAKE YOU WASTE YOUR DAY OFF.
OH, DON'T BE. WE'RE THE ONES WHO INVITED YOU.
BUT IT'S SUP-POSED TO BE ABOUT YAMA-CHAN...
THAT'S OKAY.
I CAME BECAUSE I HEARD YOU WOULD BE COMING...
WHAT?
WELL, LET'S JUST HAVE FUN.

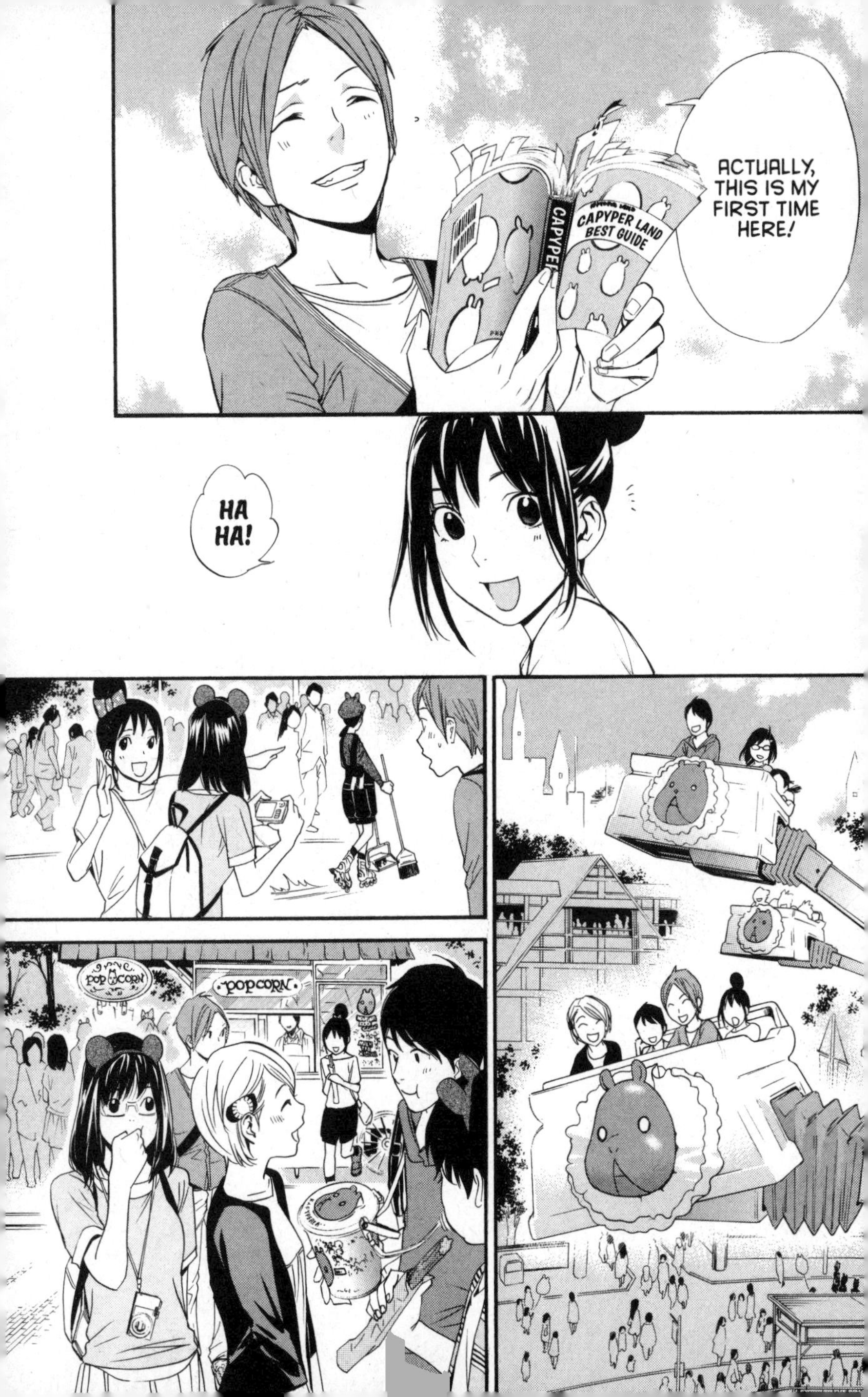
CAPYPER LAND BEST GUIDE
CAPYPE
ACTUALLY, THIS IS MY FIRST TIME HERE!
HA HA!
POPCORN
POP CORN

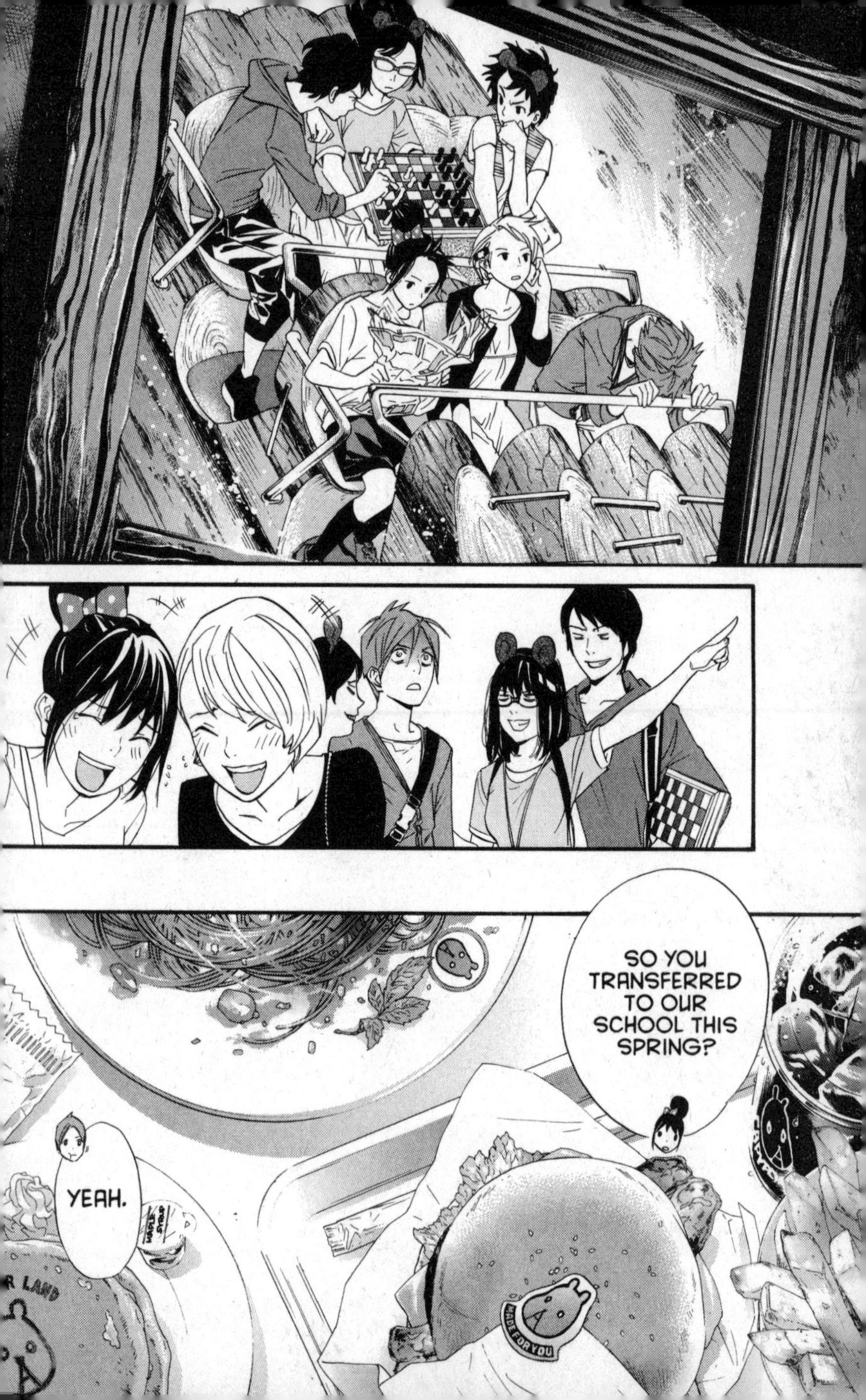
SO YOU TRANSFERRED TO OUR SCHOOL THIS SPRING?
YEAH.
MAPLE SYRUP
MADE FOR YOU

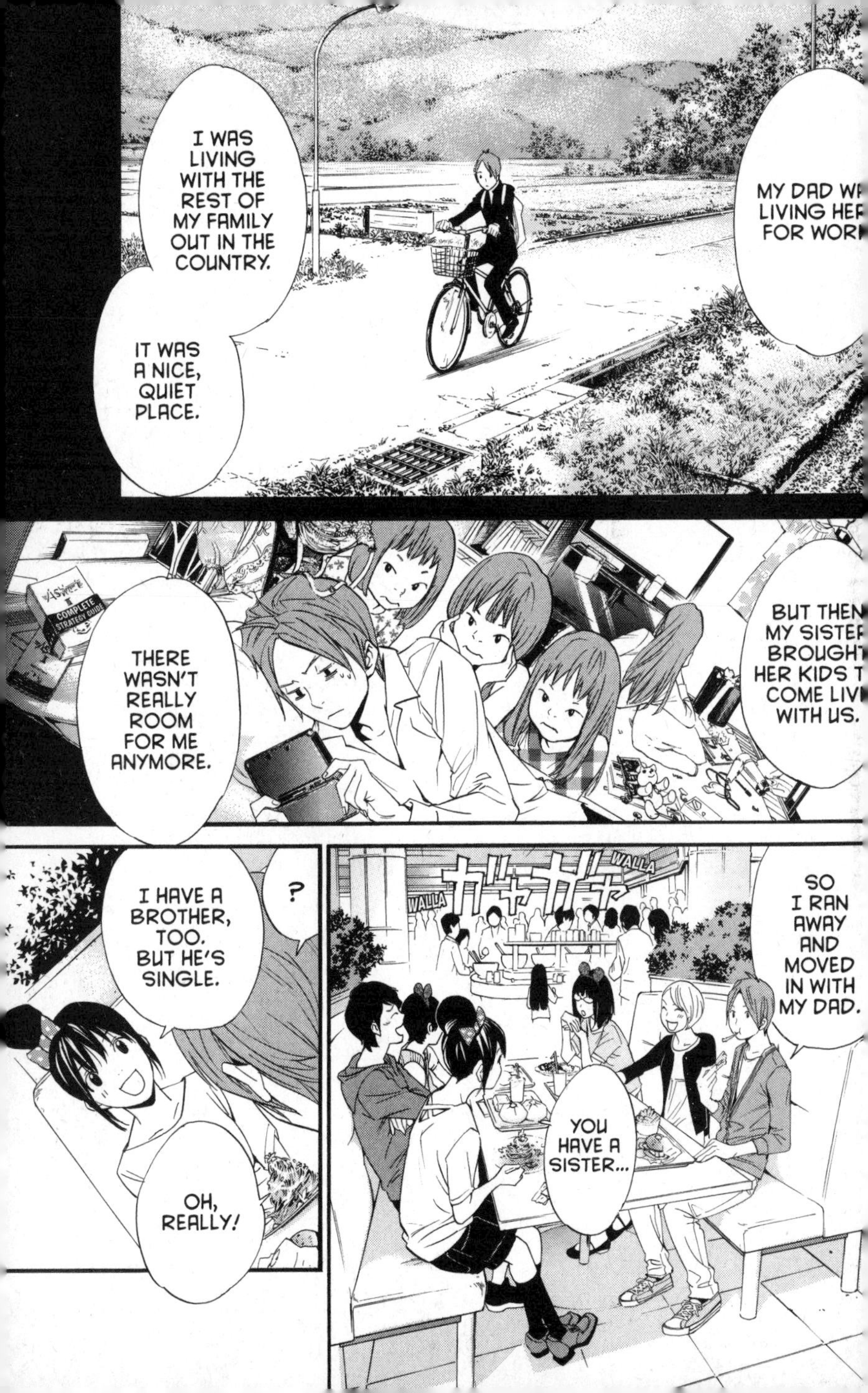

MY DAD WA LIVING HER FOR WOR
I WAS LIVING WITH THE REST OF MY FAMILY OUT IN THE COUNTRY.
IT WAS A NICE, QUIET PLACE.
BUT THEN MY SISTER BROUGHT HER KIDS T COME LIV WITH US.
COMPLETE STRATEGY GUIDE
THERE WASN'T REALLY ROOM FOR ME ANYMORE.
SO I RAN AWAY AND MOVED IN WITH MY DAD.
ガヤガヤ
WALLA
WALLA
YOU HAVE A SISTER...
?
I HAVE A BROTHER, TOO. BUT HE'S SINGLE.
OH, REALLY!

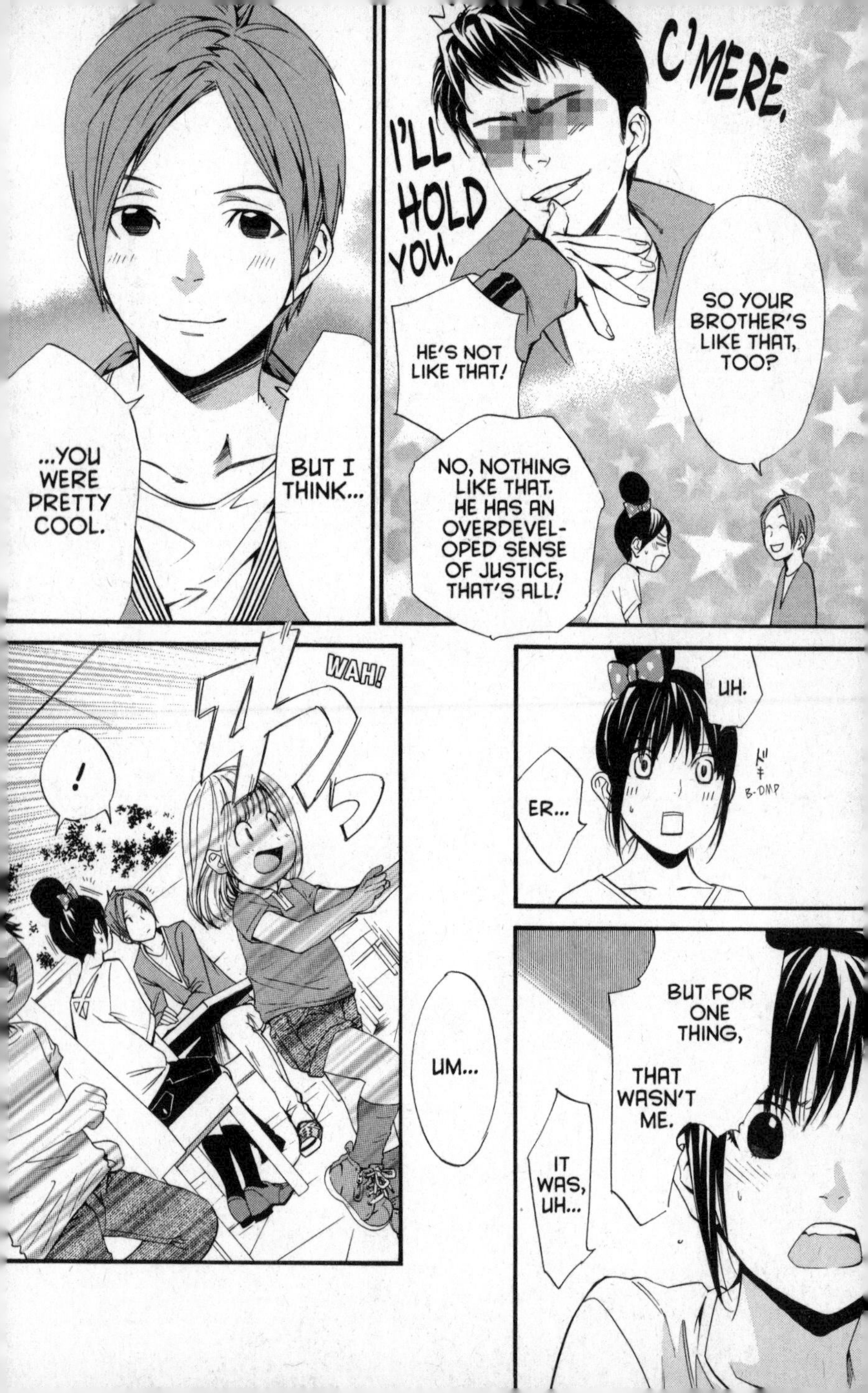
C'MERE,
I'LL HOLD YOU.
SO YOUR BROTHER'S LIKE THAT, TOO?
HE'S NOT LIKE THAT!
NO, NOTHING LIKE THAT. HE HAS AN OVERDEVEL-OPED SENSE OF JUSTICE, THAT'S ALL!
BUT I THINK...
...YOU WERE PRETTY COOL.
UH.
B-DMP
ER...
BUT FOR ONE THING,
THAT WASN'T ME.
IT WAS, UH...
UM...
WAH!
!

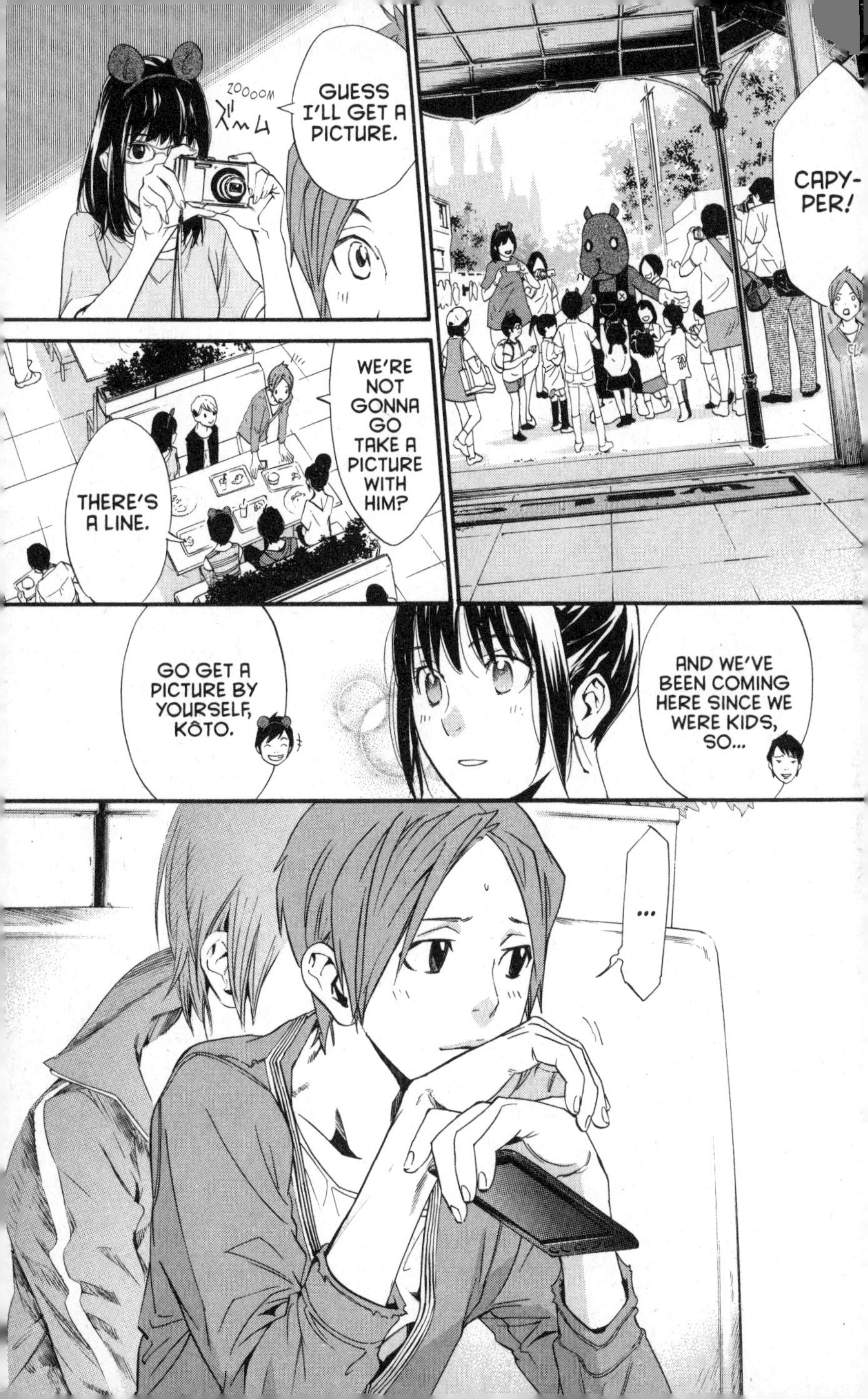
CAPY-PER!
GUESS I'LL GET A PICTURE.
ZOOOOM
WE'RE NOT GONNA GO TAKE A PICTURE WITH HIM?
THERE'S A LINE.
AND WE'VE BEEN COMING HERE SINCE WE WERE KIDS, SO...
GO GET A PICTURE BY YOURSELF, KÔTO.
...

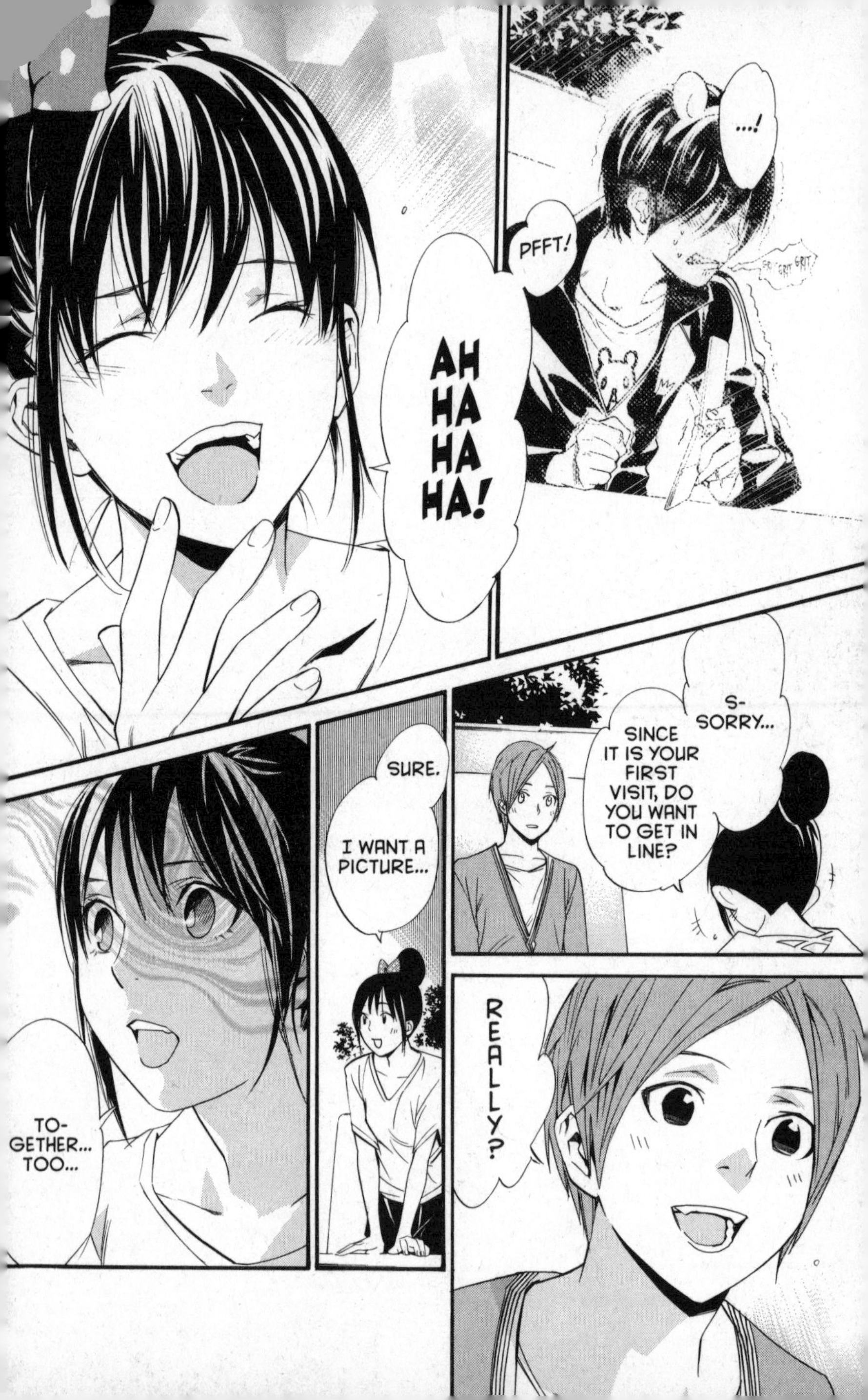

...!
PFFT!
GRIT GRIT GRIT
AH HA HA HA HA!
S-SORRY...
SINCE IT IS YOUR FIRST VISIT, DO YOU WANT TO GET IN LINE?
REALLY?
SURE.
I WANT A PICTURE...
TO-GETHER... TOO...

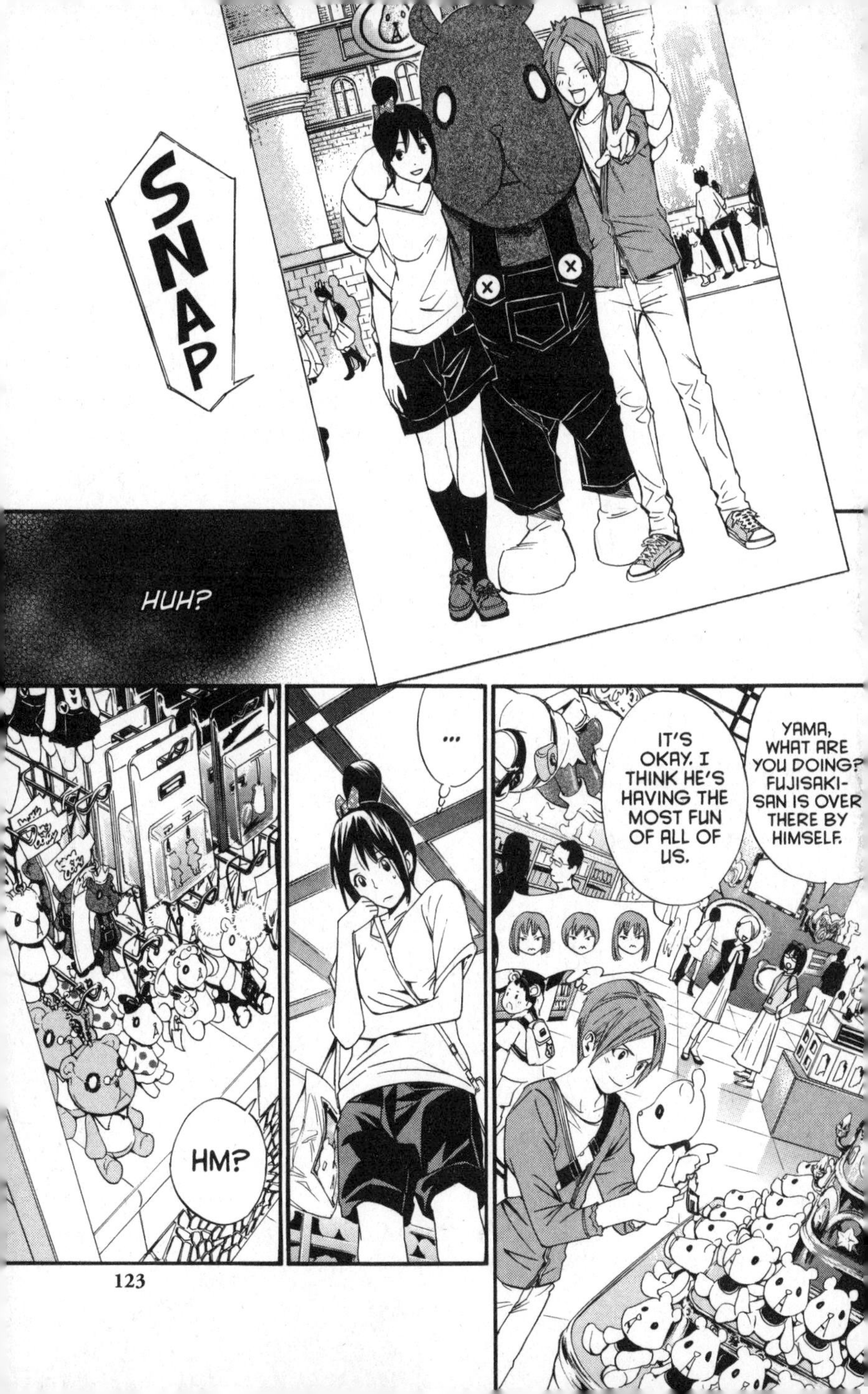
SNAP
HUH?
YAMA, WHAT ARE YOU DOING? FUJISAKI-SAN IS OVER THERE BY HIMSELF.
IT'S OKAY. I THINK HE'S HAVING THE MOST FUN OF ALL OF US.
...
HM?

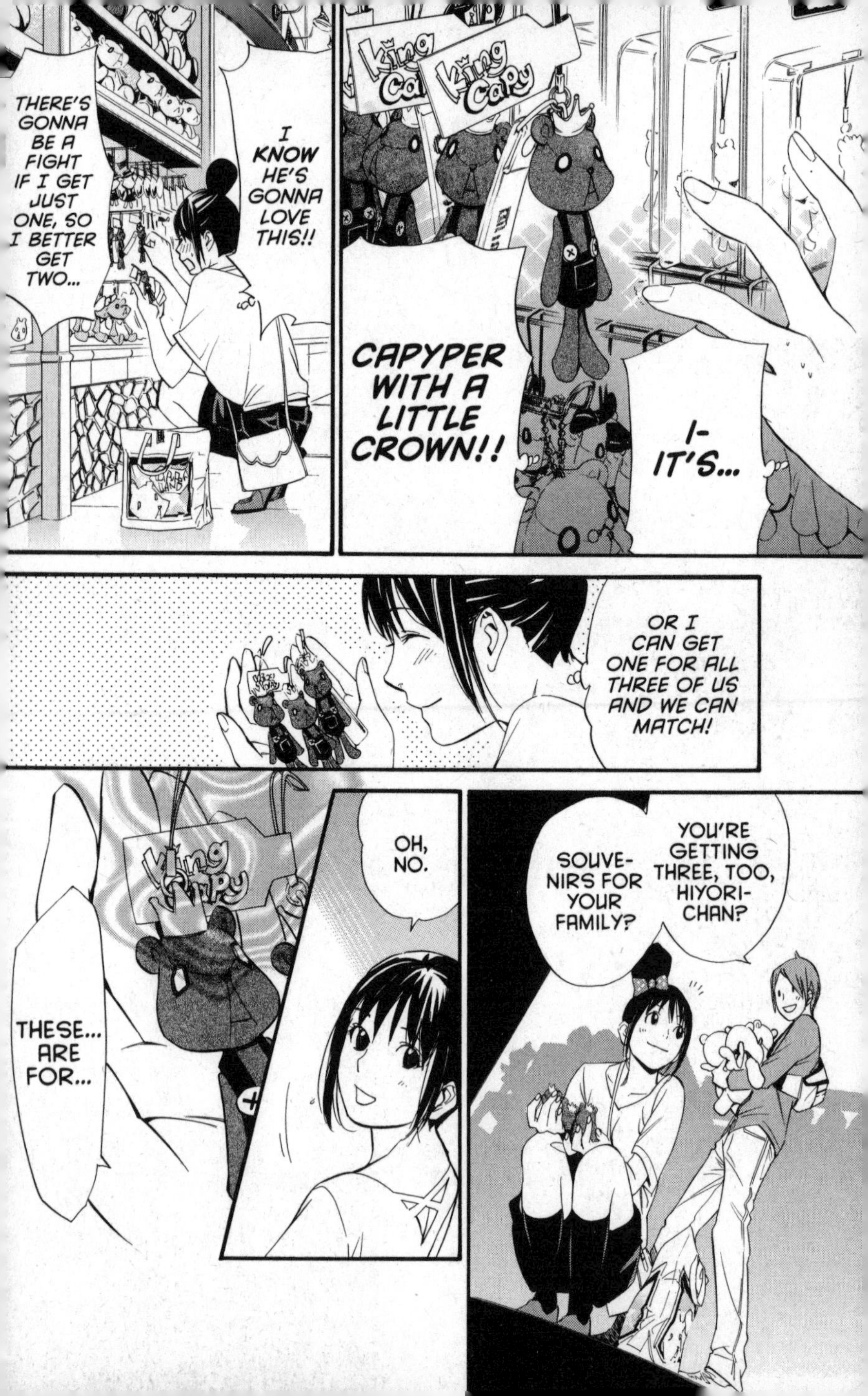
King Capy
I- IT'S...
CAPYPER WITH A LITTLE CROWN!!
I KNOW HE'S GONNA LOVE THIS!!
THERE'S GONNA BE A FIGHT IF I GET JUST ONE, SO I BETTER GET TWO...
OR I CAN GET ONE FOR ALL THREE OF US AND WE CAN MATCH!
YOU'RE GETTING THREE, TOO, HIYORI-CHAN?
SOUVE-NIRS FOR YOUR FAMILY?
OH, NO.
THESE... ARE FOR...

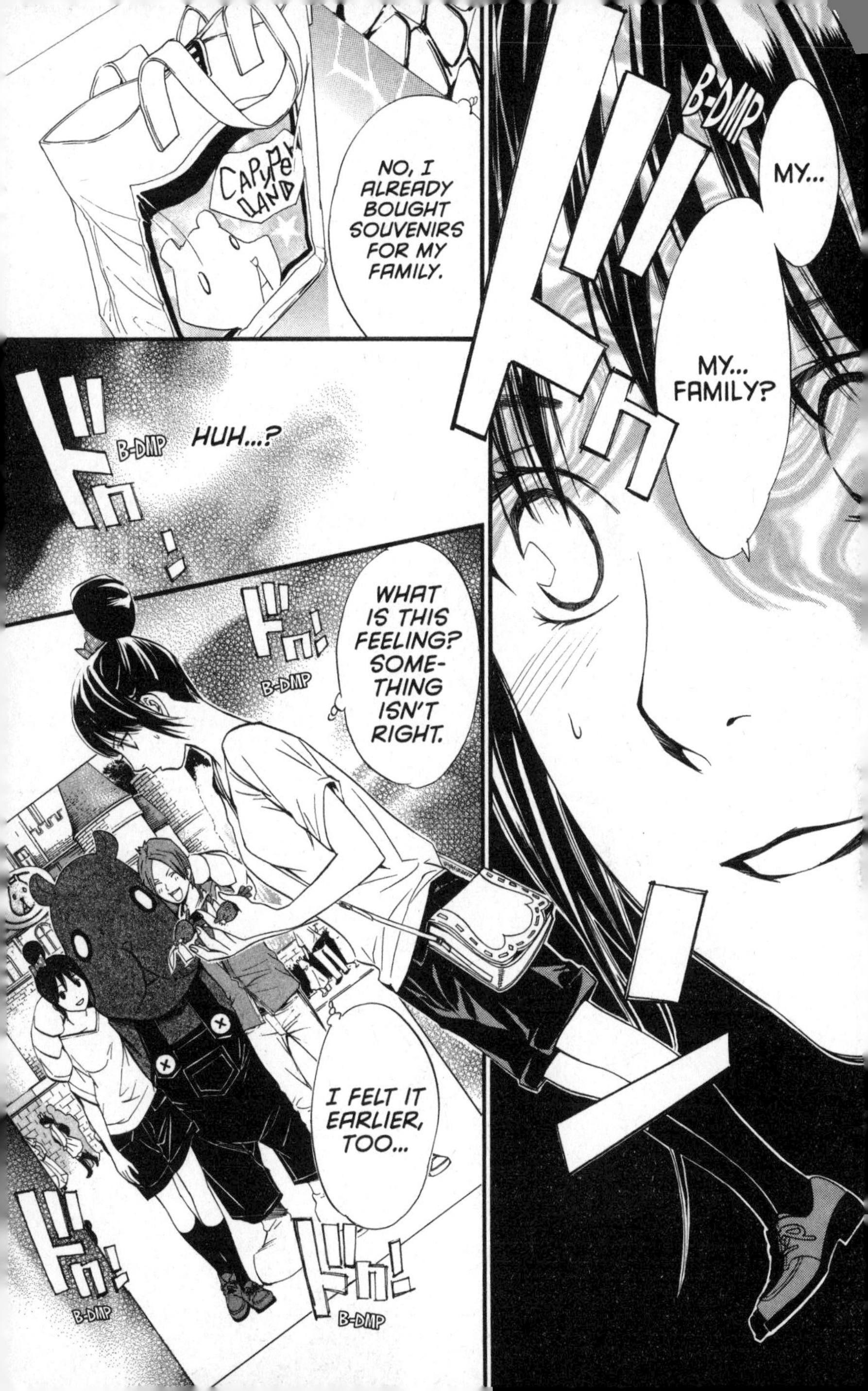
B-DMP
MY...
MY... FAMILY?
NO, I ALREADY BOUGHT SOUVENIRS FOR MY FAMILY.
HUH...?
B-DMP
WHAT IS THIS FEELING? SOME-THING ISN'T RIGHT.
B-DMP
I FELT IT EARLIER, TOO...
B-DMP
B-DMP

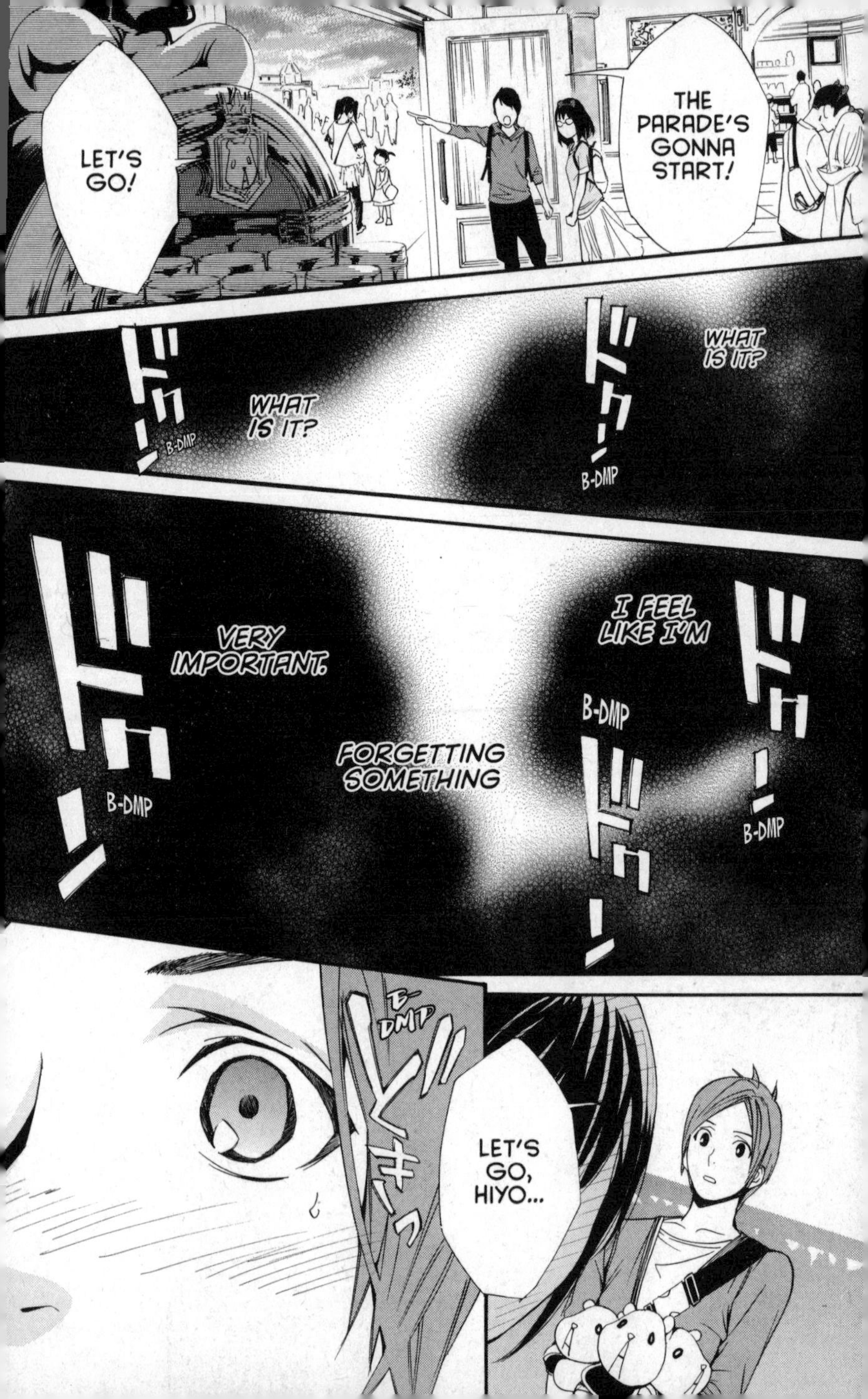
THE PARADE'S GONNA START!
LET'S GO!
WHAT IS IT?
B-DMP
WHAT IS IT?
B-DMP
I FEEL LIKE I'M
B-DMP
B-DMP
FORGETTING SOMETHING
VERY IMPORTANT.
B-DMP
B-DMP
LET'S GO, HIYO...

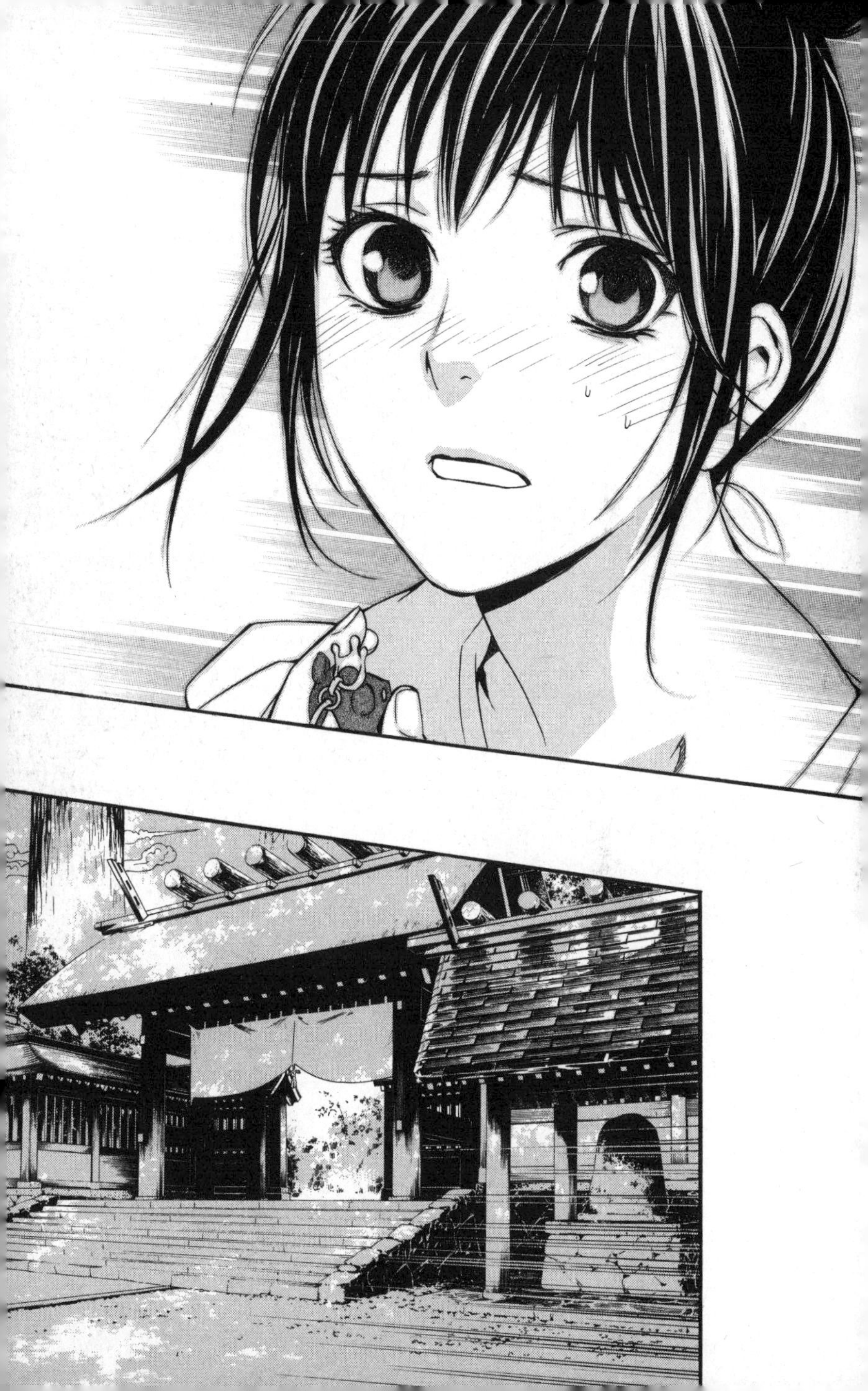

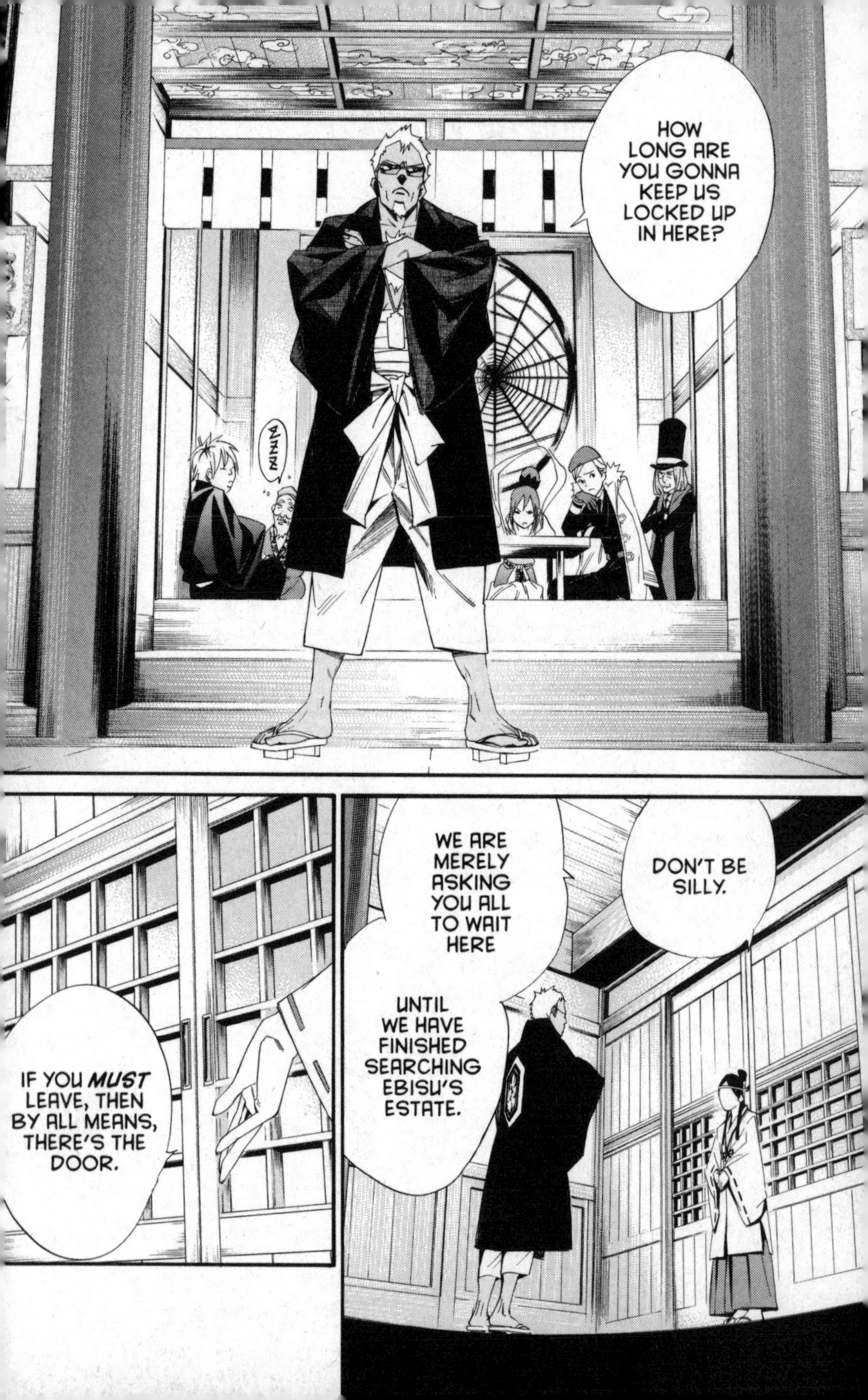
HOW LONG ARE YOU GONNA KEEP US LOCKED UP IN HERE?
DON'T BE SILLY.
WE ARE MERELY ASKING YOU ALL TO WAIT HERE
UNTIL WE HAVE FINISHED SEARCHING EBISU'S ESTATE.
IF YOU *MUST* LEAVE, THEN BY ALL MEANS, THERE'S THE DOOR.

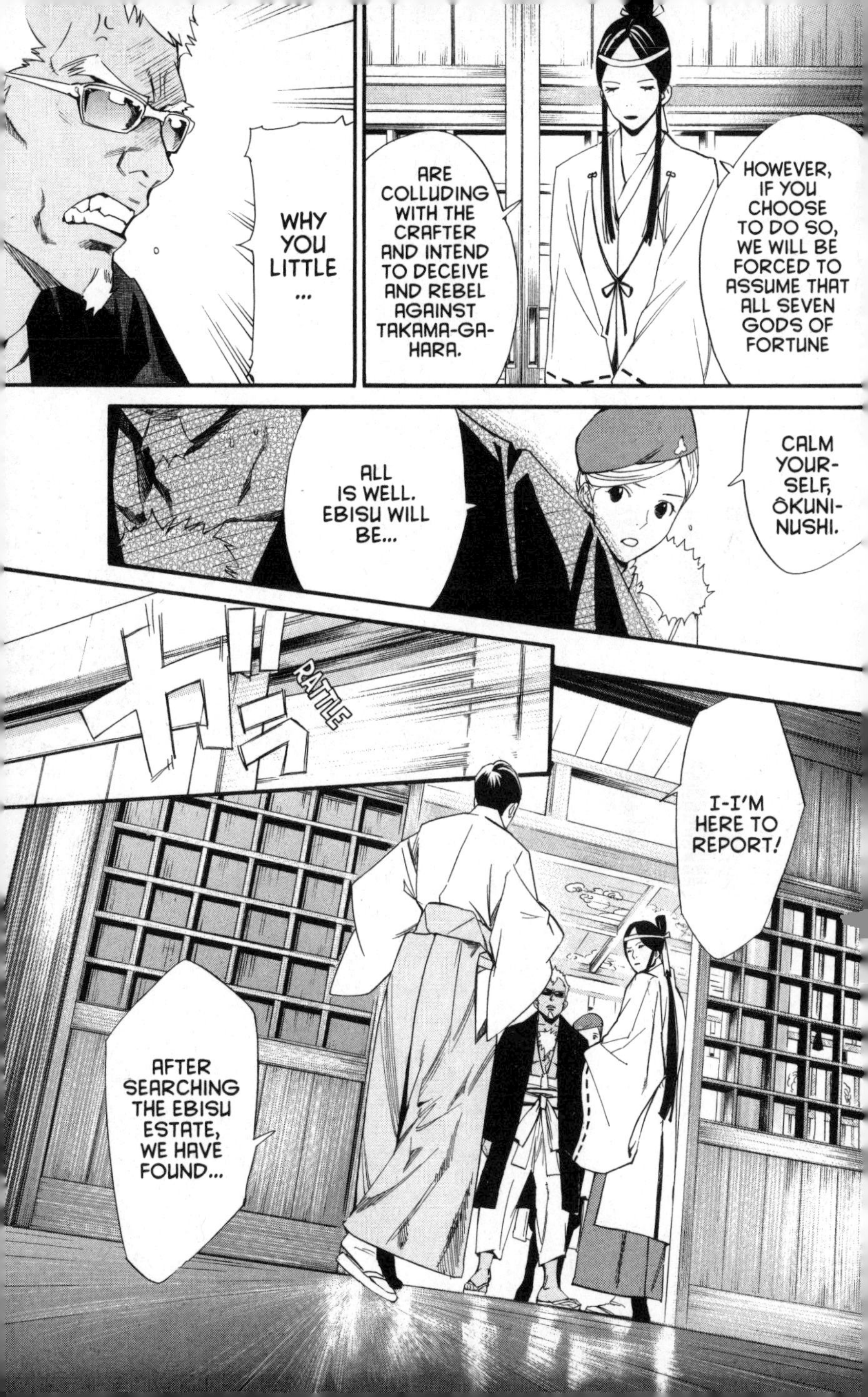
HOWEVER, IF YOU CHOOSE TO DO SO, WE WILL BE FORCED TO ASSUME THAT ALL SEVEN GODS OF FORTUNE
ARE COLLUDING WITH THE CRAFTER AND INTEND TO DECEIVE AND REBEL AGAINST TAKAMA-GA-HARA.
WHY YOU LITTLE ...
CALM YOURSELF, ÔKUNI-NUSHI.
ALL IS WELL. EBISU WILL BE...
RATTLE
I-I'M HERE TO REPORT!
AFTER SEARCHING THE EBISU ESTATE, WE HAVE FOUND...

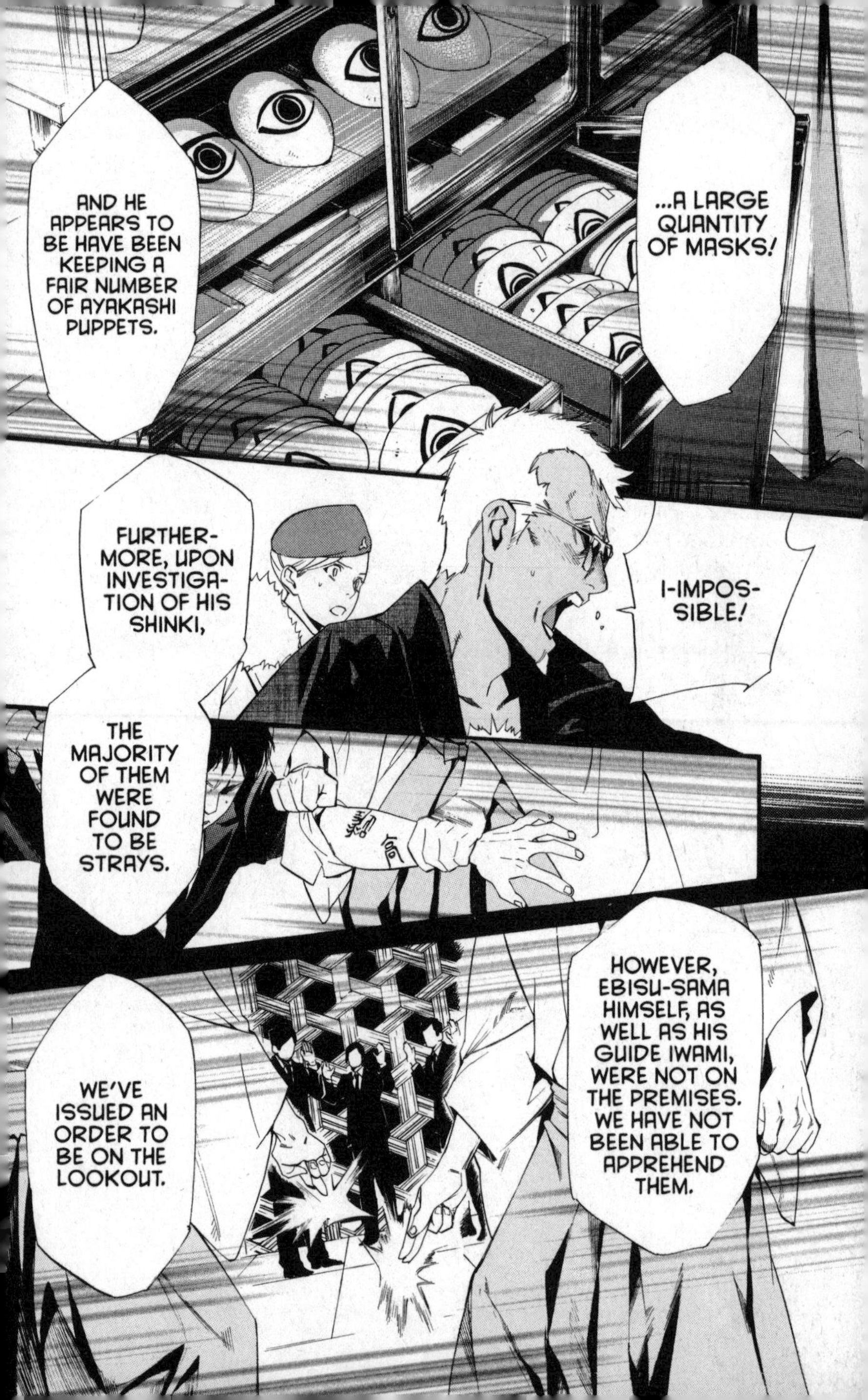
...A LARGE QUANTITY OF MASKS!
AND HE APPEARS TO BE HAVE BEEN KEEPING A FAIR NUMBER OF AYAKASHI PUPPETS.
I-IMPOSSIBLE!
FURTHERMORE, UPON INVESTIGATION OF HIS SHINKI,
THE MAJORITY OF THEM WERE FOUND TO BE STRAYS.
HOWEVER, EBISU-SAMA HIMSELF, AS WELL AS HIS GUIDE IWAMI, WERE NOT ON THE PREMISES. WE HAVE NOT BEEN ABLE TO APPREHEND THEM.
WE'VE ISSUED AN ORDER TO BE ON THE LOOKOUT.

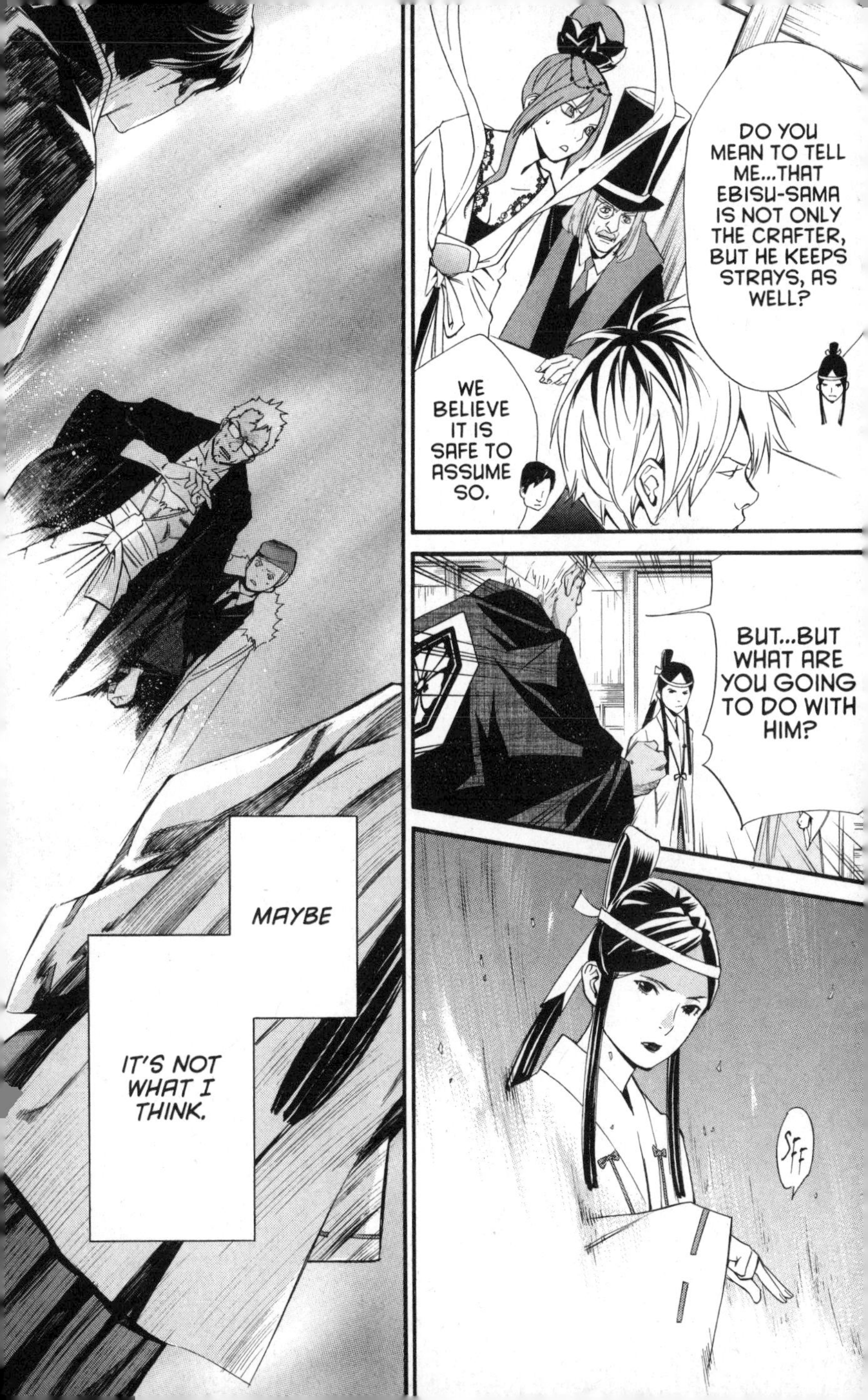
DO YOU MEAN TO TELL ME...THAT EBISU-SAMA IS NOT ONLY THE CRAFTER, BUT HE KEEPS STRAYS, AS WELL?
WE BELIEVE IT IS SAFE TO ASSUME SO.
BUT...BUT WHAT ARE YOU GOING TO DO WITH HIM?
SFF
MAYBE
IT'S NOT WHAT I THINK.

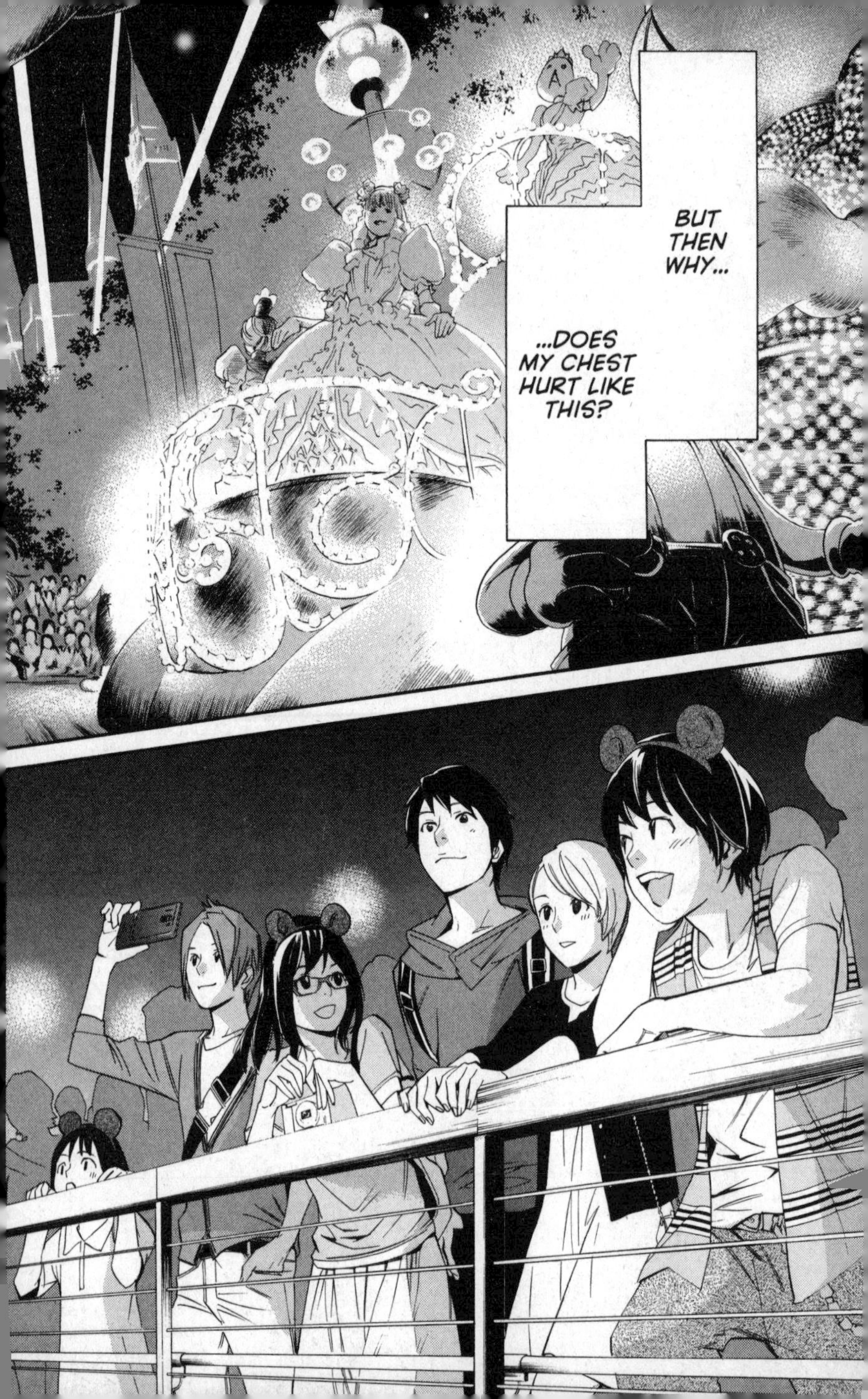
BUT THEN WHY...
...DOES MY CHEST HURT LIKE THIS?

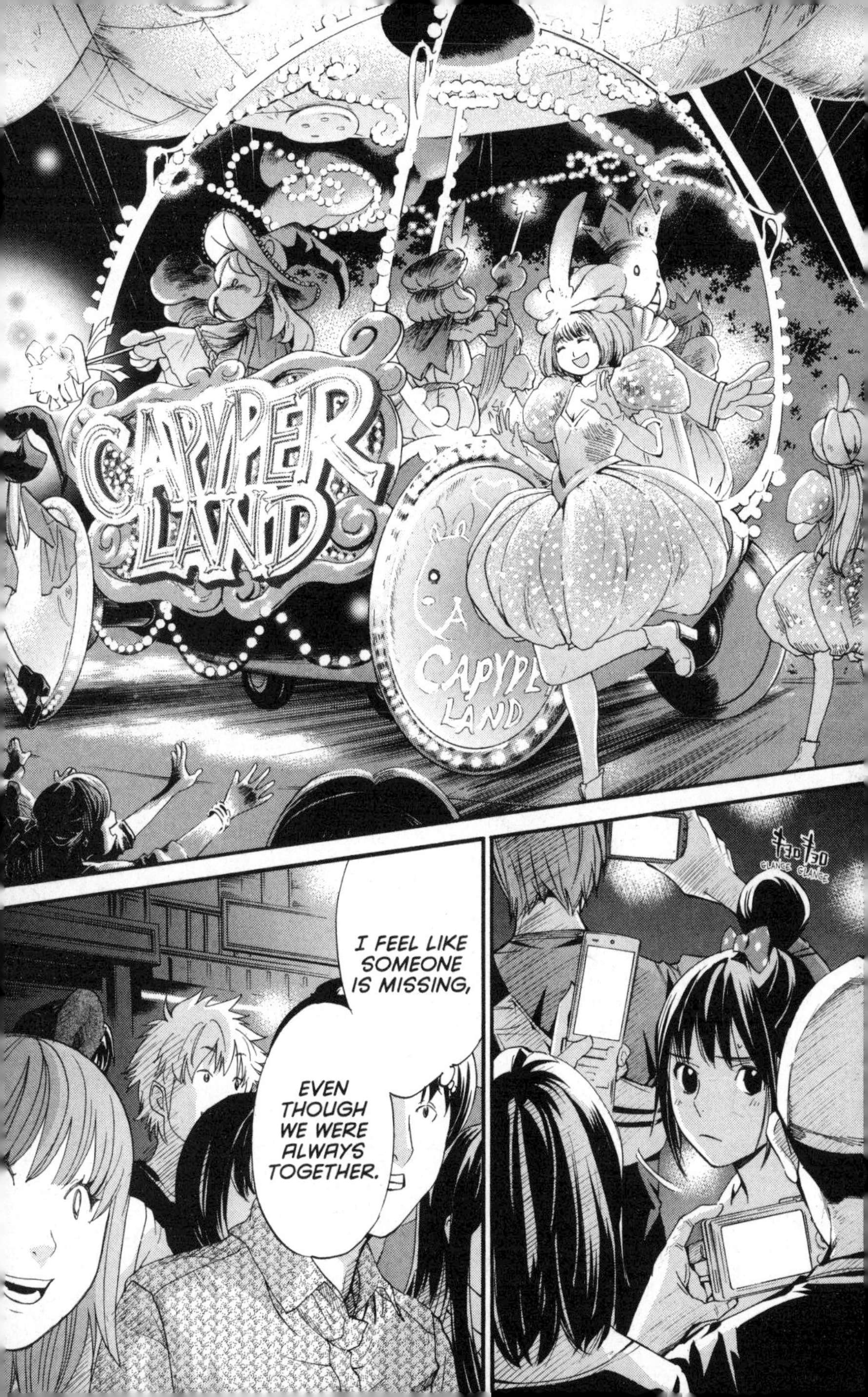
CAPYPER LAND
GLANCE GLANCE
I FEEL LIKE SOMEONE IS MISSING,
EVEN THOUGH WE WERE ALWAYS TOGETHER.

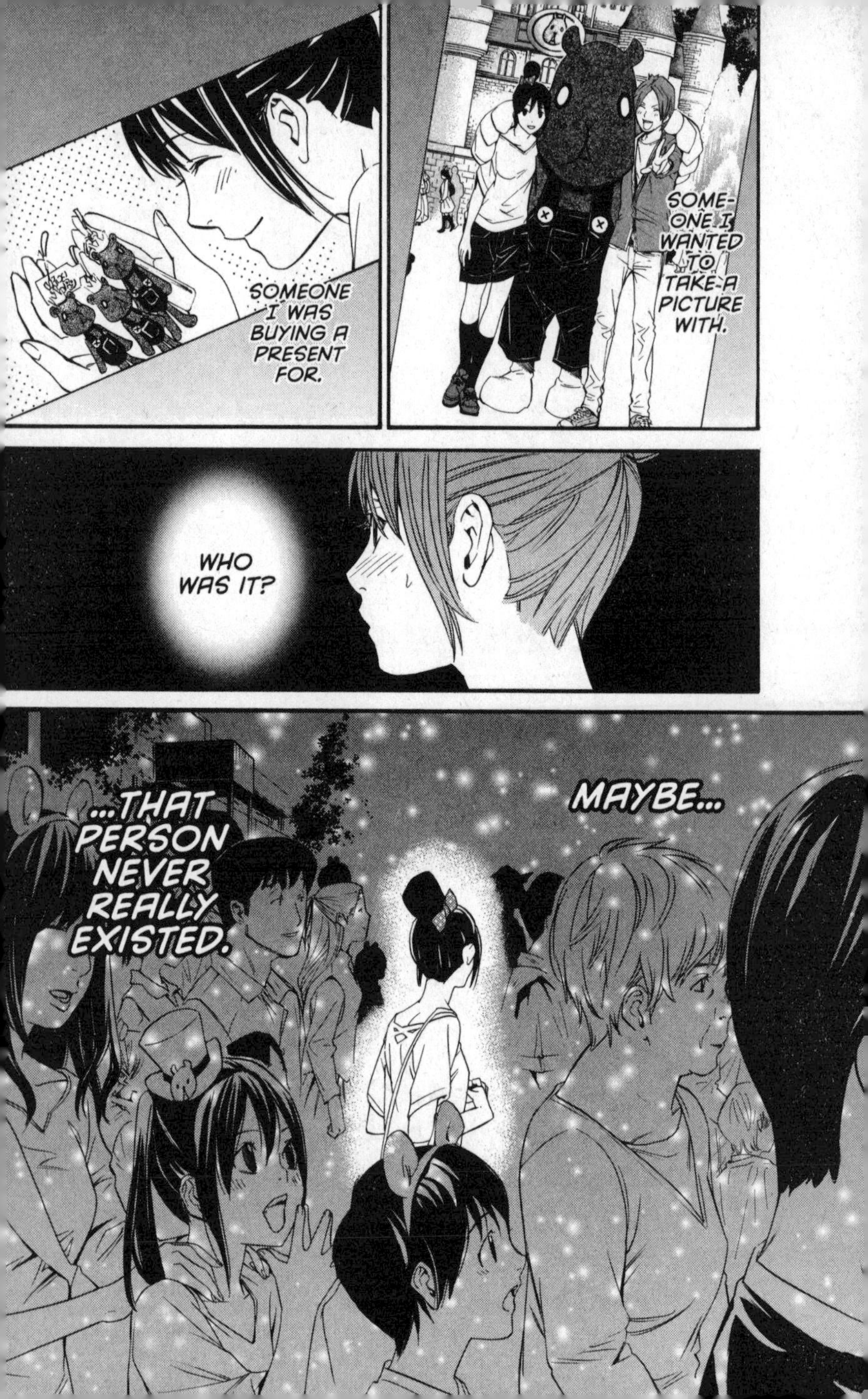
SOME-ONE I WANTED TO TAKE A PICTURE WITH.
SOMEONE I WAS BUYING A PRESENT FOR.
WHO WAS IT?
MAYBE...
...THAT PERSON NEVER REALLY EXISTED.

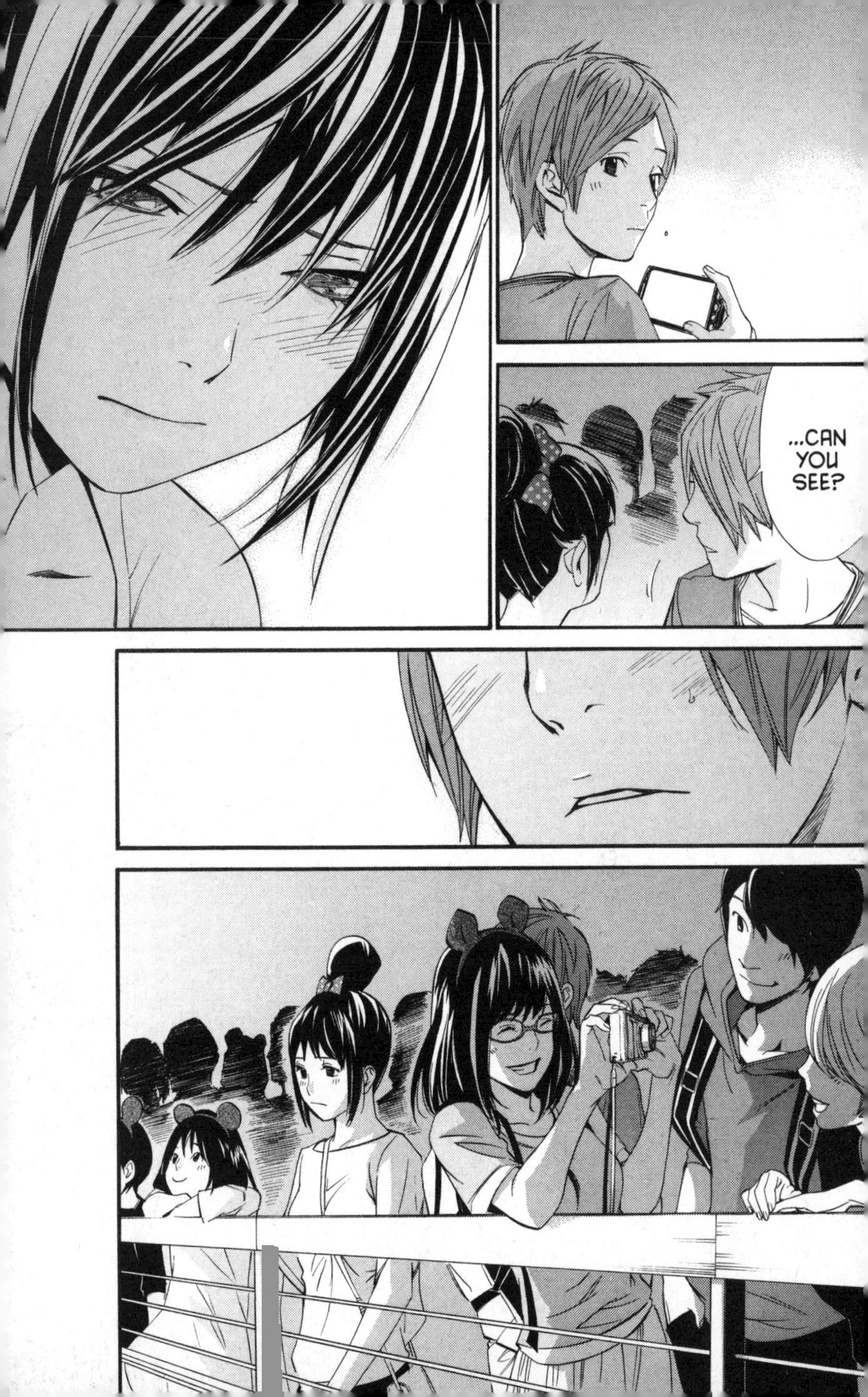
...CAN YOU SEE?

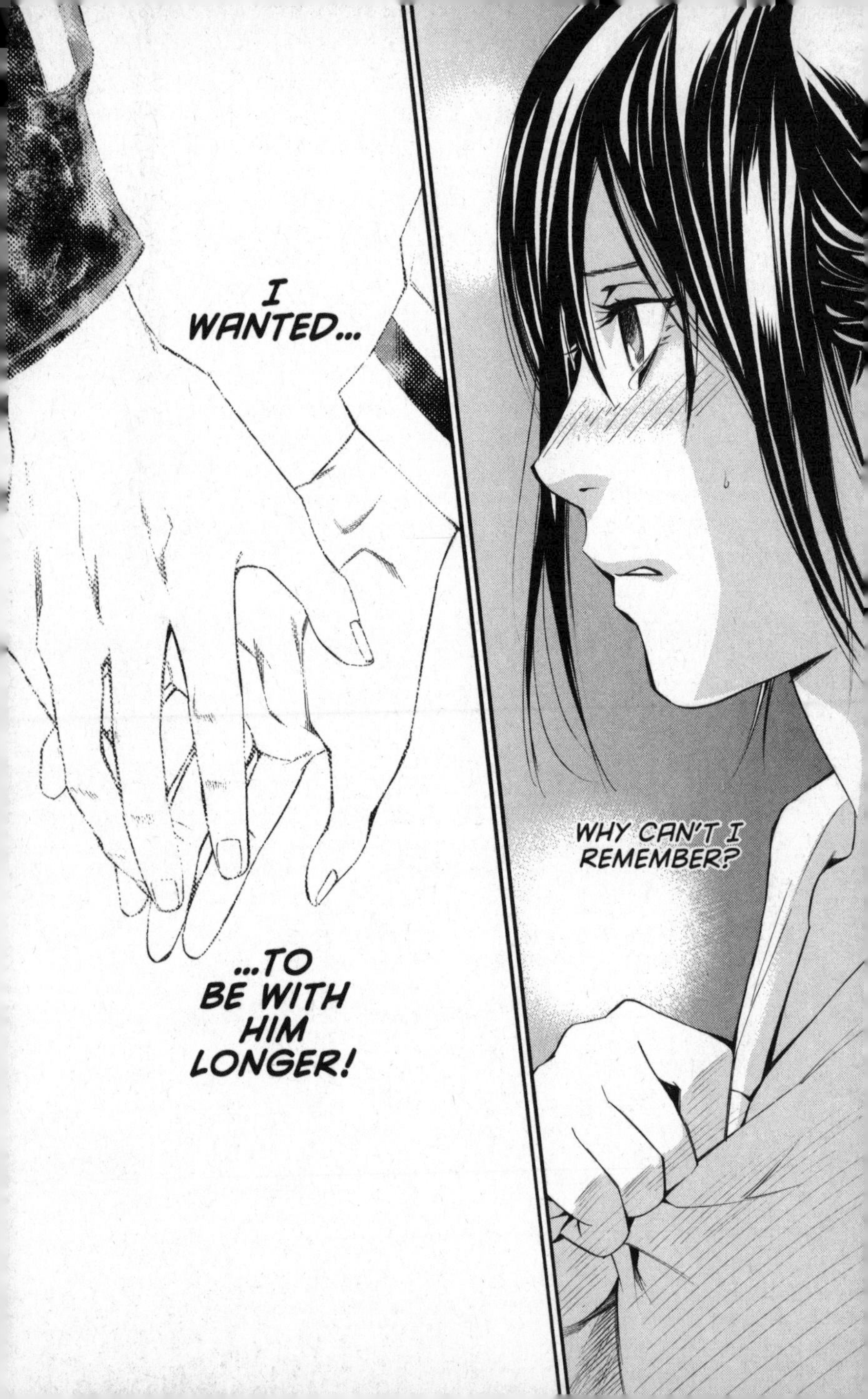
WHY CAN'T I REMEMBER?
I WANTED...
...TO BE WITH HIM LONGER!

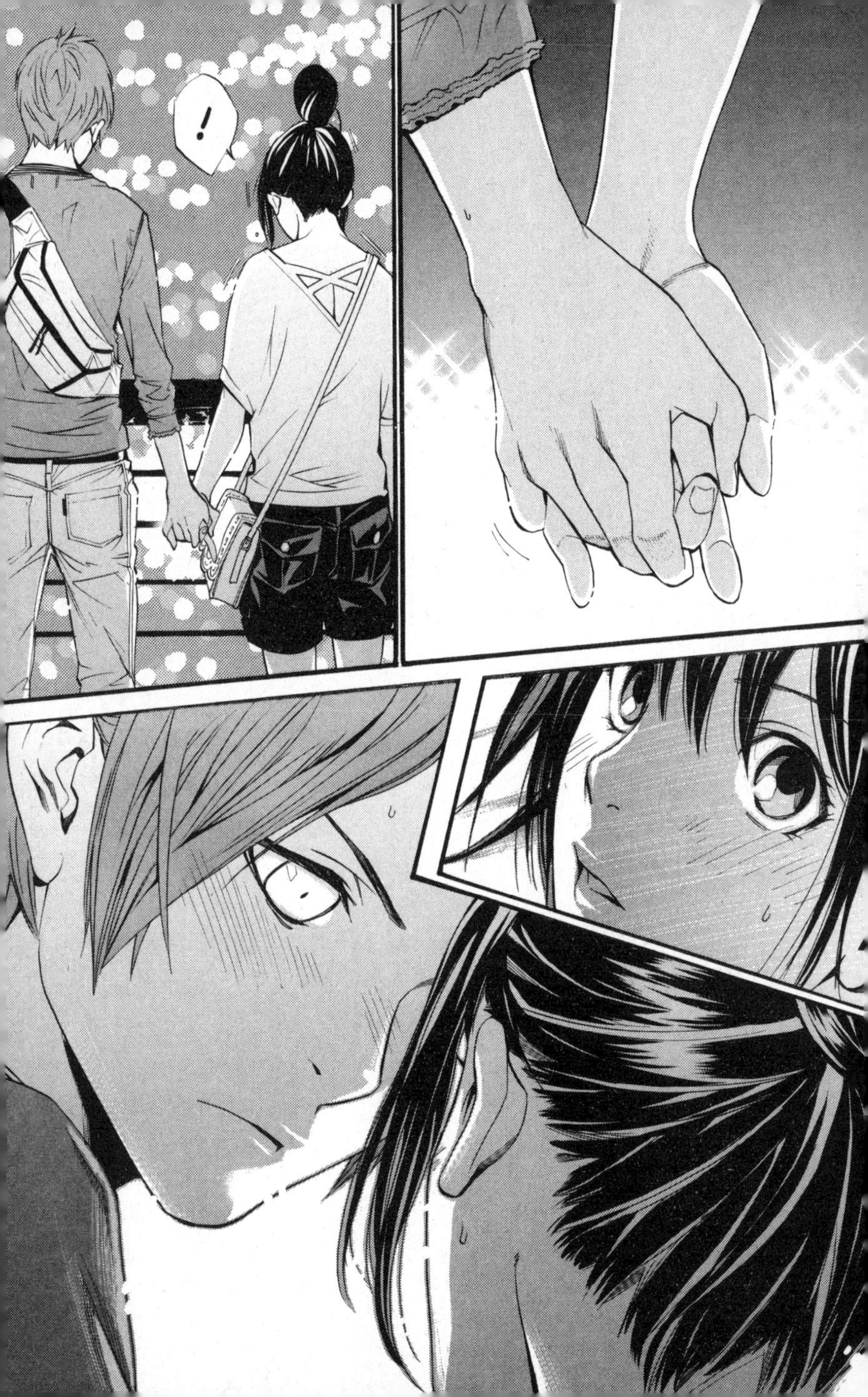
!

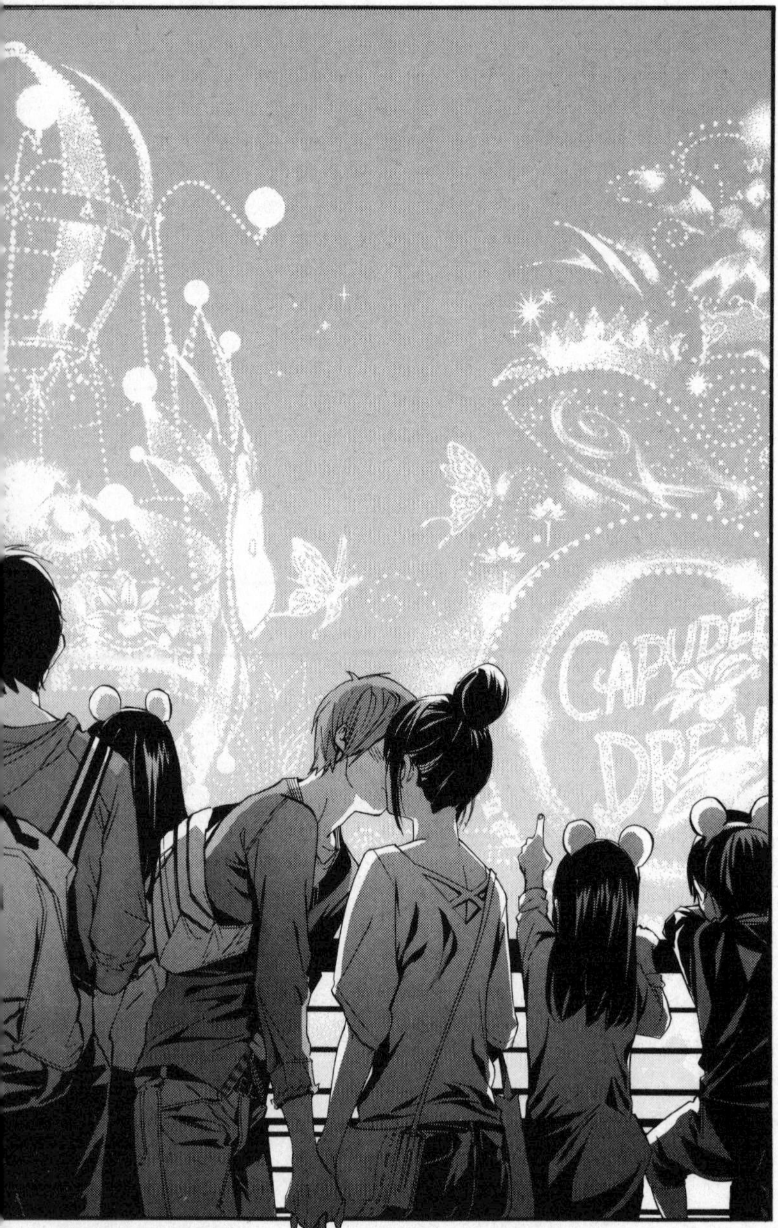

CHAPTER 30 / END

野

兔

神

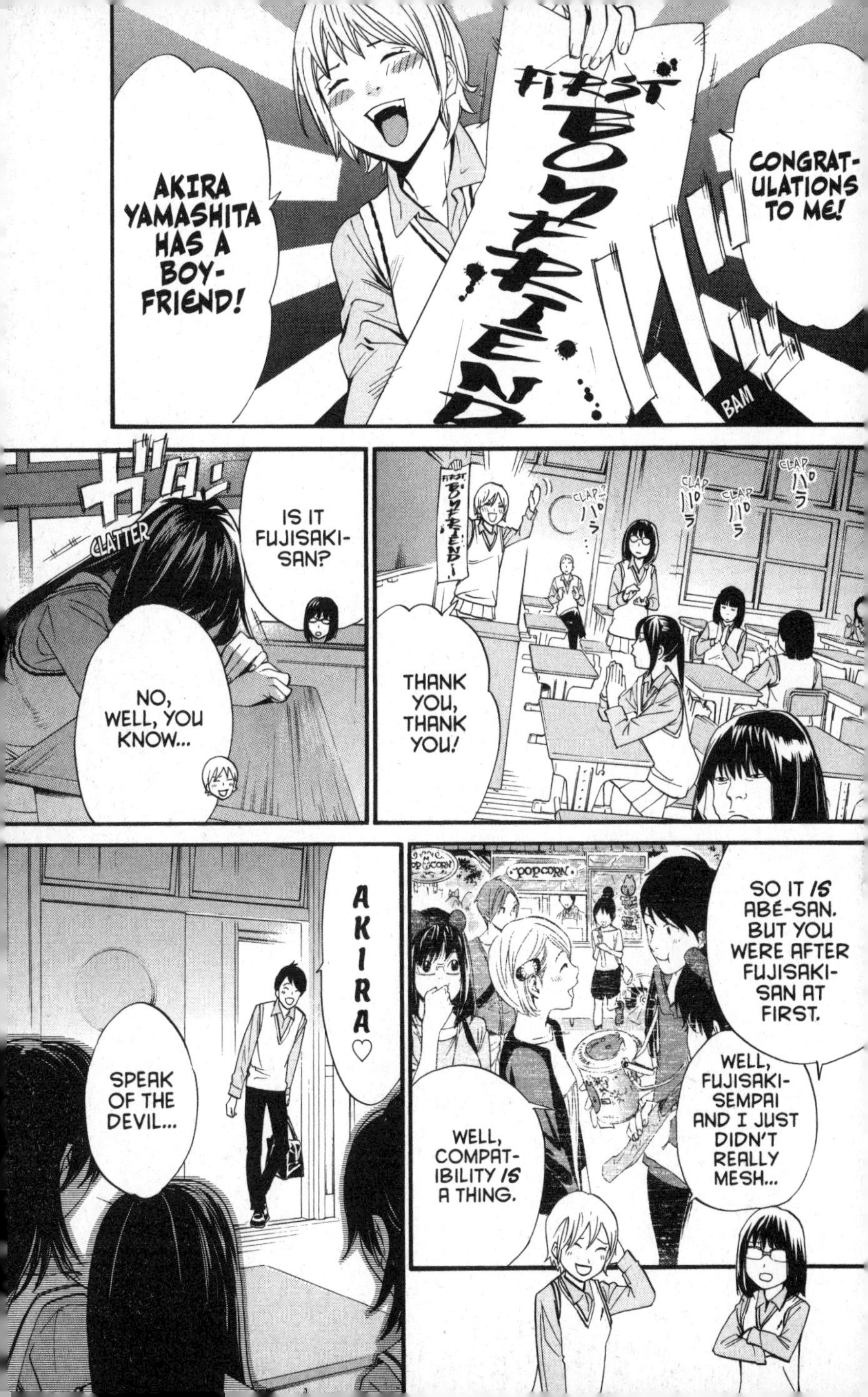
CONGRAT-ULATIONS TO ME!
FIRST BOYFRIEND
BAM
AKIRA YAMASHITA HAS A BOY-FRIEND!
CLAP CLAP CLAP CLAP
THANK YOU, THANK YOU!
FIRST BOYFRIEND
CLATTER
IS IT FUJISAKI-SAN?
NO, WELL, YOU KNOW...
SO IT *IS* ABÉ-SAN. BUT YOU WERE AFTER FUJISAKI-SAN AT FIRST.
POPCORN
WELL, FUJISAKI-SEMPAI AND I JUST DIDN'T REALLY MESH...
WELL, COMPAT-IBILITY *IS* A THING.
AKIRA♡
SPEAK OF THE DEVIL...

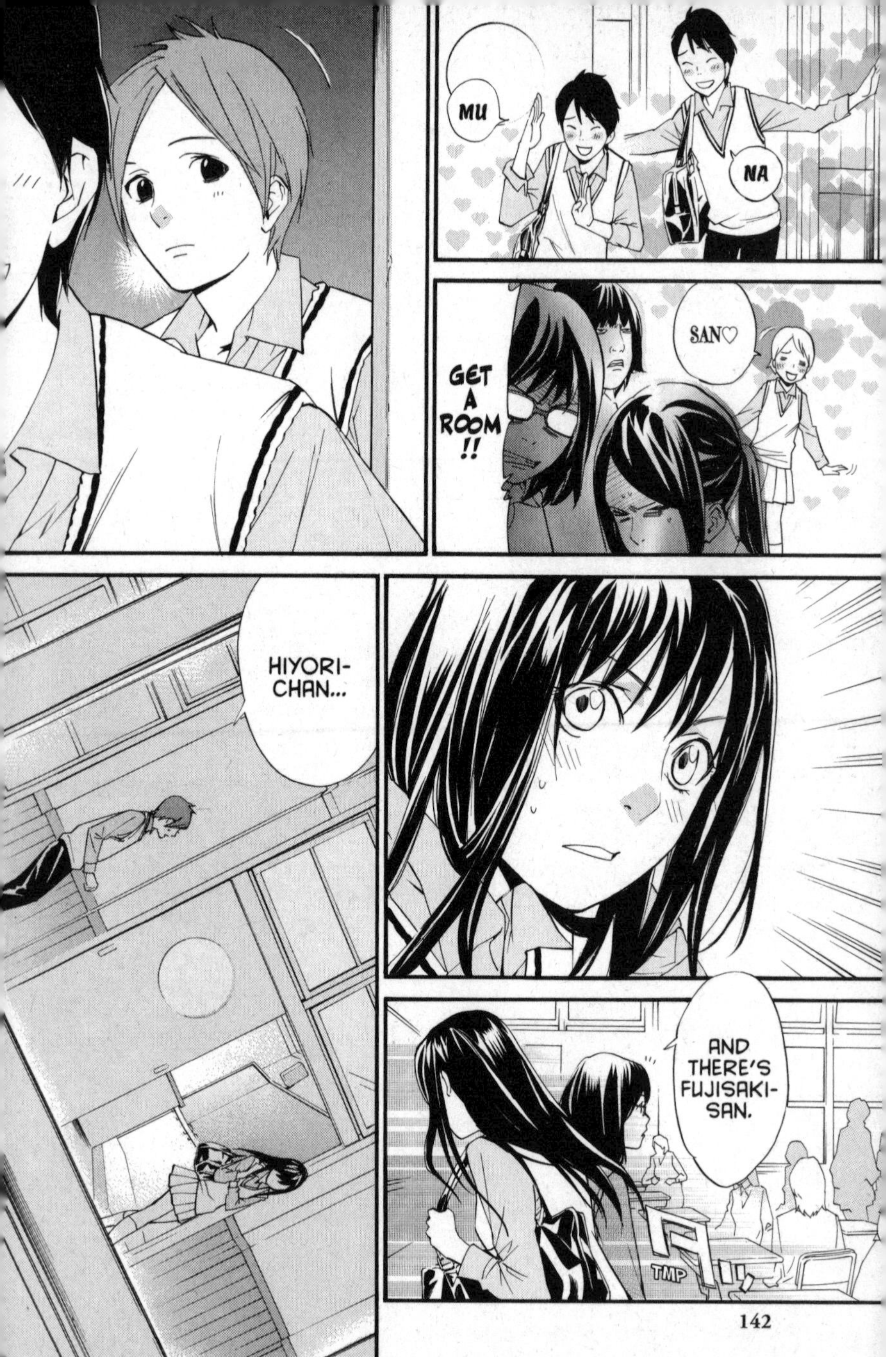
MU
NA
SAN♡
GET A ROOM!!
AND THERE'S FUJISAKI-SAN.
TMP
HIYORI-CHAN...

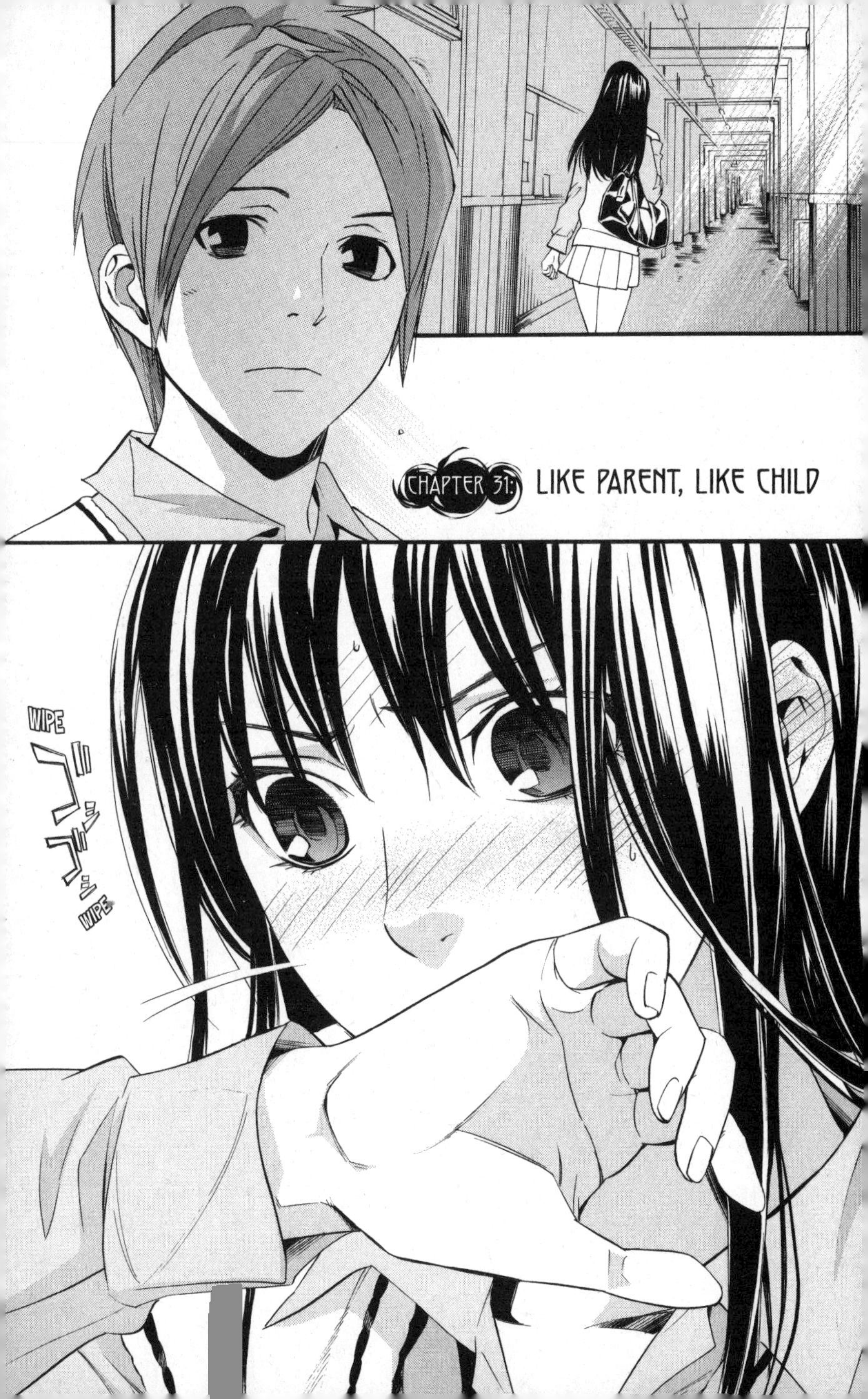
CHAPTER 31: LIKE PARENT, LIKE CHILD
WIPE
WIPE

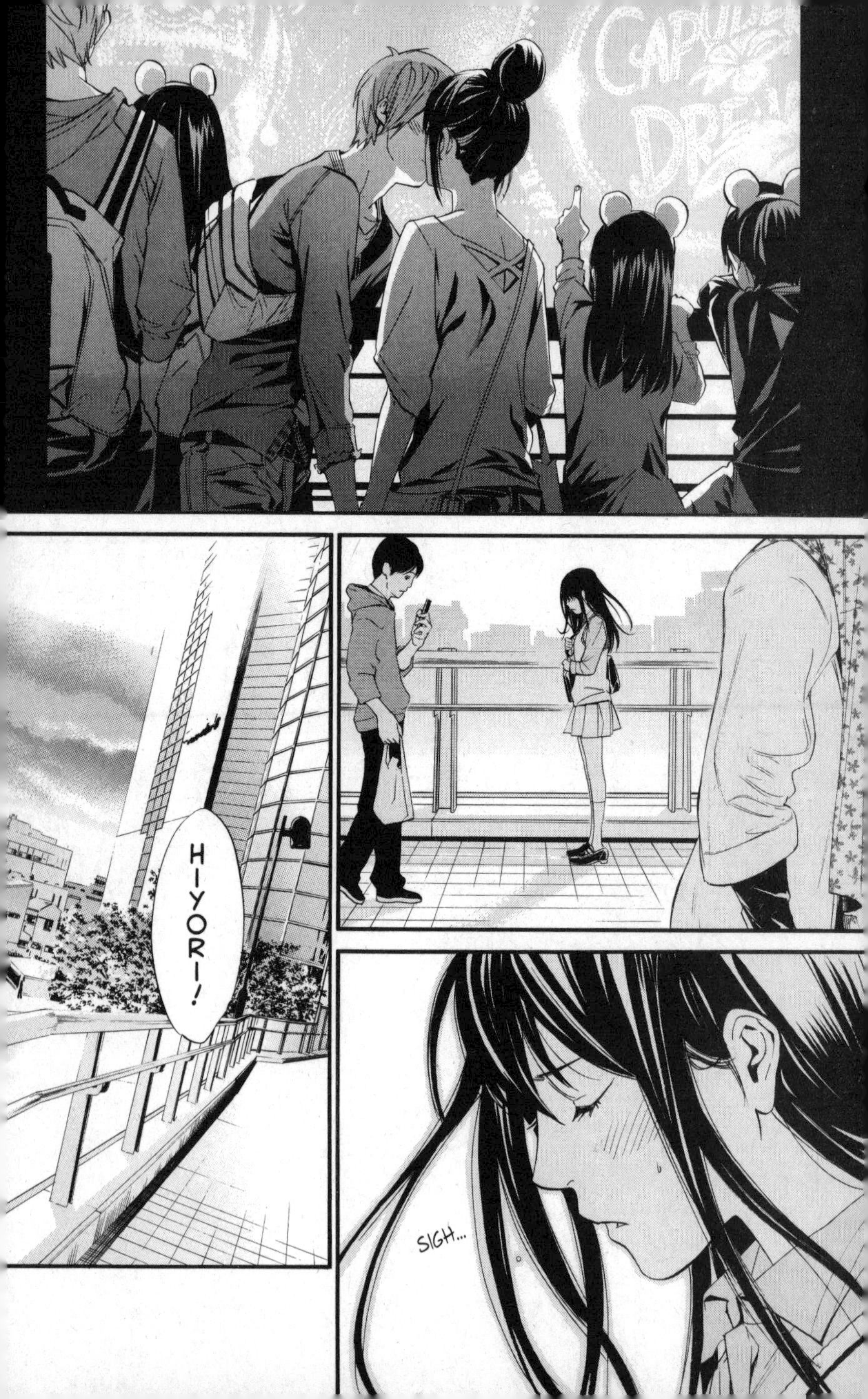
SIGH...
HIYORI!

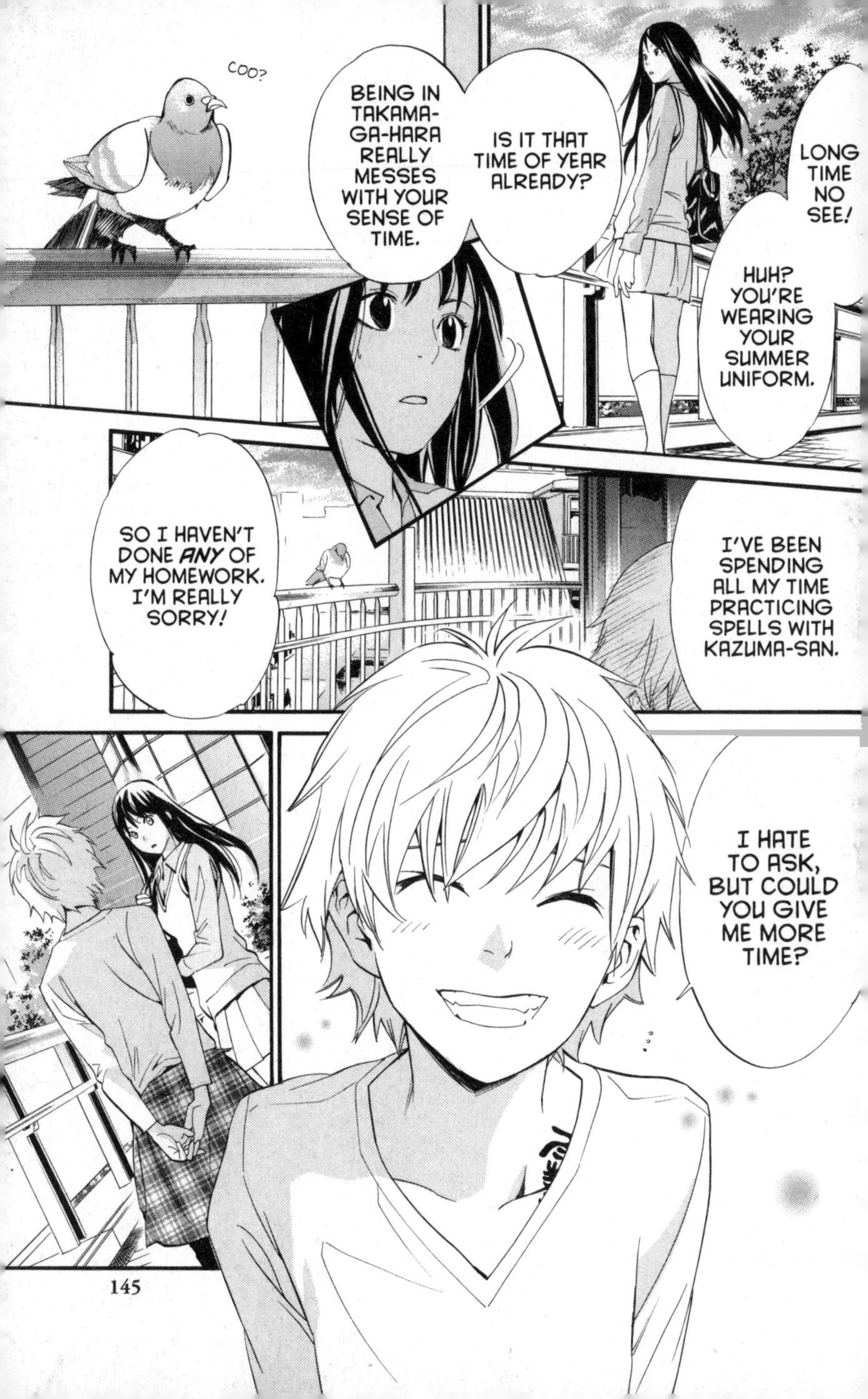
LONG TIME NO SEE!
HUH? YOU'RE WEARING YOUR SUMMER UNIFORM.
IS IT THAT TIME OF YEAR ALREADY?
BEING IN TAKAMA-GA-HARA REALLY MESSES WITH YOUR SENSE OF TIME.
COO?
I'VE BEEN SPENDING ALL MY TIME PRACTICING SPELLS WITH KAZUMA-SAN.
SO I HAVEN'T DONE *ANY* OF MY HOMEWORK. I'M REALLY SORRY!
I HATE TO ASK, BUT COULD YOU GIVE ME MORE TIME?

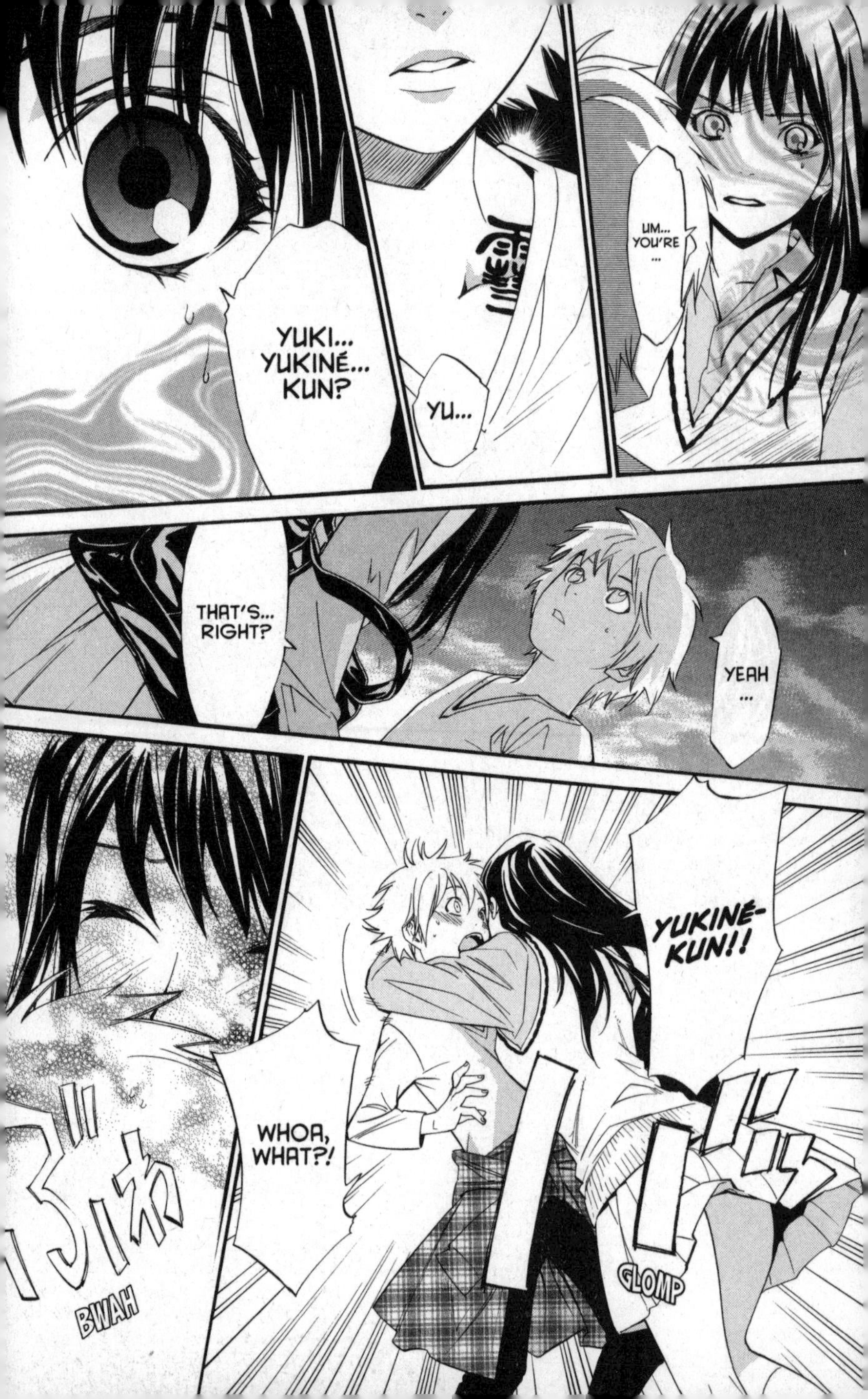
UM... YOU'RE ...
YU...
YUKI... YUKINÉ... KUN?
THAT'S... RIGHT?
YEAH ...
YUKINE-KUN!!
GLOMP
WHOA, WHAT?!
ぶわ
BWAH

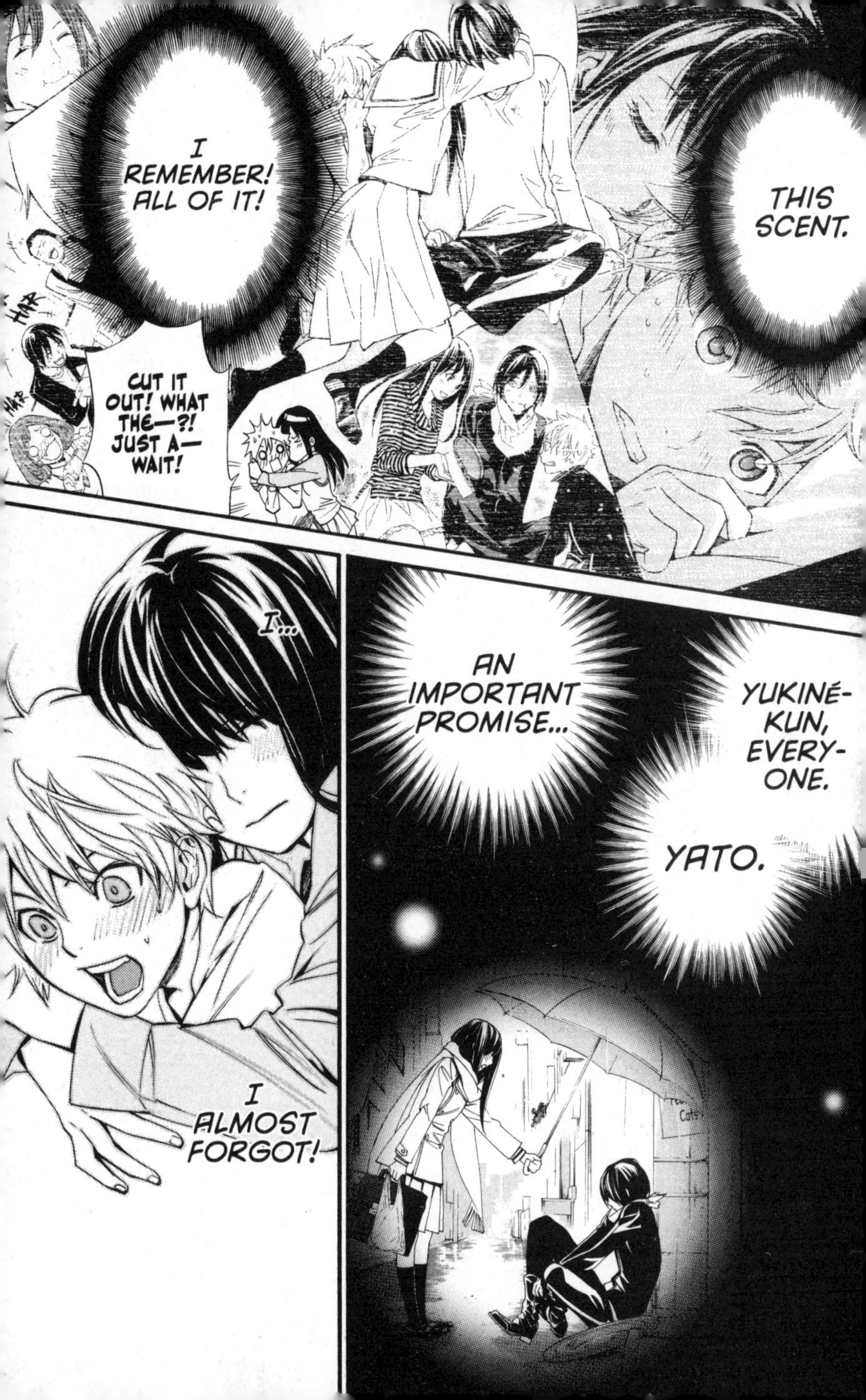
THIS SCENT.
I REMEMBER! ALL OF IT!
CUT IT OUT! WHAT THE—?! JUST A—WAIT!
HAR
HAR
YUKINÉ-KUN, EVERY-ONE.
YATO.
AN IMPORTANT PROMISE...
I...
I ALMOST FORGOT!

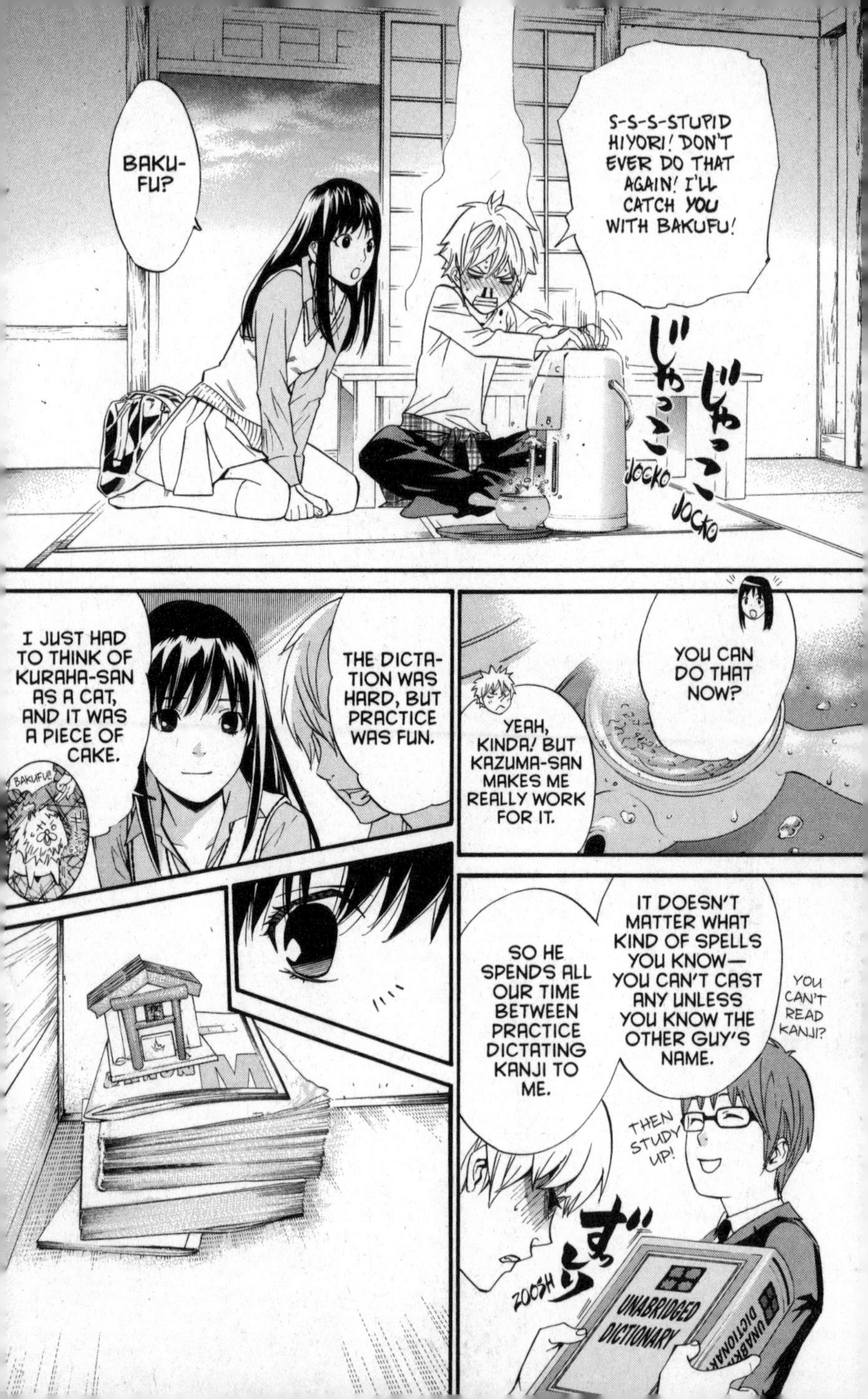
S-S-S-STUPID HIYORI! DON'T EVER DO THAT AGAIN! I'LL CATCH YOU WITH BAKUFU!
BAKU-FU?
じゃっこ JOCKO
じゃっこ JOCKO
YOU CAN DO THAT NOW?
YEAH, KINDA! BUT KAZUMA-SAN MAKES ME REALLY WORK FOR IT.
THE DICTA-TION WAS HARD, BUT PRACTICE WAS FUN.
I JUST HAD TO THINK OF KURAHA-SAN AS A CAT, AND IT WAS A PIECE OF CAKE.
BAKUFU!!
YOU CAN'T READ KANJI?
IT DOESN'T MATTER WHAT KIND OF SPELLS YOU KNOW— YOU CAN'T CAST ANY UNLESS YOU KNOW THE OTHER GUY'S NAME.
SO HE SPENDS ALL OUR TIME BETWEEN PRACTICE DICTATING KANJI TO ME.
THEN STUDY UP!
ずらっ ZOOSH
UNABRIDGED DICTIONARY

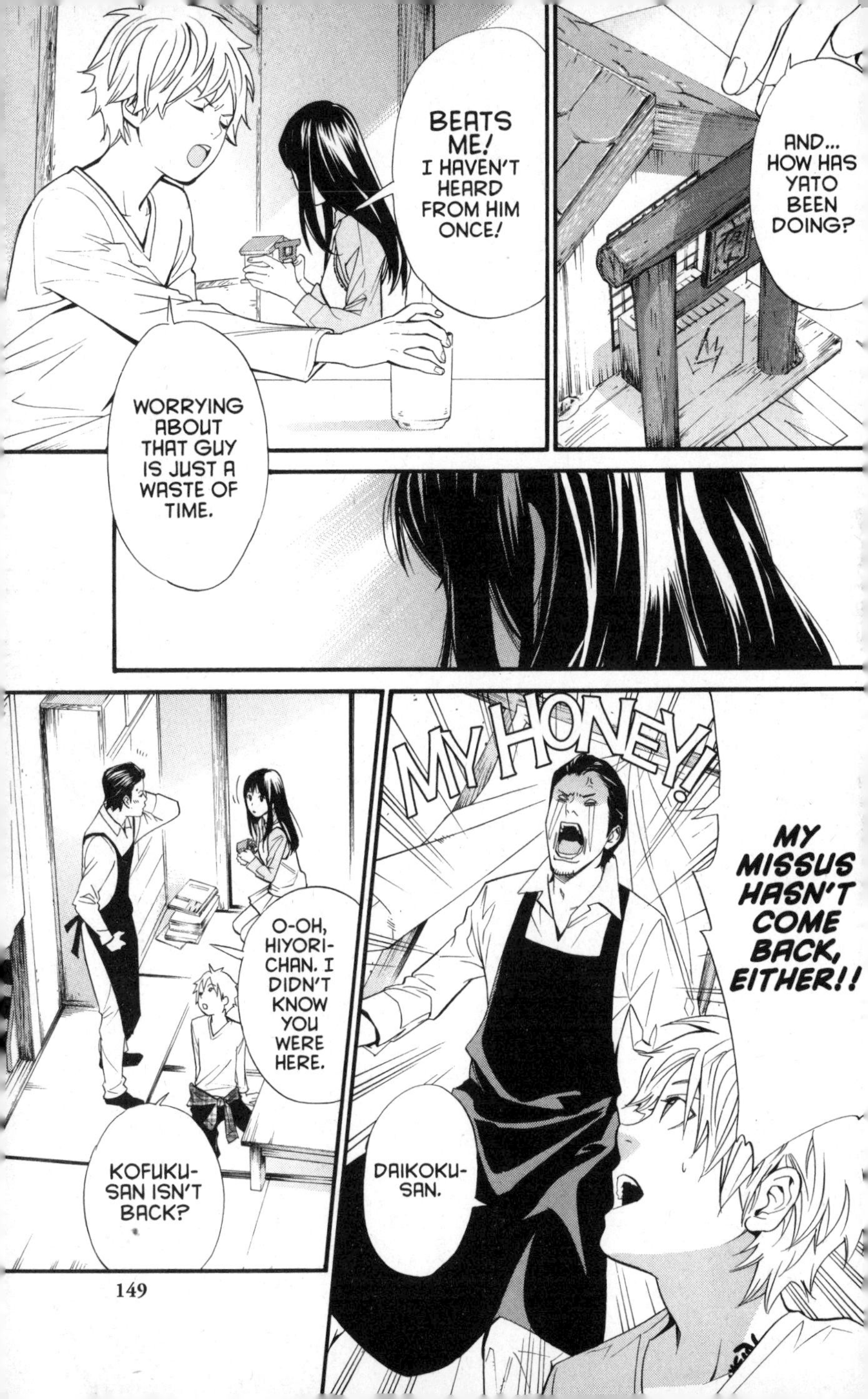
AND... HOW HAS YATO BEEN DOING?
BEATS ME! I HAVEN'T HEARD FROM HIM ONCE!
WORRYING ABOUT THAT GUY IS JUST A WASTE OF TIME.
MY HONEY!!
MY MISSUS HASN'T COME BACK, EITHER!!
DAIKOKU-SAN.
O-OH, HIYORI-CHAN. I DIDN'T KNOW YOU WERE HERE.
KOFUKU-SAN ISN'T BACK?

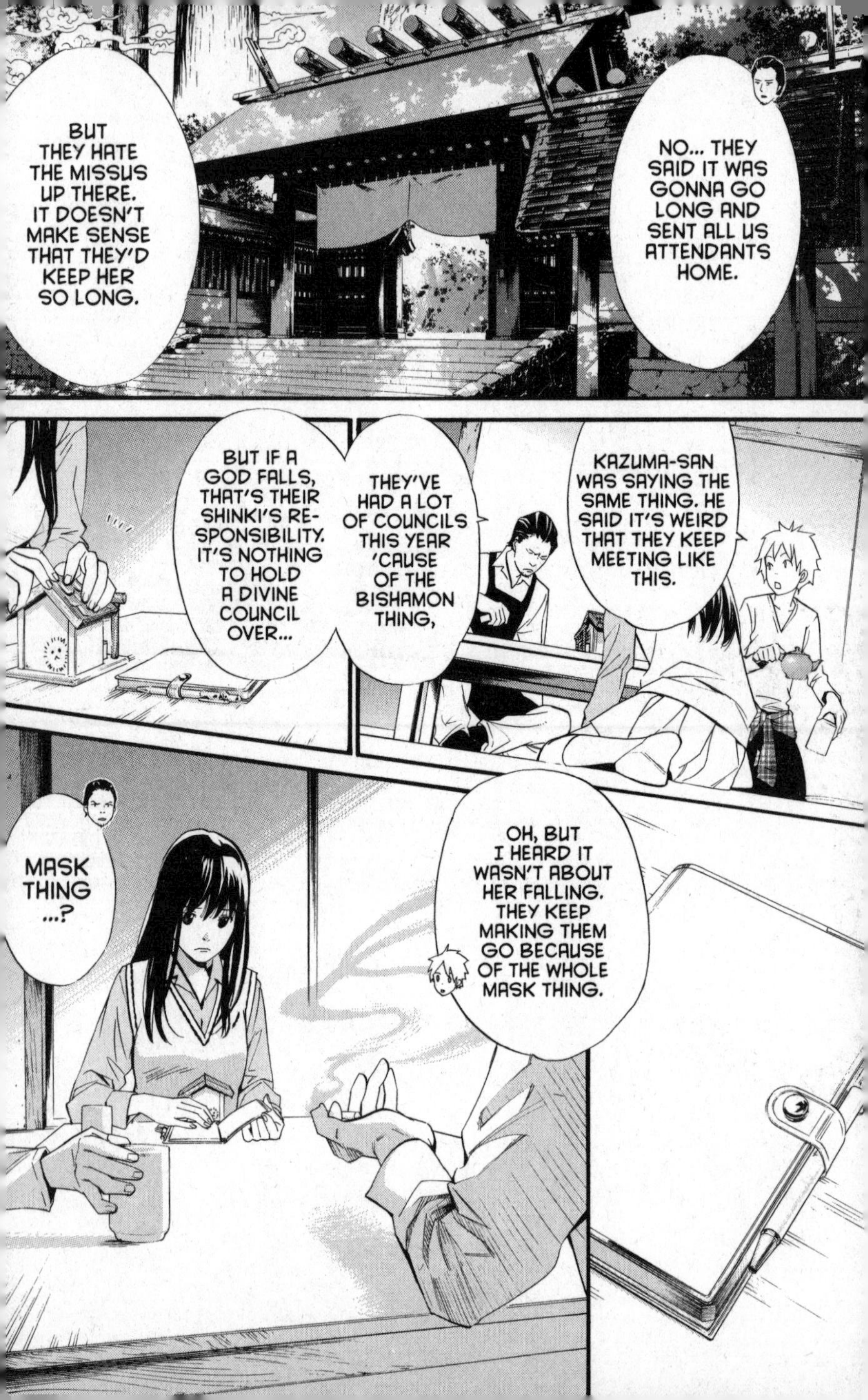
NO... THEY SAID IT WAS GONNA GO LONG AND SENT ALL US ATTENDANTS HOME.
BUT THEY HATE THE MISSUS UP THERE. IT DOESN'T MAKE SENSE THAT THEY'D KEEP HER SO LONG.
KAZUMA-SAN WAS SAYING THE SAME THING. HE SAID IT'S WEIRD THAT THEY KEEP MEETING LIKE THIS.
THEY'VE HAD A LOT OF COUNCILS THIS YEAR 'CAUSE OF THE BISHAMON THING,
BUT IF A GOD FALLS, THAT'S THEIR SHINKI'S RE-SPONSIBILITY. IT'S NOTHING TO HOLD A DIVINE COUNCIL OVER...
OH, BUT I HEARD IT WASN'T ABOUT HER FALLING. THEY KEEP MAKING THEM GO BECAUSE OF THE WHOLE MASK THING.
MASK THING ...?

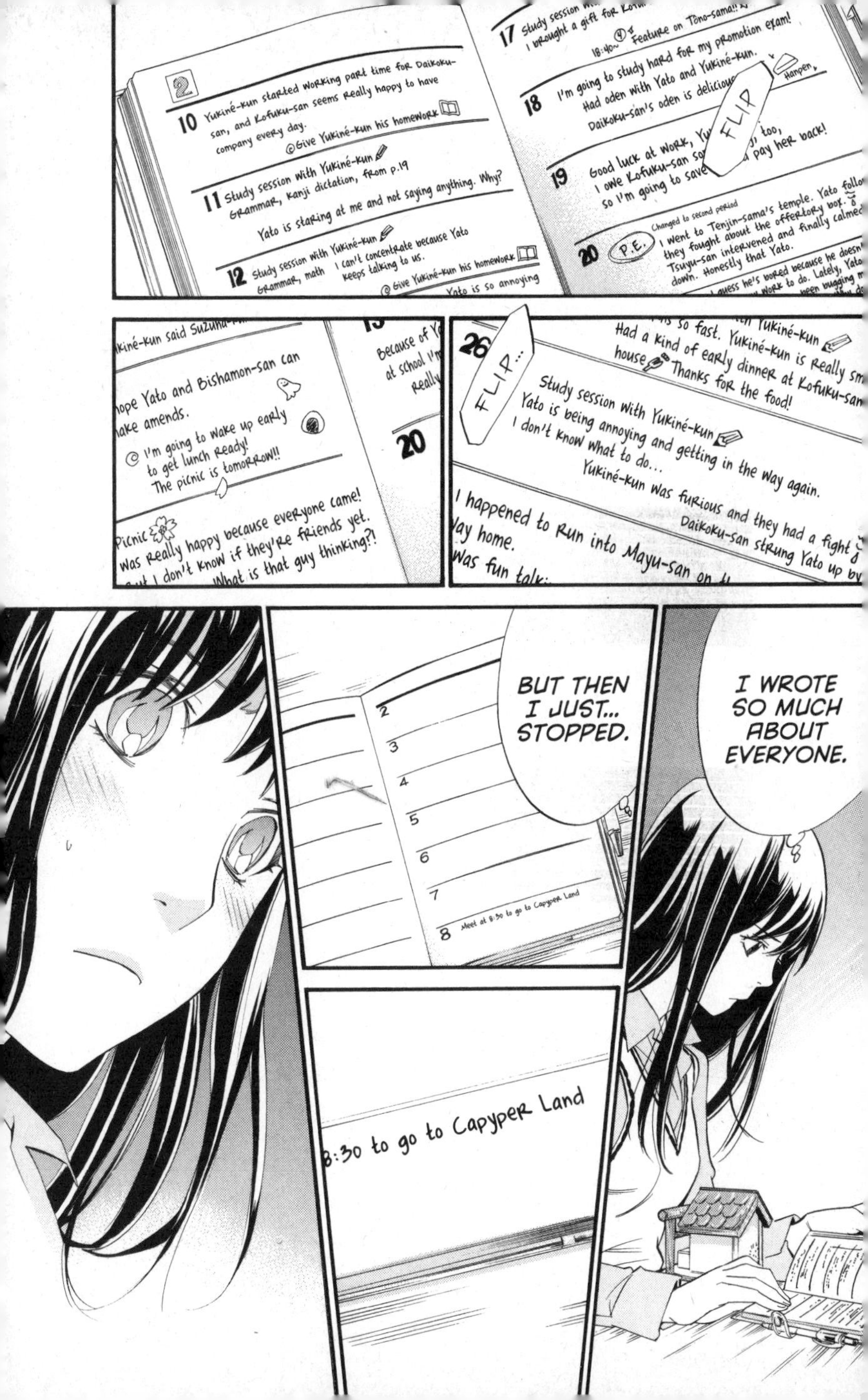
2
10 Yukiné-kun started working part time for Daikoku-san, and Kofuku-san seems really happy to have company every day.
◎Give Yukiné-kun his homework
11 Study session with Yukiné-kun
Grammar, kanji dictation, from p.19
Yato is staring at me and not saying anything. Why?
12 Study session with Yukiné-kun
Grammar, math
I can't concentrate because Yato keeps talking to us.
◎Give Yukiné-kun his homework
Yato is so annoying
17 Study session
I brought a gift for
18:40~ ④ Feature on Tōno-sama!!
I'm going to study hard for my promotion exam!
18 Had oden with Yato and Yukiné-kun.
Daikoku-san's oden is delicious
Hanpen,
FLIP
19 Good luck at work,
I owe Kofuku-san
so I'm going to save
pay her back!
Changed to second period
20 P.E.
I went to Tenjin-sama's temple. Yato
they fought about the offertory box.
Tsuyu-san intervened and finally calmed
down. Honestly that Yato.
I guess he's bored because he doesn't
have work to do.
FLIP...
26
Had a kind of early dinner at Kofuku-san's house
Thanks for the food!
Study session with Yukiné-kun
Yato is being annoying and getting in the way again.
I don't know what to do...
Yukiné-kun was furious and they had a fight
Daikoku-san strung Yato up by
I happened to run into Mayu-san on
way home.
Was fun talk
Yukiné-kun said Suzuha
hope Yato and Bishamon-san can
make amends.
◎ I'm going to wake up early to get lunch ready!
The picnic is tomorrow!!
Picnic
Was really happy because everyone came!
But I don't know if they're friends yet.
What is that guy thinking?!
Because of
at school
20
I WROTE SO MUCH ABOUT EVERYONE.
BUT THEN I JUST... STOPPED.
2
3
4
5
6
7
8 Meet at 8:30 to go to Capyper Land
8:30 to go to Capyper Land

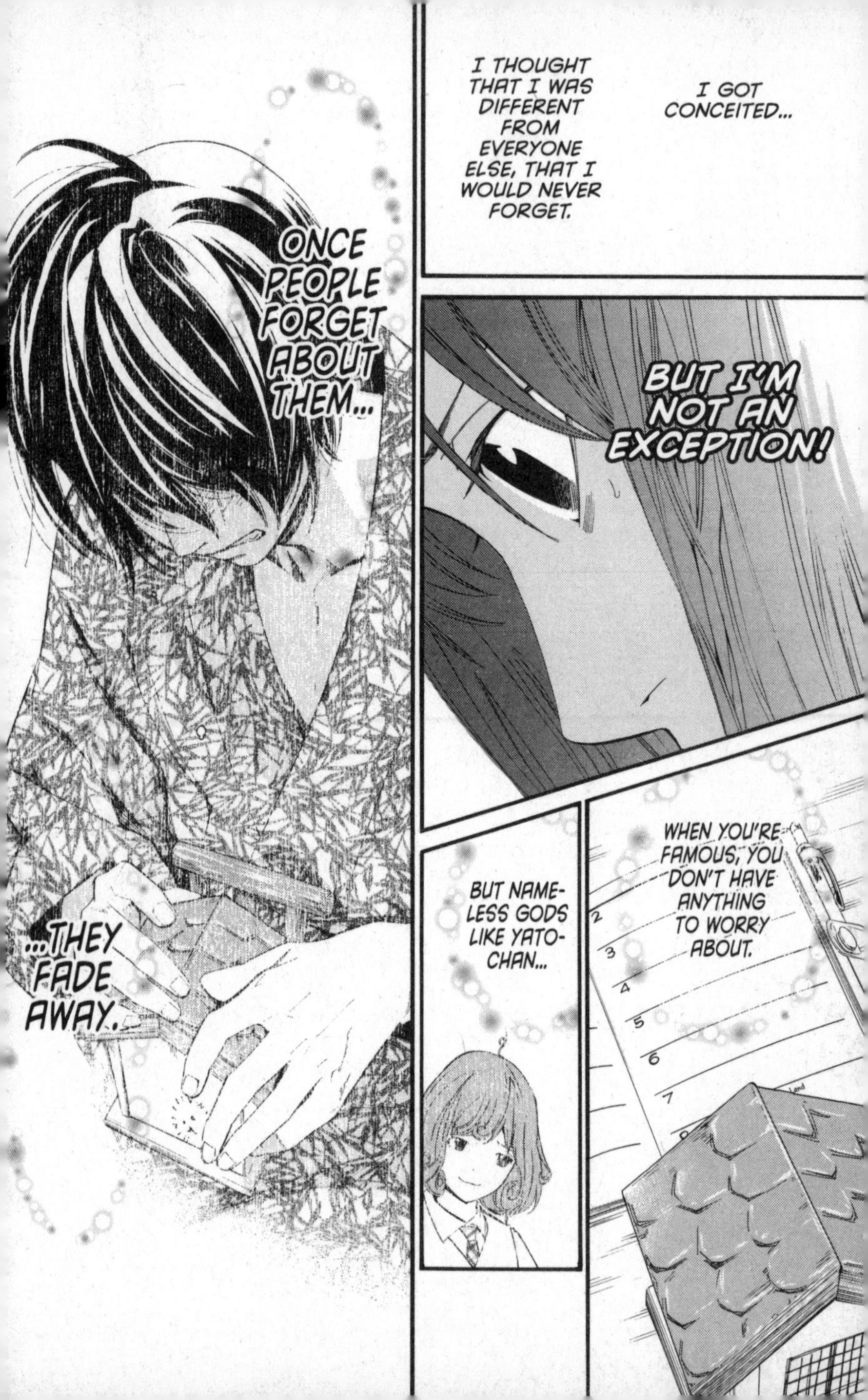
I GOT CONCEITED...
I THOUGHT THAT I WAS DIFFERENT FROM EVERYONE ELSE, THAT I WOULD NEVER FORGET.
BUT I'M NOT AN EXCEPTION!
WHEN YOU'RE FAMOUS, YOU DON'T HAVE ANYTHING TO WORRY ABOUT.
BUT NAME-LESS GODS LIKE YATO-CHAN...
ONCE PEOPLE FORGET ABOUT THEM...
...THEY FADE AWAY.

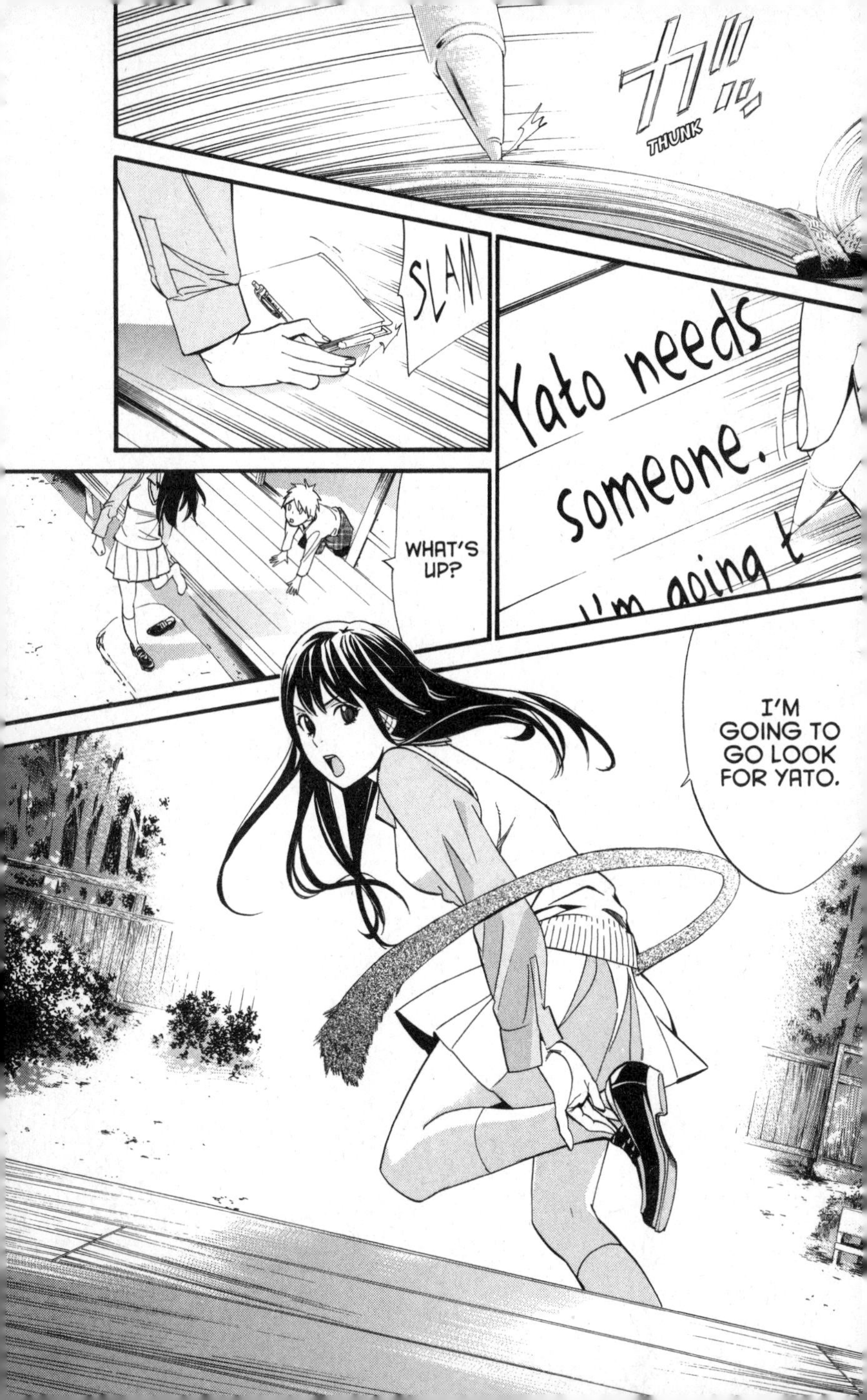
THUNK
Yato needs someone. I'm going t
SLAM
WHAT'S UP?
I'M GOING TO GO LOOK FOR YATO.

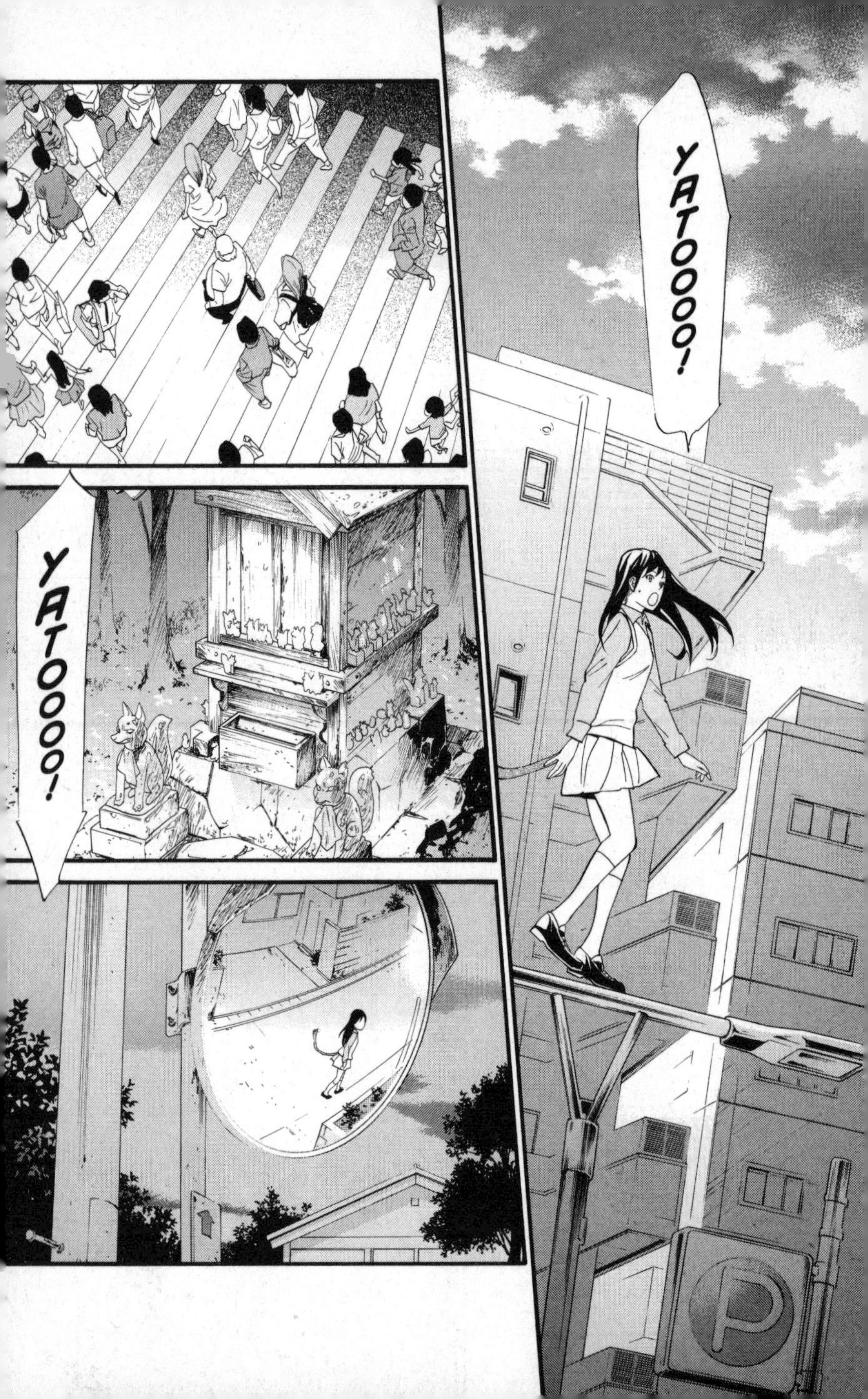
YATOOOOO!
YATOOOOO!

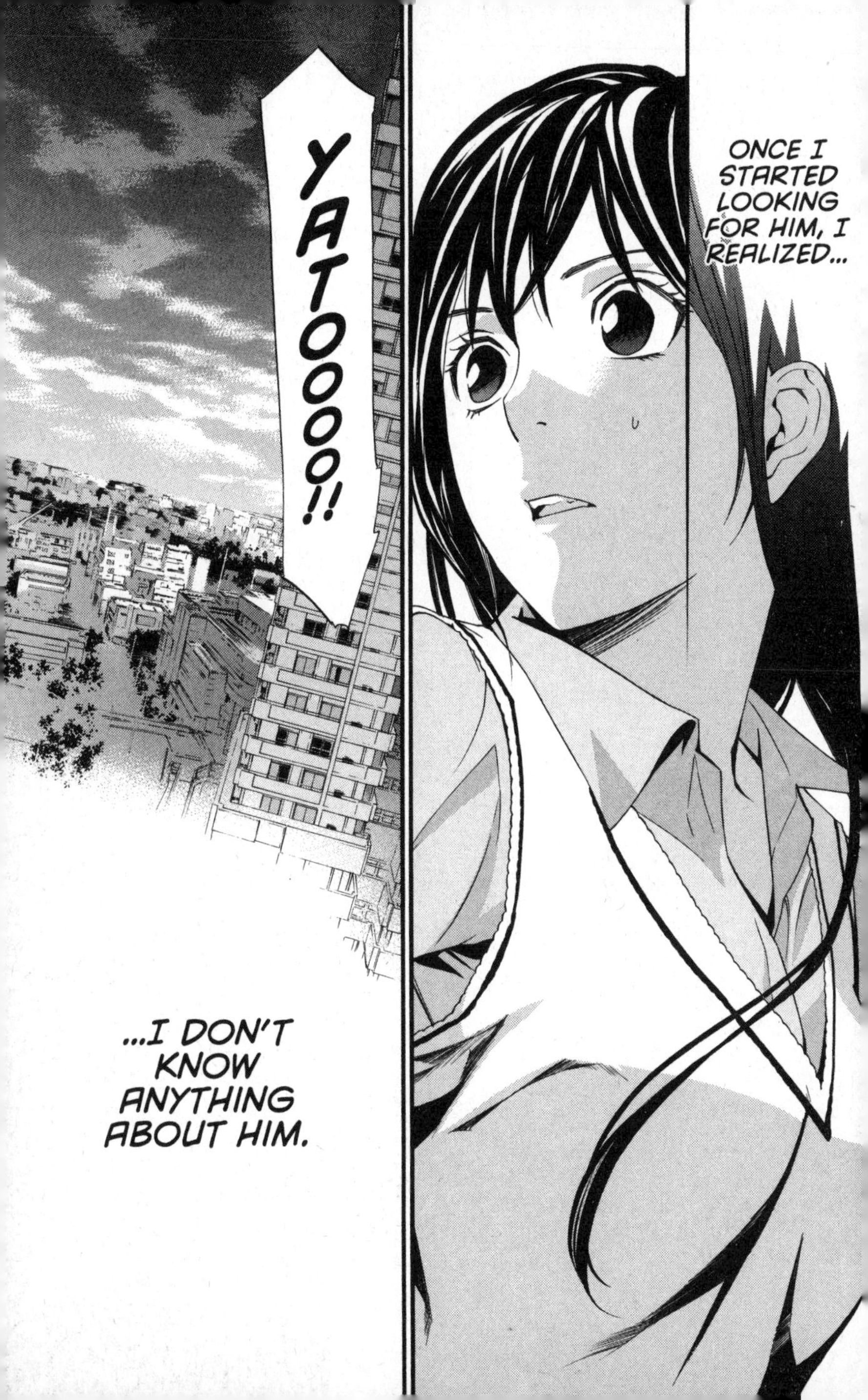
ONCE I STARTED LOOKING FOR HIM, I REALIZED...
YATOOOOO!!
...I DON'T KNOW ANYTHING ABOUT HIM.

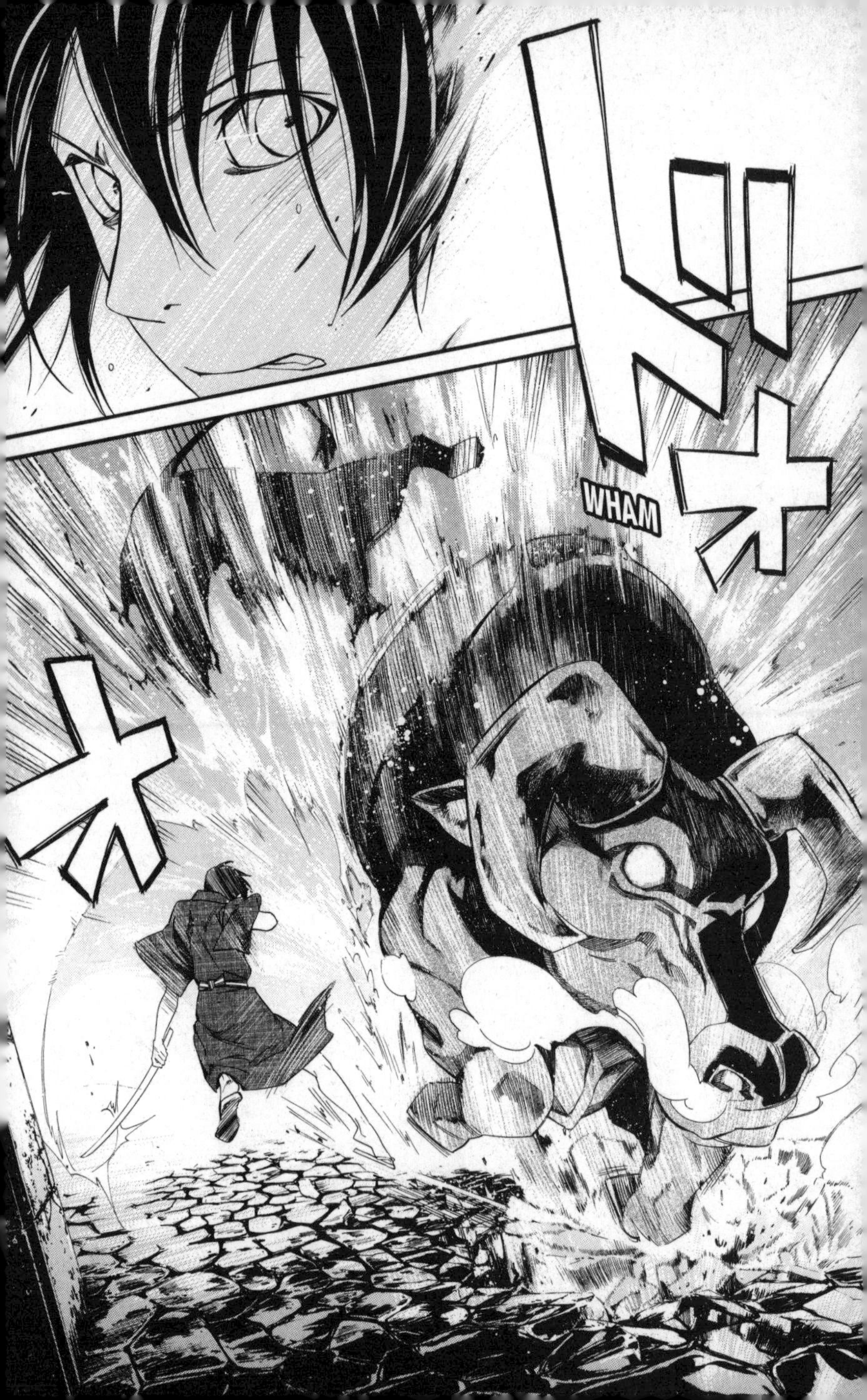
WHAM

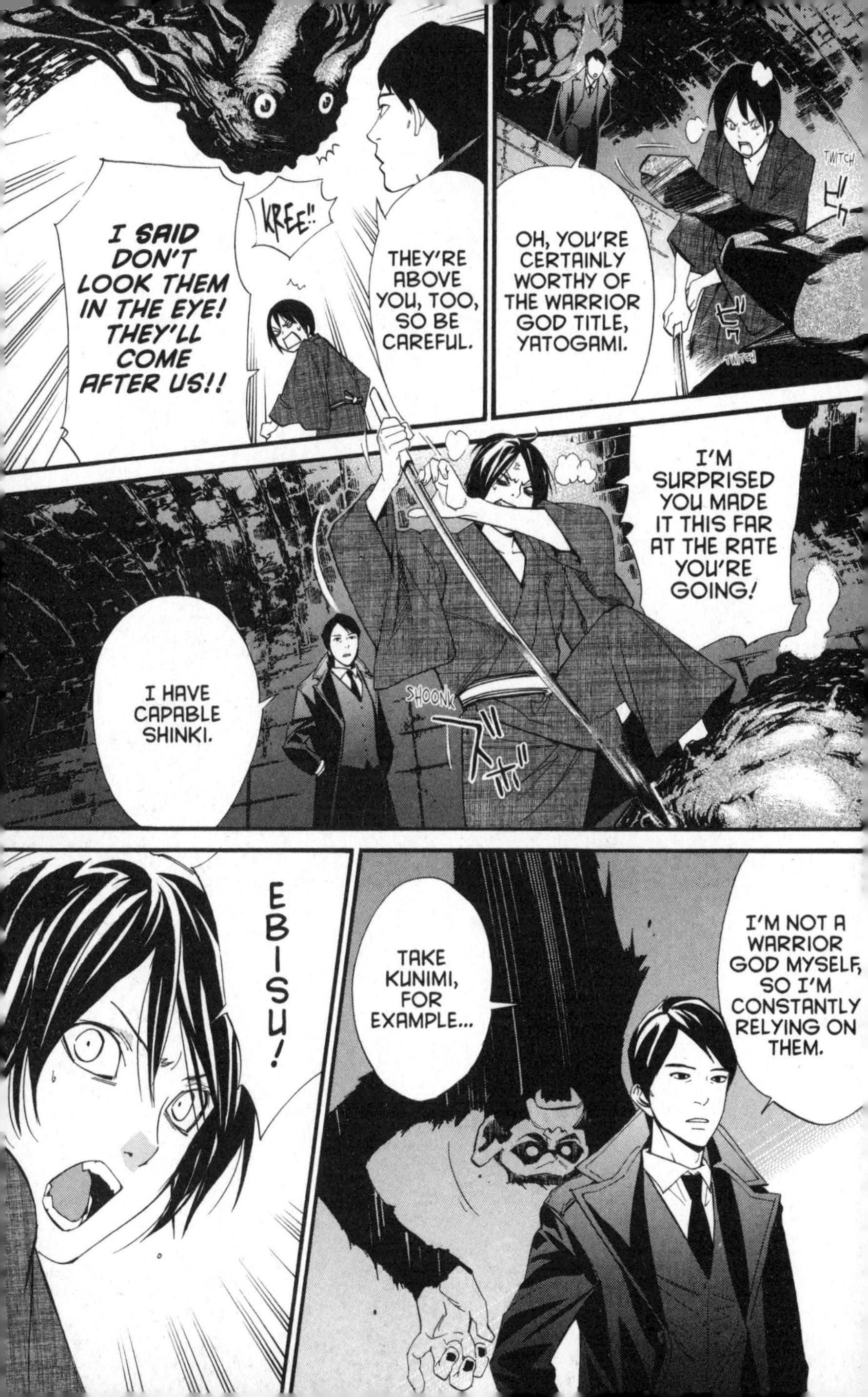

TWITCH
OH, YOU'RE CERTAINLY WORTHY OF THE WARRIOR GOD TITLE, YATOGAMI.
TWITCH
THEY'RE ABOVE YOU, TOO, SO BE CAREFUL.
KREE!!
I SAID DON'T LOOK THEM IN THE EYE! THEY'LL COME AFTER US!!
I'M SURPRISED YOU MADE IT THIS FAR AT THE RATE YOU'RE GOING!
SHOONK
I HAVE CAPABLE SHINKI.
I'M NOT A WARRIOR GOD MYSELF, SO I'M CONSTANTLY RELYING ON THEM.
TAKE KUNIMI, FOR EXAMPLE...
EBISU!

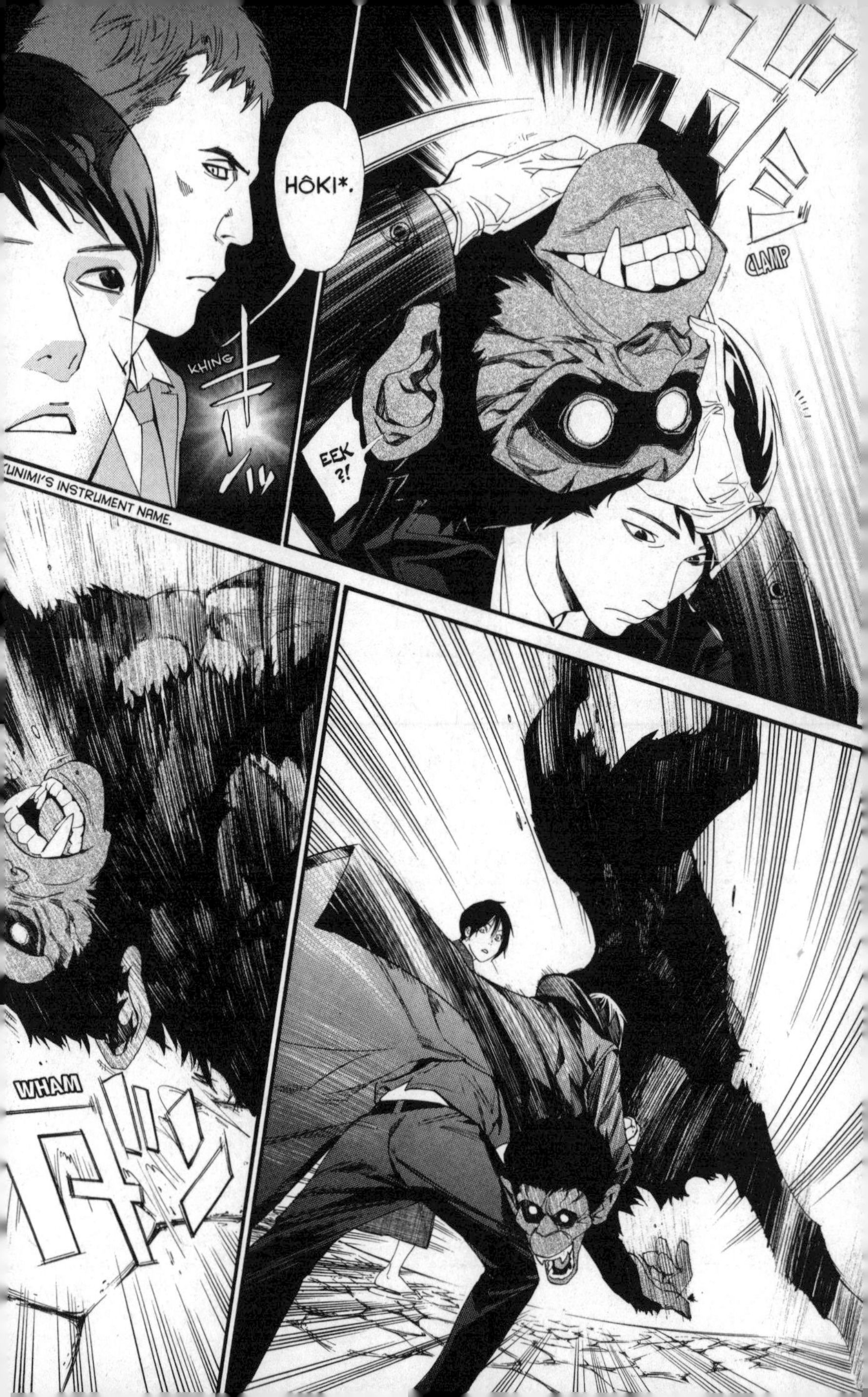
CLAMP
EEK ?!
HÔKI*.
KHING
*KUNIMI'S INSTRUMENT NAME.
WHAM

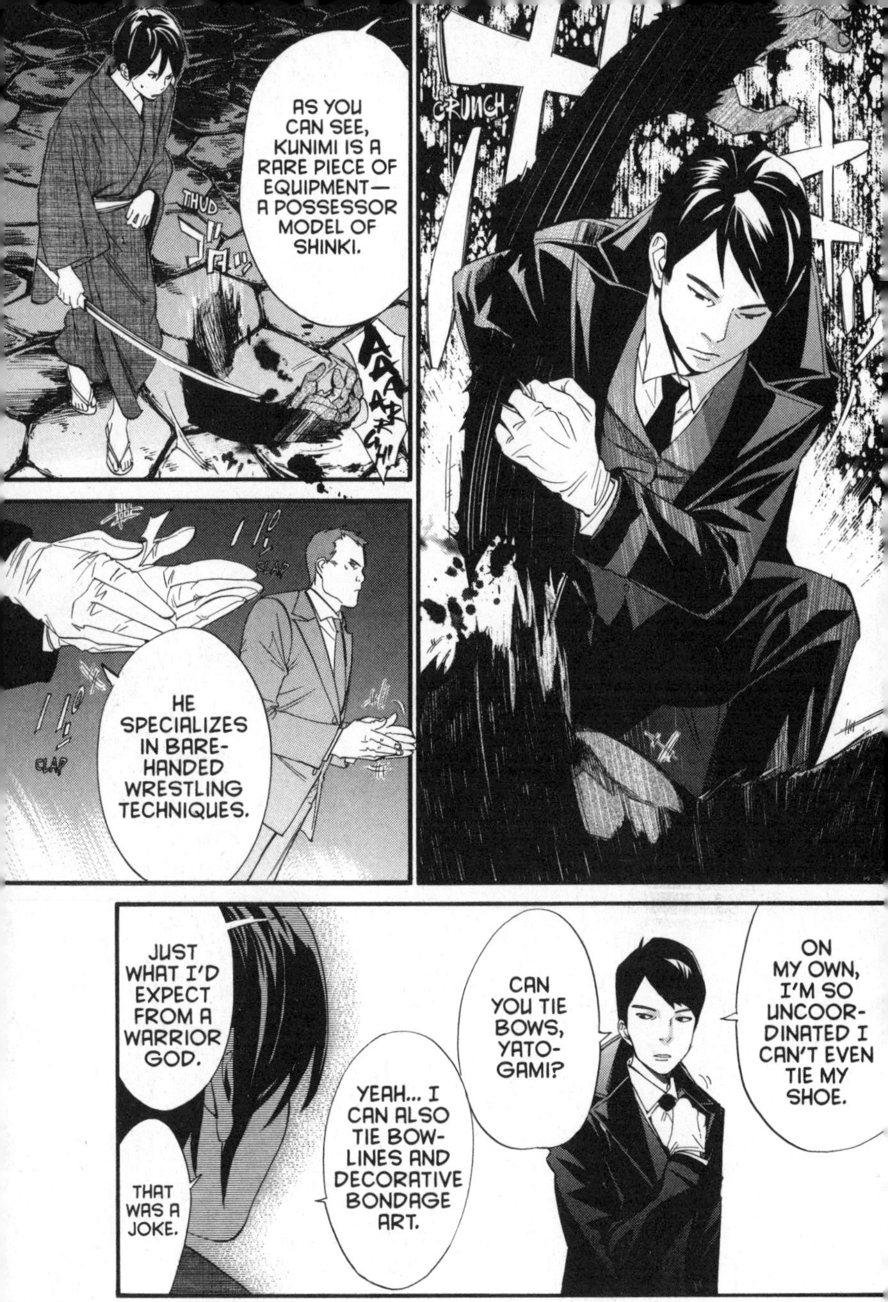
CRUNCH
AS YOU CAN SEE, KUNIMI IS A RARE PIECE OF EQUIPMENT— A POSSESSOR MODEL OF SHINKI.
THUD
AAAARRGH!
CLAP
HE SPECIALIZES IN BARE-HANDED WRESTLING TECHNIQUES.
CLAP
ON MY OWN, I'M SO UNCOOR-DINATED I CAN'T EVEN TIE MY SHOE.
CAN YOU TIE BOWS, YATO-GAMI?
YEAH... I CAN ALSO TIE BOW-LINES AND DECORATIVE BONDAGE ART.
JUST WHAT I'D EXPECT FROM A WARRIOR GOD.
THAT WAS A JOKE.

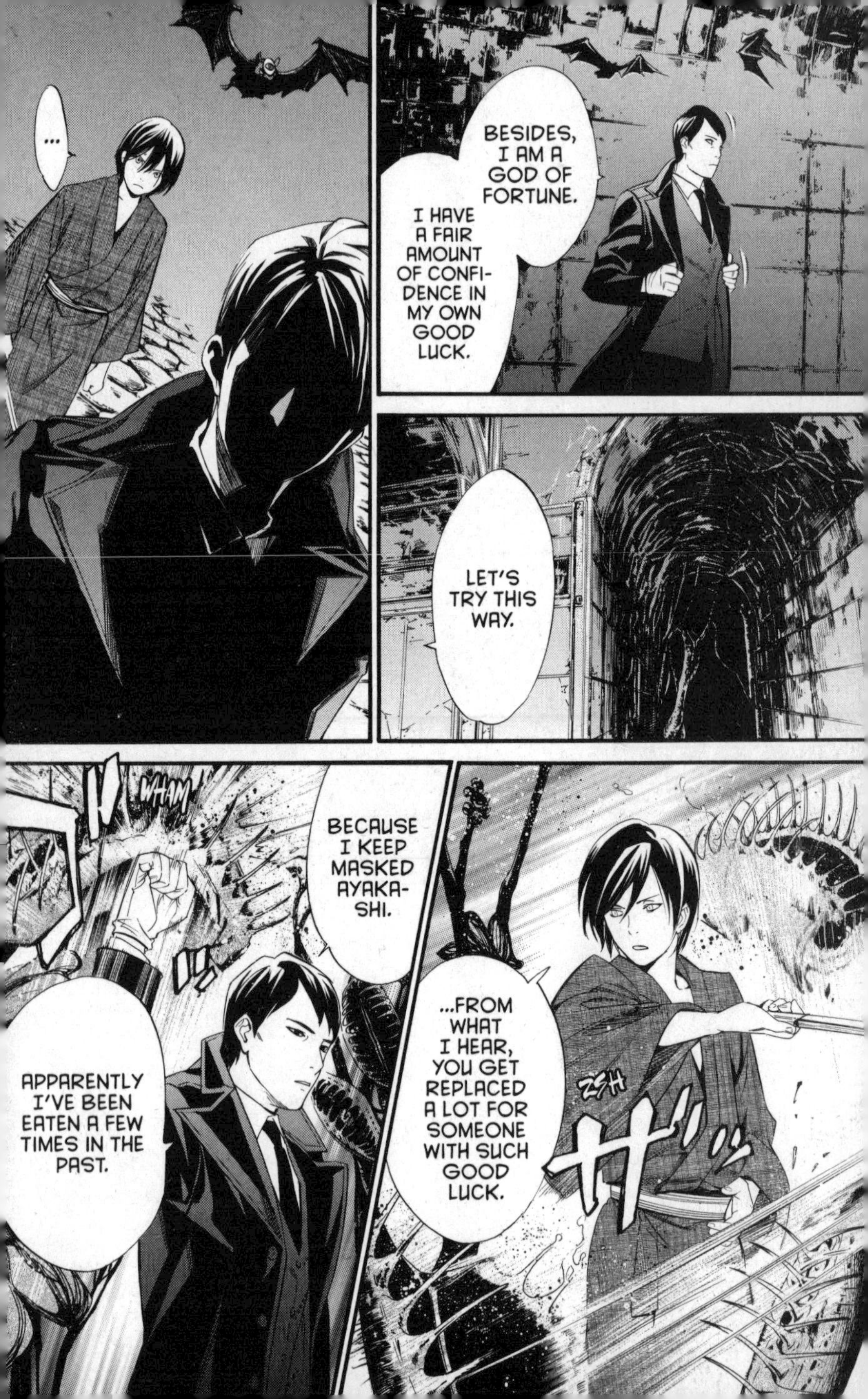
BESIDES, I AM A GOD OF FORTUNE.
I HAVE A FAIR AMOUNT OF CONFIDENCE IN MY OWN GOOD LUCK.
LET'S TRY THIS WAY.
...
...FROM WHAT I HEAR, YOU GET REPLACED A LOT FOR SOMEONE WITH SUCH GOOD LUCK.
ZSH
WHAM
BECAUSE I KEEP MASKED AYAKA-SHI.
APPARENTLY I'VE BEEN EATEN A FEW TIMES IN THE PAST.

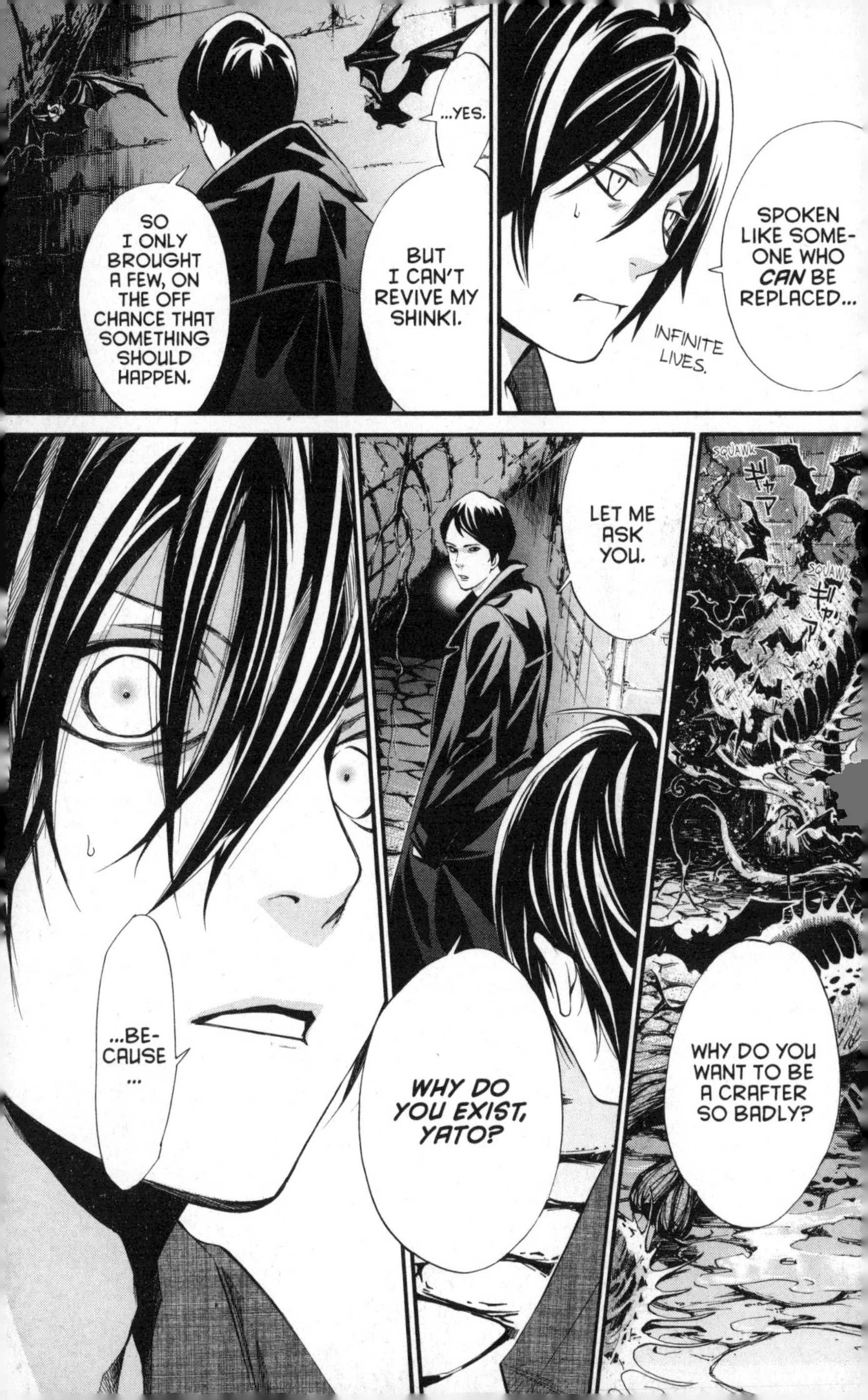
SPOKEN LIKE SOME-ONE WHO *CAN* BE REPLACED...
INFINITE LIVES.
...YES.
BUT I CAN'T REVIVE MY SHINKI.
SO I ONLY BROUGHT A FEW, ON THE OFF CHANCE THAT SOMETHING SHOULD HAPPEN.
SQUAWK
ギャア
SQUAWK
ギャア
WHY DO YOU WANT TO BE A CRAFTER SO BADLY?
LET ME ASK YOU.
WHY DO YOU EXIST, YATO?
...BE-CAUSE ...

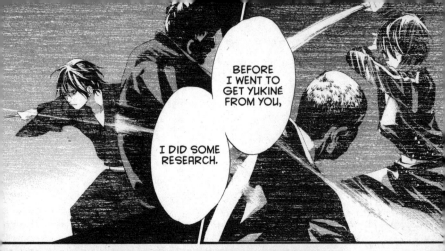

BEFORE I WENT TO GET YUKINÉ FROM YOU,
I DID SOME RESEARCH.
FORMALLY, YOU ARE KNOWN AS A WAR GOD.
BUT SOME SOURCES CALL YOU A GOD OF CALAMITY.
IT GOES WITHOUT SAYING THAT YOU HAVE NO SHRINE, BUT YOU WEREN'T REGISTERED IN THE HEAVENS, EITHER.
THE ONLY MENTION OF YOUR NAME WAS IN A FEW ORAL TRADITIONS
AND YOUR OWN SOCIAL MEDIA PROFILES.
MURMUR
SOCIAL MEDIA?
SOCIAL MEDIA?!
YOU COULD DISAPPEAR AT ANY MOMENT. WHAT KIND OF WORK HAS BEEN KEEPING YOU...

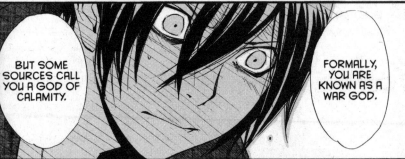

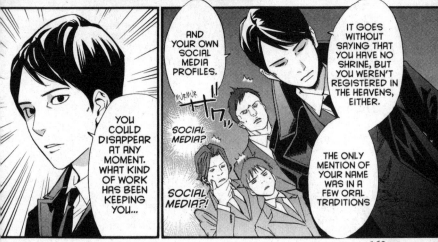

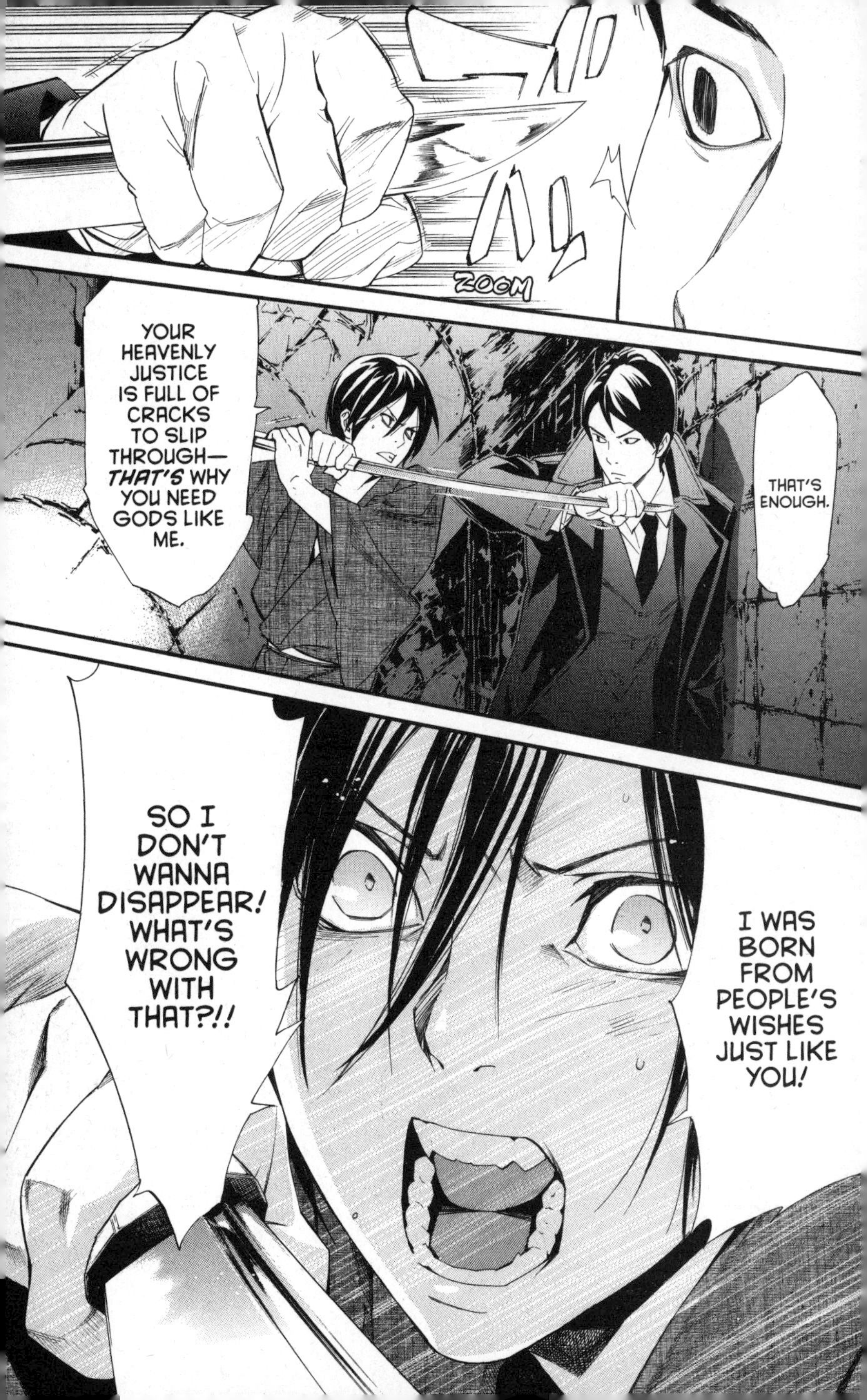

ZOOM
THAT'S ENOUGH.
YOUR HEAVENLY JUSTICE IS FULL OF CRACKS TO SLIP THROUGH—*THAT'S* WHY YOU NEED GODS LIKE ME.
I WAS BORN FROM PEOPLE'S WISHES JUST LIKE YOU!
SO I DON'T WANNA DISAPPEAR! WHAT'S WRONG WITH THAT?!!

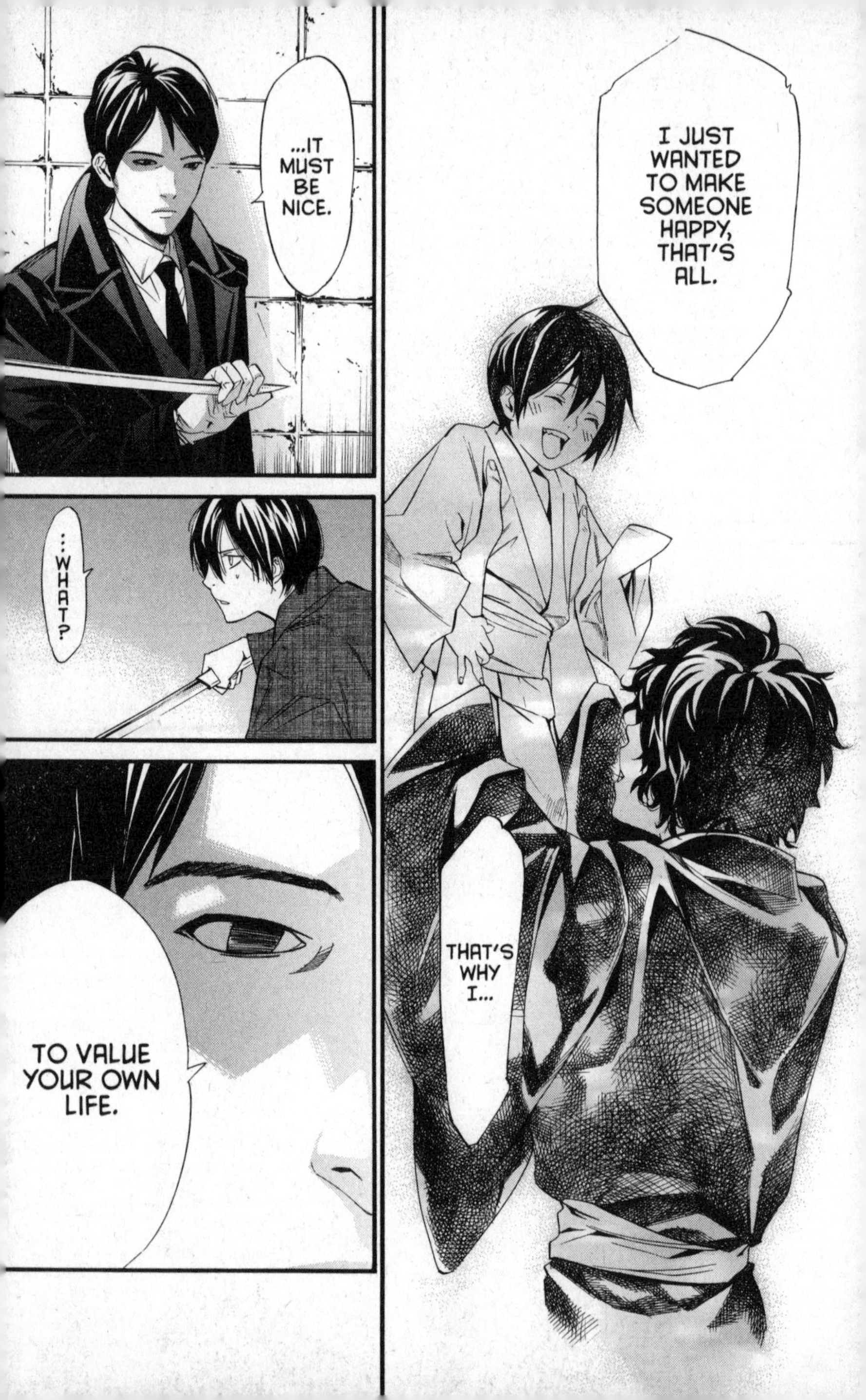
I JUST WANTED TO MAKE SOMEONE HAPPY, THAT'S ALL.
THAT'S WHY I...
...IT MUST BE NICE.
...WHAT?
TO VALUE YOUR OWN LIFE.

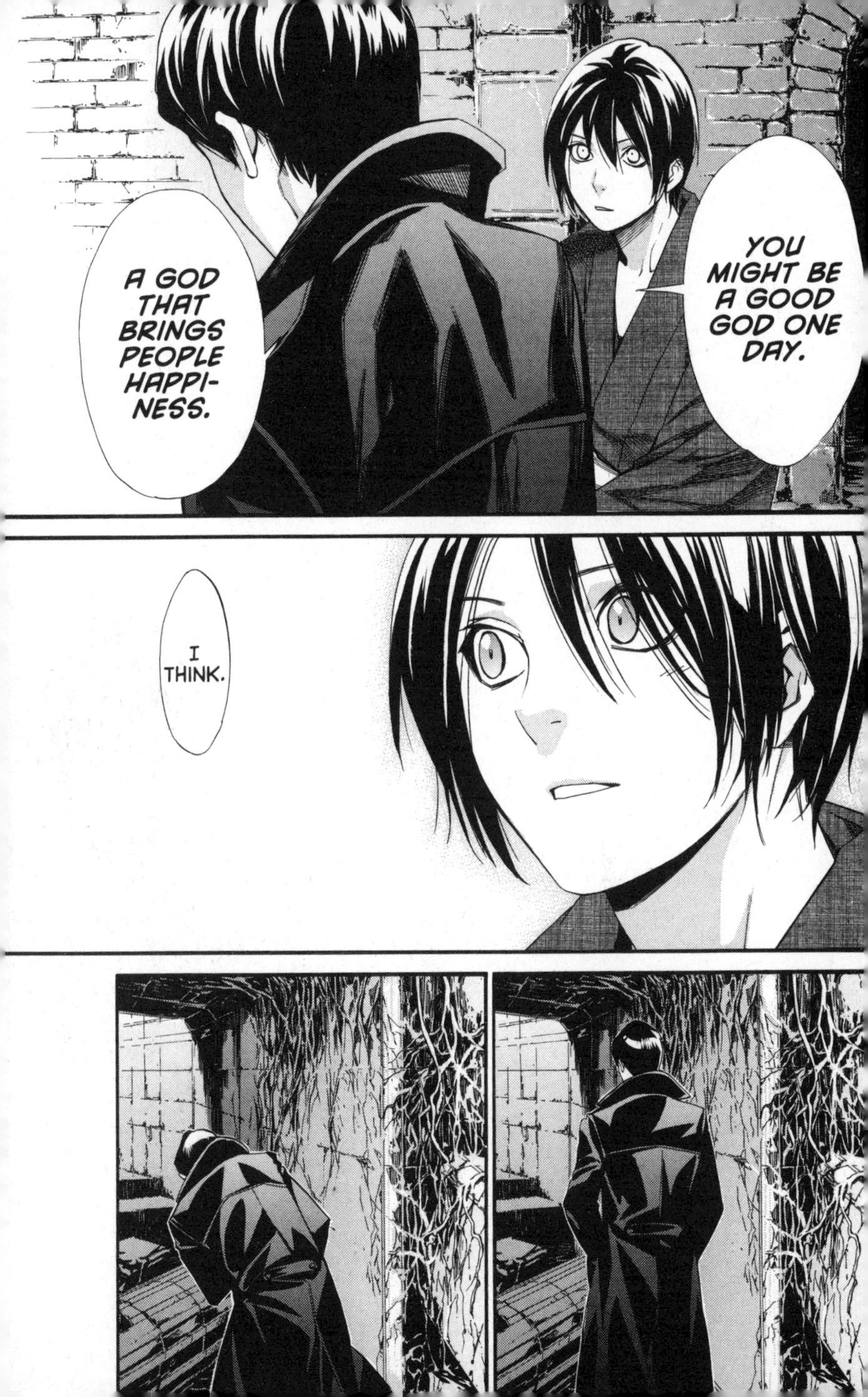
YOU MIGHT BE A GOOD GOD ONE DAY.
A GOD THAT BRINGS PEOPLE HAPPINESS.
I THINK.

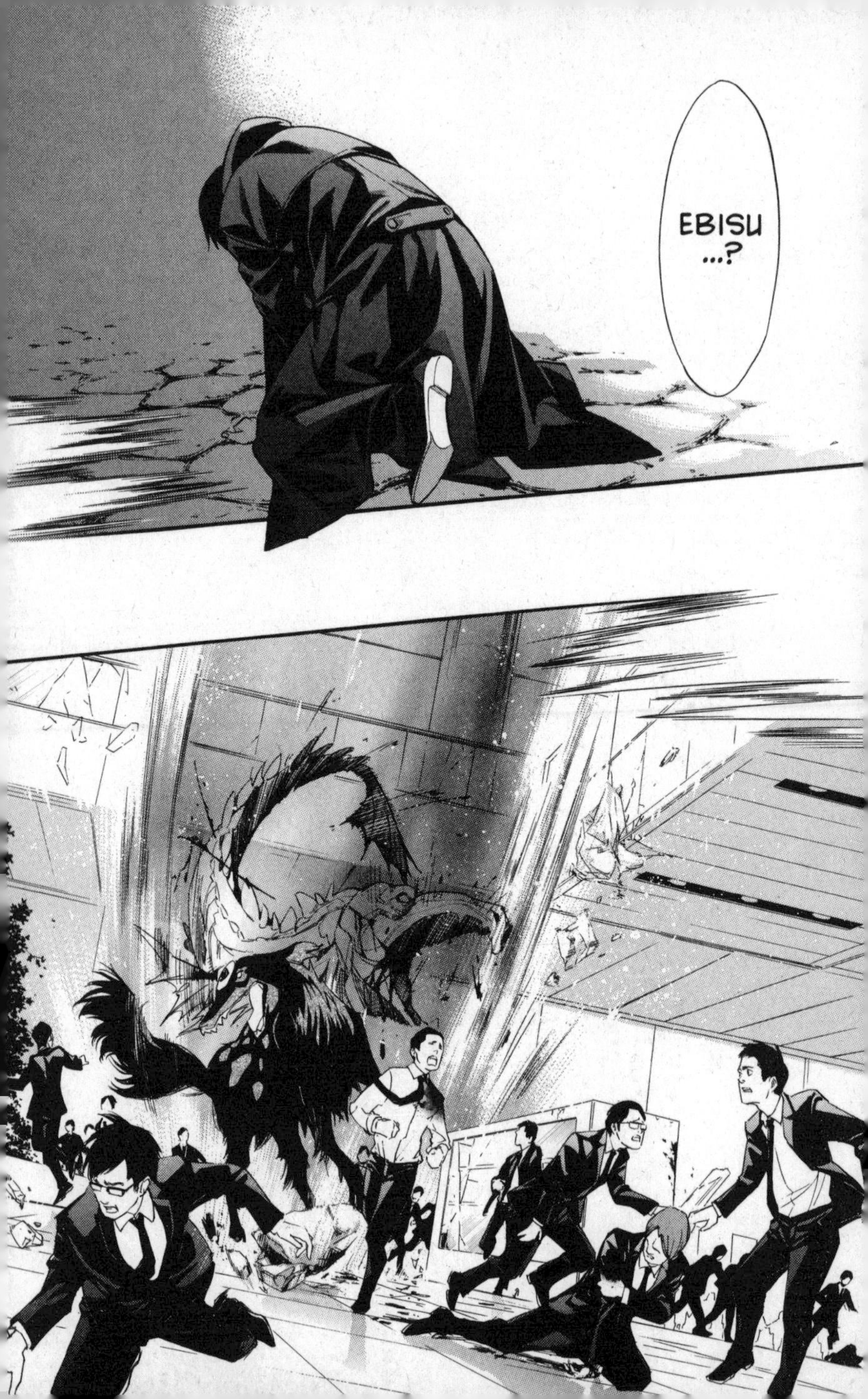
EBISU
...?

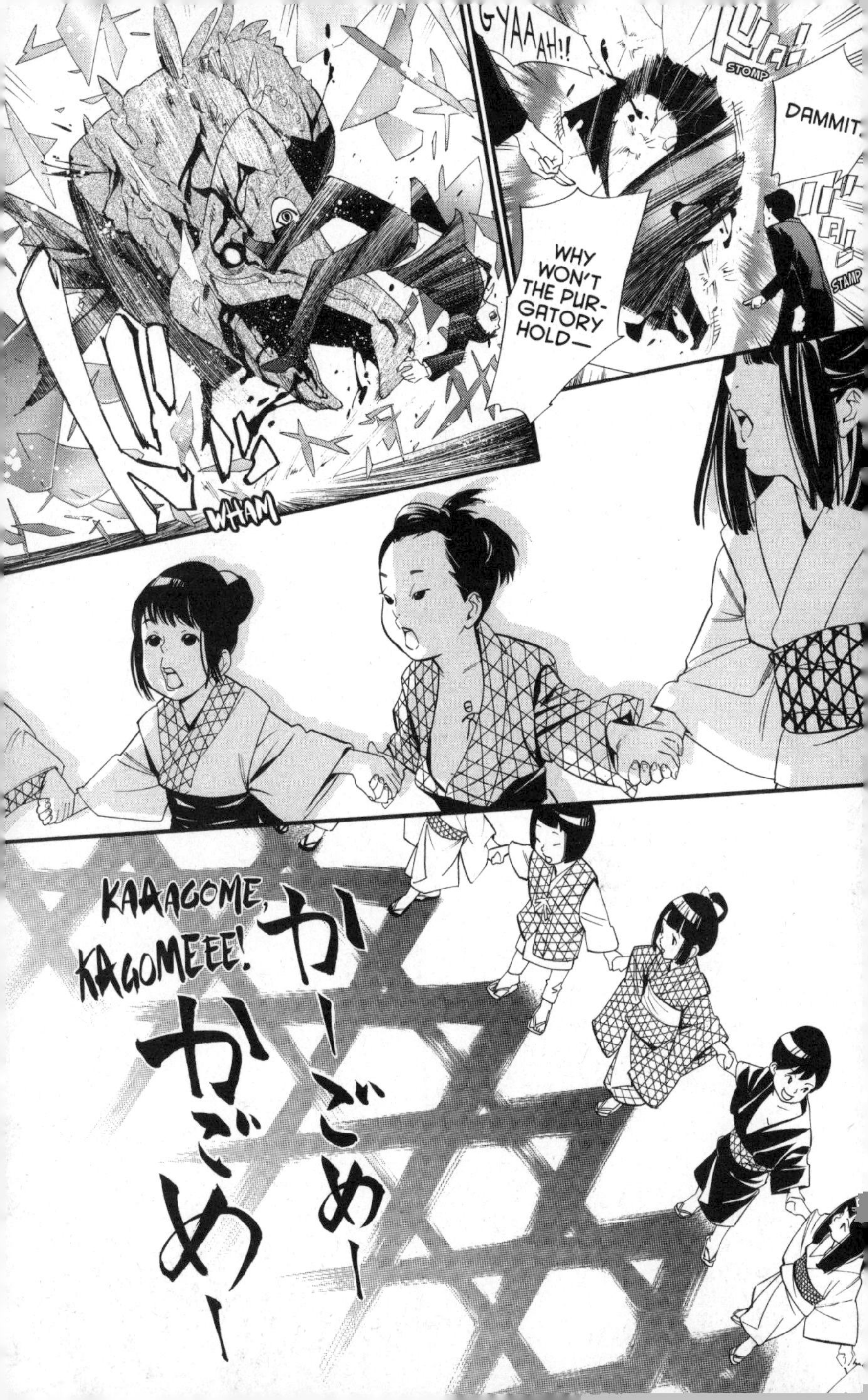
STOMP
DAMMIT
STAMP
GYAAAH!!
WHY WON'T THE PURGATORY HOLD—
WHAM
KAAAGOME, KAGOMEEE!
かーごめー
かごめー

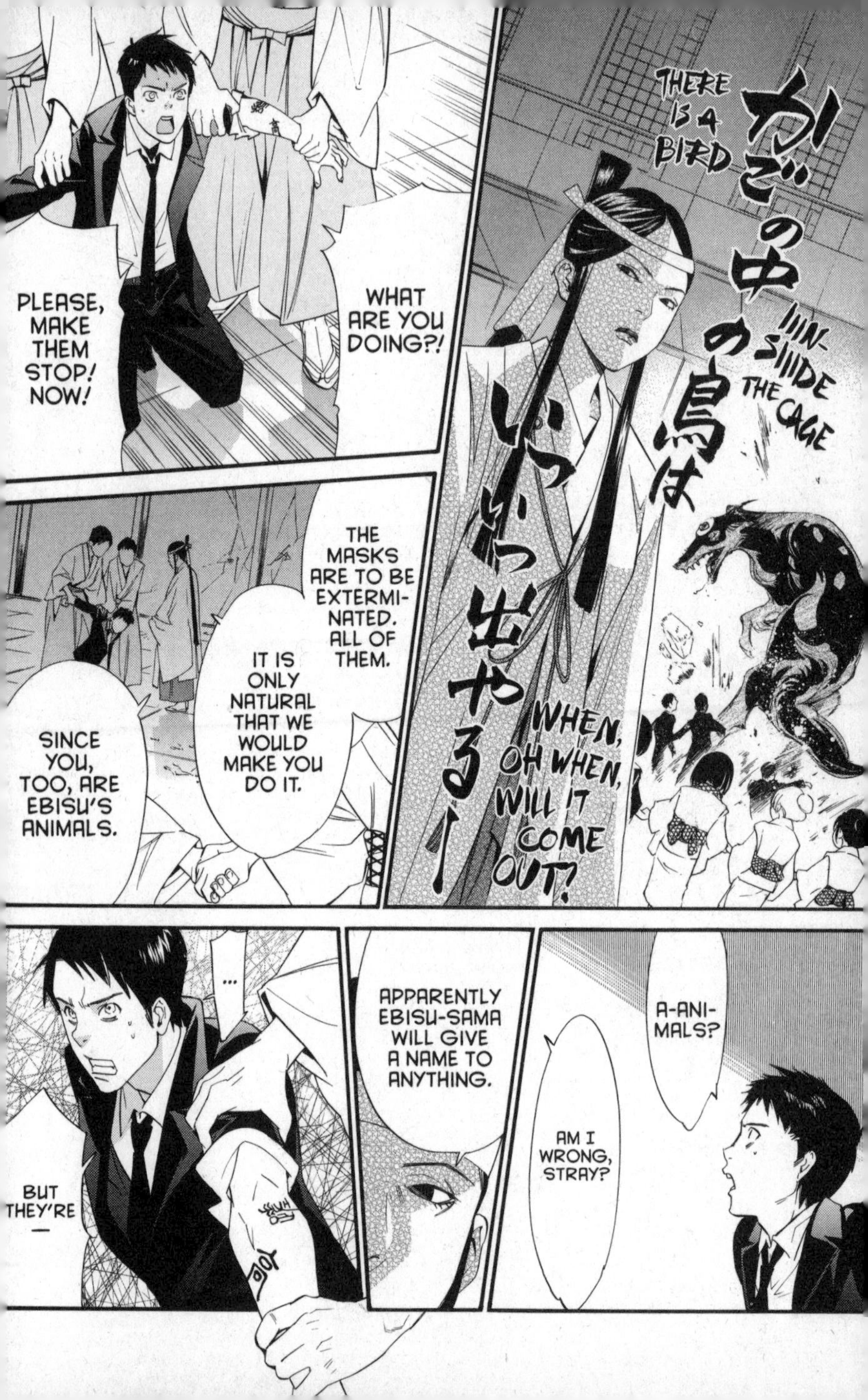
かごの中の鳥は
いついつ出やる！
THERE IS A BIRD
IIIN-SIIIDE THE CAGE
WHEN, OH WHEN, WILL IT COME OUT?!
WHAT ARE YOU DOING?!
PLEASE, MAKE THEM STOP! NOW!
THE MASKS ARE TO BE EXTERMINATED. ALL OF THEM.
IT IS ONLY NATURAL THAT WE WOULD MAKE YOU DO IT.
SINCE YOU, TOO, ARE EBISU'S ANIMALS.
A-ANIMALS?
AM I WRONG, STRAY?
APPARENTLY EBISU-SAMA WILL GIVE A NAME TO ANYTHING.
...
BUT THEY'RE —

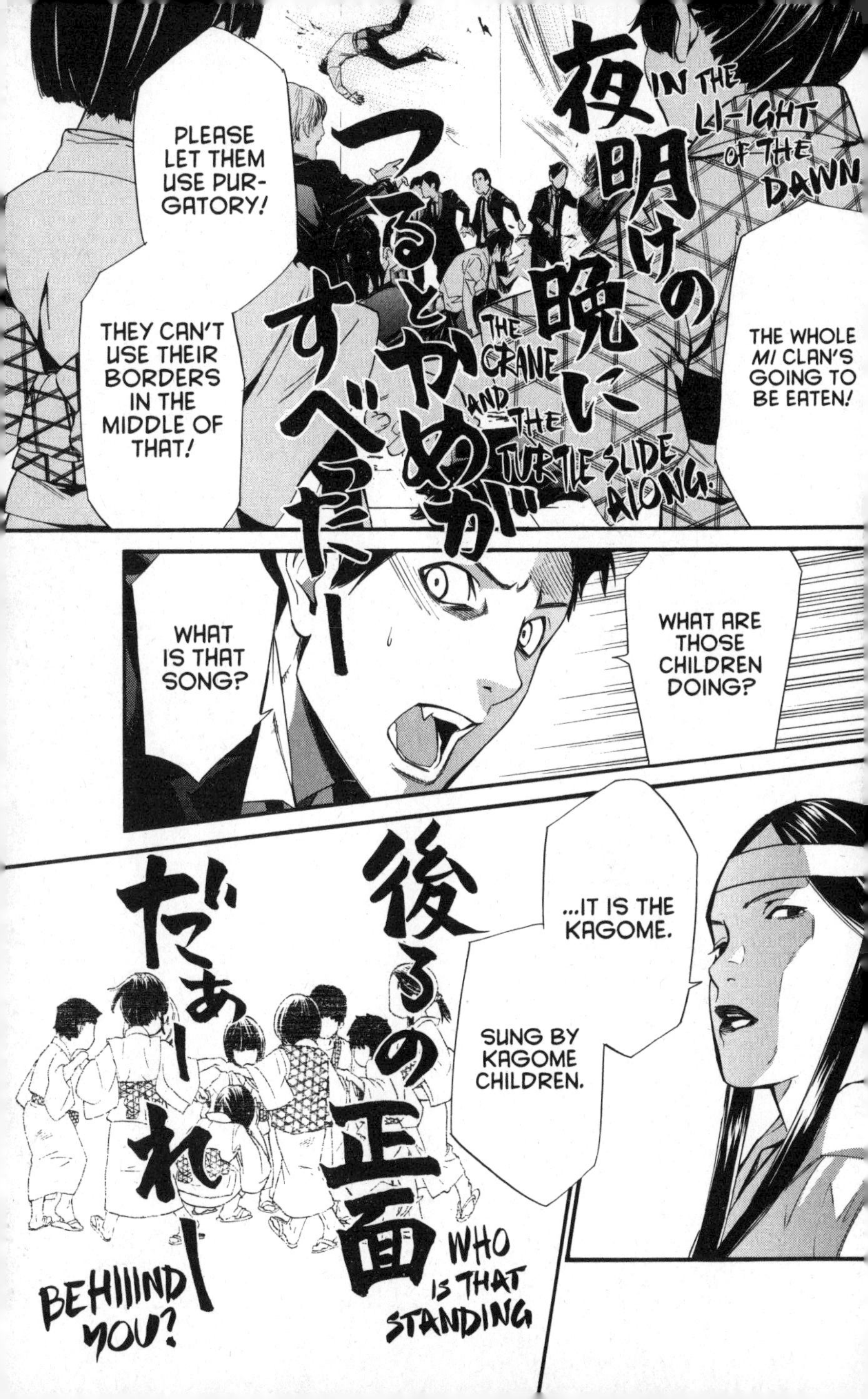

夜明けの晩に
IN THE LI-IGHT OF THE DAWN
THE WHOLE *MI* CLAN'S GOING TO BE EATEN!
つるとかめがすべったー
THE CRANE AND THE TURTLE SLIDE ALONG.
PLEASE LET THEM USE PUR-GATORY!
THEY CAN'T USE THEIR BORDERS IN THE MIDDLE OF THAT!
WHAT ARE THOSE CHILDREN DOING?
WHAT IS THAT SONG?
...IT IS THE KAGOME.
SUNG BY KAGOME CHILDREN.
後ろの正面
WHO IS THAT STANDING
だあーれー
BEHIIIIND YOU?

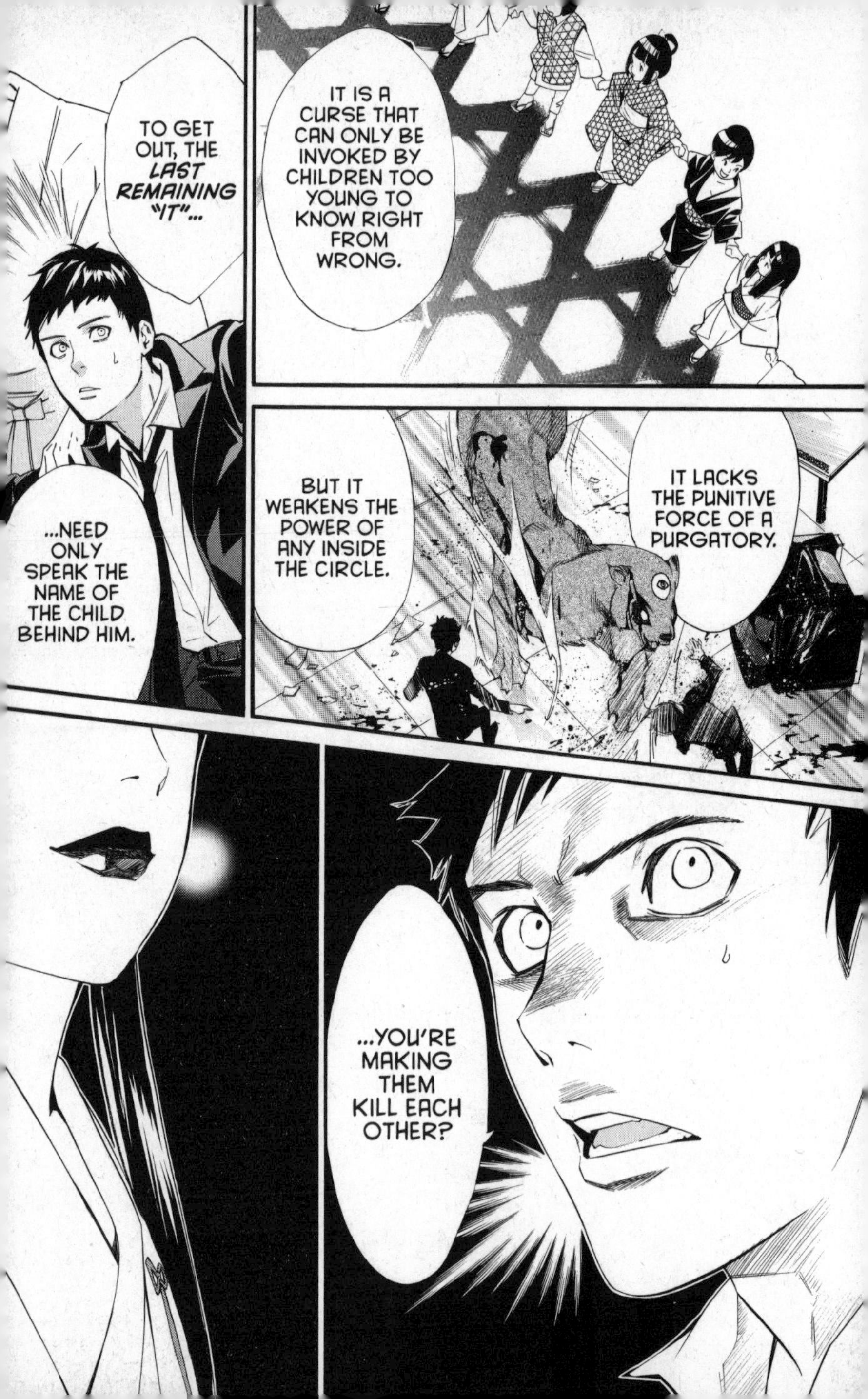
IT IS A CURSE THAT CAN ONLY BE INVOKED BY CHILDREN TOO YOUNG TO KNOW RIGHT FROM WRONG.
IT LACKS THE PUNITIVE FORCE OF A PURGATORY.
BUT IT WEAKENS THE POWER OF ANY INSIDE THE CIRCLE.
TO GET OUT, THE *LAST REMAINING "IT"*...
...NEED ONLY SPEAK THE NAME OF THE CHILD BEHIND HIM.
...YOU'RE MAKING THEM KILL EACH OTHER?

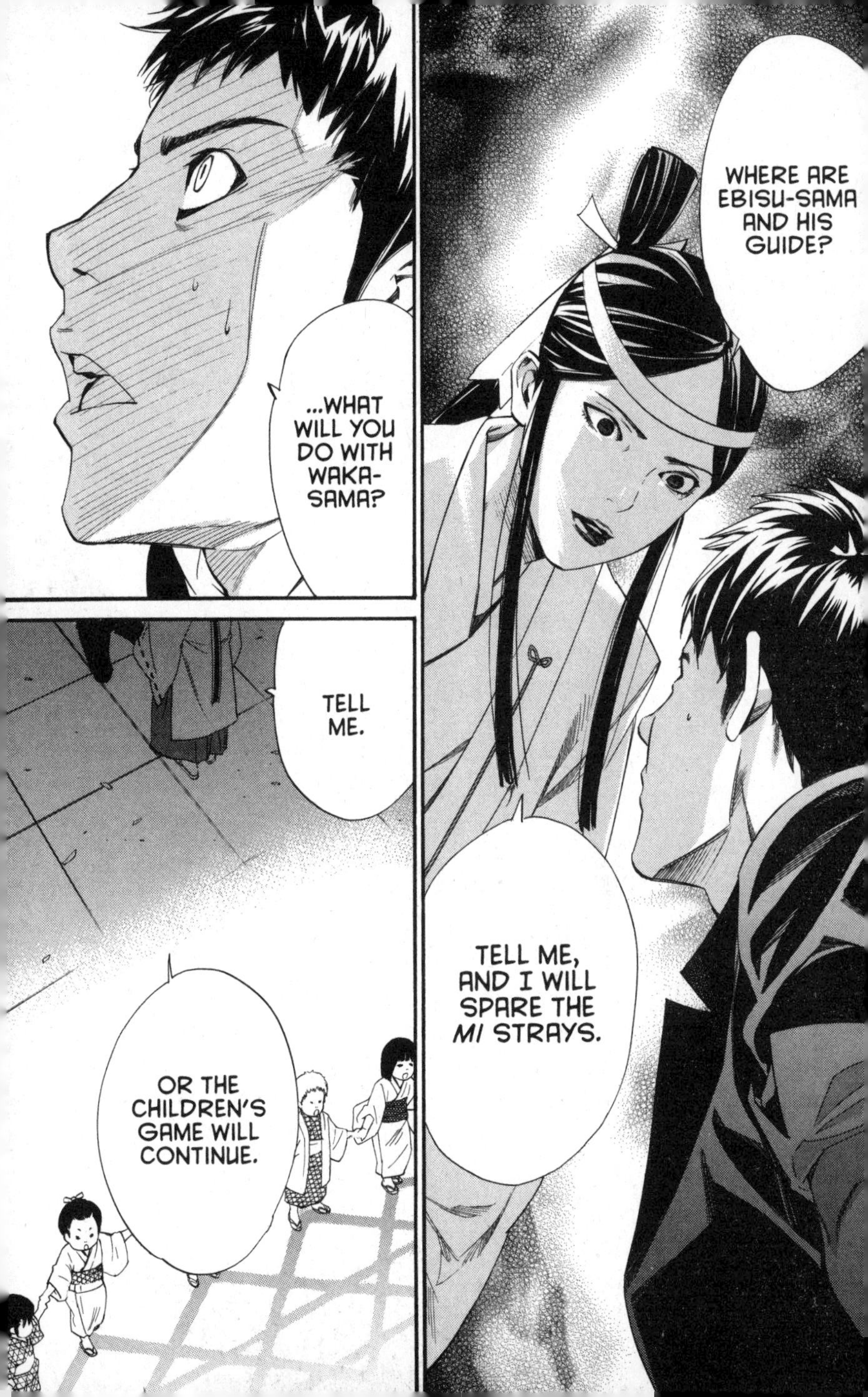
WHERE ARE EBISU-SAMA AND HIS GUIDE?
TELL ME, AND I WILL SPARE THE *MI* STRAYS.
...WHAT WILL YOU DO WITH WAKA-SAMA?
TELL ME.
OR THE CHILDREN'S GAME WILL CONTINUE.

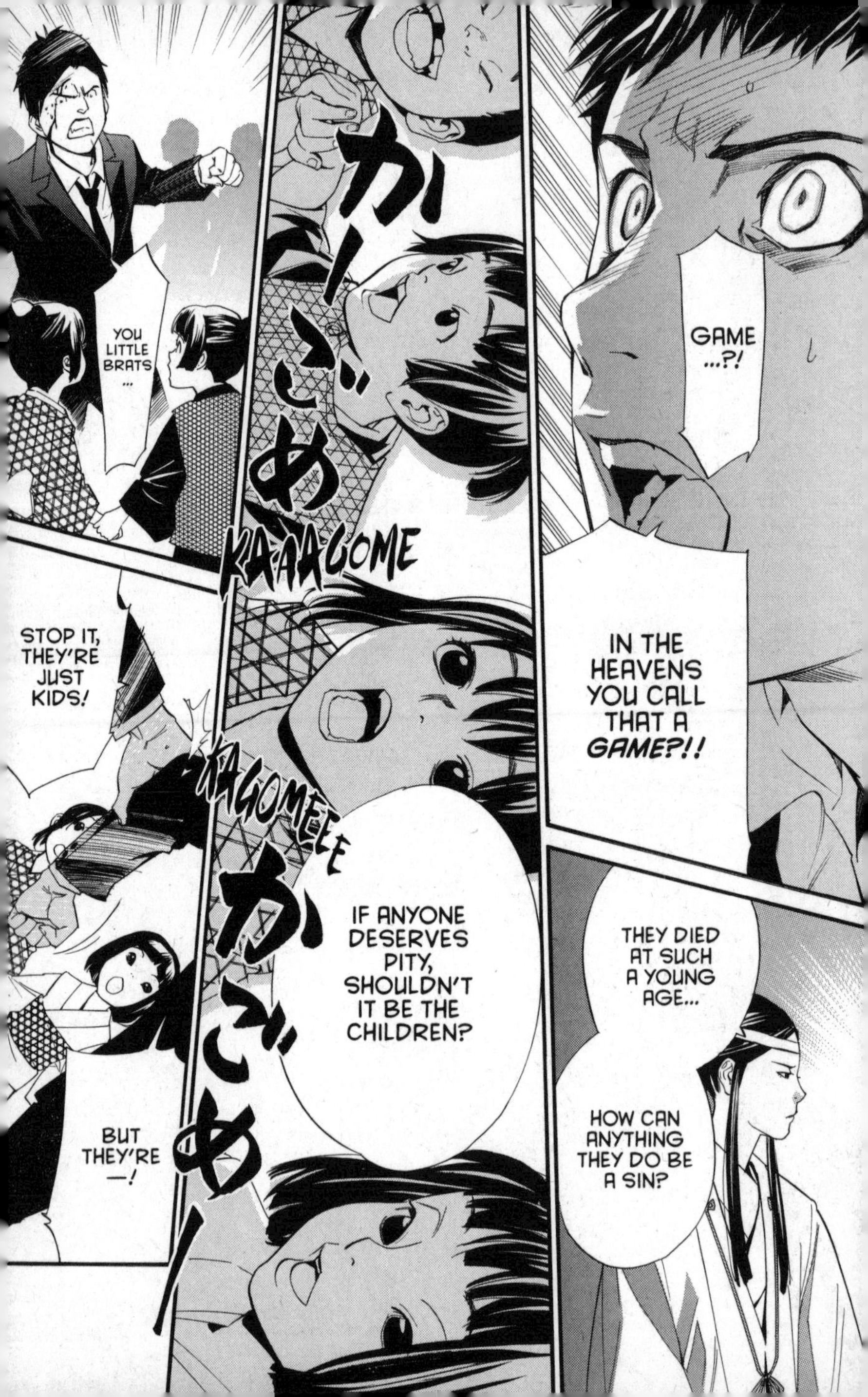
GAME ...?!
IN THE HEAVENS YOU CALL THAT A GAME?!!
THEY DIED AT SUCH A YOUNG AGE...
HOW CAN ANYTHING THEY DO BE A SIN?
IF ANYONE DESERVES PITY, SHOULDN'T IT BE THE CHILDREN?
かーごめ
KAAAGOME
かごめ
KAGOMEEE
YOU LITTLE BRATS ...
STOP IT, THEY'RE JUST KIDS!
BUT THEY'RE —!

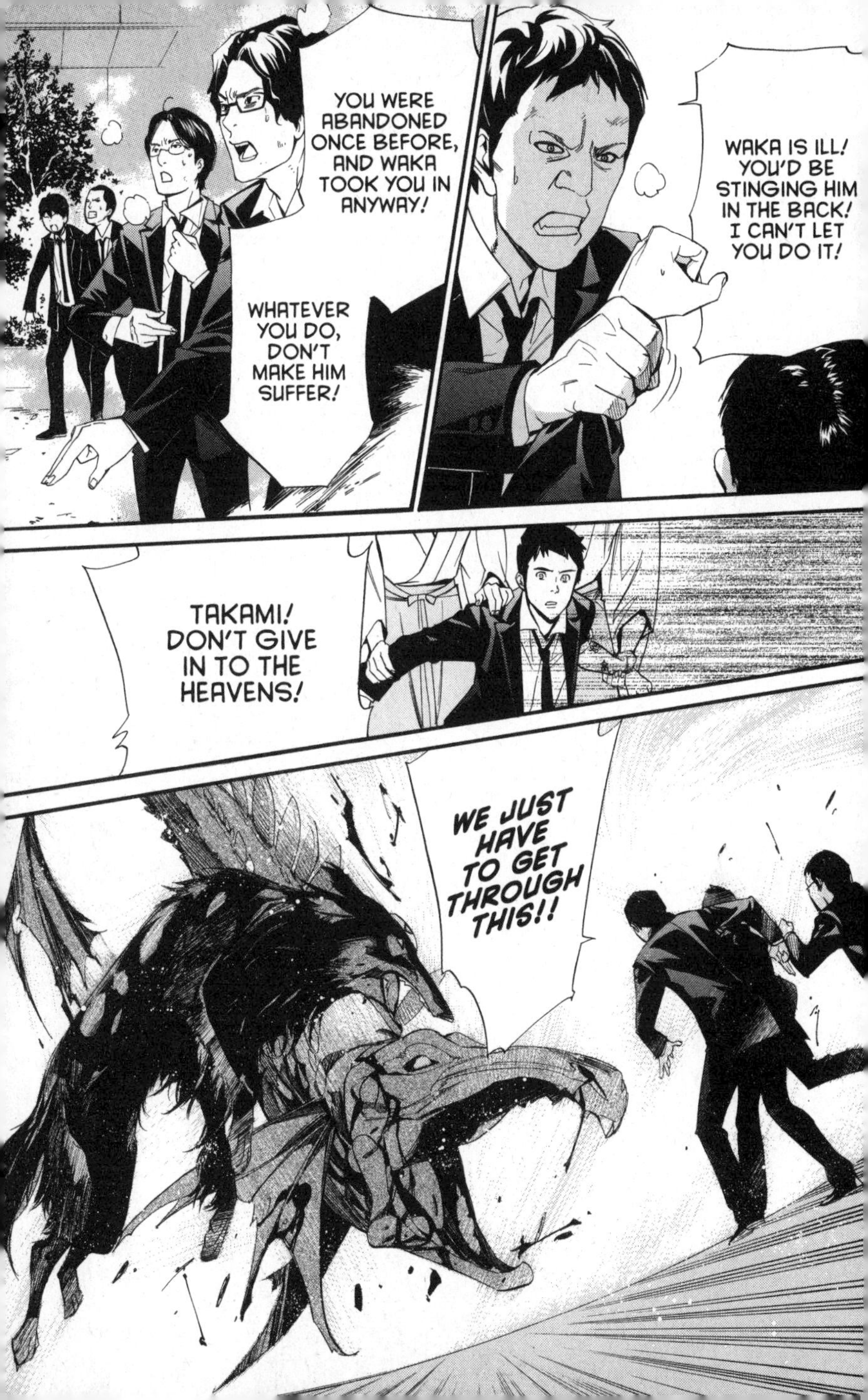
WAKA IS ILL! YOU'D BE STINGING HIM IN THE BACK! I CAN'T LET YOU DO IT!
YOU WERE ABANDONED ONCE BEFORE, AND WAKA TOOK YOU IN ANYWAY!
WHATEVER YOU DO, DON'T MAKE HIM SUFFER!
TAKAMI! DON'T GIVE IN TO THE HEAVENS!
WE JUST HAVE TO GET THROUGH THIS!!

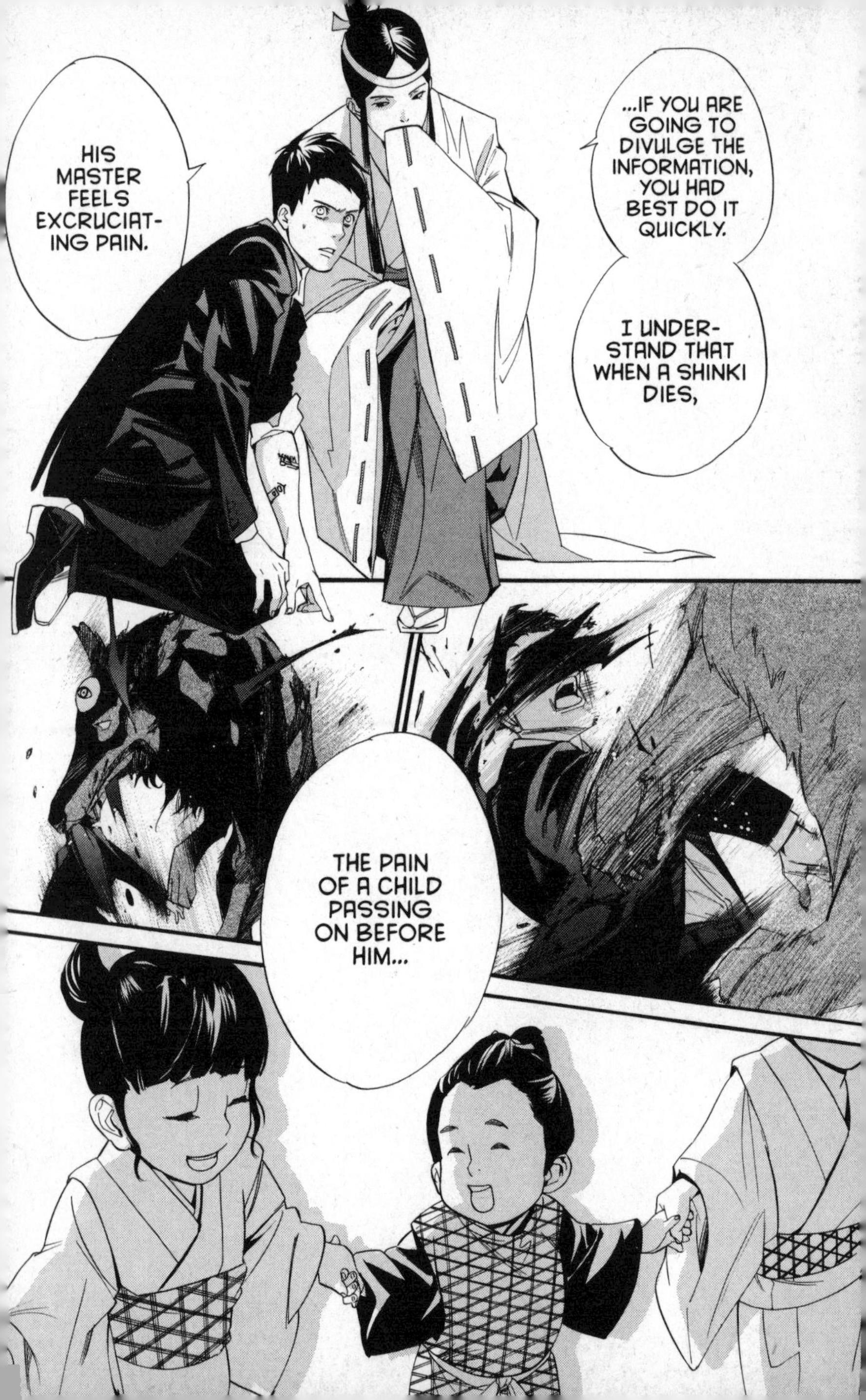
...IF YOU ARE GOING TO DIVULGE THE INFORMATION, YOU HAD BEST DO IT QUICKLY.
I UNDER-STAND THAT WHEN A SHINKI DIES,
HIS MASTER FEELS EXCRUCIAT-ING PAIN.
THE PAIN OF A CHILD PASSING ON BEFORE HIM...

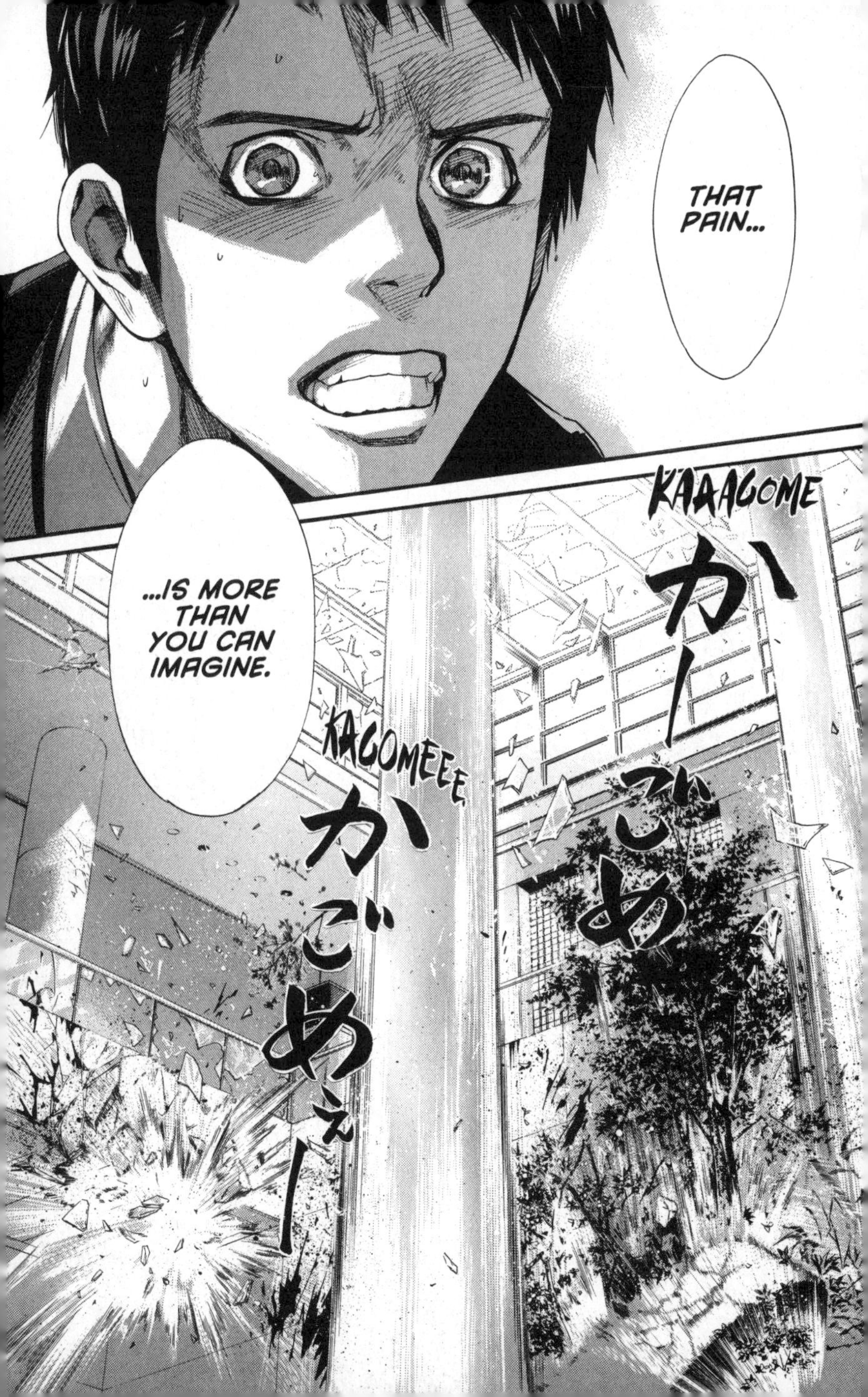
THAT PAIN...
...IS MORE THAN YOU CAN IMAGINE.
KAAAGOME
かーごめ
KAGOMEEE
かごめぇー

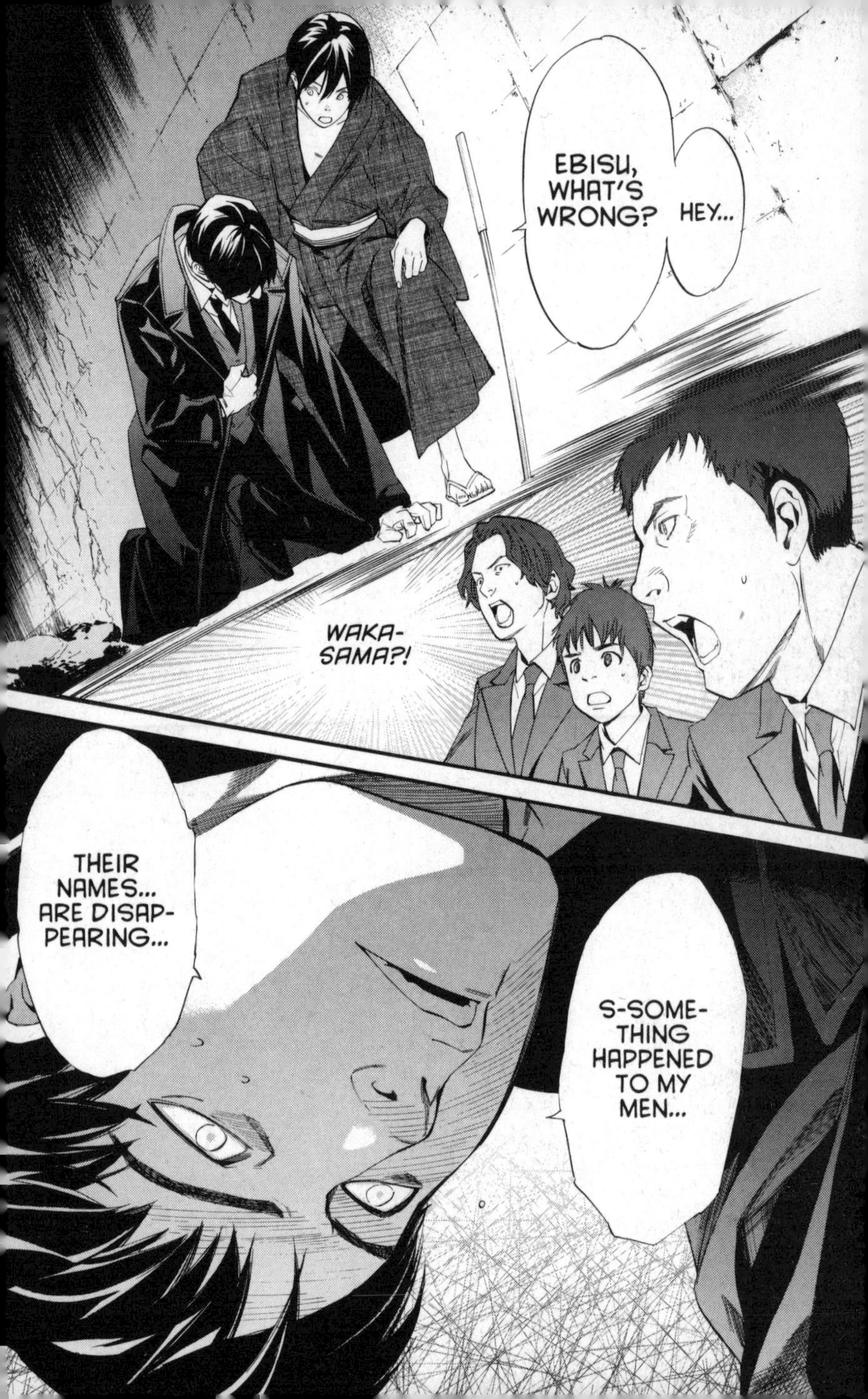
EBISU, WHAT'S WRONG? HEY...
WAKA-SAMA?!
S-SOMETHING HAPPENED TO MY MEN...
THEIR NAMES... ARE DISAPPEARING...

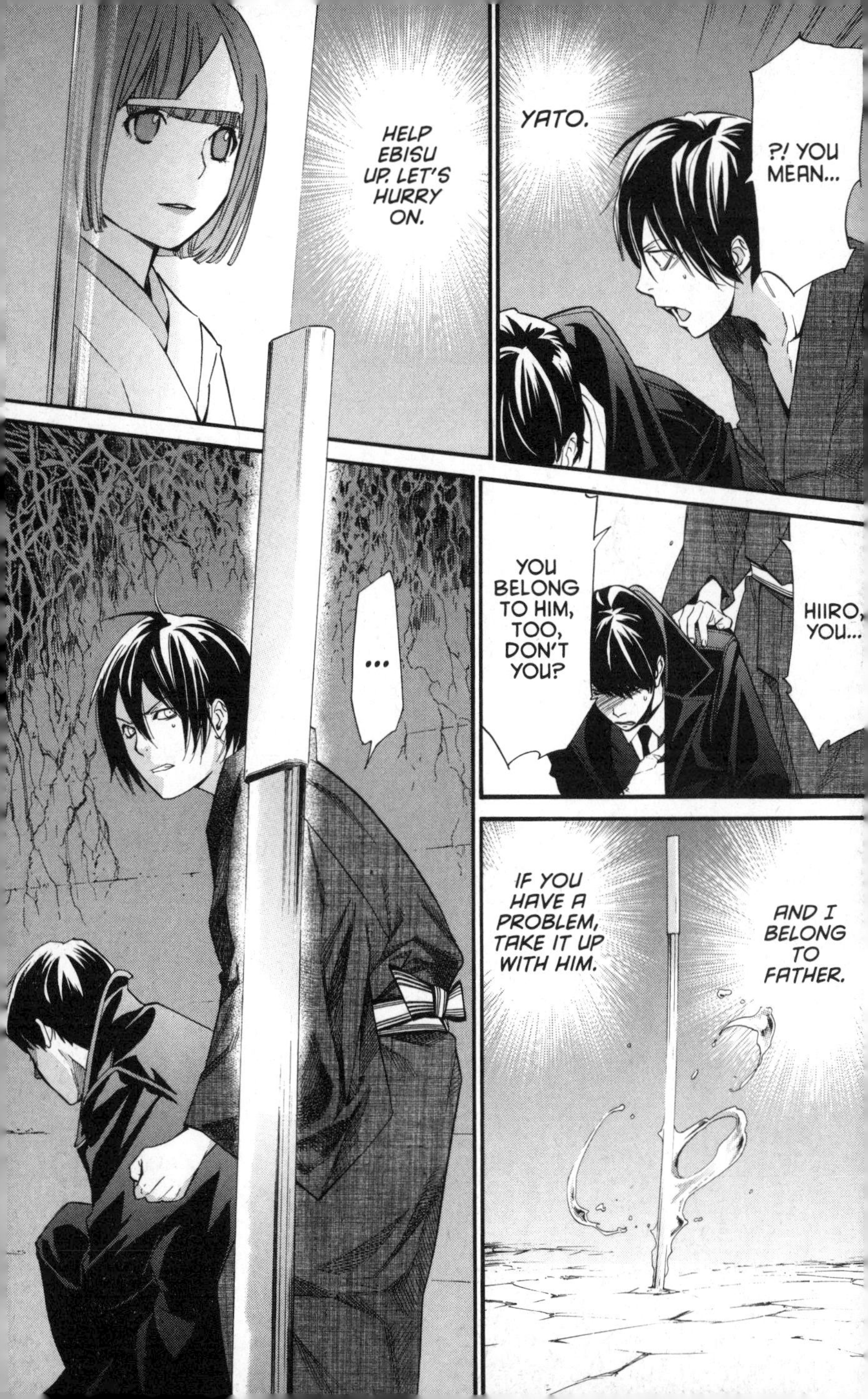
YATO.
?! YOU MEAN...
HELP EBISU UP. LET'S HURRY ON.
HIIRO, YOU...
YOU BELONG TO HIM, TOO, DON'T YOU?
AND I BELONG TO FATHER.
IF YOU HAVE A PROBLEM, TAKE IT UP WITH HIM.
...

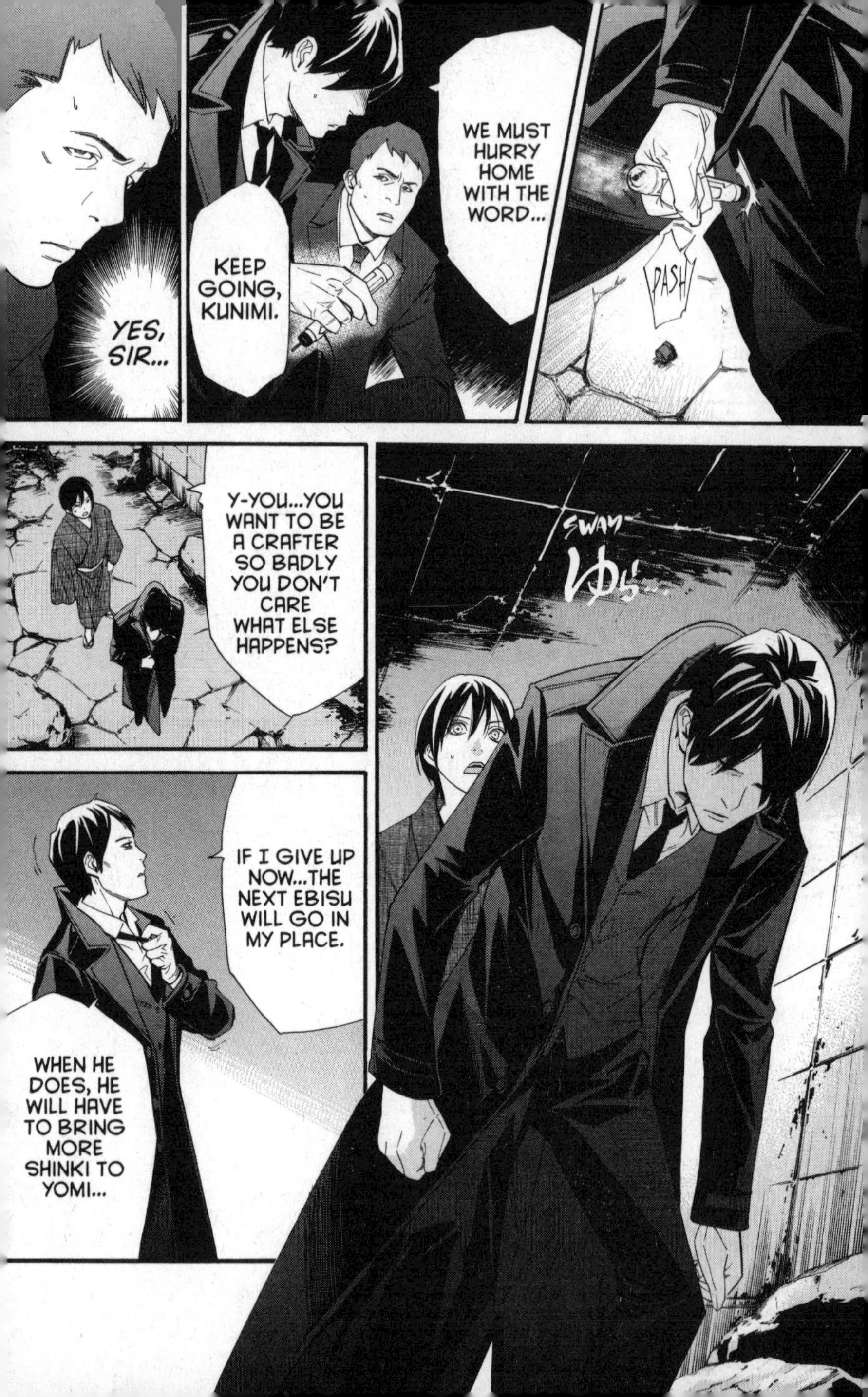
PASH
WE MUST HURRY HOME WITH THE WORD...
KEEP GOING, KUNIMI.
YES, SIR...
SWAY
ゆら…
Y-YOU...YOU WANT TO BE A CRAFTER SO BADLY YOU DON'T CARE WHAT ELSE HAPPENS?
IF I GIVE UP NOW...THE NEXT EBISU WILL GO IN MY PLACE.
WHEN HE DOES, HE WILL HAVE TO BRING MORE SHINKI TO YOMI...

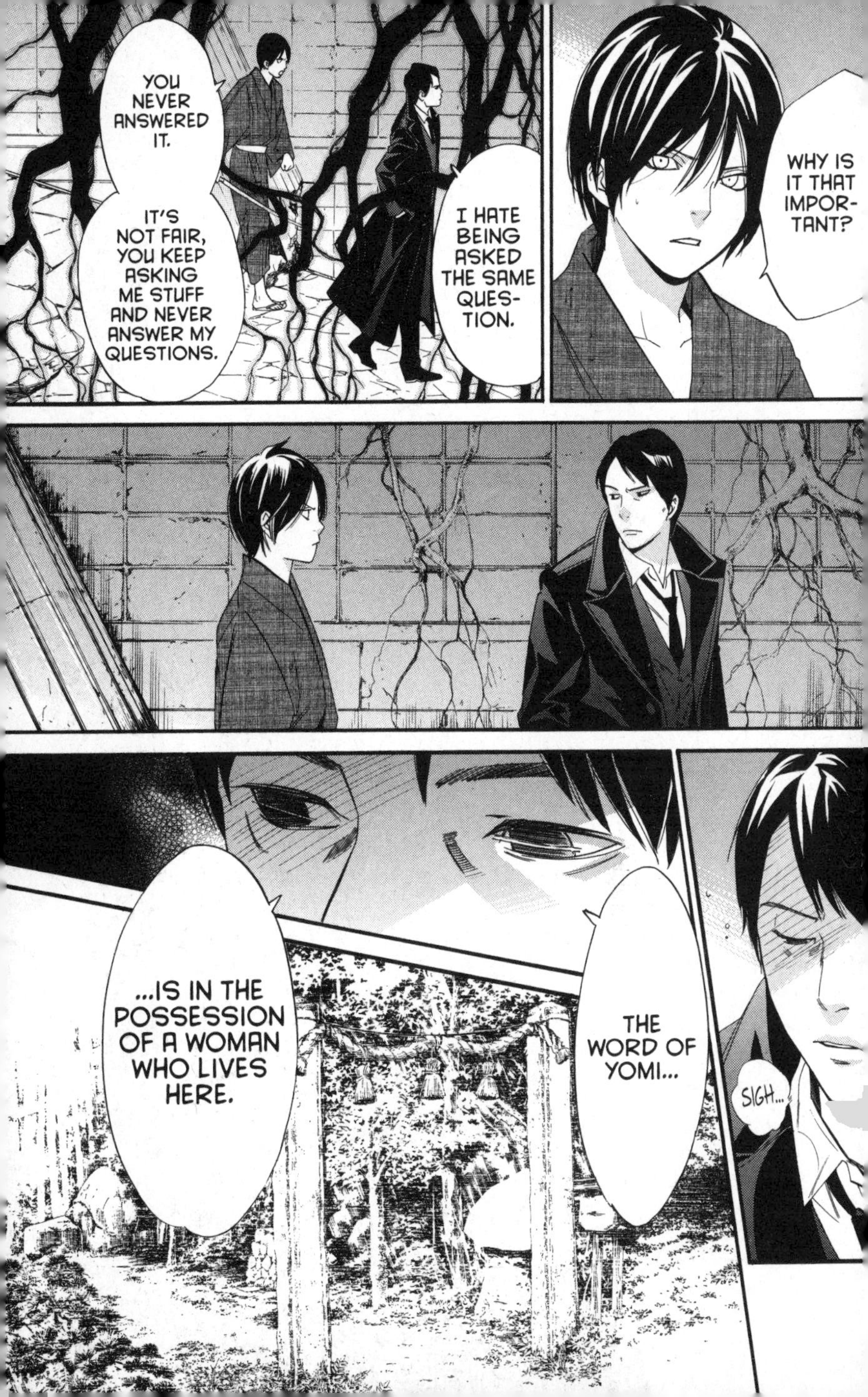
WHY IS IT THAT IMPORTANT?
I HATE BEING ASKED THE SAME QUESTION.
YOU NEVER ANSWERED IT.
IT'S NOT FAIR, YOU KEEP ASKING ME STUFF AND NEVER ANSWER MY QUESTIONS.
SIGH...
THE WORD OF YOMI...
...IS IN THE POSSESSION OF A WOMAN WHO LIVES HERE.

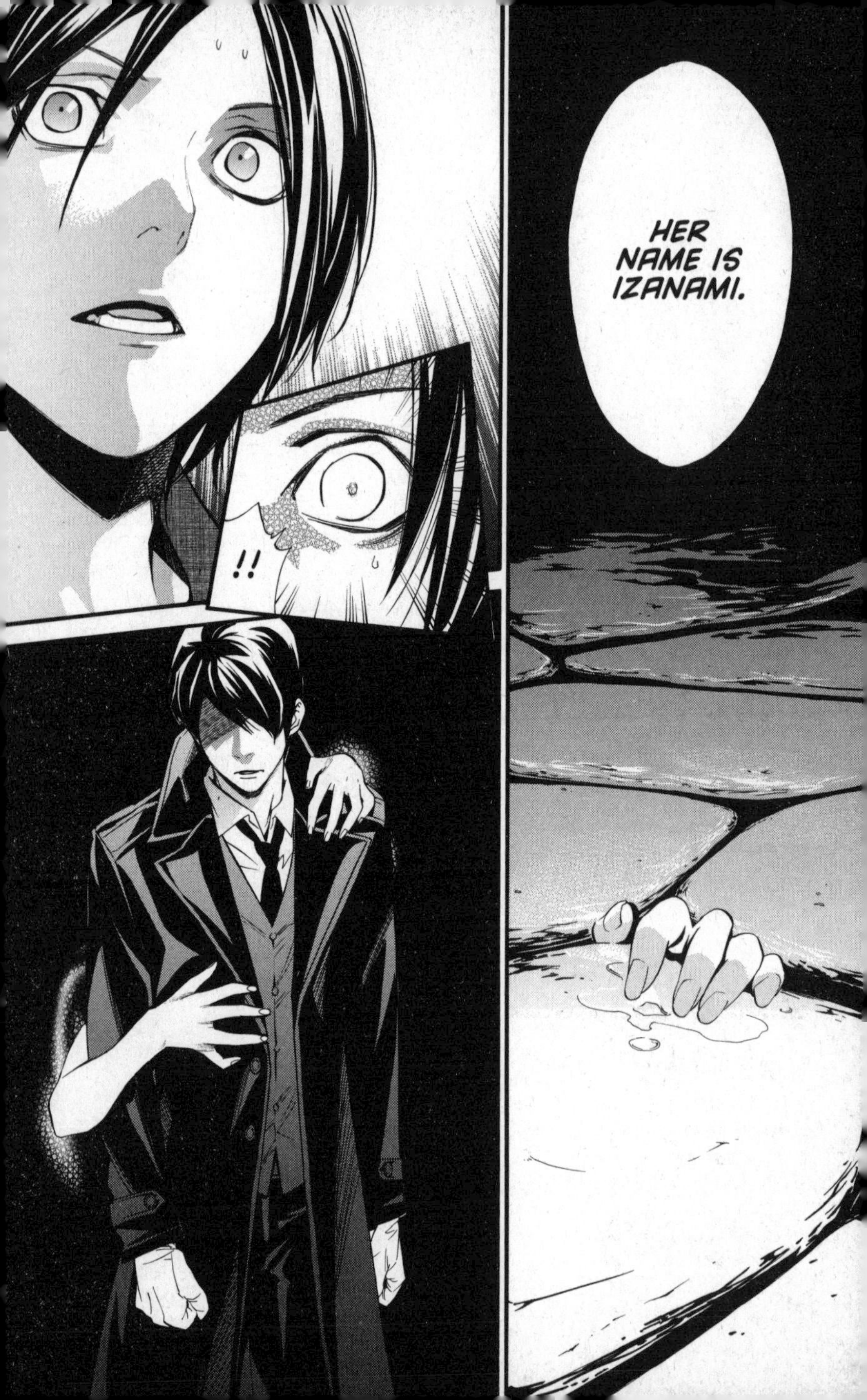
HER NAME IS IZANAMI.
!!

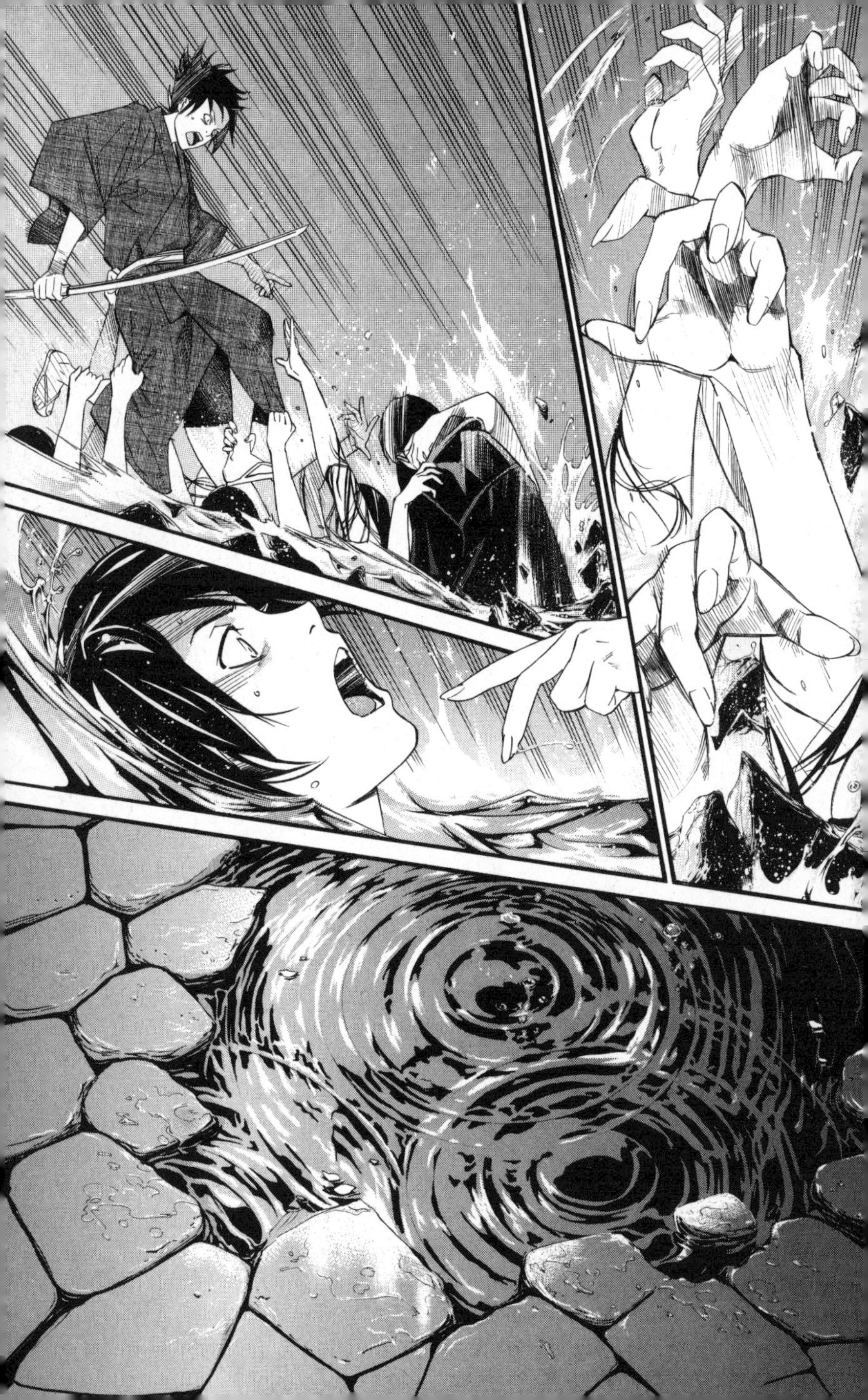

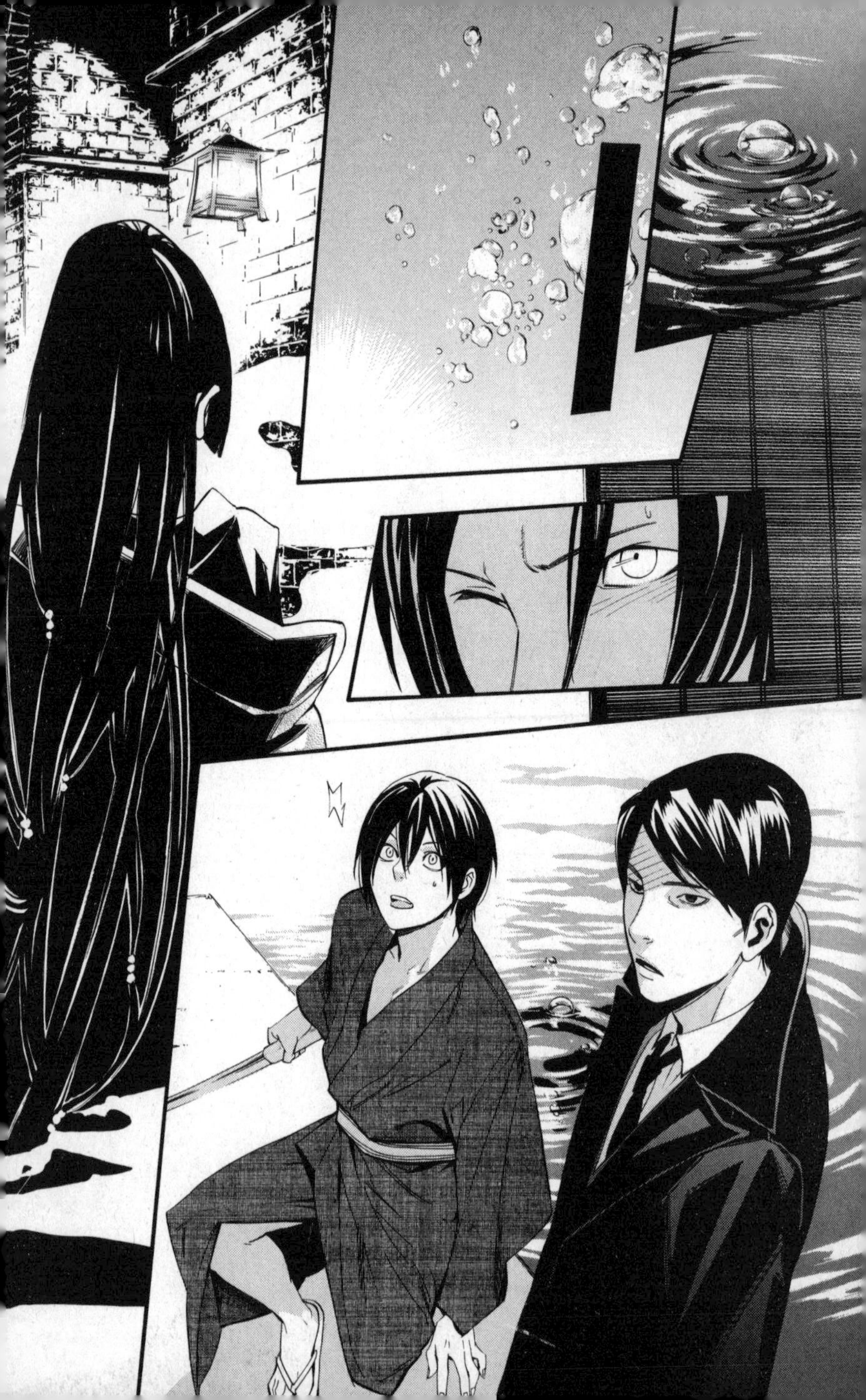

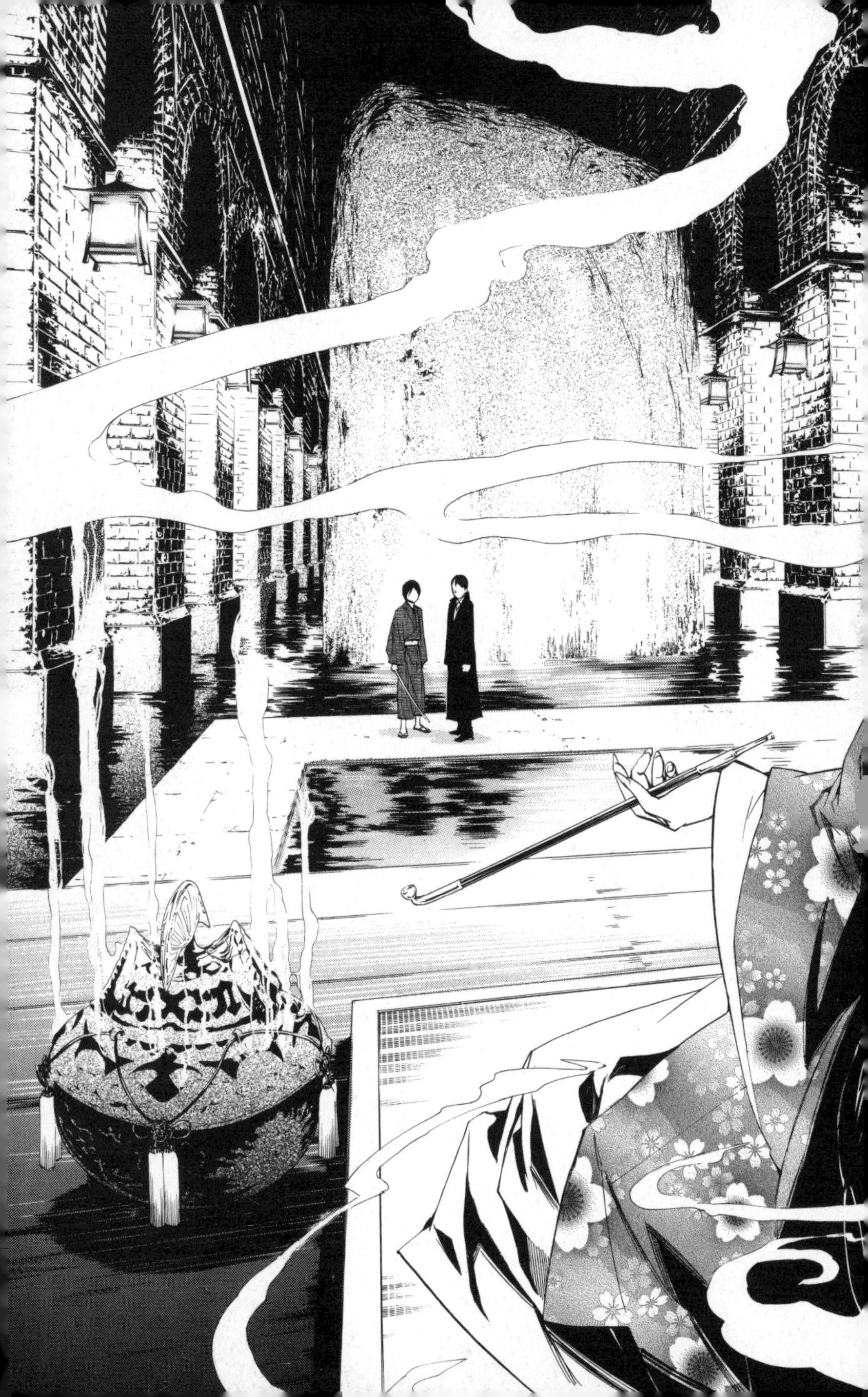

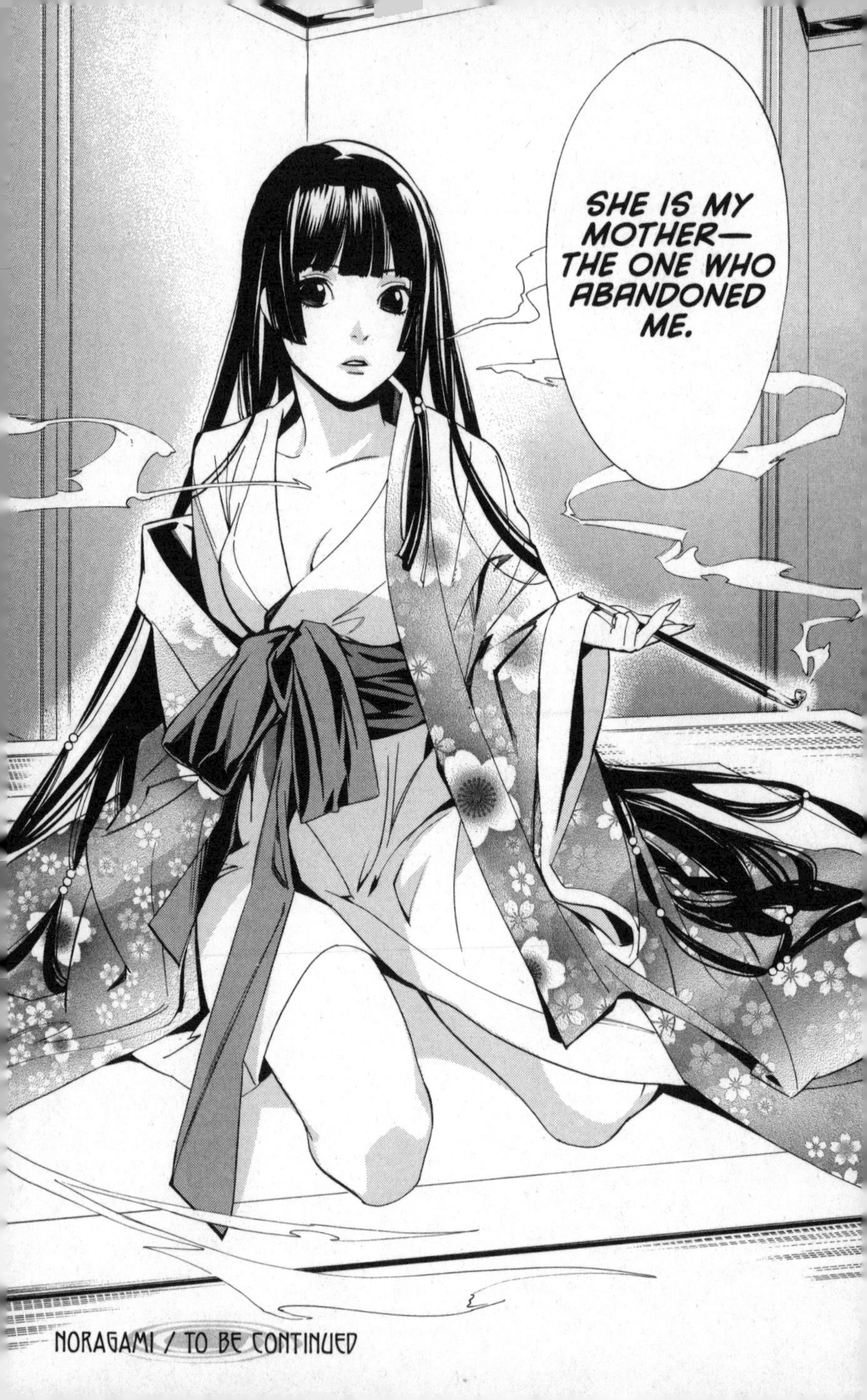
SHE IS MY MOTHER—THE ONE WHO ABANDONED ME.
NORAGAMI / TO BE CONTINUED

野

兑

神

ATROCIOUS MANGA

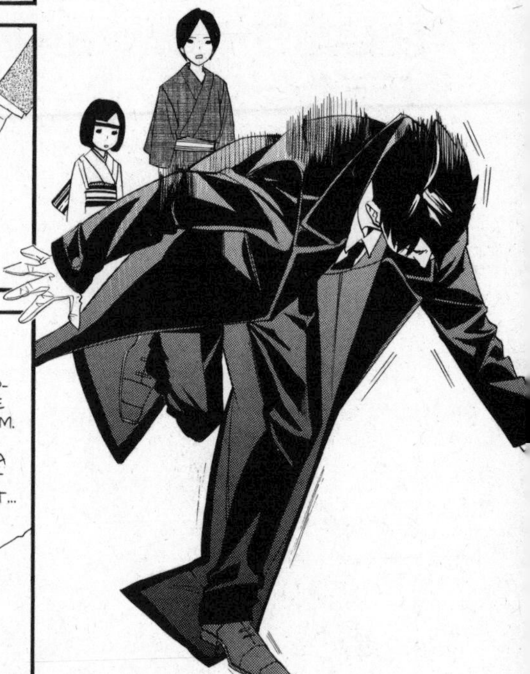

GET WELL SOON, OKAY?

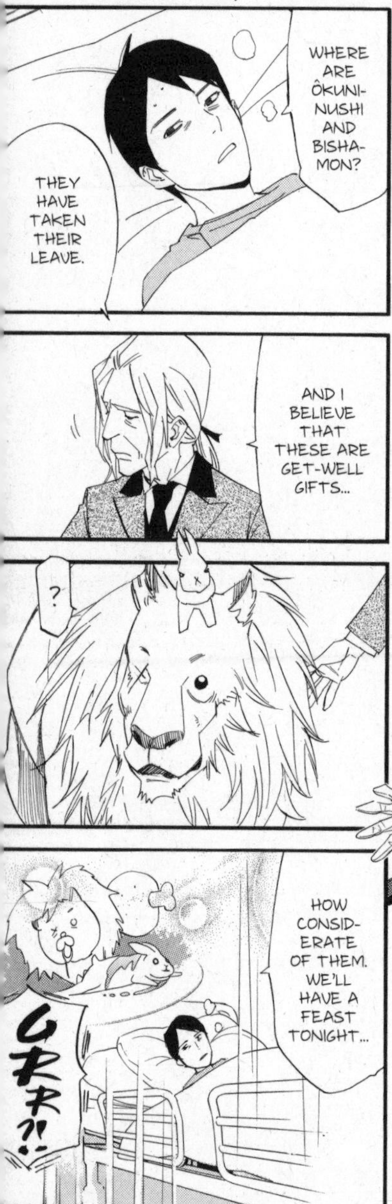
WHERE ARE ÔKUNINUSHI AND BISHAMON?
THEY HAVE TAKEN THEIR LEAVE.
AND I BELIEVE THAT THESE ARE GET-WELL GIFTS...
?
HOW CONSIDERATE OF THEM. WE'LL HAVE A FEAST TONIGHT...
GRR?!

OUR BONE

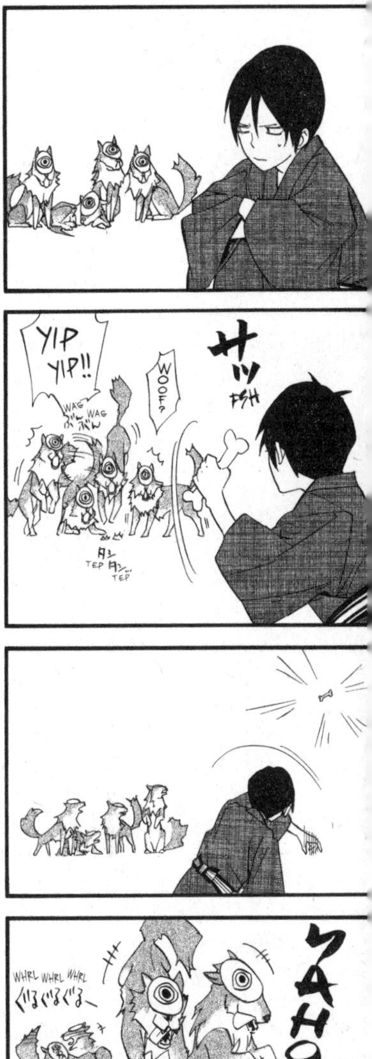
YIP YIP!!
WOOF?
WAG WAG
サッ
FSH
TEP TEP
WHRL WHRL WHRL
ぐるぐるぐる
YAHOO!!
AAAAUGHHH!

YATO'S

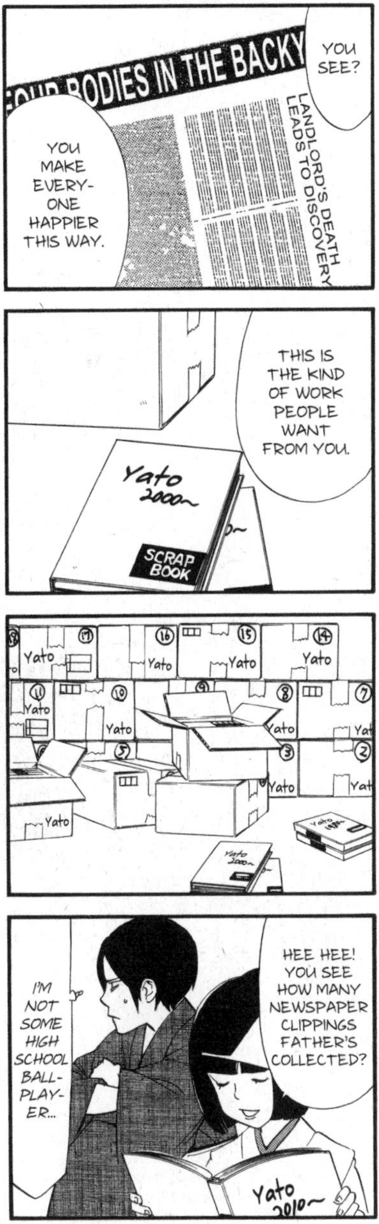
YOU SEE?
BODIES IN THE BACKY
LANDLORD'S DEATH LEADS TO DISCOVERY
YOU MAKE EVERYONE HAPPIER THIS WAY.
THIS IS THE KIND OF WORK PEOPLE WANT FROM YOU.
Yato 2000~
SCRAP BOOK
HEE HEE! YOU SEE HOW MANY NEWSPAPER CLIPPINGS FATHER'S COLLECTED?
I'M NOT SOME HIGH SCHOOL BALL-PLAYER...
Yato 2010~

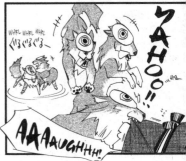

HATE IT WITH EVERY FIBER OF MY BEING!!

MY "MASTER" WON'T COME HOME, SO I'M REALLY BORED WITH NO WORK TO DO.
YOU'RE LUCKY, GOING TO SCHOOL.
ARE YOU HAVING FUN AT SCHOOL, HIYORI?
...ARE YOU HAVING PROB-LEMS?
THEN YOU CAN ASK YATO TO...
Noooooo...
もくもく SILENT SILENT
もくもく SILENT SILENT
CAPYPER LAND
!!!
EWAM
スパーン
HI-SSSSSSSS!!
...HIYORI, DO YOU HATE HIM THAT MUCH?
TRASH
BUT I KNOW HOW YOU FEEL.
THE SECRET TO PACHINKO!!
Secret Tricks of the Pros
READ NOW FOR GOOD LUCK
SPECIAL BONUS LUCKY CHARM
Everything will go your way!
ニコッ GRIN
ドォーン B-DMP
WHAT?! WHAT DO YOU KNOW, YUKINE-KUN?!

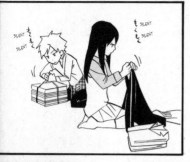

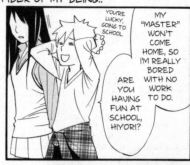

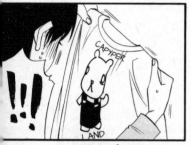

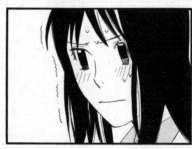

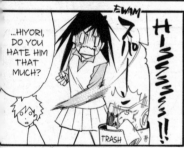

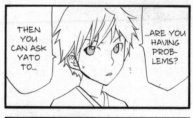

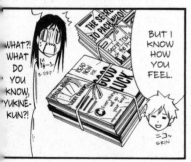

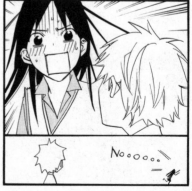

EVEN EBISU IS OUT OF IDEAS

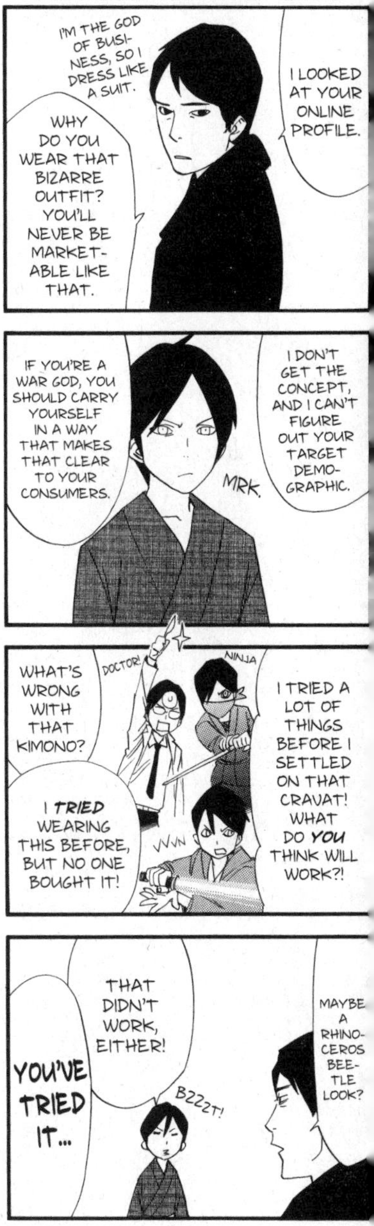
I LOOKED AT YOUR ONLINE PROFILE.
I'M THE GOD OF BUSINESS, SO I DRESS LIKE A SUIT.
WHY DO YOU WEAR THAT BIZARRE OUTFIT? YOU'LL NEVER BE MARKETABLE LIKE THAT.
I DON'T GET THE CONCEPT, AND I CAN'T FIGURE OUT YOUR TARGET DEMOGRAPHIC.
MRK.
IF YOU'RE A WAR GOD, YOU SHOULD CARRY YOURSELF IN A WAY THAT MAKES THAT CLEAR TO YOUR CONSUMERS.
NINJA
I TRIED A LOT OF THINGS BEFORE I SETTLED ON THAT CRAVAT! WHAT DO *YOU* THINK WILL WORK?!
DOCTOR!
WHAT'S WRONG WITH THAT KIMONO?
I ***TRIED*** WEARING THIS BEFORE, BUT NO ONE BOUGHT IT!
VVVN
MAYBE A RHINOCEROS BEETLE LOOK?
THAT DIDN'T WORK, EITHER!
BZZZT!
YOU'VE TRIED IT...

PREVENTING LAWSUITS

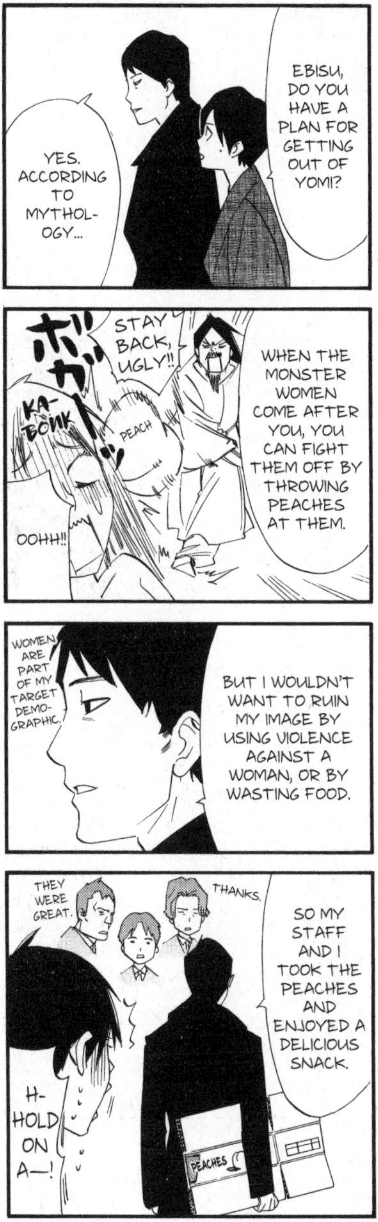
EBISU, DO YOU HAVE A PLAN FOR GETTING OUT OF YOMI?
YES. ACCORDING TO MYTHOLOGY...
WHEN THE MONSTER WOMEN COME AFTER YOU, YOU CAN FIGHT THEM OFF BY THROWING PEACHES AT THEM.
STAY BACK, UGLY!!
KA-BONK
PEACH
OOHH!!
BUT I WOULDN'T WANT TO RUIN MY IMAGE BY USING VIOLENCE AGAINST A WOMAN, OR BY WASTING FOOD.
WOMEN ARE PART OF MY TARGET DEMOGRAPHIC.
SO MY STAFF AND I TOOK THE PEACHES AND ENJOYED A DELICIOUS SNACK.
THANKS.
THEY WERE GREAT.
PEACHES
H-HOLD ON A—!

THANK YOU TO EVERYONE WHO READ THIS FAR!!

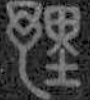

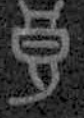

TRANSLATION NOTES

Japanese is a tricky language for most Westerners, and translation is often more art than science. For your edification and reading pleasure, here are notes on some of the places where we could have gone in a different direction in our translation of the work, or where a Japanese cultural reference is used.

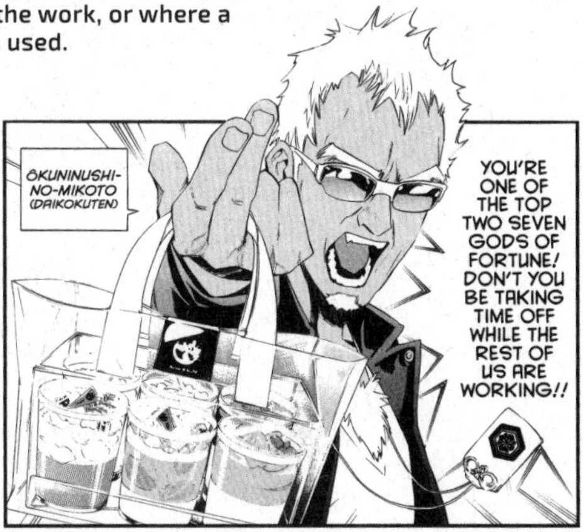
YOU'RE ONE OF THE TOP TWO SEVEN GODS OF FORTUNE! DON'T YOU BE TAKING TIME OFF WHILE THE REST OF US ARE WORKING!!
ÔKUNINUSHI-NO-MIKOTO (DAIKOKUTEN)

Ôkuninushi aka Daikokuten, page 23

As shown here, Daikokuten, one of the Seven Gods of Fortune, is also known as Ôkuninushi. Ôkuninushi is a Shinto deity that features prominently in Japan's mythological history as the first ruler of Izumo, which is where all the gods meet for the Divine Council (he was later replaced). Daikokuten is a Buddhist deity derived from the Hindu god Shiva. Since his introduction to Japan, he has been intertwined with Ôkuninushi, and the two have come to be seen as the same god. This is because the *kanji* characters for *ôkuni* can also be pronounced *daikoku*.

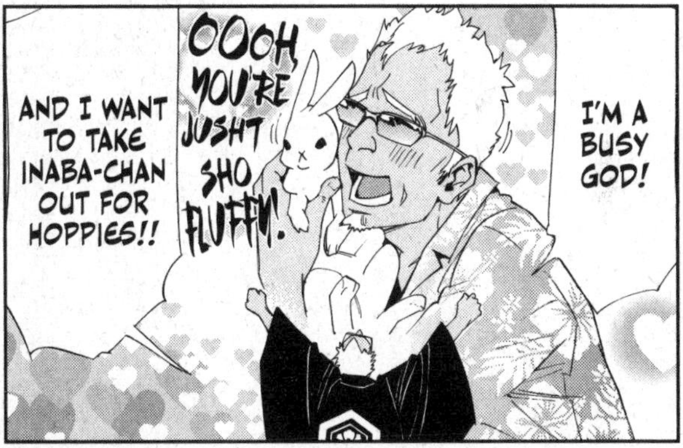
I'M A BUSY GOD!
OOOH, YOU'RE JUSHT SHO FLUFFY!
AND I WANT TO TAKE INABA-CHAN OUT FOR HOPPIES!!

Taking Inaba-chan out for hoppies, page 49

A big part of the legend of Ôkuninushi is the tale of the White Hare of Inaba. In a nutshell, Ôkuninushi comes across an injured rabbit and helps it, and the rabbit predicts his future success. That being the case, it's no wonder that Ôkuninushi would have a beloved pet rabbit, which he takes out for walks. The Japanese word for this kind of walk is *sanpo*, which Ôkuninushi combines with the word for rabbit (*usagi*), making it *usanpo*, or a bunny walk. The translators attempted to replicate the cuteness of his word choice by using "hoppies" instead of "walkies."

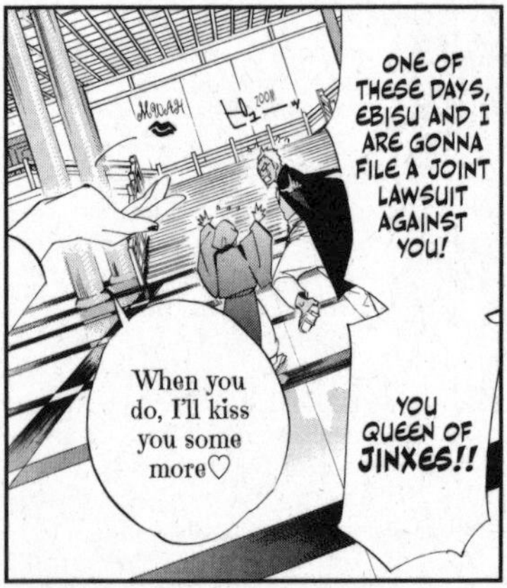
ONE OF THESE DAYS, EBISU AND I ARE GONNA FILE A JOINT LAWSUIT AGAINST YOU!
YOU QUEEN OF JINXES!!
When you do, I'll kiss you some more♡

Queen of jinxes, page 51

Specifically, Ôkuninushi calls Kofuku the "queen of *sageman*," where *sageman* is a slang term referring to a woman who brings bad luck to her boyfriend.

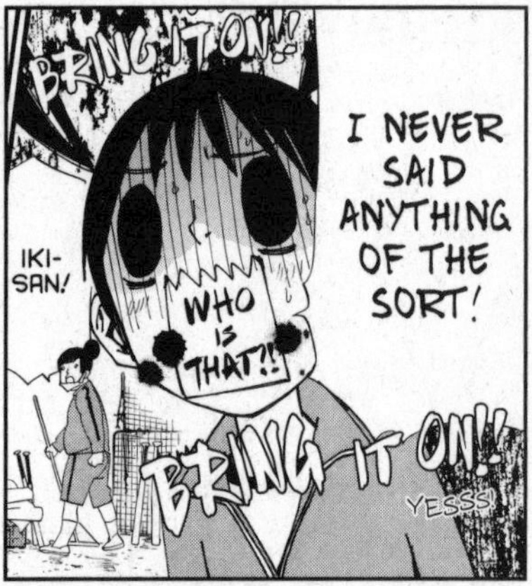
BRING IT ON!!
I NEVER SAID ANYTHING OF THE SORT!
WHO IS THAT?!
IKI-SAN!
BRING IT ON!!
YESSS!

Bring it on, page 63

Here the baseball team uses a baseball-specific Japanese word for "bring it on." The word is *bachikoi*, which is short for *battaa koi*, meaning roughly, "bring it, batter!"

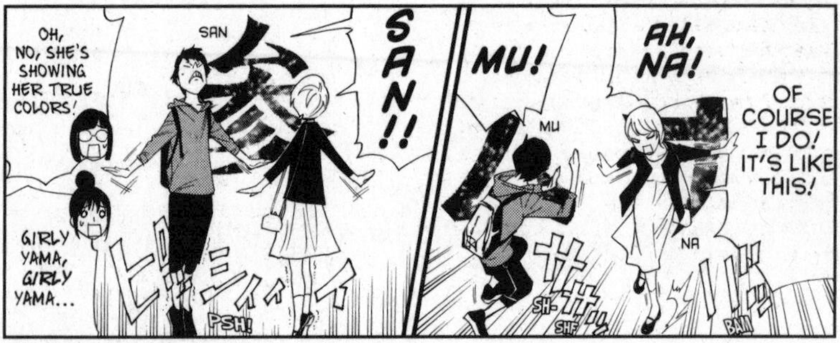
AH, NA!
OF COURSE I DO! IT'S LIKE THIS!
MU!
MU
NA
SH-
SHF
BAM
SAN!!
SAN
OH, NO, SHE'S SHOWING HER TRUE COLORS!
GIRLY YAMA, GIRLY YAMA...
PSH!

Na mu san, page 115

Namusan is an abbreviation of *namusanpô*, which means roughly, "I believe in the Three Treasures of Buddhism!" and was originally a plea for mercy uttered by someone who has failed or been surprised. It has since lost some of its meaning and mostly used in the same vein as phrases such as, "Good heavens!" and, "Damn it!"

Apparently Yama's favorite band likes to recite the phrase while posing to mimic the characters that spell out *na*, *mu*, and *san*.

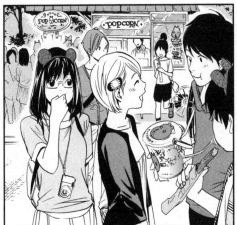

Popcorn, page 117

POPCORN
POP CORN

Readers have surely noticed the strong resemblance between Capyper Land and certain famous amusement park franchise. In the Tokyo-based park, the popcorn is one of the main attractions to the point that if you tell a Tokyo native that you've been to the famous theme park, they may very well respond with, "Did you try the popcorn?" This is partly because of the variety of popcorn flavors—different popcorn stands have different flavors, such as butter, caramel, honey, and even curry—and partly because of the wide array of collectible popcorn buckets.

MU
NA
SAN♡
GET A ROOM!!

Get a room, page 142

While these aren't the exact words expressed by Yama's classmates, the translators feel it captures the sentiment fairly well. What they actually said was *bakappuru*, which is a combination of the Japanese word *baka* (stupid) and the English couple, Japan-ified to *kappuru*. The word refers to a couple that is overly affectionate in public, and, in this case, probably with an extra helping of stupid.

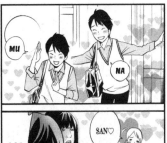

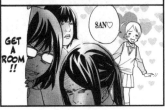

That was a joke, page 159

A more literal translate of Yato's line is, "retort [to what I just said]." In other words, Yato knows that what he just said is outlandish, and he was hoping Ebisu would give a more appropriately shocked reaction. This is all to say that his statement was not necessarily untrue, just that he was hoping for a different reaction.

ON MY OWN, I'M SO UNCOORDINATED I CAN'T EVEN TIE MY SHOE.
CAN YOU TIE BOWS, YATOGAMI?
YEAH... I CAN ALSO TIE BOWLINES AND DECORATIVE BONDAGE ART.
JUST WHAT I'D EXPECT FROM A WARRIOR GOD.
THAT WAS A JOKE.

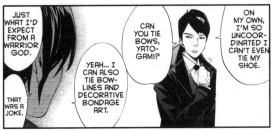

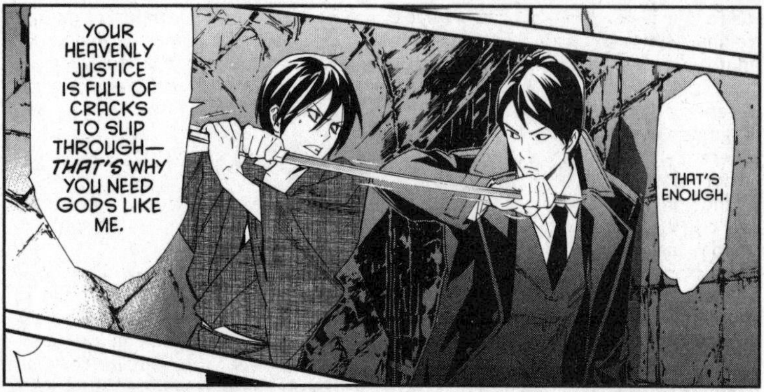
THAT'S ENOUGH.
YOUR HEAVENLY JUSTICE IS FULL OF CRACKS TO SLIP THROUGH—*THAT'S* WHY YOU NEED GODS LIKE ME.

Heavenly justice, page 163

In Japanese, Yato referred to "heaven's net", which is supposed to capture all evil deeds and evildoers. Yato calls it "sieve," implying that it's not as inescapable as it purports to be, and someone has to clean up the mess it leaves behind. The translators wanted to render his line as, "Your heavenly net is full of holes," but Western readers may not be familiar with the concept of heaven's net, and so it would leave more confusion as to what exactly Yato was needed for.

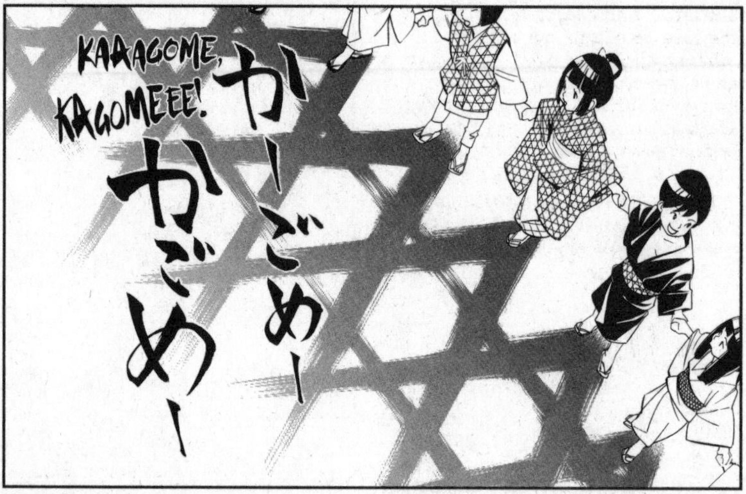
かーごめー
かごめー
KAAAGOME, KAGOMEEE!

Kagome Kagome, page 168

Kagome Kagome is a children's game with accompanying song. Like many such games, the meaning of the song's lyrics have been debated for ages. In this game, children stand in a circle with one blindfolded in the middle, who is "it," referred to as the *oni* (ogre) in Japanese. The children walk in a circle around "it" while singing the song, and when they get to the end, "it" has to guess who is standing behind him or her.

As for the lyrics, the translators used a mostly literal translation in this manga, taking a few liberties in an attempt to match the rhythm of the song. When multiple meanings could be applied, they chose the one they felt was most appropriate to this particular version of the game. Here they are again, for reference:

Kagome Kagome
There is a bird inside the cage
When, oh when, will it come out?
In the light of dawn,
the crane and the turtle slide along.
Who is that standing behind you?

Kagome means "the eyes of a basket," and generally refers to a particular pattern of basket weave which can be seen on the clothing of the children singing the *kagome* song. The bird (*tori*) in the cage is specifically a chicken, but can symbolize many things, such as the *torii* gate of a shrine, the unborn child of a pregnant woman, or a prisoner awaiting execution. Based on the treatment of Ebisu's shinki, the translators believe the latter is the most fitting. The cage (*kago*, which also means "basket") can be the chicken coop, the fence surrounding the shrine, the womb, or the fence surrounding the execution ground—the barrier imprisoning Ebisu's shinki.

Yoake no ban, here rendered as "the light of dawn" is more literally translated as "the evening of dawn," which can mean many things, including the end of dawn, the middle of the night, or the time from dawn to dusk. It may also refer to the *yoake no bannin*, or the "watchman of the dawn," i.e. a rooster.

The crane and the turtle are both symbols of good luck. The verb describing their action is *suberu*, which can either mean "slip" or "control, supervise." The latter would indicate that good luck rules the day, which is certainly not the case here (although the god supervising the children's game may feel otherwise). So more likely, these symbols of good luck have lost their footing and slipped, which would be a sign of bad luck. Furthermore, as symbols of longevity, their fall can represent death.

The last line seems rather straightforward, but it, too, has a few other interpretations, which mainly point to the idea that whoever is standing behind "it" is "its" killer or executioner.

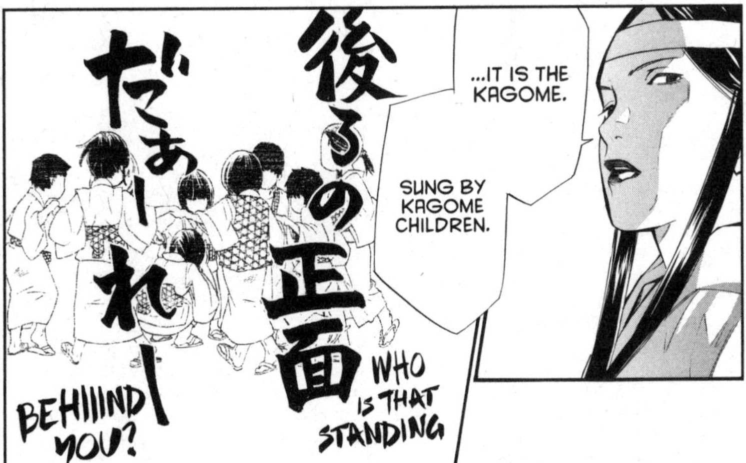
...IT IS THE KAGOME.
SUNG BY KAGOME CHILDREN.
後ろの正面
だあーれー
WHO IS THAT STANDING
BEHIIIND YOU?

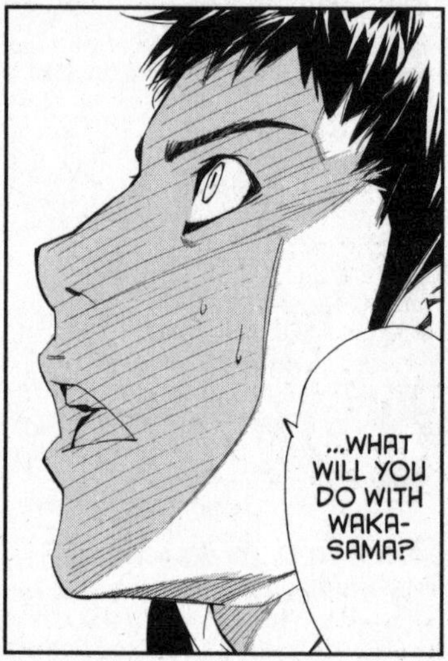
...WHAT WILL YOU DO WITH WAKA-SAMA?

Waka-sama, page 171

Ebisu's shinki refer to their master as *Waka* or *Waka-sama*. Literally, waka means "young" or, as a title, "young one." *Waka-sama* means "honorable young one" or "young master." Incidentally, Ebisu uses *mi* as the unifying name for his shinki. Like most shinki name suffixes, it has a few different meanings, one of which being "more and more," perhaps indicating Ebisu's businesslike desire to increase all of his assets.

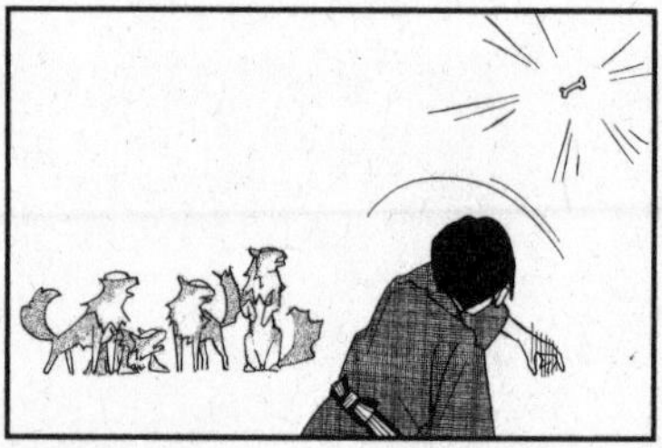

Our Bone, page 187

This is a parody of *Gonta no Honekko*, or "Gonta's Bone," which is a brand of dog chew bones. In one commercial, we see Gonta the dog listing his daily activities, most of which include chewing on his bone treat.

The rhinoceros beetle look, page 189

This suggestion may not be as random as it appears. The Japanese word for "rhinoceros beetle" is *kabutomushi*, which literally means "helmet bug." It is so called because of its horn's resemblance to a samurai helmet. Such a helmet would be an appropriate accessory for a war god. Taking the look all the way to "beetle," however, would be somewhat extreme.

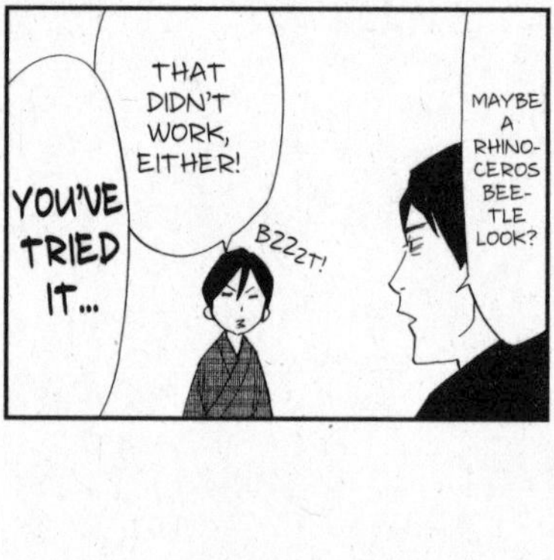
MAYBE A RHINOCEROS BEETLE LOOK?
THAT DIDN'T WORK, EITHER!
BZZZT!
YOU'VE TRIED IT...

N O R A G A M I

Thanks to all of your support, this work is being made into an anime. They let me go to the script meetings and voice recordings. I was constantly overwhelmed by all the professionals. And I would like to thank Kawashima-sensei, too. Thank you very, very much!

Adachitoka

D=EVIL SURVIVOR

デビルサバイバー

KODANSHA COMICS

AFTER DEMONS BREAK THROUGH INTO THE HUMAN WORLD, TOKYO MUST BE QUARANTINED. WITHOUT POWER AND STUCK IN A SUPERNATURAL WARZONE, 17-YEAR-OLD KAZUYA HAS ONLY ONE HOPE: HE MUST USE THE *"COMP"*, A DEVICE CREATED BY HIS COUSIN NAOYA CAPABLE OF SUMMONING AND SUBDUING DEMONS, TO DEFEAT THE INVADERS AND TAKE BACK THE CITY.

BASED ON THE POPULAR VIDEO GAME FRANCHISE B ATLUS!

Noragami: Stray God volume 8 is a work of fiction. Names, characters, places, and incidents are the products of the author's imagination or are used fictitiously. Any resemblance to actual events, locales, or persons, living or dead, is entirely coincidental.

A Kodansha Comics Trade Paperback Original.

Published in the United States by Kodansha Comics, an imprint of Kodansha USA Publishing, LLC, New York.

Publication rights for this English edition arranged through Kodansha Ltd., Tokyo.

First published in Japan in 2013 by Kodansha Ltd., Tokyo.

ISBN 978-1-63236-103-5

Printed in the United States of America.

www.kodanshacomics.com

9 8 7 6 5 4 3 2 1

Translator: Alethea Nibley & Athena Nibley
Lettering: Lys Blakeslee